First World War
and Army of Occupation
War Diary
France, Belgium and Germany

3 DIVISION
1 Northern Brigade Headquarters,
Northumberland Fusiliers 51st, 52nd and 53rd Battalions
(Y.S.Bns),
King's (Liverpool Regiment) 13th Battalion,
Prince of Wales's Own (West Yorkshire Regiment)
1/5th and 1/6thBattalions,
York and Lancaster Regiment
1/4th (Hallamshire) (T.F.) Battalion.
3 Northern Brigade Headquarters,
Durham Light Infantry 20th, 51st and 52nd Battalions
28 February 1919 - 30 May 1919

WO95/1438

The Naval & Military Press Ltd
www.nmarchive.com
Published in association with The National Archives

Published by

The Naval & Military Press Ltd

Unit 10 Ridgewood Industrial Park,

Uckfield, East Sussex,

TN22 5QE England

Tel: +44 (0) 1825 749494

www.naval-military-press.com

www.nmarchive.com

This diary has been reprinted in facsimile from the original. Any imperfections are inevitably reproduced and the quality may fall short of modern type and cartographic standards.

© Crown Copyright
Images reproduced by permission of The National Archives, London, England, 2015.

Contents

Document type	Place/Title	Date From	Date To
Heading	B.E.F. Northern Div Formerly 3 Div 1 Northern Bde 52 Northumberland Fus 1919 Mar To 1919 Oct		
War Diary			
War Diary		25/03/1919	31/03/1919
War Diary	Cologne	14/03/1919	10/06/1919
War Diary	Biesfeld	19/06/1919	20/06/1919
War Diary	Broich Camp	21/06/1919	23/06/1919
War Diary	Cologne	01/07/1919	31/10/1919
Heading	B.E.F. Northern Div Formerly 3 Div Northern Bde 51 Northumberland Fus 1919 Mar To 1919 Oct		
War Diary	Suly Cologne	17/03/1919	29/03/1919
Miscellaneous	To 1st. Northern Brigade.	30/04/1919	30/04/1919
War Diary	Suly Cologne	01/04/1919	31/10/1919
Heading	To 8th Infy Bde.		
Heading	B E F Northern Div Fromerly 3 Div 1 Northern Bde H.Q. 1919 Apr To 1919 Sept		
War Diary	Cologne.	01/04/1919	31/05/1919
Miscellaneous	Appendix 2 To War Diary 1st Northern Brigade Administrative Instructions No. 1	28/05/1919	28/05/1919
Miscellaneous	Appendix 2 To War Diary 1st Northern Brigade Group. Instruction No. 1	27/05/1919	27/05/1919
Miscellaneous	To Accompany 1st Northern Brigade Instructions No. 1		
Miscellaneous	Appendix 2 To War Diary 1st Northern Brigade. G. 1600/8/1	03/06/1919	03/06/1919
Miscellaneous	1st Northern Brigade Defence Scheme.		
Miscellaneous	Details Of Guards Fusiliers By "A" Battalion 1st Northern Brigade.		
Miscellaneous	Addendum No. 1	09/05/1919	09/05/1919
Miscellaneous	Amendment And Addendum No. 2	26/05/1919	26/05/1919
Miscellaneous	Defence Scheme in the event of Civil Disturbances in Cologne.	31/05/1919	31/05/1919
Miscellaneous	Appendix "A" to 1st Northern Brigade Defence Scheme. Signal Communications.		
Miscellaneous	Appendix "B" Medical Arrangements.		
War Diary	Cologne	01/06/1919	20/06/1919
War Diary	Kurten Area	21/06/1919	30/06/1919
Miscellaneous	Appendix I 1st Northern Brigade Instructions for Arrangements.	17/06/1919	17/06/1919
Miscellaneous	1st Northern Brigade. G. 100/2/4	18/06/1919	18/06/1919
Miscellaneous	1st Northern Brigade Instructions for Advance No. 3 Appendix 2	18/06/1919	18/06/1919
Miscellaneous	1st Northern Brigade. G. 100/2/5 Appendix 3	19/06/1919	19/06/1919
Miscellaneous	Location List. Appendix 4	20/06/1919	20/06/1919
Diagram etc	Sketch Map Showing Dispositions Of Units 1st Northern Brigade Group		
Miscellaneous	Addendum No. 2 to 1st Northern Brigade Instructions No. 2 Appendix 5	24/06/1919	24/06/1919
Miscellaneous	Amendment No. 1 To 1st Northern Brigade Instructions for Advance No. 2 Signal Arrangements. Appendix 5	23/06/1919	23/06/1919
Operation(al) Order(s)	1st Northern Brigade Order No. 1 Appendix 6	27/06/1919	27/06/1919

Type	Description	Start	End
Miscellaneous	Move Of 1st Northern Brigade Personnel By Lorry. To Accompany 1st Northern Brigade Order No. 1	27/03/1919	27/03/1919
Miscellaneous	Table B. To Accompany 1st Northern Brigade Order No. 1		
Miscellaneous	Cologne Guards to be taken over by 51st Battalion Northumberland Fusiliers, in accordance with para. 7 of 1st Northern Brigade Order No. 1		
Miscellaneous	Appendix "A" A. Lorries.		
Miscellaneous	Addendum No. 1 to 1st Northern Brigade Order No. 1	27/06/1919	27/06/1919
Operation(al) Order(s)	Appendix No. 2 to 1st Northern Brigade Order No. 1 of 27/6/19	28/06/1919	28/06/1919
War Diary	Cologne	01/07/1919	26/08/1919
Miscellaneous	Subject. Training Of Lewis Gunners.	20/08/1919	20/08/1919
Miscellaneous	Amendment And Addendum No. 1 to 1st Northern Brigade Defence Scheme dated 27/4/19	28/08/1919	28/08/1919
Miscellaneous	1st Northern Brigade. G. 1000/143		
War Diary			
War Diary	Cologne.	14/08/1919	30/08/1919
Miscellaneous	Instructions for Relief of the 16th Bn. Lancashire Fusiliers. Bruhl. by 53rd Bn. Northumberland Fus. Appendix I	19/09/1919	19/09/1919
Miscellaneous	Instructions for Taking Over Artillery Barracks, Bonner Strasse by 52nd. Bn. Northumberland Fus. Appendix 2	19/09/1919	19/09/1919
Heading	B E F Northern Div. Formerly 3 Div 2 Northern Inf Bde 1/5 W. Yorks 1919 Feb To 1919 Oct From 49 Div 146 Bde		
War Diary	1/5 Battalion Prince of Wales's Own (West Yorkshire) Regt. War Diary. Period From February 29th 1919 To 31st March 1919		
War Diary	Moncheaux	28/02/1919	02/03/1919
War Diary	In The Train	03/03/1919	03/03/1919
War Diary	Cologne	04/03/1919	31/03/1919
War Diary			
Heading	1/5th. Bn. P. W. O. (West Yorkshire). Regt. War. Diary. April. 1919		
War Diary			
War Diary	Cologne	05/04/1919	30/04/1919
Heading	1/5th Bn P W D (W Y K) Regt War Diary May 1919		
War Diary			
War Diary	Cologne	01/05/1919	09/05/1919
War Diary			
War Diary	Cologne	18/05/1919	22/05/1919
War Diary			
War Diary	Cologne	27/05/1919	31/05/1919
Heading	1/5th Bn. P. W. D. C W York Regt) War Diary June 1919		
War Diary			
War Diary	Bickendorf	11/06/1919	18/06/1919
War Diary	Dunnwald	19/06/1919	19/06/1919
War Diary	Burscheid	20/06/1919	29/06/1919
War Diary	Cologne	30/06/1919	30/06/1919
Heading	1/5th Battalion Prince Of Wales's Own. (West Yorkshire Regt.) War Diary July 1919		
War Diary			
War Diary	Cologne	08/07/1919	31/07/1919

Heading	1/5th Bn. P. W. O. (West Yorkshire) Regt War Diary. 1 To 31st August. 1919		
War Diary	Cologne	01/08/1919	22/08/1919
War Diary	Rhine Army Troops Kall.	29/08/1919	29/08/1919
War Diary	Soetenich	30/08/1919	31/08/1919
Miscellaneous	2nd Northern Infantry Brigade. Northern Division "A"	20/10/1919	20/10/1919
Miscellaneous			
Heading	1/5th Bn. Prince Of Wales's Own. (West Yorkshire Regt. War Diary for period from 1st to 30th September 1919		
War Diary			
War Diary	Soetenich	01/09/1919	03/09/1919
War Diary	Urft.	04/09/1919	30/09/1919
Heading	1/5th Bn. P. W. D (West. Yorkshire Regiment). War Diary. October 1919		
War Diary			
War Diary	Urft	17/10/1919	29/10/1919
War Diary	Cologne	30/10/1919	31/10/1919
Heading	B E F Northern Div Formerly 3 Div 2 Northern Inf Bde 13 K. L'Pool 1919 Apr. To 1919 Oct		
War Diary			
War Diary	Beuel	18/04/1919	31/07/1919
War Diary	Beuel Germany	01/08/1919	30/09/1919
War Diary			
Heading	B E F Northern Div Formerly 3 Div 2 Northern Inf Bde. 1919 Mar To 1919 Oct		
Miscellaneous	2nd Nthn. Inf. Bde. G.213 Northern Division "A".	05/05/1919	05/05/1919
War Diary			
War Diary	Cologne.	22/03/1919	31/03/1919
War Diary			
War Diary	Cologne.	01/08/1919	30/09/1919
Miscellaneous	Northern Division 'A' Diaries	04/11/1919	04/11/1919
War Diary	Cologne	06/10/1919	30/10/1919
Miscellaneous		28/10/1919	28/10/1919
Miscellaneous	2nd Northern Infantry Brigade.	28/10/1919	28/10/1919
Miscellaneous	2nd. Northern Infy. Bde. G. 728/2		
Heading	B E F Northern Div Formerly 3 Div 1 Northern Bde 53 North'd Fus 1919 Mar To 1919 Sept		
War Diary	Catterick	01/03/1919	11/03/1919
War Diary	Dunkerque	08/03/1919	10/03/1919
War Diary	Cologne.	11/03/1919	11/03/1919
War Diary	Efferen	11/03/1919	22/03/1919
War Diary	Sulz	23/03/1919	31/03/1919
Miscellaneous	Guards provided by 53rd. Bn. North'd. Fusiliers. 24th. March 1919	24/03/1919	24/03/1919
Miscellaneous	Appendix "A"		
Miscellaneous	Nominal Roll Of 53rd Bn. Northumberland Fusiliers. Proceeding Overseas.	07/03/1919	07/03/1919
War Diary	Sulz.	01/04/1919	22/04/1919
War Diary	Marienburg	23/04/1919	31/05/1919
War Diary	Cologne.	01/06/1919	19/06/1919
War Diary	Kurten	19/06/1919	01/07/1919
War Diary	Marienburg.	01/07/1919	26/07/1919
War Diary	Cologne.	31/07/1919	31/07/1919
War Diary	Marienburg. Cologne.	04/08/1919	30/08/1919
War Diary	Marienburg.	31/08/1919	31/08/1919

War Diary			
War Diary	Bruhl.	26/09/1919	29/09/1919
Heading	B E F Northern Div Formerly 3 Div 2 Northern Inf Bde 1/6 W. Yorks 1919 Mar To 1919 Oct From 49 Div 146 Bde		
War Diary	Cologne	01/03/1919	30/04/1919
Miscellaneous	2nd Nthn. Inf. Bde. Northern Division "A".	25/07/1919	25/07/1919
War Diary	Cologne	01/05/1919	11/06/1919
War Diary	Cologne & Dunwald	18/06/1919	18/06/1919
War Diary	Dunnwald Hilgen	19/06/1919	19/06/1919
War Diary	Hilgen	20/06/1919	30/06/1919
War Diary	Cologne	01/07/1919	23/07/1919
Miscellaneous	Northern Division "A".		
War Diary			
War Diary	Cologne	09/08/1919	30/09/1919
Miscellaneous	Memorandum		
War Diary	Cologne	01/10/1919	04/10/1919
Heading	B E F Northern Div Formerly 3 Div 2 Northern Bde 1/4 Y < L Regt 1919 Mar To 1919 Oct From 49 Div 149 Bde		
Heading	War Diary From 1st. To 31st. March. 1919		
War Diary	Kerpen	01/03/1919	01/03/1919
War Diary	Cologne	02/03/1919	08/03/1919
Miscellaneous	Special Order Of The Day. by Major General N. G. G. Cameron, C. E. C.M.G. Commanding 49th (West Riding) Division.	20/02/1919	20/02/1919
War Diary	Cologne	09/03/1919	23/03/1919
War Diary	Cologne (Nippes)	24/03/1919	31/03/1919
Heading	War Diary For April 1919		
War Diary	Cologne	01/04/1919	30/04/1919
Heading	War Diary For May 1919		
War Diary	Cologne	01/05/1919	19/06/1919
War Diary	Hilgen	20/06/1919	30/06/1919
War Diary	Cologne	01/07/1919	31/10/1919
Heading	B E F Northern Div Formerly 3 Div 3 Northern Inf Bde H Q. 1919 Apr To 1919 June		
War Diary	Cologne 59 Hohenstaufen Ring.	01/04/1919	30/04/1919
War Diary	Cologne.	01/05/1919	30/05/1919
Miscellaneous	Instructions for Advance, No. 1		
Miscellaneous	March Table		
Miscellaneous	Appendix "A" to Accompany 3rd Northern Brigade B. 3493 Signal Arrangements.		
Miscellaneous	3rd Northern Brigade.		
Miscellaneous	Reference Map. Sheet Cologne. 1/200,000	29/05/1919	29/05/1919
Miscellaneous	March Table For J 1 D. Y.		
Miscellaneous	3rd. Northern Bde. B3493/2	30/05/1919	30/05/1919
Miscellaneous	Reference Map. Sheet Cologne 1/200,000	30/05/1919	30/05/1919
Miscellaneous	March Table For J-1 Day.		
Miscellaneous	To Accompany 1st Northern Brigade Instructions No. 1 Appendix 3	30/05/1919	30/05/1919
Miscellaneous	Northern Division "G".	06/07/1919	06/07/1919
War Diary	Cologne	01/06/1919	18/06/1919
War Diary	Wermelskirchen	19/06/1919	30/06/1919
Miscellaneous	3rd Northern Brigade No. 8.3493/2	01/06/1919	01/06/1919
Miscellaneous	3rd Northern Brigade B.M. 133	26/06/1919	26/06/1919

Miscellaneous	March Table to Accompany 3rd Northern Brigade B.M. 133	26/06/1919	26/06/1919
Miscellaneous	3rd Northern Infantry Brigade.		
Heading	B E F Northern Div Formerly 3 Div 3 Northern Inf Bde 20 Dur. L. I. 1919 Mar To 1919 June From 41 Div 124 Bde		
War Diary	Barracks Riehl	01/03/1919	19/06/1919
War Diary	Billets Wermelskirchen	20/06/1919	30/06/1919
Operation(al) Order(s)	20th Bn. Durham Light Infantry Operation Order No. 116	30/06/1919	30/06/1919
Miscellaneous	Operation Orders.	18/06/1919	18/06/1919
Heading	B E F Northern Div Formerly 3 Div 3 Northern Bde. 51 Dur L. I. 1919 Mar To 1919 June		
War Diary	Hipswell Camp Catterick	01/03/1919	07/03/1919
War Diary	Cologne	08/03/1919	30/04/1919
Miscellaneous	Northern Division.	04/06/1919	04/06/1919
War Diary	Cologne	01/05/1919	30/06/1919
Heading	B E F Northern Div Formerly 3 Div 3 Norhern Inf Bde 52 Dur L. I. 1919 Mar To 1919 June		
Heading	War Diary 52nd Battn. D. L. I. March 1919		
War Diary	Catterick	02/03/1919	03/03/1919
War Diary	France	03/03/1919	04/03/1919
War Diary	Belgium	05/03/1919	05/03/1919
War Diary	Germany	06/03/1919	25/03/1919
War Diary	Cologne	28/03/1919	31/03/1919
Miscellaneous	Lovement Orders by. Lieut. Colonel J.B. Liur D.S.O. Collanding 52nd Bn. Durham Infantry. Appendix 1	01/03/1919	01/03/1919
Miscellaneous	52nd Battn Durham Light Infantry Nominal Roll Of Officers. Appendix 2		
Miscellaneous	52nd Battalion Durham Light Infantry.		
Heading	52 Bn D. L. I. War Diary For April 1919		
War Diary	Cologne	04/04/1919	23/04/1919
Miscellaneous	O.C. 52nd Bn. Durham L. I. Appendix 1	12/04/1919	12/04/1919
Miscellaneous	52nd Battalion Durham Light Infantry Nominal Roll Of Officers Left The Battalion During April, 1919	01/05/1919	01/05/1919
Miscellaneous	52nd Battalion Durham Light Infantry Nominal Roll Of Officers Joined The Battalion During April, 1919	01/05/1919	01/05/1919
War Diary	Cologne	01/05/1919	19/06/1919
War Diary	Wermelskirchen	20/06/1919	29/06/1919
War Diary	Cologne	30/05/1919	30/05/1919

B.E.F.

NORTHERN DIV
formerly 3 DIV

1 NORTHERN BDE

52 NORTHUMBERLAND FUS

1919 MAR to 1919 OCT

WAR DIARY or INTELLIGENCE SUMMARY

Army Form C. 2118.

Northern Div.
R3rr
52nd Bn. Northumberland Fusiliers
WD II

	Summary of Events and Information	Remarks and references to Appendices
	Battalion entrained. Train left at 07.00. Arrived Dover 18.35. Stayed the night at Rest Camp	
	Embarked Admiralty Pier. "Princess Elizabeth". Arrived Dunkirk 15.45. Occupied No.4 Rest Camp for the night.	
	Entrained	
	Still in Train	
	Arrived Cologne. Occupied Billets.	
	Billets as above. Occupied Billets, Bergerather Strasse and Luxemberg Strasse. Schools	
do	Inspected by General Plumer.	
do	Billets as above. Strength 44 Officers 654 Other Ranks.	
do	do	
do	do	
do	do	9 Officers and 130 Other Ranks taken on Strength from 1st. N.F.
do	do	
do	do	Strength 54 Officers 783 Other Ranks
do	do	
do	do	Inspection by D.D.S Division Major General Deverell.
do	do	Guard on Docks increased to 3 Officers 1 W.M.C.O. and 68 Other Ranks. Football match against 9.D.R.J. we lost by 2 Goals to 5 Goals. Licar. Demobilisation
do	do	Stopped for time.
do	do	Church Parade 9. A.M. Strength 54 Officers 790 Other Ranks.
do	do	Received order to Perform for move. Same order cancelled in afternoon Brigadier General Kennedy visited Battalion 11.30.A.M. Battalion stood to arms 2 p.m. until 4.30 p.m.

Army Form C. 2118.

WAR DIARY
or
INTELLIGENCE SUMMARY.
(Erase heading not required.)

Instructions regarding War Diaries and Intelligence Summaries are contained in F. S. Regs., Part II. and the Staff Manual respectively. Title pages will be prepared in manuscript.

Place	Date	Hour	Summary of Events and Information	Remarks and references to Appendices
	25.3.19		Billets as above. Capt. P.J.M. Palmer took over duties of Brigade Field Officer for week ending 31.3.19. Capt. J.M. Settle proceeded to England for course Berkhampstead.	
	26.3.19		Billets as above.	
	27.3.19		do	
	28.3.19		do	
	29.3.19		do. 1 German shot and 6 taken prisoners at Doebo by Docho Guard. 6 to toy the Elbe.	
	30.3.19 9.30am		do Church Parade.	
	31.3.19		do Strength return. 49 Officers 789 Other Ranks.	

MReed R
Lodg 52nd Bn Northumberland Fusiliers

WAR DIARY or INTELLIGENCE SUMMARY

Army Form C. 2118.

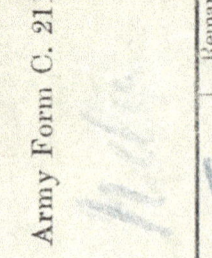

	Summary of Events and Information	Remarks and references to Appendices

Battalion entrained. Left Durham 04.00, arrived Dover 18.35. Stayed the night at No.2 Rest Camp. Embarked Admiralty Pier on "Princess Elizabeth". Arrived Dunkirk 15.45. No.4 Rest Camp for the night. Entrained for Cologne via Armentieres, Mons, Courtrai, Namur, Huy, Aix-la-Chapelle. Crossed German frontier. Arrived Cologne, occupied billets in Sülz, Berrenrather & Luxemburger Strasses.

" As above

" Inspected by General Plumer 09.45 in Remigius Str. Strength 46 Officers 654 other ranks

" Church Parade in Gymnasium.

" Canteen, Supper Bar & Reading Room opened in Remigius Str.

" 9 Officers & 130 other ranks taken on strength from 1st Batln North'd Fus. Guards found by Batln in billets Sud Brucke 2NCO's 12.O.R. Dom Hotel 2NCO's 8.O.R. Luxemburger Nall 1NCO 3.O.R. Docks. 1 Officer 6NCO's 29.O.R. R.E.Dump 1NCO 3.O.R. Schnurgasse 2NCO's 8.OR Quarter Guard 2NCO's 8.O.R.

WAR DIARY or INTELLIGENCE SUMMARY

Army Form C. 2118.

Place	Date	Hour	Summary of Events and Information	Remarks and references to Appendices
COLOGNE 14.3.19	14.3.19		Billets as above. Route march, about 4 miles.	
do	15.3.19		" " Strength 54 Officers 983 other ranks.	
do	16.3.19	10.00	" " Church Parade in Corps Lecture Hall.	
do	17.3.19		" " Platoon & Coy Training 4 hrs each morning, 1 hr in afternoon, 2 afternoons Recreation.	
do	18.3.19		" " Route march about 8 miles.	
do	19.3.19		" " Training as above.	
do	20.3.19		" " Inspected by G.O.C. Division. Major General DEVERELL.	
do	21.3.19		" " Training as above.	
do	22.3.19		" " Docks Guard increased to 3 Officers, 14 NCO's & 68 other ranks. Other guards as before.	
do			" " Football Match v. 9th DLI. Lost by 2 goals to 5 goals. Leave & Demob. stopped pro tem.	
do	23.3.19	09.00	Billets as above. Church Parade. Strength 54 officers 990 other ranks.	
do	24.3.19		" " Ordered to prepare to move to new billeting area. Same order cancelled in afternoon.	
do	25.3.19		" " G.O.C. Brigade, Brigadier General KENNEDY visited Battn. 11.30 Battalion stood to arms 14.00 until 19.30, as disturbances were probable amongst civil population.	
do	26.3.19		" " Guards found by Battn. as follows: Docks 3 Officers 90 other ranks. SUDBRUCKE 2 NCO's 12 O.R. RTO's Train Guards 2 NCO's 24 O.R. Quarter Guard 2 NCO's 8 O.R. A.P.M's Picquet 1 NCO 10 D.R.	

Army Form C. 2118.

WAR DIARY
or
INTELLIGENCE SUMMARY.
(Erase heading not required.)

Instructions regarding War Diaries and Intelligence Summaries are contained in F. S. Regs., Part II. and the Staff Manual respectively. Title pages will be prepared in manuscript.

Place	Date	Hour	Summary of Events and Information	Remarks and references to Appendices
COLOGNE	27.3.19		Billets as above. Training as above	
do	28.3.19		" "	
do	29.3.19		{ 1 German shot & taken in act of stealing by Day's GUARD. C Coy of this Battn.	
			{ Great issue of 6 hours leave to this Battn. 3 officers 4 O.R.	
do	30.3.19		Church Parade 09.30.	
do	31.3.19		Strength 49 officers 989 Other ranks.	
do	1.4.19		Capt JSN Palmer promoted A/MAJOR. Lt J.A. Luke promoted A/CAPTAIN.	
do	2.4.19		Battalion stands to ready to move to KNAPSACK at 1 hour's notice in case of BOLSHEVIK riots	
do	3.4.19		Battalion stood to ready for move as above at ½ hour's notice from 14.00 to 16.30.	
do	4.4.19		Route march 15 Kilos. Inspected by G.O.C. Brigade while on the march.	
do			Strength 49 officers 989 other ranks.	
do	5.4.19		Battalion stood to. Football Match v. 53rd North'd Fus. Lost by 2 goals to 5 goals.	
do	6.4.19		51st Battalion North'd Fusiliers took over vigilance from us. Church Parade 09.00.	
do	7.4.19		Platoon & Company training 4 hours morning, 1 hour afternoon.	
do	8.4.19		" "	
do	9.4.19		Football match v. 53rd North'd Fus. Won by 2 goals to 1 goal.	

WAR DIARY
INTELLIGENCE SUMMARY

Army Form C. 2118.

Place	Date	Hour	Summary of Events and Information	Remarks and references to Appendices
COLOGNE	10.4.19		Billets as above. Route March 16 Kilo.	
do	11.4.19	"	Strength 48 officers 990 other ranks (including interpreter).	
do	12.4.19	"	" " " " " " " "	
do	13.4.19	"	Church Parade 10.45.	
do	14.4.19	"	Education 8 hours per week in definite progress, in addition to military training.	
do	15.4.19	"	" " " " " " "	
do	16.4.19	"	Name of higher formation changed from 8th Bde 3rd Division to 1st Bde, Northern Division.	
do	17.4.19	"	Route march about 10 Kilo. Battalion stood to for 48 hours.	
do	18.4.19	"	Good Friday. Church Parade 09.30. Strength 48 officers 989 other ranks.	
do	19.4.19	"	Football Match v 51st North'n Div, lost by 1 goal to 4 goals.	
do	20.4.19	"	Church Parade 09.45.	
do	21.4.19	"	All guards found as on 26.3.19 and in addition LUXEMBURGER WALL 1NCO & 3.O.R. SEHNUR GASSE 2NCO's 8.O.R. Extra Train Guard 1NCO 8 O.R. Capt Whense, Lt Ruffle Lt Minnow, Lt Brookes, 2Lt Pearce, 2Lt Penrose, 2Lt Hill, b 2 Lt Ackerman ordered to be posted to Battalions of their own regiments.	
do	22.4.19	"	Pleasure trip on RHINE for 150 O.R.	
do	23.4.19	"	St George's Day. Red & White rose worn by all ranks. Muster Parade, and lecture by C.O. on "History of the Regiment", followed by Ceremonial Parade and Inspection	

WAR DIARY or INTELLIGENCE SUMMARY.

Continued

by G.O.C. Brigade. Special dinner for men. Holiday afternoon. Football match v 51st North'd Fusiliers, won by 4 goals to 1. Concert in Gymnasium at night. Billets as above.

" " " Route March 10 Kilos.

" " " New Rota of Bde duties, enabling Battalion to train at full strength for 2 weeks at a 3, only finding QUARTER GUARD 1 NCO & 3 O.R. and BDE HDQRS GUARD 2 NCO's 8 O.R.

" " " Strength 38 officers 435 O.R. London Personal Rations 2 Corp attached.

" " " London Personal Rations 2 Corp attached.

" " " Football Match v. Royal Scots. Won by 1 goal to nil. Concert in Gym at night.

J.H.Evans Lt Col
Comdg 52 N'th: Fus

Army Form C. 2118.

WAR DIARY
or
INTELLIGENCE SUMMARY.

(Erase heading not required.)

Instructions regarding War Diaries and Intelligence Summaries are contained in F. S. Regs., Part II. and the Staff Manual respectively. Title pages will be prepared in manuscript.

Place	Date	Hour	Summary of Events and Information	Remarks and references to Appendices
COLOGNE	MAY 1919		52nd Northumberland Fusiliers.	
	1/5/19		Billets. Sülz, COLOGNE. Strength 35 Officers, 734 O.R.	
"	3/5/19		" " Football Match v 9th D.L.I. won by 4 goals to 1.	
"	4/5/19		" " Church Parade 09.45, parties leaving billeting area ordered to carry rifles.	
"	5/5/19		" " Battalion paraded 09.00. and proceeded in motor lorries to EXERCIER PLATZ, north of COLOGNE, where the Division was inspected by G.O.C., Major General Deverell. Returned by motor lorry to billets at 14.00. Whist Drive at night in Gymnasium.	
"	6/5/19		Billets as above, Company Training and Education.	
"	7/5/19		" " Battn practised ceremonial drill in morning, G.O.C. Brigade, Brig. General Kennedy being present. Recreation in afternoon. Strength 34 officers 734 O.R.	
"	8/5/19		Battalion paraded as on May 5th, and took part in inspection of the Division by His Royal Highness the Duke of Connaught, returning to billets by motor lorry at 14.00.	
"	9/5/19		Billets as above. Gas training inspected by Divisional Gas Officer. Capt Spicer, D.L.I., Adjutant since May 1917, left to join a battalion of his own regiment under cooperating orders. Capt Steel, North'd Fusiliers, taking over the duties of Adjutant. Lt. Colonel J.C. HARTLEY, D.S.O. Royal Fusiliers took over command of the Battalion.	
"	10/5/19		Battalion took over Brigade duties as follows for ensuing week:-	G.J.M.

WAR DIARY
or
INTELLIGENCE SUMMARY

(Erase heading not required.)

Army Form C. 2118.

Place	Date	Hour	Summary of Events and Information	Remarks and references to Appendices
COLOGNE	10/5/19.		Guards detached for the week. DOCKS. 3 Officers, 12 NCO's & 73 O.R. SUD BRUCKE 2 NCO's & 102 O.R. SCHNUR GASSE 2 NCO's & 120 O.R. LUXEMBURGER WALL 1 NCO & 3 O.R. POWDER FACTORY 4 Officers, 10 NCO's & 90 O.R. FORT VII. 2 Officers, 3 NCO's & 26 O.R. VOLKSGARTEN. 2 NCO's & 8 O.R. VORGEBIRGE STR. 2 NCO's & 8 O.R. BONN TOR GOODS STATION 2 NCO's & 8 O.R. E.F.C. GUARD. BAYERN STR. 2 NCO's & 8 O.R. ALTER BURGER WALL 2 NCO's & 8 O.R. 44th C.C.S. 2 NCO's & 10 O.R. TOTAL DETACHED. 9 Officers, 42 NCO's, 246 O.R. Guards detailed from Hdqrs daily. 3 TRAIN GUARDS, each 1 NCO & 120 O.R. WORKING PARTY AT ARSENAL 1 Officer, 3 NCO's & 24 O.R. BRIGADE HDQRS GUARD 2 NCO's & 8 O.R. REGT'L QUARTER GUARD 1 NCO & 30 O.R. TOTAL DAILY DUTIES. 1 Officer, 9 NCO's, 74 O.R. Billets. SULZ. COLOGNE. Church Parade for details at 10.15.	
"	11/5/19.		" " " Construction of 30 yds range commenced on Parade Ground.	
"	12/5/19.		" " "	
"	13/5/19.		" " " Battalion education programme in abeyance, but Education Officer visited each guard during the week and lectured on the Peace Terms.	
"	14/5/19.		As above. Strength 33 Officers & 734 O.R.	
"	16/5/19.		Major G.L. THOMPSON, North'd Fusiliers, reported for duty as 2nd in Command.	
"	19/5/19.		Lt Col. H.E. PEASE. D.S.O., 2nd in Command since January 1917, and Commanding Officer	G.J.M.

Army Form C. 2118.

(3)

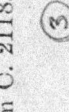

WAR DIARY
or
INTELLIGENCE SUMMARY.
(Erase heading not required.)

Instructions regarding War Diaries and Intelligence Summaries are contained in F. S. Regs., Part II. and the Staff Manual respectively. Title pages will be prepared in manuscript.

Place	Date	Hour	Summary of Events and Information	Remarks and references to Appendices
COLOGNE	17/5/19		from 12/2/19 to 9/5/19 left under cross-posting order to join a battalion of his own regiment, the D.L.I.	
"	18/5/19		Battalion relieved of Brigade Duties by 53rd North'd Fusiliers, and re-assembled in billets. Billets as above, Church Parade 09.45. ~~Fire Piquets found nightly. Total strength 2 Officers 7NCO's 745 O.R.~~	
"	20/5/19		A & D Coy proceeded to LACHEM & RIEHL respectively as detachments to fire G.M.C.	
"	21/5/19		Camera Club initiated as educational hobby. total Strength 33 Officers 734. O.R.	
"	22/5/19		Route March 10 Kilometres.	
"	24/5/19		Draft of 124 O.R. from 4th York & Lancs Regt.	
"	25/5/19		Church Parade 09.45. Further draft 46 O.R. from York & Lancs Regt. Fire Piquets found nightly for ensuing week. Total strength 2 Officers, 9 NCO's & 48 O.R. Also daily Bde Hdqr Guard 2NCO's & 10 O.R. and Quarter Guard 1NCO & 3 O.R.	
"	26/5/19.		Bde Hdqr Guard mounted by this battalion commenced in Bde Orders as the best of the week. 2 Lt W.J.B unke detached to 8th Trench Mortar Battery.	
"	27/5/19.		Battalion billets inspected by G.O.C. VIth Corps, Lieut. Gen Sir. A. HALDANE. K.C.B. DSO. A & D Corps returned from musketry detachments. One Company stood to arms, and remainder of battalion confined to billets owing to general strike of civil population, from 16.00 to 21.00.	
"	28/5/19.		Battalion visited by G.O.C. Brigade, Brigadier General Kennedy. First match of Cologne	C.J.M.

WAR DIARY
or
INTELLIGENCE SUMMARY.
(Erase heading not required.)

Army Form C. 2118.

Place	Date	Hour	Summary of Events and Information	Remarks and references to Appendices
COLOGNE	28/5/19		Cricket Cup Competition, Battalion beat 3rd Cavalry Division Field Ambulance by 81 runs to 66.	
"	29/5/19		Route March 10 Kilo. Strength 34 Officers 849 O.R.	
"	30/5/19		Battalion took over Brigade duties for ensuing week as follows:— Guards detached for the week:— Powder Magazine 4 Officers 10 NCO's 85 O.R. Bonn Jcr Goods Station 2 NCO's 10 O.R. Aldenburger Wall 2 NCO's 10 O.R. Schnur Gasse 2 NCO's 10 O.R. Fort VII. 2 Officers 3 NCO's 24 O.R. Volksgarten 2 NCO's 10 O.R. Vorgebirge Strasse 2 NCO's 10 O.R. Eifel Jcr Goods Station 1 Officer 3 NCO's 41 O.R. Luxemburger Wall 1 NCO 3 O.R. 44th C.C.S. 2 NCO's 10 O.R. Karthaus Wall 1 NCO 6 O.R. No 3 Coy Train 1 NCO 3 O.R. Docks 4 Officers 12 NCO's 930 R. E.F.C. Guard 2 NCO's 10 O.R. Altenburg Brewery 2 NCO's 80 R. Guards detailed daily from Adapr:— Train Guards 2 NCO's 16 O.R. Quarter Guard 1 NCO 3 O.R. Guard on detached empty billet. 1 NCO 3 O.R. 19 Guards in all with total strength 11 Officers 51 NCO's 325 O.R.	Q.J.M.

Army Form C. 2118.

June 1919 (1)

WAR DIARY
or
~~INTELLIGENCE SUMMARY~~

52nd Northumberland Fusiliers.

Place	Date	Hour	Summary of Events and Information	Remarks
COLOGNE.	JUNE. 1919 1/6/19		Billets SÜLZ, COLOGNE. Battalion doing Bde duties as detailed under entry 31/5/19. Church Parade for composite company of details 10.30 hrs. Training hours diminished to 4 hours per day for summer in the morning, afternoons to be free for recreation or voluntary education. Morning training to include 6 hours per week compulsory education.	
"	2/6/19.		Education staff initiated discussions in the various guardrooms on the "Govt Housing proposals", and therefrom furnished a report that had been called for on the opinion of the troops as to same.	
"	3/6/19.		Details at Adqrs observed the King's Birthday by giving the Royal Salute at 09.00 hours, followed by three cheers for His Majesty. Rest of day observed as holiday. Strength 34 Officers 895 O.R.	
"	4/6/19.		Cologne Cricket Cup Competition, match versus 51st North'd Fusiliers, won by 69 runs to 64.	
"	5/6/19.		No definite education in progress except with details at Adqrs, but Education Officer lectured to various guards on "The Crossings of the Atlantic".	
"	7/6/19.		All guards returned to billets, being relieved by 53rd North'd Fusiliers.	
"	8/6/19.		Church Parade 11.00 hrs.	
"	9/6/19.		General holiday, inter-company cricket matches morning and afternoon.	
"	10/6/19.		One hour each morning given to compulsory Education as follows. Arithmetic 1 hour. Mental Arith ½ hr. Spelling ½ hr. Letter-writing 1 hr. Geography 1 hour. Civics 1 hour. History 1 hour. Voluntary classes.	G.J.M.

WAR DIARY
INTELLIGENCE SUMMARY

Army Form C. 2118.

June 1919. ②

Cont'd.

were held in afternoon as follows. German. Music. Drawing & Design. Shorthand. Book-keeping. Type-writing. Camera Club.   Strength 34 officers. 934 other ranks.

Under London Gazette dated 3/6/19, Rev. W. Allen. C.F. was awarded the Military Cross on detachment. B & C Coys proceeded to LACHEM & RIEHL Ranges respectively to fire General Musketry Course. Cologne Cricket Cup Competition, Match v Divisional Cavalry Ammunition Column, Won by 56 runs to 49. Church Parade 10.30 hrs.

Reference secret orders issued in preparation for advance into Germany in case Peace Terms not signed, battalion warned that this was J-3 day. Preparations for move made accordingly. B & C coys recalled from Musketry detachment.

J-2 day. Preparations for move completed. Lorry convoy arrived, also detachment of 2 officers & 11 O.R. of R.F.A. personnel with one 18 pounder gun to accompany the battalion in the two central motor lorries.

Battalion with detachment of R.F.A. embussed and moved off as part of B Brigade convoy. Strength 24 officers 626 O.R. Infantry. 2 officers 11 O.R. & one eighteen pounder gun R.F.A. Route. The Walls. Bayen Strasse. New Bridge. DEUTZ. MULHEIM. BERG GLADBACH. BIESFELD, where the battalion bivouacked for the night alongside the road. Details

E.J.M.

WAR DIARY
or
INTELLIGENCE SUMMARY
(Erase heading not required.)

Army Form C. 2118.

June 1919 (3)

Place	Date	Hour	Summary of Events and Information	Remarks and references to Appendices
Continued BIESFELD	19/6/19		of unfit men, band etc were left in COLOGNE to follow after the battalion with the Horse Transport. Strength of this party, 1 Officer 42 O.R. Strength of Transport 1 Officer 43 O.R.	
BIESFELD	20/6/19	14.00.	As the advance into Germany was postponed, battalion embarked and proceeded to new camping ground (on roadside 1½ mile S. of KÜRTEN (BROICH), and thus nearer the perimeter. Bivouacked here, and joined by details and transport. Swimming pool constructed at once by damming the stream near the camp.	
BROICH CAMP	21/6/19		Battalion practised Outpost schemes by Coys in the morning, baseball, swimming etc in afternoon.	
"	22/6/19		Church Parade. 10.00 hrs. Tents arrived and bivouac done away with.	
"	23/6/19	06.30	Battalion route-marched to LAUDENBERG and occupied a practise outpost position. The Commander in Chief, British Army of the Rhine, GENERAL SIR WILLIAM ROBERTSON passing in his car, got out and watched the men bathing.	
		15.00		
		19.00	Message from Brigade that Germans had asked for 1 day's extension of armistice and had been refused, and that our next message would be to move or not forward into Germany. Certain steps taken in view of former possibility.	
		21.45	Message that Germans had promised to sign peace terms, and in consequence all orders for move forward into Germany were cancelled.	E.J.M.

Army Form C. 2118.

WAR DIARY
or
INTELLIGENCE SUMMARY
(Erase heading not required.)

June 1919 (4)

Summary of Events and Information	Remarks and references to Appendices
Battalion route-marched towards WIPPERFURTH and practised outpost scheme. Afternoon recreation. Company tactical schemes during morning, swimming, baseball etc and band performance afternoon. As on 25.6.19. Training as on 25.6.19. Strength 35 officers 892 O.R., of whom 9 officers and 155 O.R. were away from the battalion on detached employment, courses, hospital, leave etc. Preliminary orders for return to COLOGNE issued. At 6 p.m. message received that Peace was signed. Church Parade 10.00 hrs. Embussed and left for COLOGNE, all but a guard of 1 Officer 2 NCO's and 12 men left with the tents which were left standing to dry. Arrived former billets SUEZ, COLOGNE at 16.05 hrs.	G.J.M.

J.H.... ...

WAR DIARY
or
INTELLIGENCE SUMMARY.
(Erase heading not required.)

Army Form C. 2118.

July 1919

Place	Date	Hour	Summary of Events and Information	Remarks and references to Appendices
COLOGNE	1/7/19		5 2nd Bn. Northumberland Fusiliers.	
"	2/7/19		Billets BERGENRATHER STR. SULZ, COLOGNE.	
"	3/7/19		'B'+'C' Coys. to LAACHEM & RIEHL respectively to complete firing of E.M.C.	
"			General Holiday by order G.O.C. in C. – Peace signed.	
"	4/7/19	1630hrs	Miss Lena Ashwells Concert Party visits the Bn. and plays in School Gymnasium.	
"			1500 Officers men proceed on RHINE TRIP. Left COLOGNE 07.45 hrs & entrained at Bonn. Returned 1900 hrs.	
"	5/7/19		Battalion assume the duties of 13th Battalion – Projects.	
"	6/7/19		Church Parade.	
"	7/7/19		'B' & 'C' Coys return from Musketry Camps.	
"	8/7/19		Coys. proceed to Laachem to fire E.M.C. (2140. & OR.) Bath. Strength 34 Officers 890. O.R.	
"	12/7/19		Battalion assume duties of 'A' Bn. (Guards) Strength supplied 8 Officers 225 OR.	
"	13/7/19		Church Parade for details.	
"	15/7/19		Bn. on Guards. Strength 34 Officers 890 O.R.	
"	18/7/19		Rhine Trip: 50 Officers rotc. from details left behind.	
"	19/7/19		Ends return to Billets being relieved by 51st Bn. Dorth'd Fus. Strength 34 Officers 889 O.R.	
"			General Holiday for Peace Celebration.	
"	20/7/19		Church Parade.	

WAR DIARY or INTELLIGENCE SUMMARY

Army Form C. 2118.

2nd Bn. Northumberland Fusiliers.

July 1919

Syllabus of training & Education came into operation: 2 Corps 2 whole mornings a week education, whole mornings training: other 2 Corps all 4 whole days: Wednesday ½ holiday for Bn.: Saturday & Sunday for Interior Economy: Large numbers admitted to Corps & Army Schools. Lunch for those outside: ½ morning on Education with the Bn. "A" "B" "C" Corps Education, "C" "D" Corps Training. Strength 34 Officers 889 O.R.

Training & Education: Bn. Sports due to be held had to be cancelled owing to heavy rain.

"A" Corps Platoon & Company Drill: Details to Rifle Practice 19 E.M.C. Air and Rifle in the morning.

Battalion assumed duties of "B" Bn. (Projects) Another Project is added from this date Details to circulate in THIEBOLD SASSE & AGRIPPA STR. on Saturdays & Sundays only. Strength 34 Officers 886 O.R.

Church Parades.

"B" "C" Corps inoculated: "C" & "D" Carry out training: New N.C.Os chosen under 2/Lt. RODGER Commence "D" Corps inoculated.

Training as for programme: Coy. Sports in afternoon; Duties to pic. and parties to LOCHEM by train. Strength 34 Officers 886 O.R.

Army Form C. 2118.

August 1919.

WAR DIARY
or
INTELLIGENCE SUMMARY.
(Erase heading not required.)

52nd Bn. Northumberland Fusiliers.

Place	Date	Hour	Summary of Events and Information	Remarks and references to Appendices
COLOGNE	1/8/19		Billets BERRENRATHER STR. SULZ. COLOGNE	
"	2/8/19		A & B Coys. Training. Lecture by Bn. Ed. Officer 1130 hrs. Bn. Cinema in Gym.	
"	3/8/19		C & D Coys. Parade with inoculation. All coys. Medical & Dermatological Schools.	
"	4/8/19		Bn assumes duties "A" Batl. Guards mounts in Remagier St. unmarked Pl. 0530 hrs. Church Parade for details left from Guards.	
"	5/8/19		Observed as holiday as far as possible. VI Corps Torch Light Tattoo 2100 hrs at STADTWALD.	
"	6/8/19		Training & Education as per programme. EIFFELTOR Guard. 2 eoffr Gr B.N. Coy & 5 men return ex STADTWALD. VI Corps Torchlight Tattoo in STADTWALD. W.O. & 51 of N.F. Elementary made by special Officer at 1200hrs. VI Corps Torchlight Tattoo in review in SPIELPLATZ. Cadre match afternoon Officers v. O.R's all available men practice on SPIELPLATZ.	
"	7/8/19		Training & Education as per programme. Officers & N.C.O's visit Practice new Gas.	
"	8/8/19		Training & Education as per programme. Coy Cmdrs at lecture Corps school on Education. Cricket match against 53rd N.F. unknown they won.	
"	9/8/19		Guards relieved Medical inspection Baths. Cricket inter-Junior P.Bn. A.A.	
"	10/8/19		Church Parades.	
"	11/8/19		Training & Ceremonial Parade	

Army Form C. 2118.

August 1919

WAR DIARY
or
INTELLIGENCE SUMMARY.
(Erase heading not required.)

Place	Date	Hour	Summary of Events and Information	Remarks and references to Appendices
COLOGNE	12/8/19		Continued.	
"	12/8/19		Training + Lectures to Bn by Coffr. – at Corps school.: Through 1st Battn. 3 Officers attended lectures on Civics in afternoon. Cricket match. Officers v. O.R.'s. Tea served on ground.	
"	13/8/19		Training + Brigade review in the morning. Lecture on New Savings to O.R. corps in afternoon. another lecture on civics to same Officers as before.	
"	14/8/19		Education + Training. Last lecture on civics in afternoon.	
"	15/8/19		Brigade Review by Maj. Gen. Kennedy.	
"	16/8/19		Lectures + Eng. Exam. – cadets. Inspection by C.O.	
"	17/8/19		Church Parades.	
"	18/8/19		Review in _____ by Army Council. 15 Officers + 45 + OR's on Parade.	
"	19/8/19		assumed duties of "B" battalion. Disposal: 1 Off. 13 O.R.'s. Guard on Military Gov[ernor]. Training v Education as per Programme.	
"	20/8/19		Training, Etc. "C" Coy: "AT HOME" – Guard. 200 OR attended.	
"	21/8/19		Training. Rendezvous as per Programme.	
"	22/8/19		assumed duties of "A" Battalion. Parade Regimental Strength 45 Off. 29 W.O.s. 175 O.R.s.	
"	23/8/19		Church Parade. VI Corps school. 11.35 hrs.	
"	24/8/19		Training + August all-night.	
"	25/8/19			

Army Form C. 2118.

WAR DIARY
or
INTELLIGENCE SUMMARY.
(Erase heading not required.)

August 1919

	Summary of Events and Information	Remarks and references to Appendices

...continued

Training & Education as Per Programme
" " " " "
" " " " "
" " " " "
" " " " "

1-8-19 Relieved of all guards by 57th N.Z. ammun. C. battln entrain. Church Parade VI corps school march passed corps comnd.

J. Huntly Lt. Col.
Comdg 52nd North ambulance tups

Army Form C. 2118

WAR DIARY or **INTELLIGENCE SUMMARY**
(Erase heading not required.)

September 1919

Remarks and references to Appendices

52nd Batt. Northumberland Fusiliers.

Battn. Bombardier Lt. Litz. Colyn.

Training Education. Full morning was inspection by C.O. & A & B Coy in Rupenwiesen.
Afternoon in Buttgarten B & C Coy dance in Gym. 2000hrs.
Battalion Sports in POLLER WIESEN Grounds. Began swimming 1430hrs.
Prize presented by M.T. & arty. "C" Coy winner. D Coy chased Cup.
Inspection of A. & D Coys by C.O. A + D Coys whist drive in Gym.
Training Education. Steen Pergli whist drive in Gym at 2015hrs.
Batt C. Coys football match at 1400hrs. C winning 4 goals score.

Church Parade. — Battalion
Training Education. D+C football match C winning. Brigade Cinema in Gym.
Training Area School.

do.

Days thrown in Gym. attendance good. 200hrs.
Armed duties by "A" Battalion during 53rd N.F. Drill Guards
from Army Rifle meeting winner up in N.º 4 tea event. Cpl Roberts

Army Form C. 2118.

No. 71

WAR DIARY
or
INTELLIGENCE SUMMARY.
(Erase heading not required.)

Place	Date	Hour	Summary of Events and Information	Remarks and references to Appendices
COLOGNE	14.9.19		52nd Bn. N.F./Northumberland Fusiliers	
"	15.9.19		Church Parade VI Corps school	
"	16.9.19		Training & Education	
"	17.9.19		do	
"	18.9.19		do	
"	19.9.19		do	
"	20.9.19		Relieved Jail Guards by 57th N.F.	
"	21.9.19		Church Parade VI Corps School	
"	22.9.19		Lecture by Adj. Battalion Officers	
"	23.9.19		Moved from billets by route march relieving 53rd N.F. in ARTILLERY Barracks. BONNER STRASS. MORIENBURG	
"	24.9.19		Coys. cleaning Barracks Etc.	
"	25.9.19		Training & Education. Football match v. Barracks. A+B Coys. "B" winning 6-0	
"	26.9.19		do do do C & D Coys. D winning 4-0.	
"	27.9.19		Assumed duties of "A" Bat. relieving 57th N.F. Guard mounting Parade in Barrack Foot-ball Match. 1430 hrs. Batt v. R.E's. Batt winning 3-0	

Army Form C. 2118.

WAR DIARY
or
INTELLIGENCE SUMMARY.
(Erase heading not required.)

September 1919

Place	Date	Hour	Summary of Events and Information	Remarks and references to Appendices
COLOGNE	28.9.19		52nd Bn. Northumberland Fusiliers	
"	29.9.19		Church Parade in Barracks	
"	30.9.19		Training & Education Music Parade in Barracks at 9.45am	
			do	

30-9-19.

J.V. Hardy Lt. Col.
Comdg. 52nd Bn. Northumberland Fusiliers

WAR DIARY or INTELLIGENCE SUMMARY

Army Form C. 2118.

October 1919.

Place	Date	Hour	Summary of Events and Information	Remarks and references to Appendices
	Oct 1919 1st		Training (Barrack Square)	
	2nd		Training & Education. Football match Officers v Sgts. Sgts won 3 to 1.	
	3rd		Training & Education.	
	4th		Relieved of all Guards & assumed duties of "B" Battalion. Football match with 51st N.F. Lost 2 to 1.	
	5th		Church Parade on Barrack Square by Senior Chaplain.	
	6th		Training and Education. Football match in afternoon. Received word Railway strike had been settled.	
	7th		Training & Education. Soccer match Probables v Probables on Barrack Ground.	
	8th		Route march. First 2 Platoon football matches.	
	9th		Training & Education. Football match with A.V.C. Drawn 2-1.	
	10th		Training & Education.	
	11th		Assumed duties of "A" Battalion relieving 51st N.F. of all Bde Guards.	
	12th		Church Parades.	
	13th		Training & Education. Composite Company	

Army Form C. 2118.

October 1919

WAR DIARY
or
INTELLIGENCE SUMMARY
(Erase heading not required.)

Instructions regarding War Diaries and Intelligence Summaries are contained in F.S. Regs., Part II. and the Staff Manual respectively. Title pages will be prepared in manuscript.

Place	Date	Hour	Summary of Events and Information	Remarks and references to Appendices
	Oct. 1919			
	14th		Training and Education. Football match 51st Sqds v 52nds Sqds. 52nd won 5-2	
	15th		Training and Education.	
	16th		Training and Education.	
	17th		Training and Education. Platoon football matches.	
	18th		Relieved of all Guards by 51st N.F. and assumed duties of "B" Bn.	
	19th		Church Parade. Padre preached his last sermon to the Unit - Rev. W. Sellers. C.F.	
	20th		Training and Education.	
	21st		Received draft from 53rd N.F. of 86 O.R's.	
	22nd		Training and Education as per programme.	
	23rd		Training of Education "Smoker" held at night by Sgts. Invitation sent to officers accepted.	
	24th		Training and Education.	
	25th		Mounted Part of Rde Guards. Hockey match in afternoon Bn v Cyclists. Result Bn won 5 to NIL.	
	26th		Church Parade. Football match in afternoon. Blues v Reds - Draw.	

Army Form C. 2118.
October 1919.

WAR DIARY
or
INTELLIGENCE SUMMARY
(Erase heading not required.)

Instructions regarding War Diaries and Intelligence Summaries are contained in F. S. Regs., Part II. and the Staff Manual respectively. Title pages will be prepared in manuscript.

Place	Date	Hour	Summary of Events and Information	Remarks and references to Appendices
	Oct. 1919. 27th		Training & Education.	
	28th		"B" Company & part of "A" Company proceeded to Antwerp to take over Guard duties etc. 5 Officers 200 O.R's.	
	29th		"D" proceeded to Barracks for Patrol and Police duty etc under D.A.P.M. 3 Officers 108 O.R's.	
	30th		"C" Company took over Police Duty etc. under D.A.P.M. 2 Officers 122 O.R's.	
	31st		Barracks in Roman Gr., taken over by 19th Middlesex.	

J. Murphy Lt. Col.
Cmdg 52nd Northumberland Fus.

BEF

Northern Div
formerly 3 Div.

Northern Bde

51 Northumberland Fus

1919 Mar to 1919 Oct.

To 2 Inft Bde
Rhine Garrison

WAR DIARY
or
INTELLIGENCE SUMMARY.
(Erase heading not required.)

Army Form C. 2118.

Place	Date	Hour	Summary of Events and Information	Remarks and references to Appendices
July Cologne	March 1919			
	17th	Morning	Demonstration of Guard Duties. Educational Training	
		Afternoon	Football Training i.e. Platoon Practice. One company bathing	
	18th	Morning	Battalion carried out training as per syllabus	
		Afternoon	One company recreational training; One company bathing; two companies general education.	
	19th	Morning	Battalion Ceremonial & Close Order Drill.	
		Afternoon	One company bathing. Remainder Platoon Football Practice. Brigadier General A.A. Kennedy C.M.G. took over command of Brigade today.	
	20th	Morning	One company Education. Remainder carried out training as per syllabus. The Divisional Commander inspected the various guards.	
		Afternoon	One company bathing. General Education. Platoon Football Practice	
	21st	Morning	One company Education. One company detached guard. Two companies carried out Route March.	
		Afternoon	Companies paying out.	

Army Form C. 2118.

WAR DIARY
or
INTELLIGENCE SUMMARY.
(Erase heading not required.)

Instructions regarding War Diaries and Intelligence Summaries are contained in F.S. Regs., Part II. and the Staff Manual respectively. Title pages will be prepared in manuscript.

Place	Date	Hour	Summary of Events and Information	Remarks and references to Appendices
Sully Cologne	March 22nd	Morning	Battalion carried out interior economy and medical inspections.	
		Afternoon	Battalion on sports.	
	23rd	Sunday	Battalion on Church Parade.	
	24th	Morning	Battalion on Education. Lecture on Cycles Slavedom Tournaments By Lieut. T. Hunterbrigg. The lecture was thoroughly appreciated by officers and men.	
		Afternoon	Battalion carried out training as per syllabus.	
	25th	Morning	Battalion on Education.	
		Afternoon	Battalion Stand by in case of Bolshevist Rising.	
	26th	Morning	Battalion on Education.	
		Afternoon	Half holiday. One Company Bathing.	
	27th	Morning	Battalion on Recreational & Educational training and one company bathing.	
		Afternoon	Recreational, Educational training and one company bathing.	
	28th	Morning	Owing to inclemency of the weather battalion carried out drill in barracks.	
		Afternoon	Companies kept in.	
	29th	Morning	Commanding Officer inspected "B" Coy. A lecture was given by Colonel J.G. Adams, Chief Dental Surgeon, his subject being "Prevention". This was very instructive and both officers and men learnt a great deal from it.	
		Afternoon	Half holiday. Owing to inclement weather men could not carry out sports.	

(A8041) Wt W1771/M2031 750,000 5/17 Sch. 53 Forms/C2118/14
D. D. & L., London, E.C.

Army Form C. 2118.

WAR DIARY
or
INTELLIGENCE SUMMARY.
(Erase heading not required.)

Summary of Events and Information	Remarks and references to Appendices

Sunday Battalion on Church Parade.

Monday a. was programme of training will as usual at promulgated including to day morning training carried out in usual weekly educational work.

Afternoon M.C D.C class under Adjutant. Sports arranged.

31.3.19.

Nicholson. C. Lt.
Commanding 51st North'd. Fus.

To Ist. Northern Brigade,

Herewith WAR DIARY for month of APRIL.

[signature] Lt. Col.
Commanding 5Ist. Northumberland Fusiliers

Cologne
30/4/19.

Army Form C. 2118.

WAR DIARY
or
INTELLIGENCE SUMMARY.
(Erase heading not required.)

Vol 2 Nov?

5th B— Northumberland Fus.

Place	Date	Hour	Summary of Events and Information	Remarks and references to Appendices
Suzy Bologne	April 1919			
	1st	Morning	Battalion "Standing to". A Lecture on Temperance was given by Colonel Sanders R.A. and Capt. Weeks R.A.M.C. Officers and men greatly interested.	
		Afternoon	Football.	
	2nd	Morning	Training in billets. Lecture by Mr. J.E. King. Subject "How the Navy helped the Army to win the war." This promises to be a very instructive lecture to officers and men.	
		Afternoon	Inter Platoon football. Battalion teams played 63rd & 12th M.F. Score drawn.	
	3rd	O.O.		
		Morning	Battalion carried out training as per programme. One company Education. J.O.C. inspected Rev. Bradford.	
		Afternoon	One company education. One company bathing.	
	4th	Morning	Ceremonial Drill.	
		Afternoon	Companies paying out.	
	5th	Morning	C.O. inspecting billets.	
		Afternoon	Half Holiday. Sports.	
	6th	Sunday	Battalion Church Parade.	

Army Form C. 2118.

5/1st Northumberland Inn

WAR DIARY
or
INTELLIGENCE SUMMARY.
(Erase heading not required.)

Instructions regarding War Diaries and Intelligence Summaries are contained in F. S. Regs., Part II. and the Staff Manual respectively. Title pages will be prepared in manuscript.

Place	Date	Hour	Summary of Events and Information	Remarks and references to Appendices
Lule Colge	April 1919 7th	Morning	Battalion carried out training as per syllabus. Lt. Col. A.E. Greenwell took over command of Battalion 13-day.	
		Afternoon	One company Bathing. Remainder on Sports.	
	8th	Morning	Battalion carried out training as per syllabus. Changing of Warsaw guard.	
		Afternoon	One company bathing. Remainder on Sports.	
	9th	Morning	Battalion on Company Drill. Lt. Col. L.S.E. Worden proceeded to England.	
		Afternoon	Inter-Platoon Football competition.	
	10th	Morning	Battalion carried out training as per syllabus.	
		Afternoon	One company bathing. Remainder on Sports.	
	11th	Morning	A Futur 11th & Battalion were to as by Capt J.G. Adams. 147 men have proceeded Zup 4 the Rhine. Phil were drawing by night.	
	12th	Afternoon	Companies payed out.	
			games among Companies.	
		Afternoon	Sports. The Batter beat the 53rd by two goals to nil.	
	13th	Sunday	Batt. on Church Parade	
	14th	Morning	Education & Drill "A" Coy. Coy. by M.E.	
		Afternoon	Drill and Sports.	

Army Form C. 2118.

WAR DIARY
or
INTELLIGENCE SUMMARY.
(Erase heading not required.)

51st Northumberland Fus.

Place	Date	Hour	Summary of Events and Information	Remarks and references to Appendices
Cologne	April 1919 15th	Morning	Training as per syllabus	
		Afternoon	Sports	
	16th	Morning	Education & military training	
		Afternoon	Sports Programme carried out	
	17th	Morning	Route march weather failed/programme carried at same	
		Afternoon	Training on Monday	
	18th		Good Friday. Battalion on Church Parade. Sports Programme arranged by all battalion. Battalion beat the Rest	
	19th	Morning	Lorries brought Bn away. Brought J. Normale guard.	
		Afternoon	Sports Battn beat 52nd 4-1	
	20th	Sunday	Battn on Church Parade.	
	21st	Morning	Battn training as per syllabus "A" by firing	
		Afternoon	Sports	

Army Form C. 2118.

51st Northumberland Div

WAR DIARY
or
INTELLIGENCE SUMMARY.
(Erase heading not required.)

Instructions regarding War Diaries and Intelligence Summaries are contained in F. S. Regs., Part II. and the Staff Manual respectively. Title pages will be prepared in manuscript.

Place	Date	Hour	Summary of Events and Information	Remarks and references to Appendices.
Lully Troops	April 1919 22nd		Morning Training as per Syllabus. Afternoon Recreational Training from 3.0 p.m.	
	23rd		St George's Day. "The Red & White Rose" was worn by everyone in the Battn. A Special Dinner was given. At 2-0 we began the sports. A football match agst the 62nd Bn resulted in a win 4-1 for the 52nd. The 52nd lost the wrestling match in Mules & we beat them agn at the tug of war. A mule race provided much amusement. After the sports a High Tea was given. At 6-45 the Battn Brass Party gave an excellent concert, the day was completed by the new having a splendid supper.	
	24th		Morning Training as per syllabus. Afternoon Drill & Recreational training. Lecture by Rev. J.H. Hazlett on the origin & prevention of Venereal Disease	
	25th		Morning Education P.T. and Platoon Drill. Afternoon Recreational & Companies joined out.	

Army Form C. 2118.

WAR DIARY
or
INTELLIGENCE SUMMARY.
(Erase heading not required.)

1/1st Northumberland Yeo.

Instructions regarding War Diaries and Intelligence Summaries are contained in F. S. Regs., Part II. and the Staff Manual respectively. Title pages will be prepared in manuscript.

Place	Date	Hour	Summary of Events and Information	Remarks and references to Appendices
Sidi Bishr	April 1919			
	26th	Morning	Interior Economy	
		Afternoon	Inclement weather prevented Sports	
	27th	Sunday	Divine Service	
	28th	Morning	Training as per syllabus	
		Afternoon	Drill & one company bathing	
	29th	Morning	Lecture by Lord Morris on Palestine. G.O.C's Inspection	
		Afternoon	Musketry & Gas Drill. One Company bathing.	
	30th	Morning	Education and Ceremonial Drill.	
		Afternoon	Sports.	

Rolaque
30.4.19.

[signature]
Lt. Col.
Commanding 1/1st Bn. Northd. Fus.

51st Northumberland Fusiliers

Army Form C. 2118.

WAR DIARY
or
INTELLIGENCE SUMMARY.
(Erase heading not required.)

Instructions regarding War Diaries and Intelligence Summaries are contained in F. S. Regs., Part II. and the Staff Manual respectively. Title pages will be prepared in manuscript.

Place	Date	Hour	Summary of Events and Information	Remarks and references to Appendices
Sulz. Cologne	May 1919 1st.		Morning Lecture on Submarine Warfare by Commdr. Everrard. Drill. Afternoon One Company Bathed remainder on Drill and Recreation.	
	2nd.		Morning Education and Drill. Afternoon Companies paying out.	
	3rd.		Saturday Interior Economy. Anticipated Billet Inspection by G. in C. Sir W. Robertson. Battalion takes over Guard Duties. B and C Companies being detached.	
	4th.		Sunday A Company Divine Service.	
	5th.		Monday A Company reports to O.C. 52nd. Northumberland Fusiliers. to form Composite Brigade for Inspection by Divisional General.	
	6th.		Morning General Routine. Afternoon Lecture on Peace Conference.	
	7th.		Wednesday General Routine. Recreation.	
	8th.		Morning Review by Duke of Connaught. A Company supplied 50 O.R. Afternoon General Routine. Guards etc.	
	9th.		Friday General Routine. Companies paying out.	
	10th.		Saturday Battalion relieved from Guard Duties. Soccer Team beaten by West Kents 2-1	
	11th.		Sunday Divine Service.	
	12th.		B and C Companies firing G.M.C. A Company finding reliefs. D Company for training.	
	13th.		General Routine. Sig. Moom L. R. Drowned in HOHENSTAUFENRING BATHS.	
	14th.		Morning A.D.M.S. inspected billets. Afternoon D Company on Recreation.	

51st Northumberland Fusiliers

Army Form C. 2118.

WAR DIARY
or
INTELLIGENCE SUMMARY.
(Erase heading not required.)

	Summary of Events and Information	Remarks and references to Appendices
	General Routine. One Company's Training.	
Morning	General Routine.	
Afternoon	Lecture by Venn Archdeacon Jones. Subject Pioneers of Social Reform. (Wilberforce- Shaftesbury- Peel.) G.O.C. Inspected Transport.	
Morning	Battalion becomes B Battn. and takes over Picquets. Interior Economy.	
Afternoon	Recreation Cricket.	
Sunday	Divine Service.	
Monday	B&C Companies firing. A Company finding butt parties and reliefs.	
Tuesday	B & C Companies return.	
Wednesday	B & C Companies at Company Commanders disposal. A Company removed to Fire Station.	
Thursday.	Route March.	
Friday	General Routine. Companies paying out.	
Saturday.	Battalion takes over guard duties.	
Sunday.	Divine Service.	
Monday.	One Company training.	
Tuesday	Battn. on guard duties.	
Wednesday	Brigade Cinema opened. Picquet called out to help A.P.M.'S Staff. in Aegidius Strasse	
Thursday.	General Routine.	

Army Form C. 2118.

WAR DIARY
or
INTELLIGENCE SUMMARY.
(Erase heading not required.)

Summary of Events and Information	Remarks and references to Appendices

Friday Companies paying out.

Saturday Battalion relieved of Guard Duties.

Cologne
31/5/19

[signature]
Lieut. Colonel
Commanding 51st. Northumberland Fusiliers.

51st Battalion Northumberland Fusiliers.

Army Form C. 2118.

JUNE 1919.
WAR DIARY
or
INTELLIGENCE SUMMARY.
(Erase heading not required.)

Instructions regarding War Diaries and Intelligence Summaries are contained in F. S. Regs., Part II. and the Staff Manual respectively. Title pages will be prepared in manuscript.

Place	Date	Hour	Summary of Events and Information	Remarks and references to Appendices
Sulz.				
Cologne.	1st.	Sunday.	Divine Service.	
	2nd.	Monday.	"A" and "D" Companies practising for Musketry Course.	
	3rd.	Tuesday.	Kings Birthday General Holiday. Platoon Football Competitions final :- 5 Platoon "B" Coy. 4. 9 Platoon "C" Coy. 5.	
	4th.	Wednesday.	Training as per programme.	
	5th.	Thursday.	"A" and "D" Companies firing. "B" and "C" finding reliefs.	
	6th.	Friday.	Training for "B" and "C" Companies as per programme.	
	7th.	Saturday.	Interior Economy, Sports and Recreation.	
	8th.	Sunday.	Divine Service.	
	9th.	Monday.	General Holiday.	
	10th.	Tuesday.	General Routine.	
	11th.	Wednesday.	Morning. Training as per syllabus. Afternoon. Recreation.	
	12th.	Thursday.	General Routine. "A" and "D" Companies finish firing.	
	13th.	Friday.	"A" and "D" Companies return.	
	14th.	Saturday.	Battalion becomes "A" Battalion and takes over Guards accordingly.	
	15th.	Sunday.	Divine Service.	
	16th.		General Routine.	
	17th.		General Routine.	
	18th.	Wednesday.	Battalion preparing to move forward. All Guards relieved by 9th London Regiment.	
	19th.	Thursday.	Battalion moved forward. Embussed at 0826 and proceeded to DURSCHIED via HEUMAR, NEUE BRUCKE, BERG GLADBACH. Battalion Bivouacked on Field S.W. of Village. Battalion Headquarters situated in Custos House.	
	20th.	Friday.	Morning. Companies parade for training. Musketry, P.T. etc. Afternoon. Battalion embussed at 2 p.m. and embussed for BROICH arriving at 1515 hours. Men bivouacked. Officers and Orderly Room accommodated in tents.	
	21st.	Saturday.	Morning. Companies training. Afternoon. Recreation etc.	
	22nd.	Sunday.	Tents arrive from Brigade H.Q. and are erected. Divine Service.	
	23rd.	Monday.	Battalion paraded at 8.30 and proceeded on Brigade Outpost Scheme. "A", "C" and "D" Companies on outpost. "B" Company in reserve. Battalion Headquarters at EICHHOF. Recreation etc. in afternoon.	

Army Form C. 2118.

WAR DIARY
or
INTELLIGENCE SUMMARY.

51st Battalion Northumberland Fusiliers

(Erase heading not required.)

	Summary of Events and Information	Remarks and references to Appendices

...day. **Morning.** Interior Economy.
Afternoon. Recreation etc.

...sday. Commanding Officer proceeded on leave.
Companies parade for Instructional Outpost Scheme.

...day. Brigade Signal Scheme. Companies carry on training in Camp.
Sports etc. in afternoon.

...y. Demonstration of attacking a strong point.
Sports etc. in the afternoon.

...day. Companies training. Sports etc. in afternoon.
Peace signed and Battalion prepares to move back to Cologne.

...y. Battalion embussed at 0900 hours for Cologne. Arrived at Sulz at 1115. Guard left with tents etc.

...y. Battalion takes over Guards from 9th London Regiment

G.G. Carpenter
MAJOR
Commanding 51st Bn. Northd. Fusrs.

Army Form C. 2118.

51st Battalion Northumberland Fusiliers.

WAR DIARY
or
INTELLIGENCE SUMMARY.
(Erase heading not required.)

JUNE 1919

Instructions regarding War Diaries and Intelligence Summaries are contained in F. S. Regs., Part II. and the Staff Manual respectively. Title pages will be prepared in manuscript.

Place	Date	Hour	Summary of Events and Information	Remarks and references to Appendices
Sulz. Cologne.	1st.	Sunday.	Divine Service.	
	2nd.	Monday.	"A" and "D" Companies practising for Musketry Course.	
	3rd.	Tuesday.	Kings Birthday General Holiday. Platoon Football Competitions final :- 5 Platoon "B" Coy. 2. 9 Platoon "C" Company 5.	
	4th.	Wednesday.	Training as per programme.	
	5th.	Thursday.	"A" and "D" Companies firing. "B" and "C" finding reliefs.	
	6th.	Friday.	Training for "B" and "C" Companies as per programme.	
	7th.	Saturday.	Interior Economy, Sports and Recreation.	
	8th.	Sunday.	Divine Service.	
	9th.	Monday.	General Holiday.	
	10th.	Tuesday.	General Routine.	
	11th.	Wednesday.	Morning. Training as per syllabus. Afternoon. Recreation.	
	12th.	Thursday.	General Routine. "A" and "D" Companies finish firing.	
	13th.	Friday.	"A" and "D" Companies return.	
	14th.	Saturday.	Battalion becomes "A" Battalion and takes over Guards accordingly.	
	15th.	Sunday.	Divine Service.	
	16th.	General Routine.		
	17th.	General Routine.		
	18th.	Wednesday.	Battalion preparing to move forward. All Guards relieved by 9th London Regiment.	
	19th.	Thursday.	Battalion moved forward. Embussed at 0826 and proceeded to DURSCHED via HEUMARKT, NEUF "RUCKE, BERG GLADBACH. Battalion Bivouacked on Field S.W. of Village. Battalion Headquarters situated in Custers House.	
	20th.	Friday.	Morning. Companies parade for training. Musketry, P.T. etc. Afternoon. Battalion embussed at 2 p.m. and embussed for BROICH arriving at 1515 hours. Men bivouacked. Officers and Orderly Room accomodated in tents.	
	21st.	Saturday.	Morning. Companies training. Afternoon. Recreation etc.	
	22nd.	Sunday.	Tents arrive from Brigade H.Q. and are erected. Divine Service.	
	23rd.	Monday.	Battalion paraded at 8.30 and proceeded on Brigade Outpost Scheme. "A", "C" and "D" Companies on outpost. "B" Company in reserve. Battalion Headquarters at EICHHOF. Recreation etc. in afternoon.	

51st Battalion Northumberland Fusiliers. Army Form C. 2118.

JUNE 1919.

WAR DIARY or INTELLIGENCE SUMMARY.

(Erase heading not required.)

Place	Date	Hour	Summary of Events and Information	Remarks and references to Appendices
Sulz. Cologne.	24th.Tuesday.		Morning. Interior Economy. Afternoon. Recreation etc.	
	25th.Wednesday.		Commanding officer proceeded on leave. Companies parade for Instructional Outpost Scheme.	
	26th.Thursday.		Brigade Signal Scheme. Companies carry on training in Camp. Sports etc. in afternoon.	
	27th.Friday.		Demonstration of attacking a strong point. Sports etc. in the afternoon.	
	28th.Saturday.		Companies training. Sports etc. in afternoon. Peace signed and Battalion prepares to move back to Cologne.	
	29th.Sunday.		Battalion embussed at 0900 hours for Cologne. Arrived at Sulz at 1115. Guard left with tents etc.	
	30th.Monday.		Battalion takes over Guards from 9th London Regiment	

G.J. Capenter
Major
Commanding 51st Bn. Northd. Fusrs.

51st Battalion NORTHUMBERLAND FUSILIERS.

WAR DIARY
or
INTELLIGENCE SUMMARY.
(Erase heading not required.)

Army Form C. 2118.

Instructions regarding War Diaries and Intelligence Summaries are contained in F. S. Regs., Part II. and the Staff Manual respectively. Title pages will be prepared in manuscript.

Place	Date	Hour	Summary of Events and Information	Remarks and references to Appendices
Sulz, Cologne.	July 1919.			
	1st.		Quarterly Audit Board held. President:- Major C.G.Arkwright M.C. Battalion on Guard duties.	
	2nd.		Battalion on Guard duties.	
	3rd.		Holiday to celebrate the signing of Peace.	
	4th.		Battalion on Guard duties.	
	5th.		Battalion becomes "C" Battalion and hands over Guard duties.	
	6th.		Divine Service. Brigadier General J.W.Sandilands C.B.,C.M.G.,D.S.O. assumed Command of Brigade on this date.	
	7th.		Battalion Parade. General Routine.	
	8th.		Training as per Programme.	
	9th.		Casuals firing G.M.C. at Reihl. Remainder General Routine.	
	10th.		Route March.	

51st Battalion NORTHUMBERLAND FUSILIERS.

WAR DIARY
or
INTELLIGENCE SUMMARY.
(Erase heading not required.)

Army Form C. 2118.

Place	Date	Hour	Summary of Events and Information	Remarks and references to Appendices
Sulz. Cologne.	July 1919. 11th.		Training as per syllabus.	
	12th.		Battalion becomes "B" Battalion and takes over picquets.	
	13th.		Divine Service.	
	14th.		Lecture by Mr.James Burns M.A. Subject:- An hour at the National Gallery. This lecture was thoroughly appreciated by all ranks of this Battalion who attended. Lieut.Col.A.C.Girdwood C.M.G.,D.S.O., Captain Pigg D.S.O.,M.C., Allied Victory March, Paris. and 4 N.C.Os. of this Battalion were present.	
	15th.		Examination at VIth Corps School for candidates sitting for 3rd Class Army Certificate.	
	16th.		Training as per programme.	
	17th.		Heats for Sports run off in the afternoon.	
	18th.		Battalion Sports Day. Weather very fine. The Band of 52nd Battalion Northumberland Fus. played selections in the afternoon. Events went off very well. Prizes presented by the Divisional General. A concert was given by the Battalion Concert Party in the evening which was greatly appreciated. Smoking Concert in Sergeant's Mess.	6

Army Form C. 2118.

51st Battalion NORTHUMBERLAND FUSILIERS.

WAR DIARY
or
INTELLIGENCE SUMMARY.
(Erase heading not required.)

Place	Date	Hour	Summary of Events and Information	Remarks and references to Appendices
Sulz, Cologne.	July 1919. 19th.		Battalion becomes "A" Battalion and takes over Guard duties.	
	20th.		Divine Service.	
	21st.		Guard Duties.	
	22nd.		Guard duties. Removal of Transport from Durener Strasse to Eifel Tor.	
	23rd.		Guard Duties.	
	24th.		Guard Duties.	
	25th.		Guard Duties.	
	26th.		Battalion hands over Guard duties and becomes "C" Battalion. Casuals proceed to Fort 2 to fire G.M.C.	
	27th.		Divine Service. 66666	
	28th.		Training as per programme.	

51st Battalion NORTHUMBERLAND FUSILIERS.

WAR DIARY
or
INTELLIGENCE SUMMARY.

(Erase heading not required.)

Army Form C. 2118.

	Summary of Events and Information	Remarks and references to Appendices
	Training as per programme.	
	Ceremonial Drill takes place of Route March.	
	Trainign as per programme.	

y. Cartwright Major.
Commanding 51st Battalion Northumberland Fusiliers.

Army Form C. 2118.

51st. Battalion Northumberland Fusiliers.

WAR DIARY
or
INTELLIGENCE SUMMARY.

(Erase heading not required.)

Instructions regarding War Diaries and Intelligence Summaries are contained in F. S. Regs. Part II. and the Staff Manual respectively. Title pages will be prepared in manuscript.

Place	Date	Hour	Summary of Events and Information	Remarks and references to Appendices
Sulz. Cologne.	AUGUST. 1919. 1st.		Training as per Programme. Practice for Torchlight Tattoo in the evening.	
	2nd.		General Routine. Battalion becomes "B" Battalion and takes over Picquets. Guard for Military Governor's House taken over for 1 week.	
	3rd.		Divine Service. (Collection for Gordon Boys' Homes.)	
	4th.		Training suspended (Bank Holiday) Capt.N.B.Pigg. D.S.O. M.C. and Lieut.G.P.Gale and 80 O.R. to repsent the Battalion in the VI Corps Torchlight Tattoo in evening. Casuals return from LACHEM after firing G.M.C.	
	5th.		Training as per Programme. Torchlight Tattoo again carried out.	
	6th.		Commanding Officer's Ceremonial Parade.	
	7th.		Practice ceremonial parade for Corps Review at Exercier Platz, MERHEIM. Battalion proceeded by lorry. Sgt.G.WAKE. receives the Special Army Education Certificate, Congratulated by G.O.C.Brigade and Commanding Officer.	

Army Form C. 2118.

51st.Battalion Northumberland Fusiliers.

WAR DIARY
or
INTELLIGENCE SUMMARY.
(Erase heading not required.)

Instructions regarding War Diaries and Intelligence Summaries are contained in F. S. Regs., Part II. and the Staff Manual respectively. Title pages will be prepared in manuscript.

Place	Date	Hour	Summary of Events and Information	Remarks and references to Appendices
Sulz COLOGNE.	AUGUST.1919. 8th.		Training as per Programme. Battalion Cross Country Run, Winner :- Pte.Norcliffe, "B" Company.	
	9th.		Battalion becomes "A" Battalion and takes over all Brigade Guards for week.	
	10th.		Divine Service.	
	11th.		Battalion on Guard duties.	
	12th.		Battalion on Guard duties. Lieut.C.D.Lockwood takes over command of "A" Company from Capt. W.E.Richardson.	
	13th.		Battalion On Guard duties.	
	14th.		Battalion on Guard duties.	
	15th.		Battalion on Guard duties. Practice for VI Corps Torchlight Tattoo.	
	16th.		Battalion on Guard duties. Docks Guard taken over from 2nd.Northern Brigade. All Brigade Guards to remain on until 19th. instead of being relieved to-day.	

Army Form C. 2118.

51st. Battalion Northumberland Fusiliers.

WAR DIARY
INTELLIGENCE SUMMARY.
(Erase heading not required.)

Place	Date	Hour	Summary of Events and Information	Remarks and references to Appendices
Sulz. COLOGNE.	AUGUST. 1919. 17th.		Battalion on Guard duties. Divine Service.	
	18th.		Battalion on Guard duties. Brigadier General C.D. Hamilton Moore. C.M.G. D.S.O. takes over Command of this Brigade. Duties of Adjutant taken over by 2/Lieut. J.W. Hunt. VI Corps reviewed by Army Council.	
	19th.		Battalion becomes "C" Battalion and hands over all Brigade Guards to 53rd. Battalion Northumberland Fusiliers. Transport takes 1st. Prize at RHINE ARMY HORSE SHOW for Mess Carts (Mule drawn).	
	20th.		All companies clean up, bathe etc. Casuals proceed to LACHEM to fire G.M.C.	
	21st.		Training as per Programme. Regimental Lewis Gun Class commences under Lewis Gun Officer. Regimental Sergeant Major's Class commences. Regimental colours issued to Companies. Concert by Battalion Concert Party in the evening.	
	22nd.		Training as per Programme.	
	23rd.		General Routine.	

Army Form C. 2118.

51st. Battalion Northumberland Fusiliers.
WAR DIARY
or
INTELLIGENCE SUMMARY.
(Erase heading not required.)

Place	Date	Hour	Summary of Events and Information	Remarks and references to Appendices
Sulz. COLOGNE.	AUGUST. 1919.			
	24th.		Divine Service.	
	25th.		Training as per Programme. Adjutant's Lecture to all N.C.Os.	
	26th.		Training as per Programme. Brigade Cinema Show in Gymnasium.	
	27th.		Battalion Route March.	
	28th.		Training as per Programme. Divisional Eliminating Athletic Meeting. Battalion athletic team ties for 2nd.place and so qualify for Corps trials. Concert by Battalion Concert Party.	
	29th.		All training suspended to enable men to scrub and blanco equipment as ordered by G.O.C.Brigade.	
	30th.		Battalion becomes "A" Battalion and takes over all Brigade Guards from 52nd. Battalion Northumberland Fusiliers. All Picquets taken over.	

51st. Battalion Northumberland Fusiliers.

WAR DIARY
or
INTELLIGENCE SUMMARY.
(Erase heading not required.)

Army Form C. 2118.

Place	Date	Hour	Summary of Events and Information	Remarks and references to Appendices
	AUGUST.1919.			
Sulz. COLOGNE.	31st.		Battalion on Guard and Picquets duties. Divine Service.	

G.G. Carpenter
Major.
Commanding 51st. Battalion Northumberland Fusiliers.

51st Battalion NORTHUMBERLAND FUSILIERS.
WAR DIARY
or
INTELLIGENCE SUMMARY.
(Erase heading not required.)

Army Form C. 2118.

Instructions regarding War Diaries and Intelligence Summaries are contained in F.S. Regs., Part II. and the Staff Manual respectively. Title pages will be prepared in manuscript.

Place	Date	Hour	Summary of Events and Information	Remarks and references to Appendices
SULZ, COLOGNE.	September 1919. 1st.		Battalion "A" Battalion and finding all Brigade Guards.	
	2nd.		Battalion on Guard duties.	
	3rd.		Battalion on Guard duties.	
	4th.		Battalion on Guard duties. Major C.Pannall D.S.O.,M.C. takes over Command of the Battalion. Musketry details return from Fort 11.	
	5th.		Battalion on Guard duties.	
	6th.		Battalion is relieved of Brigade Guards by 52nd Northumberland Fusiliers and becomes "B" Battalion.	
	7th.		Divine Service.	
	8th.		General Routine.	
	9th.		Commanding Officer Inspects "A" and "B" Companies. General Routine.	
	10th.		Battalion on Route March. Sports in afternoon.	

Army Form C. 2118.

Sheet 2.
WAR DIARY
or
INTELLIGENCE SUMMARY.
(Erase heading not required.)

Instructions regarding War Diaries and Intelligence Summaries are contained in F. S. Regs., Part II. and the Staff Manual respectively. Title pages will be prepared in manuscript.

Place	Date	Hour	Summary of Events and Information	Remarks and references to Appendices
SULZ, COLOGNE.	11th.		General Routine. Sports in afternoon.	
	12th.		Commanding Officer Inspects "C" Company and Transport. General Routine. VIth Corps Cross Country Championship Run held in afternoon.	
	13th.		General Routine.	
	14th.		General Routine. Lecture to Battalion by Medical Officer at 2 p.m.	
	15th.		General Routine.	
	16th.		Battalion Lewis Gun Course Commences. "B" Company immersed in Gas Chamber.	
	17th.		"A" Company immersed in Gas Chamber. Remainder General Routine.	
	18th.		"C" Company and ½ Transport immersed in Gas Chamber. Remainder General Routine.	
	19th.		"D" Company immersed in Gas chamber and remainder of Transport. General Routine.	
	20th.		Battalion becomes "A" Battalion and takes over all Guards and Picquets.	
	21st.		Battalion on Guard duties. Divine Service.	

Army Form C. 2118.

Sheet 3.
WAR DIARY
or
INTELLIGENCE SUMMARY.
(Erase heading not required.)

Instructions regarding War Diaries and Intelligence Summaries are contained in F. S. Regs., Part II. and the Staff Manual respectively. Title pages will be prepared in manuscript.

Place	Date	Hour	Summary of Events and Information	Remarks and references to Appendices
SULZ, COLOGNE.	22nd.		Details of all Companies on Education etc.	
	23rd.		Examination for 3rd Class Army Certificates Commences. Details of Coys. on Education.	
	24th.		General Routine. Battalion on Guard duties.	
	25th.		General Routine. Battalion on Guard duties.	
	26TH.		General Routine. Battalion on Guard duties.	
	27th.		Battalion hands over Brigade Guards to 52nd N.F.s and becomes "B" Battalion. Hockey Match in afternoon "C" Company v The Rest.	
	28th.		Divine Service.	
	29th.		General Routine.	
	30th.		General Routine.	

(signature)
Major.
Commanding 51st Battalion Northumberland Fusiliers.

51st Battalion Northumberland Fusiliers.
WAR DIARY
or
INTELLIGENCE SUMMARY.
(Erase heading not required.)

Army Form C. 2118.

Place	Date	Hour	Summary of Events and Information	Remarks and references to Appendices
October 1919. Sulz, Cologne.	1st. Wed.		General Routine.	
	2nd Thur.		General Routine. Lecture to Officers in Star Theatre by Sir H.M.Thompson K.C.M.G.,D.S.O.,A.M.S.	
	3rd Fri.		General Routine.	
	4th Sat.		Battalion becomes "A" Battalion and takes over all Brigade Guards. Regimental Football Team played 52nd Battalion Northumberland Fus. at Marienburg.	
	5th Sun.		CHURCH PARADE FOR DETAILS OF ALL COMPANIES. Battalion on Guard duties.	
	6th Mon.		Battalion on Guard duties.	
	7th Tue.		Battalion on Guard duties.	
	8th Wed.		Battalion on Guard duties.	
	9th Thus.		Battalion on Guard duties.	
	10th Fri.		Battalion on Guard duties. Pte.J.Benyon (Shot whilst on Guard) Buried at SUDFIEDHOF.	

51st Battalion Northumberland Fusiliers.

WAR DIARY
or
INTELLIGENCE SUMMARY.
(Erase heading not required.)

Army Form C. 2118.

Place	Date	Hour	Summary of Events and Information	Remarks and references to Appendices
Sulz. Cologne.	October 11th.	1919. Sat.	Battalion relieved of Guards and becomes "B" Battalion. Sports in afternoon.	
	12th.	Sun.	Divine Service.	
	13th.	Mon.	General Routine.	
	14th.	Tue.	General Routine. Lieut.Col.W.P.S.Foord assumed Command of the Battalion. Football Match:- Sgt's Mess 51st N.Fus. v Sgt's Mess 52nd Northd.Fus.	
	15th.	Wed.	General Routine.	
	16th.	Thur.	General Routine. Football Match between Regimental Team and 36th C.C.S.	
	17th.	Fri.	General Routine.	
	18th.	Sat.	Battalion becomes "A" Battalion and takes over all Guards. Hockey Match:- Sgts 51st N.Fus. v Sgts 52nd D.L.I.	
	19th.	Sun.	Church Parade for details of all Companies.	
	20th.	Mon.	Battalion on Guard duties.	

Army Form C. 2118.

51st Battalion Northumberland Fusiliers.

WAR DIARY
or
INTELLIGENCE SUMMARY.
(Erase heading not required.)

Instructions regarding War Diaries and Intelligence Summaries are contained in F. S. Regs., Part II. and the Staff Manual respectively. Title pages will be prepared in manuscript.

Place	Date	Hour	Summary of Events and Information	Remarks and references to Appendices
Sulz. Cologne.	21st	Tues.	Battalion on Guard duties. 370 men drafted to Battalion from 53rd Battalion Northumberland Fusiliers.	
	22nd	Wed.	Battalion on Guard duties.	
	23rd	Thur.	Battalion on Guard duties. Tattoo altered from 2230 to 2200 hours.	
	24th	Fri.	Battalion on Guard duties.	
	25th	Sat.	Some of Brigade Guards relieved by 52nd Northd. Fus.	
	26th	Sun.	Divine Service.	
	27th	Mon.	General Routine and Guard duties.	
	28th	Tue.	All Guards re-taken over from 52nd N.Fus. General Routine.	
	29th	Wed.	General Routine and Guard duties.	
	30th	Thur.	General Routine and Guard duties.	
	31st	Fri.	General Routine and Guard duties.	

C. Anstey Lt. Maj.
COMDG. 51st Bn. NORTHUMBERLAND FUS.

To 8th Inf Bde

I beg to enclose copy of War Diary for month of March.

Nicholson Lt. Col.
Commanding 51st North'd Fus.

31.3.19.

GD/164
1/4/19

BEF

NORTHERN DIV
~~formerly~~ 3 DIV

1 NORTHERN BDE H.Q

1919 APR to 1919 SEPT

WAR DIARY

INTELLIGENCE SUMMARY

8th Infantry Brigade.

Army Form C. 2118.

Place	Date	Hour	Summary of Events and Information	Remarks and references to Appendices
COLOGNE.	APRIL 1st		Location of Battalions :-	
			2nd The Royal Scots Rhiel Barracks, EHRENFELD Area, COLOGNE.	
			1st Royal Scots Fusiliers KRIELER STRASSE School, LINDENTHAL AREA, COLOGNE.	
			7th K.S.L.I. RHIEL Barracks, EHRENFELD Area, COLOGNE.	
			51st Northumberland Fusiliers REDWITZ STRASSE Schools, SULZ Area, COLOGNE.	
			52nd Northumberland Fusiliers BERRENRATHER STRASSE School, SULZ Area, COLOGNE.	
			53rd Northumberland Fusiliers MANDERSCHEIDER School, BERRENRATHER STRASSE, SULZ Area, COLOGNE.	
			51st Northumberland Fusiliers "standing to" in event of strikes at HURTH.	
			Col. FAWKES R.A. and Capt. WEEKS R.A.M.C. gave addresses to Battalions.	
	2nd		Mr. T.E. WING lectured to the Brigade on "How the Navy helped the Army to win the War".	
			52nd Northumberland Fusiliers "standing to" in event of strikes at HURTH.	
			Divine Services.	
	6th.		51st Northumberland Fusiliers "standing to" in event of strikes at HURTH.	
	7th.		7th K.S.L.I. moved from EHRENFELD to BRAUWEILER.	
			2nd The Royal Scots moved from RIEHL to FREMERSDORF.	
	8th		Battalions in training.	
	9th.		53rd Northumberland Fusiliers held Guard Mounting Competition which was judged by B.G.C. 1st Northern Brigade.	
	10th		52nd Northumberland Fusiliers "standing to" in event of strikes at HURTH.	

Army Form C. 2118.

WAR DIARY
~~INTELLIGENCE SUMMARY~~

(Erase heading not required.)

Page 2.

Instructions regarding War Diaries and Intelligence Summaries are contained in F.S. Regs., Part II. and the Staff Manual respectively. Title pages will be prepared in manuscript.

Place	Date	Hour	Summary of Events and Information	Remarks and references to Appendices
COLOGNE.	April 11th		Prof. F.J.ADKINS lectured to the Brigade on "What Belgium means to us".	
	12th		51st Northumberland Fusiliers "standing to" in event of strikes at HURTH.	
			Battalions in training.	
	13th		Divine services.	
	14th		52nd Northumberland Fusiliers "standing to" in event of strikes at HURTH.	
			Battalions in training.	
	15th		G.O.C. Northern Division inspected all cook-houses of the Brigade.	
			Nomenclature of the Brigade changed from 8th Infantry Brigade to 1st Brigade Northern Division.	
	16th		51st Northumberland Fusiliers "standing to" in event of strikes at HURTH.	
	17th		Battalions in training.	
	18th		52nd Northumberland Fusiliers "standing to" in event of strikes at HURTH.	
	19th		Battalions in training.	
	20th		Divine Services.	
			51st Northumberland Fusiliers "standing to" in event of strikes at HURTH.	
	21st		Brigade took over all Guards found by 52nd Sherwood Foresters, 3rd Midland Brigade.	
	22nd		53rd Northumberland Fusiliers moved from MANDERSCHEIDER School to ARTILLERIE CASERNE, MARIENBURG, COLOGNE.	

Army Form C. 2118.

WAR DIARY

(Erase heading not required.)

Page 3.

Place	Date	Hour	Summary of Events and Information	Remarks and references to Appendices
COLOGNE.	April 22nd		Captain B.W.W.Gostling, M.C. Brigade Major posted to IX Corps, Major A.E.Sanderson D.S.O. took over duties of Brigade Major.	
	23rd		52nd Northumberland Fusiliers "standing to" in event of strikes at HURTH.	
			St. Georges Day. Red and white roses were worn by all ranks of the Northumberland Fusiliers in the Brigade. Church Services were held in the forenoon and 52nd Northumberland Fusiliers held Sports in the afternoon.	
	24th		Rev. G.H.Heaslett, B.A. lectured to the Brigade on the danger and prevention of Venereal Disease.	
	25th		Dr.W.J.Tyson lectured to the Brigade on "British Empire - A Doctor's point of view".	
			51st Northumberland Fusiliers "standing to" in event of strikes at HURTH.	
	26th		Battalions in training.	
	27th		Divine Services.	
			Order to have one Battalion "standing to" under one hour's notice in event of strikes at Hurth withdrawn.	
	28th		Battalions in training.	
	29th		Lord Morris lectured to the Brigade on "Patriotism". "NEWFOUNDLAND".	
	30th		Battalions in training.	

signature

Major.

Brigade Major, 1st Brigade, Northern Division.

Army Form C. 2118.

WAR DIARY
INTELLIGENCE SUMMARY.
(Erase heading not required.)

Instructions regarding War Diaries and Intelligence Summaries are contained in F. S. Regs., Part II. and the Staff Manual respectively. Title pages will be prepared in manuscript.

Place	Date	Hour	Summary of Events and Information	Remarks and references to Appendices
COLOGNE.	May 1st		Location of Units of 1st Northern Brigade:-	
			1st Northern Brigade H.Q. 107 Bachemer Strasse, LINDENTHAL, COLOGNE.	
			51st Northumberland Fus. VOLKS SCHULE, REDWITZ STRASSE. SULZ.	
			52nd Northumberland Fus. BERRENRATHER SCHOOL, SULZ, "	
			53rd Northumberland Fus' ARTILLERY BARRACKS, MARIENBURG, "	
			8th Trench Mortar Battery. Fire Station, GLEUER STRASSE, LINDENTHAL, COLOGNE.	
			2nd The Royal Scots. FRIEMERSDORF.	
			1st Royal Scots Fusiliers. KRIELER STRASSE, LINDENTHAL. COLOGNE.	
			7th K.S.L.I. BRAUWEILER.	
			1 Company 51st Northumberland Fusiliers held in readiness for immediate action in case of any trouble or disorder in connection with Labour Demonstrations held.	
			Lieut. Commander EVERARD, R.N., lectured to the Brigade, on "Submarines in Warfare".	
	2nd		Battalions in training.	
	3rd		Battalions in training, and in readiness for inspection of billets by C-in-C. This was, however, postponed indefinitely.	
			51st Northumberland Fusiliers took over all Guards found by this Brigade.	
	4th		Divine services.	
	5th		Preliminary Review held by G.O.C. Northern Division preparatory to Inspection by H.R.H. Duke of Connaught.	
	6th		Major H.L.Ferguson lectured to the Brigade on "Problems of the Peace Conference".	

Army Form C. 2118.

WAR DIARY

of

(Erase heading not required.)

Instructions regarding War Diaries and Intelligence Summaries are contained in F. S. Regs., Part II. and the Staff Manual respectively. Title pages will be prepared in manuscript.

Place	Date	Hour	Summary of Events and Information	Remarks and references to Appendices
	May			
	7th		Battalions in training.	
	8th.		H.R.H. Duke of Connaught held Review and inspected all Units of Northern Division.	
	9th		Major H.Hely Pounds lectured to the Brigade on "British Empire".	
	10th		52nd Northumberland Fusiliers took over all Guards found by the Brigade. 388 N.C.Os. and Men of the Brigade on Guard. Fighting strength of the Brigade, 100 Officers, 1893 O.R.	
	11th		Divine Services.	
	12th		Cadres of 2nd The Royal Scots and 1st Royal Scots Fusiliers proceeded to England. Two Companies 51st Northumberland Fusiliers commenced firing G.M.C., one Company at each of RIEHL and LACHEM Ranges.	
	13th		Battalions in training. Sigt. MOON, L.R., 51st Northumberland Fusiliers drowned whilst bathing in HOHENSTAUFEN RING Baths, COLOGNE.	
	14th		Battalions in training.	
	15th		Battalions in training. Brigadier held Conference of Battalion Commanders to discuss training and general welfare of Battalions.	
	16th		Marshal FOCH visited COLOGNE. 53rd Northumberland Fusiliers detailed to line part of the Rhine bank to cheer him on arrival of the flotilla.	

Army Form C. 2118.

WAR DIARY

~~INTELLIGENCE SUMMARY~~

(Erase heading not required.)

Instructions regarding War Diaries and Intelligence Summaries are contained in F. S. Regs., Part II. and the Staff Manual respectively. Title pages will be prepared in manuscript.

Place	Date	Hour	Summary of Events and Information	Remarks and references to Appendices
	May			
	17th		Ven. Archdeacon Jones lectured Brigade on "Pioneers of Social Reform. (Wilberforce, Shaftesbury Peel). 53rd Northumberland Fusiliers took over all Guards found by the Brigade. 372 N.C.Os. and Men of the Brigade on Guard. Fighting Strength of the Brigade. 99 Officers, 1934 Men.	
	18th		Divine services.	
	19th		Brigadier-General F.G.STONE, C.M.G., lectured Brigade on "Economics of Reconstruction".	
	20th		Battalions in training. Two Companies of 52nd Northumberland Fusiliers commenced firing G.M.C. relieving similar Companies of 51st Northumberland Fusiliers.	
	21st		Battalions in training. Cadre of 7th K.S.L.I. entrained for England.	
	22nd		Battalions in training.	
	23rd		Battalions in training. Northern Division "Instructions for Advance" received.	
	24th		Battalions in training. 51st Northumberland Fusiliers took over all Guards found by the Brigade, with the exception of SUD BRUCKE taken over by 1st London Brigade. 320 N.C.Os. and Men of the Brigade on Guard duties. Fighting Strength of the Brigade, 99 Officers, 2090 Men.	
	25th		Divine services.	
	26th		Battalions in training.	

Army Form C. 2118.

WAR DIARY

~~INTELLIGENCE SUMMARY~~

(Erase heading not required.)

Instructions regarding War Diaries and Intelligence Summaries are contained in F. S. Regs., Part II. and the Staff Manual respectively. Title pages will be prepared in manuscript.

Place	Date	Hour	Summary of Events and Information	Remarks and references to Appendices
Cologne.	May 27th		Corps Commander inspected men in training and quarters of the three Battalions, and expressed his satisfaction with all he had seen in the Brigade. Two Companies 53rd Northd. Fus. proceeded to ranges to commence firing G.M.C. and relieving similar Companies of 52nd Northd.Fus. 1 Sergt. and 6 men from 51st Bn. Northd.Fus. detailed to Guard Cold Storage, No. 2/6 GROSSENSPITZEN GASSE. COLOGNE. This was later reinforced by 1 L/Corporal and 6 men. Brigade Instructions No. 1 for advance on "J" day issued. Appendix 1.	
	28th		Guard of 1 N.C.O. and 3 men detailed by 51st Northd.Fus. over Brigade Supply Dump at WEISSHAUS. LUXEMBURGER STRASSE. SULZ.	
		14.30.	One Company 52nd Northd.Fus. "standing to" at half hours notice owing to Demonstrations in COLOGNE.	
		16.50.	Orders received confining all troops, except those on duty, to billets, prepared for eventuality of electric light being cut off.	
		18.10	Orders received for 1 Platoon to proceed to junction of ZUGWEG and BONNER WALL. COLOGNE to protect workmen who were willing to work under protection. 52nd Northd.Fus. detailed the platoon, which marched off at 18.30 hours.	
		20.00	Order "resume normal conditions" received.	

Army Form C. 2118.

WAR DIARY

~~INTELLIGENCE SUMMARY~~

(Erase heading not required.)

Instructions regarding War Diaries and Intelligence Summaries are contained in F. S. Regs., Part II. and the Staff Manual respectively. Title pages will be prepared in manuscript.

Place	Date	Hour	Summary of Events and Information	Remarks and references to Appendices
Cologne	May 28th	23.35	Platoon returned reporting all quiet.	
	29th	18.05	Orders received to remove Guard on Cold Storage, SPETZENGASSE.	
			Northern Division Defence Scheme received.	
	30th		Battalions in Training.	
			Administrative Instructions No. 1 (issued in conjunction with Instructions No. 1) for advance issued. Appendix 2.	
			Notes on probable ~~advance~~ *action* of Brigade in Advance issued. Appendix 3.	
	31st.		Mr. R. Pape Cowl lectured 51st and 52nd Bn. Northd. Fus. on "Finland".	
			52nd. Bn. Northd. Fus. took over all Guards found by the Brigade. 398 N.C.Os. and men of Brigade on Guard duties. Fighting Strength of Brigade 103 Officers. 2274 O.R.. Appendix 4.	
			Brigade Defence Scheme issued.	

[signature] Major.

Brigade Major, 1st Northern Brigade.

Appendix 2 to War Diary. <u>Secret</u>

1st Northern Brigade Administrative Instructions No. 1.

(issued in conjunction with Brigade Instructions No. G.100/2, dated 28/5/19.)

A. LORRY COLUMN.

1. MOVE OF LORRIES TO EMBUSSING POINT.

   Personnel lorries will be ordered to be in position at the embussing points mentioned in Brigade Instructions No. G.100/2, at 18.00 hours on J - 2 day.

2. MOVE FROM EMBUSSING POINTS.

   Move from Embussing point to form the Brigade Column will take place under instructions contained in Brigade Instructions No. G.100/2.

3. WITHDRAWAL OF PERSONNEL LORRIES.

   Personnel lorries will be withdrawn on J - 2 day, but 1st Line Transport of Units will not by that time have rejoined Units. Nothing, therefore, will be taken forward except Camp Kettles, not exceeding 2 per personnel lorry.

4. EMBUSSING AND DEBUSSING ARRANGEMENTS.

   Particular attention is to be paid to embussing and debussing discipline. Units are reminded that Lorry Columns are formed up in batches of 6 each batch occupying 80 yards road space. Troops embussing therefore should be formed up to meet these requirements.

5. RECONNOITRING OF EMBUSSING POINTS.

   Units will arrange to reconnoitre their embussing points as early as possible.

6. ALLOTMENT OF PERSONNEL LORRIES.

   Lorries for personnel are allotted on a scale of 25 (all ranks) per 3 ton lorry or bus; 20 per seated lorry.

B. SUPPLY ARRANGEMENTS.

7. IRON RATIONS.

   Iron rations will be issued to the men on J - 2 day. They will not be consumed without the authority of the Brigadier.

8. SUPPLY LORRIES.

   Supply Lorries containing 2 days supply for the Brigade Group will join the lorry columns on J - 2 day. Each Unit of the Brigade Group will detail one man to report to Brigade Supply Officer at Refilling Point at 18.00 hours on J - 2 day to take

over their Units supplies. These rations are for consumption on J+1 and J+2 days. Unconsumed portion of J-1 and rations for J day will carried by Units on their personnel lorries.

9. **RATION OF UNITS JOINING BRIGADE GROUP.**

All Units joining the Brigade Group from other formations will carry rations up to J+1 day inclusive after which they will be rationed by Northern Division.

10. **SUPPLY OF MARCHING COLUMN.**

The system of supply of the marching column will be normal.

11. All gaurds on stores left by battalions will be supplied by their units with rations for J day and J+1 day after which they will be rationed by the Light Division. Complete lists of these personnel will be rendered to these Headquarters by 11.00 hours J-2 day.

12. **WATER SUPPLY.**

Water is reported to be scarce in the forward area and care must be observed on its expenditure.

4 Garford Lorries will be attached to the Brigade Group. They will be used entirely for carrying water forward and not as store tank. Units must therefore arrange to requisition tanks for storeage from civilians. The C.R.E. has been asked to supply 4 200 gallon portable canvas tanks and if   obtained, these will be issued to battalions and will be carried by them on their personnel lorries. Battalions must be prepared to have to make use of water supply from streams and wells and so will arrange for chlorinating all water so obtained.

13. **RATION TABLE.**

The ration situation day by day from J-4 to J+4 day is shown in Table D.

C. TRANSPORT ARRANGEMENTS.

14. **BAGGAGE WAGONS.**

Baggage Wagons will report to all Units on J-3 day. They will rejoin their respective companies of the train on the evening of   . J-2 day.

15. **BARRACK STORES.**

except plates, mugs and jugs
Barrack Stores/will be handed over to the Light Division 'in situ'. Receipts will be given and taken from the relieving troops.

16. **SURPLUS KITS AND BLANKETS.**

Surplus kits, and blankets will be stored under unit arrangements in the localities already reported. Brigade Headquarters and Trench Mortar Battery surplus kit will be stored with that of the 51st.Bn.Northd.Fus. in the REDWITZ STRASSE Schools. O.C. this battalion will arrange for accomodation for these stores.

17. **GUARDS ON STORES.**

Guards over surplus stores will be left by each Battalion. Strength 2 N.C.Os. and 6 men preferably composed of men who cannot march.

- 3 -

D. AMMUNITION ARRANGEMENTS.

18. ECHELONS.

All echelons of ammunition will move full.

19. S.A.A.

2 lorries loaded with S.A.A. (Clip packed) will join the Brigade Group on J - 2 day. This will give a reserve of approx. 100 rounds per man. Machine Gun Company will arrange to carry their reserve on their personnel lorries.

20. GRENADES.

One box No. 36 Grenades will be loaded by battalions on each of their personnel lorries. These will be drawn from the mobile reserve.

21. L.G.MAGAZINES.

All L.G. magazines in possession of battalions will be carried charged on the personnel lorries.

22. A.A.L.G..

A.A.L.Guns will march with Transport Column.

V.Pistols. All Very Pistols will be carried and V.P. ammunition at the rate of 10 rounds per pistol.

23. AMMUNITION REQUIREMENTS

Ammunition requirements and expenditure will be wired daily to these Headquarters at 12.00 hours.

24. TRENCH MORTAR BATTERY.

O.C. Trench Mortar Battery will arrange to carry 600 rounds Stokes Shell on personnel lorry.

E. PERSONNEL.

25. EMBUSSING STRENGTH.

Infantry battalions will embus at a strength of 650 all ranks. All personnel surplus to this number will move by March route with the 1st Line Transport.

26. RECEPTION CAMP.

All returning leave personnel will report to the Northern Division Reception Camp formed at RIEHL BARRACKS.

27. Q.M.SERGEANTS.

All Regimental and Company Quartermaster Sergeants will accompany their battalions.

28. PRISONERS OF WAR.

Prisoners of War will be sent to Brigade Collecting Stations the location of which will be notified as soon as decided. Escort must not exceed 10 per cent of the total.

F. ORDNANCE STORES.

29. SOCKS.

On receipt of orders to move, units will draw from the Divisional Laundry to complete to the scale of 2 pairs per man.

30. FIELD DRESSINGS.

Units will wire D.A.D.O.S. as early as possible the number of Field Dressings required to complete to the scale of 1 per man. These will be drawn on J – 3 day.

G. ACCOMODATION AND BILLETS.

31. Accomodation in KURTEN Area is limited and troops will bivouac beside their de-bussing points. Battalions will arrange to draw jointed bivouac poles and string at 18.00 hours on J – 3 day from the Brigade Store.

32. Units will make all necessary arrangements for sanitary squads to carry sufficient picks and shovels with which to dig latrines. Careful attention must be paid to sanitation of all bivouacs and billets.

33. All units will have billetting parties ready detailed. These will move in the advanced lorry of the unit, except in the case of the Company of the Battalion finding the advanced guard company in which case the party will move on leading lorry of battalion's main body.

H. MISCELLANEOUS.

34. FEEDING GERMAN CIVILIANS.

In the event of German organization breaking down, the feeding of civilians will be undertaken by Army.

German labourers impressed may be given British Rations at the rate of 4 men to 1 British Ration.

35. SYSTEM OF REQUISITIONING.

The normal system of requisitioning will continue until the breaking of the Armistice when power to requisition, in advance of the occupied area is vested in Brigade Group Commanders.

36. CIVIL ADMINISTRATION.

The 1st Light Brigade will assume Civil Administration of No. 6 Sub-Area from J – 1 day inclusive. All personnel employed on Civil Duties will accompany Brigade Headquarters. Further details will be issued as soon as received.

I. MEDICAL ARRANGEMENTS.

37. Medical instructions will be issued separately.

J H Woods
Captain.

Appendix 1 to War Diary

SECRET.

Copy No. 20. [signature]

1st Northern Brigade.
G. 100 / 2.

Ref. 1/200000.
Sheets.. HANOVER.
        MUNSTER
        COLOGNE.
and PHAROS PLAN GROSS COLN.

1st Northern Brigade Group.

Instructions   No. 1.
----

1. GENERAL IDEA.

   Under certain circumstances it may be necessary for the Allied Armies to seize as rapidly as possible the RUHR basin, and to secure the Railway communications which are necessary for a further advance North Eastwards.

2. RAILWAY COMMUNICATIONS.

   The main railway communication runs COLOGNE - OHLIGS - ELBERFELD - HAGAN - UNNA.
   Important subsidiary lines are
        (a) ALTENA - PLETTENBERG - KIRCHMUNDEN - KROMBACH - SIEGEN.
        (b) SCHWERTE - ARNSBERG - MESCHEDE

3. INTENTION OF THE VI CORPS.

   The VI corps is to advance on a two Division front. The LONDON Division on the right and the NORTHERN Division on the left. The SOUTHERN Division of the 2nd corps is to advance on the left of the NORTHERN Division

4. DAY OF ADVANCE.

   The day of advance will in future be known as "J" day.

5. ACTION OF NORTHERN DIVISION.

   The Northern Division is to advance

   (a) On "J" day on a two Brigade front with the 1st NORTHERN Brigade on the right and the 3rd NORTHERN Brigade on the left.

   (b) On "J" + 1 day, on a one Brigade front, the 3rd NORTHERN Brigade leading with the 1st NORTHERN Brigade in support.

   (c) 2nd NORTHERN Brigade are in reserve.

6. OBJECTIVES.   1st NORTHERN BRIGADE.

   "J" day. The line ALTENA - LUDENSCHEID.

   "J" + 1 day Move into support on the line MENDEN - FRONDENBERG - SCHWERTE.

6. OBJECTIVES (continued)

3rd. NORTHERN BRIGADE.

"J" day.   SCHWERTE -- HAGEN.

"J"+1 day. SOEST and WERL.

LONDON DIVISION.

"J" day.   ATTENDORN.

"J"+1 day. ARNSBERG.

SOUTHERN DIVISION.

"J" day.   ELBERFELD.

"J"+2 days. Advance to HAGEN.

"J"+3 days. Advance to SCHWERTE.

"J"+4 days. Advance to DELLWIG.

7. AEROPLANE RECONNAISSANCE

The 12th Squadron R.A.F., is providing Aeroplanes to reconnoitre the country on our front.
These machines are provided with Wireless to communicate with Headquarters of the leading Brigades.

8. COMPOSITION OF 1ST NORTHERN BRIGADE GROUP.

Brigade Headquarters and 8th T.M.Battery.
51st, 52nd, 53rd.Bn.Northumberland Fusiliers.
One Squadron Hussars.
One Squadron Machine Guns (less 1 section)
231st. Field company. R.E..
One Section, 142 Field Ambulance.
Detachment cyclists (approx. 60 strong)
"A" coy., 3rd M.G.C..
One 18Pdr in lorry.

9. CONCENTRATION.

(a) "J" - 2 day The Squadron Hussars move to RIEHL Artillery Barracks.
The Squadron Machine Guns attached to the Brigade Group move to DEUTZ Barracks.
Each of the above will send two orderlies to Brigade Hdqrs on arrival.

(b) "J" -1 day. The 1st NORTHERN INFANTRY BRIGADE GROUP will concentrate along the Road from the Road junction just South of the N in KURTEN to BIESFELD.
The Mounted Troops being at DELLING with patrols in the perimeter between LINDLAR and WIPPERFELD ready to move

10. **TRANSPORT.**

 The Transport of the 1st NORTHERN BRIGADE will move in accordance with attached table "B"

11. **ADVANCE OF 1ST NORTHERN BRIGADE.**

 Notes on the intention of the Brigadier commanding the 1st NORTHERN BRIGADE GROUP for the Advance on "J" day ~~are attached~~ *to follow*. Detailed ~~orders~~ for this will be issued later.

12. Acknowledge.

 Major,
 Brigade Major, 1st Northern Brigade.

27th May 1919.

Distribution:-

1. 51st.Bn.Northd.Fus.
2. 52nd.Bn.Northd.Fus.
3. 53rd.Bn.Northd.Fus.
4. O.C. No. 3 Sect. Div. Sig. coy.
5. 8th T.M.B..
6. No. 3.coy. Div. Train.RASC.
7. Capt. Liddell. 15th Hussars.
8. Capt. King. cav. Div. M.G.Regt.
9. 231st.coy. (Field) R.E..
10. 142nd Field Ambulance.
11. VI corps cyclists.
12. "A" coy. 3rd.M.G.C.
13. C.R.A..
14. Northern Division.
15. 2nd Northern Infantry Brigade.
16. 3rd Northern Infantry Brigade.
17. Brigadier General.
18. Staff captain.
19/20. War Diary.

TABLE "A". To accompany 1st Northern Brigade Instructions No. 1.

Move of 1st Northern Brigade Group on "J" - 1 day.

Unit.	Head of Lorry column.	Time of starting of column from S.P.	Route.	Destination.	Remarks.
Squadron Hussars.	-		BENSBERG - DURCHEID - KURTEN - DELLING.	DELLING with Patrols as ordered.	To be N.E. of road junction just S. of N in KURTEN by S + 50.
Detachment Cyclists.	Junction of ROTHEHAUS Str. and VENLOER Str.	S - 20 mins.	VENLOER Str.- ZEUGHAUS Str.- KAISER FREDRICH Str - NEUE Br.	DELLING.	
53rd.Bn.M.Fus. R.E.Lorry with demolition equipment in rear.	Gate ARTILLERY Barracks, BONNER STRASSE.	S - 20	BONNER STRASSE - ALTEBURGER WALL - OBERLANDER WALL - BAYEN STRASSE - NEUE BRIDGE - BERG GLADBACH - DURSCHIED - KURTEN.	KURTEN - DURSCHEID Road.	Time to follow behind cyclists from NEUE BRIDGE.
"A" Coy. 3rd.Bn. M.G.Corps.	M.G. entrance gate to RIEHL Barracks.	S - 20	RIEHLER Str - FROHNGASSE - KAISER FRIEDRICH Str - NEUE BRIDGE thence as in Serial No 3.	Do.	Follow behind 53rd.Bn. from NEUE Bridge.
Brigade H'qrs & 8th T.M. Battery.	Junct.of GEIBEL and BACHEMAR Str.	S - 5.	BACHEMAR Str - ZULPICHER WALL - LUXEMBURGER WALL - EIFEL WALL - ULTEBURGER WALL OBERLANDER WALL - NEUE BRIDGE - Thence as Serial No. 3.	Do.	Half hour behind "A" Coy. 3rd Bn. M.G.C. at NEUE Bridge.

Unit.	Head of Lorry column.	Time of starting of column from S.P.	Route.	Destination.	Remarks.
...nd.Bn.N.Fus. ...th 1 Spr. on ...orry in middle ... Bn. column.	Junct. of AEMILIAN Str. and LUXEMBURGER STRASSE.	S + 5	LUXEMBURGER Str.— EIFEL WALL — VORGEBIRGES WALL — BONNER WALL — Thence as in Serial No. 3.	As Serial No. 3.	Follows Brigade Headqrs from NEUE Bridge.
51st.Fld.Coy.R.E. (less demolition Lorry)	Junction of VINCENZ STATZ and AСHENER STRASSE.	S - 15	ACHENER STR — LINDEN WALL — ZULPICHER WALL — LUXEMBURGER WALL — Thence as Serial No 6.	do.	Follow 52nd. N.F. from junction of LUXEMBURGER Str. and EIFEL WALL.
1st.Bn.N.Fus.	Junction of LOTHAR STRASSE and LUXEMBURGER Strasse.	S + 25.	As in Serial No. 6.	do.	Timed to pass NEUE BRIDGE ½ hour after 231 Fld.Co. R.E..
... Section 142nd. ...ield Ambulance.	Junction of ROTHEHAUS STR and VOGELSÄNGER Str.	S + 30.	As in Serial No. 2.	do.	Follows 51st.Bn.N.F. from NEUE BRIDGE.

...cer is to be placed on the front lorry of each convoy, this Officer must be acquainted with the Route ...sible that the distances are maintained.
..."S" will be communicated from Brigade Headquarters and all starting times calculated from this according ...e. (The table has been worked out taking "S" as the time at which the head of the leading convoy should ...DGE.)
...tely essential that all convoys should start exactly at the time given in the table.
... parade at the Embussing Point half an hour before the time at which the lorries are due to start.
... Officer will be at NEUE BRIDGE to regulate the convoys.

SECRET.

To accompany 1st Northern Brigade Instructions No. 1.

TABLE "B". Move of 1st Northern Brigade Transport.

Serial No.	Date.	Units Transport.	Starting Point.	Time of Passing S.P.	Destination.	Route.	Remarks.
1.	J – 1 day.	A. Coy. M.G. Bn.	Junction of ARDER SCHANG and RIEHLER STRASSE.	08.30 hours.	BERG GLADBACH.	RIEHLER STRASSE MULHEIMER Bridge.	Head to pass eastern end of MULHEIMER Bridge at 09.00 hours turn to right along FREIHEIT Str. and halt with head at junction of DEUTZER Str. & DANZIER Str. until arrival of rest of Bde. Transport when it will continue march in front.
2.	J – 1 day.	Detachment Cyclists.	Junction of ROTHEHAUS Str. and VENLOER Str.	08.40 hours.	do.	VENLOER STRASSE – FRIESEN – ZEUGHAUS – NEUE Bridge.	
3.	J – 1 day.	53rd.Bn.N.F.	MAIN GATE ARTILLERY BARRACKS.	08.35 hours.	BERG GLADBACH	BONNER STRASSE – UBIER RING – BAYEN STRASSE.	Follow Cyclists Transport from NEUE Bridge.
4.		Bde.Hdqrs.	Junction of DURENER STRASSE and AACHENER STRASSE.	09.10 hours.	do.	AACHENER STRASSE – HOHENZOLLERN RING – FRIESEN STRASSE – ZEUGHAUS STRASSE – KOMODIEN STRASSE – KAISER FRIEDRICH STRASSE – NEUE Bridge.	
5.		52nd.Bn.N.F.	do.	09.12 hours.	do.	do.	

Serial No.	Date.	Units Transport.	Starting point.	Time of Passing S.P.	Destination.	Route.	Remarks.
6.	J - 1 day.	51st.Bn.N.F.	As Serial No. 4.	09.17 hours.	As Serial No. 3.	As Serial No. 4.	
7.	J - 1 day.	231st Fld.Co. R.E..	Junction of VINCENZ STATZ and AACHENER STRASSE.	08.25 hours.	do.	do.	
8.	J - 1 day.	No. 3 Coy. Div.Train	Junction of WEISS-HAUS Str. and LUXEMBURGER Str.	09.25 hours.	do.	WEYER STR - ROTHGERBER -BACH MUHLEM BACH - AFILZEN GRAB - BAYEN STR - NEUE BRIDGE.	
9.	J day.	Brigade Group.			KURTEN.	BIESFELD.	Under orders O.C. No. 3 Coy. Train.
10.	J + 1 day.	do.			WIPPERFURTH.		Under orders C.R.A
11.	J + 2 days	do.			South East of KIERSPE	ROWSAHL.	do.
12.	J + 3 days.	do.			LUDENSCHEID.		do.
13.	J + 4 days.	do.			LETHMATHE.		do.

1. O.C. No. 3 Coy. Divisional Train will take command of the Transport of the Brigade Group after it has passed the NEUE Bridge and will issue orders for the march on "J" day - on "J" +1 day the Transport of the Brigade Group comes under the orders of C.R.A.
2. The usual halts at 10 minutes to each clock hour will be observed by units after passing their respective Starting Points.
3. Attention is directed to G.H.Q. Notes on March Discipline 22/5/19. 100 yards will be maintained between Transport of Units.

Appendix 4 to War Diary.

1st Northern Brigade.
G.1600/8/1.

1. Reference G.1600/8 dated 31/5/19.

2. Para. 7 (i) For 53rd. read 51st.

3. Para. 7 (ii) After limber add:, of Brigade Headquarter transport.

Major.

3/6/19. Brigade Major, 1st Northern Brigade.

To all recipients of No. G.1600/8 of 31/5/19.

SECRET.

G.1600/8.

Copy No.

1st NORTHERN BRIGADE DEFENCE SCHEME.

1. List of Permanent Guards and Picquets found by 1st Northern Brigade.

2. Action to be taken in the event of minor Civil disturbances in COLOGNE.

3. Action to be in the event of Civil Disturbances in COLOGNE.

   Appendix "A"   Signal Arrangements.

   Appendix "B"   Medical Arrangements

4. Throughout this Defence Scheme Battalions are described as follows, and will be detailed weekly by Brigade Headquarters.

   "A" Battalion.   That Battalion of the Brigade which is finding all Guards.

   "B" Battalion.   The Battalion which is next for duty on Guards is training and finding Picquets

   "C" Battalion.   is the complete Battalion training.

- - - - - - - - - - - - - - - -

THIS DEFENCE SCHEME cancels the 1st Northern Brigade Defence Scheme issued under G.1600/6 of 28/4/19, with the exception of the following pages, which will be retained and attached to this copy:-

List of Guards and Picquets G. 1000/30 of 7/5/19, with amendments.
Action to be taken in the event of Minor Disturbances in COLOGNE

DETAILS OF GUARD FURNISHED BY "A" BATTALION, 1st NO_____ BRIGADE.

Guards cancels that issued with Defence Scheme G.1600/6.

STRENGTH

DETAILS AS REGARDS GUARD.

Offrs.	N.C.Os.	Men.	L.G's.	
3	12	73	4	Finds Guards on DOCKS, as follows:-
				No. 1 Guard. SUD BRÜCKE (as below)
				No. 2 Guard. Southern end of DOCKS. 2 N.C.Os. 14 men. finds 3 Sentries
				No. 3 Guard. UBIER RING main gate. 2 N.C.Os. 13 men. 1 L.G. finds 3 Sentries.
				No. 4 Guard. MAIN GUARD Warehouse 15. 3 N.C.Os.12 men.1L.G. finds 3 Sentries.
				No. 5 Guard. Southern end of Power House No. 25. 3 N.C.Os. 21 men. finds 5 sentries by day and 4 by night.
				No. 6 Guard. Truck Eastern side of Warehouse No. 18b. 2 N.C.Os. 8 men. finds 3 sentries.
-	2	12	1	No. 1 Guard of DOCKS Company to be found by same Company which finds DOCKS Guard if Company not strong enough additional men must be attached to it. It will be under O.C. DOCKS Company. Officer of DOCKS Guard to thoroughly inspect abutments, piers etc., daily, report to be forwarded daily to Brigade Headquarters through Battalion Headquarters.
-	2	8	-	Finds one sentry by day, a double sentry by night.
-	1	3	-	Finds one sentry on War Material.
4	10	70	4	Finds six single sentries by day, doubled by night.
2	3	22	2	Garrison and defence of Fort VII, responsible for Guards, all Arms and Ammunition stored there. All N.C.Os and men will be trained in the way to fire the German Machine Gun which is the principal weapon in the adequate defence of this Fort, as soon after arrival as possible. Finds Main Guard at Gate of 1 N.C.O. and 6 men. (one sentry by day, double at night)

DETAILS OF GUARDS (continued)

DETAILS AS REGARDS GUARDS.

GUARD.	STRENGTH				DETAILS AS REGARDS GUARDS.
	Offrs.	N.C.Os.	Men.	L.G's.	
7. BONN TOR GOODS * STATION.		2	8	1	Responsible that no stores are removed from the warehouse and that the seals of trucks are unbroken. Finds single sentry by day, double sentry patrolling warehouse at night.
8. VOLKSGARTEN. (War material)		2	9	1	Finds a single sentry by day, double at night.
9. ALTEBURGER WALL. (Vehicle Guard)		2	8	1	Finds single sentry by day over abandoned German vehicles, double sentry by night.
10. VORGEBIRGE STRASSE. (Wagon Yard)		2	8	1	Finds single sentry by day in yard over German vehicles, double sentry by night.
11. TRAIN GUARD. (DOCKS to EIFEL TOR etc)		3	36		1 Guard of 1 N.C.O. and 12 men report R.T.O. at DOCKS at 10.30 hours and a similar Guard at 16.30 hours daily. Any other Guard required will be notified by the R.T.O. to the Battalion concerned direct.
12. ARSNEAL to FORT VII. (Arms removing party)	1	3	27		Will be detailed from Brigade when required.

* NOTE.   Position of Posts in Guards marked * are arranged by R.T.O. with whom officer or N.C.O. in command of the Guard will keep in close touch.

DETAIL OF PICQUETS FOUND BY "B" BATTALION. 1st NORTHERN BRIGADE.

	Offrs.	N.C.Os.	Men.	
HEUMARKT.	1	2	8	Report to A.P.M. COLOGNE at DOM HOTEL daily at 19.00 hours.
HOHENZOLLERN BRUCKE.	1	2	8	Report to A.P.M. COLOGNE at DOM HOTEL daily at 19.00 hours.
DOM HOTEL.		1	10	Report R.S.M. at Police Billet behind MONOPOLE HOTEL at 19.00 hours.
HOHE STRASSE.		1	12	Report R.S.M. at Police Billet behind MONOPOLE HOTEL at 19.00 hours.
COLOGNE STATION Patrol.		1	10	Report to D.A.P.M., Main Station daily at 21.30 hours.

Major,
Brigade Major, 1st Northern Brigade.

ADDENDUM No. 1.

TO DETAILS OF GUARDS FURNISHED BY "A" BATTALION, 1st NORTHERN BRIGADE.

Guards.	Offrs.	N.C.Os.	Men.	L.G.'s	Details as Regards Guard.
S...		2	10	–	Works under orders of O.C., No. 44 O.C.S.. Duty to guard prisoners admitted to O.C.S..
NERY r.	1	6	1	–	Single sentry by day, double at night. Guard to be under command of O.C. DOCKS Company. Duty to guard E.F.C. Stores and also A.D. of S.'s supplies. This Guard should be relieved every 48 hours.

Major
Brigade Major, 1st Northern
Brigade.

copies to all recipients G.1000/30 of 7/5/19.

1st Northern Brigade

G.1000/30/3.

AMENDMENT AND ADDENDUM No. 2.

to G.1000/30 of 7/5/19.   Details of Guards furnished by "A" Battalion, 1st Northern Brigade.

++=++=++=++=++=++=++=++

1. Delete:- Serial No. 9. SUD BRUCKE.

2. Delete:- Serial No. 12. ARSENAL TO FORT VII.
            (Arms removing party)

   Note. This takes effect from 27/5/19 inclusive.

3. Delete following Picquets:-

       HOHENZOLLERN BRUCKE.

       HOHE STRASSE.

   Note. This takes effect from 27/5/19 inclusive.

4. Add to list of Guards:-

		Officers.	N.C.Os.	Men.	L.G.
Serial No. 13. MARIENBURG advanced supply Depot. EIFEL TOR Goods Station.		1	3	42	2
Serial No. 14. ALTENBURG Brewery. MARIENBURG. (M.T.coy)		-	2	8	-
Serial No. 15. ORDNANCE DEPOT.MILITAR LAZARET. KARTHAUS WALL.		-	1	6	-

A. Sanderson

Major,

Brigade Major, 1st Northern Brigade.

26/5/19

SECRET.

1st Northern Brigade.

G.1600/8.

DEFENCE SCHEME in the event of Civil Disturbances in COLOGNE.

REFERENCE MAP OF COLOGNE.

1.   The Division is placed under the orders of the G.O.C. VI Corps for any action necessitated by Civil Disturbances in the City of COLOGNE.

2. GENERAL IDEA OF THE SCHEME.

   To secure certain important points and at the same time to keep a reserve in hand West of the River RHINE ready to move as required.

3. WARNING ORDER.

   In the event of Civil Disturbances the WARNING ORDER, Code Word "MOSELLE" will be sent from Brigade Headquarters.

   On receipt of this Code Message the following action will be taken.

   (a)   All troops will be at one hours notice.

   (b)   All Officers will join and remain with their troops.

   (c)   "A" Battalion will double all Guards of less than one Company in strength.

   (d)   "B" Battalion will:-

   (i)   Send 1 Platoon to the Railway Bridges over the EIFEL STRASSE.
        The duty of the Officer in Command of this Platoon on arrival, is to detail parties of not less than 1 N.C.O. and 6 men each to continually patrol the railway lines and examine the arches of all railway bridges between LUXEMBURGER STRASSE (inclusive) and VORGEBIRGE STRASSE (exclusive)
   (ii) Send 1 Platoon to BONN TOR Goods Station.
        The duty of the Officer in Command of this Platoon on arrival, is to detail parties of not less than 1 N.C.O. and 6 men each to continually patrol the railway lines and examine the arches of all bridges between VOLGEBIRGE STRASSE (inclusive) and ALTEBURGER STRASSE (inclusive)

- 2 -

4. ORDER TO MOVE.

In the event of orders being received for the Brigade to move the Code Word "RHINE" will be sent from Brigade Headquarters.

On receipt of this Code Message Units of the 1st Northern Brigade (less Guards and Detachments) will take the following action.

(a) "A" Battalion.

(i) Make up the Guard at the Packing Base at A.S.D. EIFEL TOR to a total strength of one Company.
All approaches to the Station will be picqueted in accordance with the Station Defence Scheme.
(ii) Headquarters will move to ARTILLERIE CASERNE (if not already there).

(b) "B" Battalion.

(i) One Company will be sent to reinforce the Guard at the Supply Depot of the HANSA WERFT and AGRIPPA WERFT (Docks) and will picquet all approaches thereto. On arrival at the Docks this Company will come under the orders of O.C. "A" Battalion.
(ii) Half Company will be sent to Guard the Cold Store at No. 229 SEVERIN STRASSE (LINDESEIS FABRIK) and will picquet all approaches thereto. On arrival this half Company will come under the orders of O.C. "A" Battalion.
(iii) On reaching these positions the Officer Commanding each of the above detachments will send two orderlies to report to O.C. "A" Battalion at ARTILLERIE CASERNE.

(c) The 51st and 52nd Bn. Northumberland Fusiliers will each detail one Platoon to remain behind when the remainder of the Battalion marches off.
These Platoons will guard the Barracks and Stores of their respective Battalions during the absence of these Units.

(d) "C" Battalion and "B" Battalion (less detachments mentioned in para 4 (b) and 8th Trench Mortar Battery will move to ARTILLERIE CASERNE and come into Brigade Reserve.

(e) Brigade Headquarters will be established at the ARTILLERIE CASERNE.

5. DRESS. Marching Order, Steel Helmets.

6. FIRE OR INCENDIARISM.

There are four Fire Stations in the City at the following places.

1. APOSTELNKLOSTER.   18 - 18A.
2. RATHAUS ALTERMARKT   15 - 19.
3. MELCHIOR STRASSE.   3.
4. VENDEL STRASSE.

Also one in each of the suburbs of NIPPES, EHRENFELD, and DEUTZ and at the Harbour in the neighbourhood of BAYENTURM shown on tracing to superimpose on a 1/15000 COLOGNE MAP already issued.

Fire Alarms are installed in the principal streets marked "FEUERMELDERSTELLE".

Hydrants (marked by a red plate on the wall) are at every 90 to 100 yards.

Battalions will reconnoitre the position of all Fire Stations, Alarms, and Hydrants in the Brigade Area.

In case of an outbreak of fire the 8th Light Trench Mortar Battery will co-operate with the local Fire Brigade and will take over their appliances if necessary.

Arrangements are being made for the Light Trench Mortar Battery to practice with the engines.

The O.C. Light Trench Mortar Battery will ensure that all his Officers reconnoitre the 4 Main Fire Stations in the City and know the shortest way to them.

7. TRANSPORT LINES. CASINO.

(a) On receipt of the Warning Order.
  (i) The following Unit Transport will at once proceed to the Headquarters 52nd and 53rd. Northumberland Fusiliers respectively.
        4 Lewis Gun Limbers.
        4 Cookers.
        1 Mess Cart.
        1 Maltese Cart.
  (ii) One Limber will at once proceed to Brigade Headquarters.

(b) The 51st. Bn. Northumberland Fusiliers, or if this Battalion is "A" Battalion for the week, the 52nd Bn. Northumberland Fus. will detail 1 Platoon to proceed at once to the Transport Lines CASINO, to afford protection for the Transport left behind.

(c) Except as stated in para. 7 (a) Transport of 51st and 52nd Bn. Northumberland Fusiliers will not accompany the Battalion and will not leave the CASINO Transport Lines until orders are issued for it to move.

8. TANKS.

The Division will have 1 Company 12th Tank Battalion in Divisional Reserve at REIHL Artillery Barracks.

9. MEDICAL ARRANGEMENTS.

See Appendix "B"

10. COMMUNICATION.

Arrangements for providing communication in the event of lines being cut, as per Appendix "A" attached.

11. RECONNAISSANCE.

All Units will reconnoitre the Area assigned to the Brigade and Commanding Officers will ensure that, before their Units take over a tour of duty, the Officers and N.C.Os. commanding detachments know their way to the posts they will occupy in case of Alarm.

Battalions will carry out marches to their assembly areas and report the time taken to Brigade Headquarters as soon as possible.

12. **LIGHTING.**

   All Units will arrange to keep a supply of candles for use in case the electric light is cut off.

13. ACKNOWLEDGE.

A. Sanderson Major,
Brigade Major, 1st Northern Brigade.

31/5/19.

Distribution:-

1. Brigadier.
2. 51st. Bn. Northd. Fus.
3. 52nd. Bn. Northd. Fus.
4. 53rd. Bn. Northd. Fus.
5. 8th T.M. Battery.
6. No. 3. Coy. R.A.S.C..
7. 142 Field Ambulance.
8. Brigade Major.
9. Staff Captain.
10. O.C. NO.3 Sect. Sig. Coy.
11/13. File.
14. Northern Division "G"
15. 3rd Bn. M.G.C..

APPENDIX "A" to

1st NORTHERN BRIGADE DEFENCE SCHEME.

SIGNAL COMMUNICATIONS.

1. The Civil Personnel are at present assisting British Signal Service Personnel in the upkeep of the telephone and telegraph systems in the Area.

2. In the event of Civil Disturbances, civilian assistance would undoubtedly cease at once and it is also probable that lines would be cut.

3. In the above eventually two means of communication only would be available within the Brigade viz:- (a) Runners and (b) Visual.

4. VISUAL. The following visual communication will be established and maintained as far as possible by "A" Battalion.

   (a) Central Station.   Central Tower of main building Artillery Barracks.
   (b) Fort Vll.   Direct communication with Artillery Barracks.
   (c) Docks.   Direct communication with Artillery Barracks from top of tower 100 yards S.E. of Company Headquarters.
   (d) Eifel Tor Goods Station.   From N.E. of main Warehouse direct to Artillery Barracks.

   In order to maintain this communication the following is the minimum personnel necessary.

   (a) Central Station.   1 N.C.O.. 8 Men. 3 lamps.
   (b) Fort VII.   2 Men. 1 lamp.
   (c) Docks.   2 Men. 1 lamp.
   (d) Eifel Tor Goods Station.   2 Men. 1 lamp.

   In the event of Civil Disturbances the Central Station would be manned by Brigade Headquarters personnel.

5. RUNNERS.

   Communications with all other guards will be maintained by means of runners.

6. WIRELESS.

   Communication between Brigade Headquarters and Division will be maintained by Wireless.

SECRET.

APPENDIX "B"

MEDICAL ARRANGEMENTS.

1. On receipt of Code Message "MOSELLE"

    (a) All Field Ambulances are being held at 1 hour's notice.

    (b) No. 142 and No. 7 Field Ambulances are preparing Dressing Stations in their present locations.

2. On receipt of Code Word "RHINE" No. 142 Field Ambulance will take the following action with reference to the 1st Northern Brigade.

    (a) Send 1 Stretcher Squad to each Regimental Aid Post of the 1st Northern Brigade.

    (b) Move half one bearer Sub-division and half one tent Sub-division with 1 Officer and 2 Motor Ambulance Cars to report Headquarters 1st Northern Brigade MARIENBURG Artillery Barracks and open a Collecting Station for wounded there.

    (c) Clear all casualties to Field Ambulance Headquarters or nearest C.C.S.

3. The above parties will be reinforced by Field Ambulance Commanders as circumstances require.

4. CASUALTY CLEARING STATIONS

    No. 44 C.C.S..   UBIER Ring.
    No. 64 C.C.S..   KAISER AGUSTA School, KARTHAUSER WALL.
    No. 36 C.C.S..   EVANG. HOSPITAL. WEYERTHAL.

5. All ranks of R.A.M.C.. will wear "RED CROSS" Brassards. Officers will carry revolvers.

Army Form C. 2118.

WAR DIARY

~~INTELLIGENCE SUMMARY.~~   1st Northern Brigade.

(Erase heading not required.)

Instructions regarding War Diaries and Intelligence Summaries are contained in F. S. Regs., Part II. and the Staff Manual respectively. Title pages will be prepared in manuscript.

Place	Date	Hour	Summary of Events and Information	Remarks and references to Appendices
COLOGNE	June 1st		Locations of Units:- 1st Northern Brigade H.Q. 107 BACHEMER STRASSE, LINDENTHAL, COLOGNE.	
			51st Northumberland Fus. VOLKS SCHOOL, REDWITZ STR., SULZ,	#
			52nd Northumberland Fusiliers.BERRENRATHER SCHOOL, "	#
			53rd Northumberland Fus. Artillery Barracks, MARIENBURG,	#
			1st Northern T.M.Battery. 3 KLOSTER STRASSE, LINDENTHAL,	#
			Divine Services.	
	2nd		Battalions in training.	
	3rd		King's Birthday. Battalions paraded at 09.00 hours, gave the Royal Salute and three cheers for His Majesty. The remainder of the day was observed as a holiday for all ranks.	
	4th		Battalions in training. Brig.Genl. A.A.Kennedy,C.M.G., promoted Major Genl. (King's Birthday Honours).	
	5th		Two Companies 51st Northumberland Fusiliers proceeded to Ranges at RIEHL and LACHEM to commence firing G.M.C.and relieving similar Companies 53rd Northumberland Fusiliers. Major-General A.A.Kennedy, C.M.G. proceeded on leave to U.K. Lieut.Colonel A.C.Girdwood, C.M.G.,D.S.O., 51st Northumberland Fusiliers, assumed temporary command of the Brigade.	
	6th		Battalions in training.	
	7th		53rd Northumberland Fusiliers took over all Guards found by the Brigade. 435 N.C.Os. and Men of Brigade on Guard Duties. Fighting Strength of the Brigade, 100 Officers, 2261 O.R.	
	8th		Divine Services.	

Army Form C. 2118.

Instructions regarding War Diaries and Intelligence Summaries are contained in F. S. Regs., Part II. and the Staff Manual respectively. Title pages will be prepared in manuscript.

WAR DIARY

(Erase heading not required.) Sheet 2.

Place	Date	Hour	Summary of Events and Information	Remarks and references to Appendices
COLOGNE.	June 9th		Whit Monday. Observed as a holiday for all ranks.	
	10th		Battalions in training.	
	11th		Battalions in training.	
	12th		Battalions in training.	
	13th		Two Companies 52nd Northumberland Fusiliers proceeded to Ranges at RIEHL and LACHEM to commence firing G.M.C. and relieving similar companies 51st Northumberland Fusiliers.	
	14th		51st Northumberland Fusiliers took over all Guards found by the Brigade. 376 N.C.Os. and Men on Guard duties. Fighting Strength of the Brigade. 93 Officers 2219 O.R.	
	15th		Divine Services.	
	16th		Battalions in training.	
	17th		Battalions in training. "J-3" day is to-day. Battalions informed by Brigade Major. 1st Brigade Instructions No. 2 issued to Brigade Group.	Appendix 1
			Orders received to recall Major General A.A.Kennedy C.M.G., and Lt.Col. Hartley D.S.O., Commanding 52nd Northumberland Fusiliers. 2 Companies 9th London Regiment arrived at MARIENBURG Barracks, accommodated by 53rd Northumberland Fusiliers.	
	18th		Battalions preparing to move. 1st Brigade Instructions No. 3 issued to all recipients of No.1.	Appendix 2.

Army Form C. 2118.

WAR DIARY

INTELLIGENCE SUMMARY

(*Erase heading not required.*) Sheet 3.

Instructions regarding War Diaries and Intelligence Summaries are contained in F. S. Regs., Part II. and the Staff Manual respectively. Title pages will be prepared in manuscript.

Place	Date	Hour	Summary of Events and Information	Remarks and references to Appendices
COLOGNE	June 18th		All Guards relieved by 9th London Regt. Orders received from Northern Division (No.8874/17) that moves would take place on J-1 day, but that troops would not move on "J" day until further orders were received. 1st Brigade G.100/2/5 issued.	Appendix 3.
	19th	07.00	Brigade Group moved forward in lorries to KURTEN area. Brigade H.Q. and T.M.B. established at KURTEN; 51st Northumberland Fusiliers, DURSCHEID; 52nd Northumberland Fusiliers, BIESFELD; 53rd Northumberland Fusiliers, KURTEN; M.G.Coy., KURTEN; Cyclists, DELLING; 231st Field Coy. R.E., DURSCHEID; 142nd Field Ambulance, DURSCHEID; Mounted Troops at DELLING with troops at WIPPERFELD and on BIESFELD - HARTGASSE Road. 1 Sub-Section M.G.Squadron attached each Battalion. Lieut. Colonel Girdwood visited Battalions. Orders sent out to 51st and 52nd Northumberland Fusiliers, 231st Field Coy. R.E. and 142nd Field Ambulance that the Brigade would be further concentrated round KURTEN the following day.	
	20th		Staff Captain met all C.Os. and billetting parties and allotted new areas for further concentration. Transport of Brigade Group arrived in KURTEN Area, and was directed to new billeting areas of Battalions. The Divisional Commander visited Brigade Headquarters and saw the Transport on the way. All Units arrive at new areas as per location list attached. 15 Tents issued to each Battalion ad 5 to smaller Units also 100 Petrol tins issued to each Battn. and 20 to smaller units.	Appendix 4.
	13.00			

Army Form C. 2118.

WAR DIARY

~~INTELLIGENCE SUMMARY~~

(Erase heading not required.) Sheet 4.

Place	Date	Hour	Summary of Events and Information	Remarks and references to Appendices
KURTEMA. ~~COLCUTE~~	June 21st		4300 Blankets arrived and were distributed to Units. 246 Tents arrived and were distributed to Units. 53rd Bn. Northumberland Fusiliers were the only Battalion with sufficient light to put them up. (D.A.P.M. (Lieut.ROLFE) proceeded on leave.	
	22nd		Divine Services. Major General A.A.Kennedy, C.M.G. arrived and assumed command of the Brigade. The Divisional Commander visited the Brigade. Appendix "D" received from Division, re Method of dealing with Russian Prisoners.	
	23rd		Battalions in training. The Major General visited the H.Qs. Mounted Troops, Cyclists and 3rd Hussars, also saw the 52nd Northumberland Fusiliers practising an Outpost Scheme. 51st Northumberland Fusiliers on an Advanced Guard and Outpost. Clean washing arrived for distribution to Units. The C.-in-C. visited the Brigade. The Corps Commander visited the Brigade. Amendments to Brigade Instructions No. 2 & 3 issued.	Appendix 5.
		1st wire. 2100	Division through 3rd Brigade wires that Germans have promised to sign and that no new moves would take place tomorrow. Units informed.	
		2nd wire. 22.30	Division wires that enemy have officially notified consenting to sign Peace and that troops will remain in their present positions until further orders. Signal scheme including all Battalions Signallers arranged and sent out.	
	24th		Battalions in training. Brigade Signal Scheme postponed owing to inclement weather, until tomorrow. Battalions carried out Tactical Scheme.	

Army Form C. 2118.

WAR DIARY

Sheet 5.

(Erase heading not required.)

Instructions regarding War Diaries and Intelligence Summaries are contained in F. S. Regs., Part II. and the Staff Manual respectively. Title pages will be prepared in manuscript.

Place	Date	Hour	Summary of Events and Information	Remarks and references to Appendices
KURTEN Area	June 25th		Battalions in training. Division G.8874/20 received giving instructions etc. for backward move to COLOGNE in case Peace is signed. Battalions carried out tactical Scheme and Brigade Signal Scheme.	
	26th		Battalions in training. Battalions Tactical Scheme. Brigade Signal Scheme repeated.	
	27th		Battalions in training. 1st Northern Brigade Order No. 1, G.100/23 issued to all Units. (Orders for backward move if Peace is signed.)	Appendix 6
	28th		Battalions carried out Tactical Scheme and Brigade Signal Tactical Schemes.	
	29th	1835	Division Wire No. G.B.449 received stating that Peace was signed and that A-1 day is 29th inst. Divine Services. 51st Northumberland Fusiliers left KURTEN and arrived at REDWITZ STRASSE School, COLOGNE.	
	30th		51st Northumberland Fusiliers took over COLOGNE Guards from Light Division. Major General A.AM Kennedy, C.M.G. left Brigade to take over Command of Northern Division. Lieut.Colonel W.P.S. Foord, D.S.O., 53rd Northumberland Fusiliers took over temporary command of 1st Northern Brigade. 1st Northern Brigade Group less 53rd Northumberland Fusiliers and parties left out to guard tents, moved to their original billets at COLOGNE, and Units not belonging to 1st Northern Brigade reverted to the command of their own formations. Transport of 1st Northern Brigade Group moved to Berg Gladbach. Brigade H.Q. established at GEIBEL STRASSE, LINDENTHAL, at 12.00 hours.	

Major,
Brigade Major, 1st Northern Brigade.

War Diary

Appendix 1.

H.Q. 1ST BRIGADE NORTHERN DIVISION
No. ~~~~
Date ....

SECRET.

Copy No. 21

1st Northern Brigade
Instructions for Advance No. 2.

SIGNAL ARRANGEMENTS.
----

1. **Method of Communication.**

The following means of communication will be available in case of an advance.

(a) Telegraph and Telephone.
(b) Visual.
(c) Wireless.
(d) Contact Aeroplanes.
(e) Pigeons.
(f) Mounted Orderlies and Despatch Riders.

2. **Telegraph and Telephone.**

(a) Owing to the rapid advance on the first day, it may not be possible to obtain communication by the above means.
Every effort will, however, be made to get communication by these methods during the halts made by the column both between the advance column and Brigade Headquarters and also between Brigade Headquarters and the Division.
For this purpose arrangements have been made for two men of a Corps Air Line Section to be attached to 53rd Northd. Fus. for the advance. They will join this Battalion on J-1 day in the KERTEN area.

(b) Signal Service personnel only will be allowed to tap into permanent routes. Battalion Signallers will on no account interfere with these.

(c) Care must be taken by Signal Service personnel attached to advanced troops that, before using permanent lines, they are disconnected on the enemy side. It is essential, however, that these disconnections are made good before the advance is continued. Teeing in will only be done at a pole on which a bridge over exists.

(d) Until the Security Section G.S. I has arranged for supervision and control, all civilian traffic through occupied offices must be stopped.
German personnel, and especially postmasters, will be forced to remain at their posts ready to work communication, but they are not to be allowed to touch any signal apparatus except in the presence of the representative of the Signal Service.

(e) No lines or instruments are to be destroyed. If a temporary withdrawal from unoccupied office is necessary, instruments will be removed and lines left untouched.

(f) The Officer Commanding 53rd Northumberland Fusiliers will arrange to detail his rear infantry lorry containing 1 Officer and 15 O.R. to halt at HALVER and proceed at once to the telegraph office in that town.
This party will be the guard over the Post and Telegraph Office and will remain there until relieved by a guard of the London Division, when it will rejoin the Battalion.

(g) Officer Commanding 53rd Northumberland Fusiliers on arrival at ALTENA will detail a guard over the telegraph and Post Office in that town.

(h) Officer Commanding 52nd Northumberland Fusiliers will detail a guard of 2 N.C.Os. and 10 men over the Post and Telegraph office at LUDENSCHEID on arrival.

(k) The Officers or N.C.Os. commanding the guards mentioned in sub-paras. (f),(g) and (h) will be given written orders as to where to proceed and the duty they are to perform, namely, (i) to allow nobody except Signal Service personnel and Officers on duty to enter the offices; (ii) to force the German personnel to remain in the office; (iii) to allow nobody except the personnel of the Signal Service to touch the instruments except when Germans are ordered to use the instruments in the presence of a man of the Signal Service.

(l) If the enemy offers organised resistance to the advance and fighting ensues or becomes imminent, a new situation will have arisen, and local commanders will use their discretion as to severing communication in order to prevent tactical information being conveyed along our lines to the enemy.

(m) A Corps Signal Box Car containing permanent line personnel will travel with the Brigade column on "J" day; its normal position will be with Brigade Headquarters, but it has permission to move anywhere up and down the convoy passing lorries as required.

(n) The following are the main German permanent routes in the area traversed by this Brigade.
  (i) KURTEN - WIPPERFURTH - KUPFER BERG - HALVER - OCKINGHSN - LUDENSCHEID.
  (ii) HALVER - BRECKERFELD - HAGEN.
  (iii) HALVER - BRECKERFELD - SCHWELM.
  (iv) LUDENSCHEID - HAGEN.
  (v) LUDENSCHEID - ALTENA - LEMATHE - ISERLOHN - MENDEN - NEHEIM - ARNSBERG.
  (vi) ISERLOHN - SCHWERTE.

3. Cable.

In an advance of this nature the laying of cable is a waste of labour and material and will not be carried out except under orders of the Battalion Commander, in which case the cable thus laid will either be picked up before the Battalion advances, or handed over to another unit in exchange for a similar length of wire.
It must be distinctly understood that no further supply of cable will be available for issue.
Communication on the outpost line should be, as far as possible, by visual and runner.

4. VISUAL.

During halts of the column and on arrival at destinations, every opportunity will be taken of using visual within the battn. between Battalions and Brigade Headquarters.

5. Wireless.

The following wireless sets are in possession of the 1st Northern Brigade.

(a) 1 Trench Set C.W. Mk.III. which will be used for communication between Brigade Headquarters and Division and flank Brigades when possible.
(b) 1 W/T Set, manned by R.A.F. personnel which will remain with Brigade Headquarters for use only in communication with aircraft
(c) 1 Loop Set manned by Infantry personnel under Brigade arrangements. The forward party of this set will accompany the Headquarters 53rd Northumberland Fusiliers to whom they will report on J-2 day.

The rear party will move with Brigade Headquarters.
The set will be erected at each halt of the lorry column en route.

A main wireless station is established at KURTEN.

A Corps Air Line Section consisting of about 10 lorries and 8 Motor Cyclists will travel in rear of the Brigade column on "J" day.

This section is opening a wireless station at HALVER on the afternoon of "J" day and a station at LUDENSCHEID on arrival at that place.

Attention is directed to G.H.Q. letter G.S.26/1 dated 24th April 1919 and O.B.26/1 of 30th April, with reference to endorsing messages "I.B.W. Clear" or "I.B.W. Cypher." Both these letters were forwarded to Units of the Brigade under G.1700/43 of 3rd May 1919.

6. Contact Aeroplanes.

(a) The 12th Squadron R.A.F. are co-operating with the 1st Northern Brigade.

These machines carry a black streamer on the tip of each lower plane.

(b) Communication with Contact Aeroplanes.
(i) Important matters will be communicated by aeroplanes to Brigade Headquarters by wireless.

As far as possible, however, information will be conveyed by dropping messages at Brigade Headquarters.

The O.C. No. 3 Sect. Div. Sig. Coy. will arrange at each halt of the convoy to select a suitable spot for the Brigade aeroplane dropping station and will lay out the ground signal consisting of a three-quarter circle with the letters "J.B." underneath it.

(ii) On the aeroplane calling with a KLAXON horn and firing a white light the leading cavalry, (or in the event of their falling behind at any stage of the advance, the leading Infantry) will fire one WHITE Very Light to show their position.

In the event of opposition being met with, the leading cavalry or leading infantry will fire a RED Verey light.

(iii) Battalions will carry their ground signal sheets and Popham panels, but will not lay them down as long as the advance proceeds satisfactorily.

In the event of opposition being met with and the Battalions having to deploy for action, the above will be laid out at Battalion Headquarters.

7. Pigeons.

The O.C. No. 3 Sect. Div. Sig. Coy. will arrange to draw 12 pigeons on J-1 day at KURTEN; these will be issued as follows:-

Squadron Hussars.   4 Pigeons.
Brigade Headquarters. 8 Pigeons.

8. Mounted Orderlies and Despatch Riders.

(i) The following will be available on "J" day at Brigade Hqrs.
  (a) Two motor despatch riders.
  (b) One troop Cavalry and one Section Cyclists. Instructions as to the action of these will be issued to O.C. Mounted Troops separately.

9. Personnel.

The following men from Battalions will be required to supplement the Brigade Signal Section. These men (with the exception of the Loop set personnel who are at present under training with the Section) will report to O.C. No. 3 Sect. Div. Sig. Coy. at Brigade Headquarters on J-2 day bringing with them 2 days rations.
(a) Loop Set.   51st Northd.Fus. 5 men. 52nd Northd.Fus. 3 men.
(b) Visual Panel. 2 Men from 51st Northumberland Fusiliers.
(c) Visual. 3 Signallers from 52nd Northumberland Fusiliers.
(d) Pigeoneers. 2 Trained men from 53rd Northumberland Fusiliers.

10. HEADQUARTERS.

Brigade Headquarters will be established as follows, on arrival.
J-1 day. KURTEN.

J day. LUDENSCHEID.

J+1 day. MENDEN.

Signal Offices will be established at German Post and telephone offices where these exist.
Headquarters of all Units should be established close to Signal Offices and in a house where subscribers telephones exist.

11. Reports.

(a) The following reports will be forwarded by O.C. Mounted Troops and leading Infantry Battalion on "J" day and J+1 day.
  (i) Morning Situation Report.

  By wire or D.R. to reach Brigade Headquarters by 04.30 hours.
  (ii) Evening Situation Report.

  By wire or D.R. so as to reach Brigade Headquarters by 14.30 hours. This report will include captures of Prisoners and War Material and will be accompanied by a summary of intelligence for the period 12.00 hours to 12.00 hours.

-5-

(b) All Units on arrival at ~~their destinations on J-1 day,~~ "J" day and J∤1 day will at once report to Brigade Headqrs by wire or D.R. stating the exact location of their Headqrs.

12. ACKNOWLEDGE.

A. Sanderson
Major,
Brigade Major, 1st Northern Brigade.

17th June 1919.

Distribution.

Copy No. 1 51st Northumberland Fusiliers.
" No. 2 52nd Northumberland Fusiliers.
" No. 3 53rd Northumberland Fusiliers.
" No. 4 O.C. No. 3 Sect. Div. Sig. Coy.
" No. 5 8th T. M. Battery.
" No. 6 No. 3 Coy. Div. Train, R.A.S.C.
" No. 7 O.C. Composite Hussar Squadron,
    (Capt. Liddell, 15th Hussars.)
" No. 8 O.C. M.G. Squadron, attd. 1st Northern. Bde.
    (Capt. King, Cav. Div. M.G. Regt.)
" No. 9 231st Field Coy. R.E.
" No.10 142nd Field Ambulance.
" No.11 VI Corps Cyclists.
" No.12 "A" Coy. 3rd Bn. M.G.C.
" No.13 Northern Division.
" No.14 2nd Northern Brigade.
" No.15 3rd Northern Brigade.
" No.16 C.S.O., VI Corps.
" No.17 O.C. Northern Div. Signal Coy.
" No.18 Brigadier.
" No.19 Staff Captain.
" No.20/21. War Diary.
" No. 22. Brigade Major.
" No.23. 12th Squadron, R.A.F.

War Diary

SECRET.

1st Northern Brigade.
G.1007/2/4.

1. With reference to 1st Northern Brigade Instructions No. 1, Table A, ROUTE Column.

2. After passing over the NEUE Bridge, the column will proceed straight along the DEUTZER FREIHEIT to its junction with the DEUTZ – MULHEIMER STRASSE, thence along the MULHEIMER STRASSE to its junction with the DANZIER STRASSE, thence along the DANZIER STRASSE to where the FRANKFURTER STRASSE comes into the DANZIER STRASSE at a right angle. From this point along the BERGISHT – GLADBACHER STRASSE.

3. D.A.P.M. 1st Northern Brigade will make arrangements to have one Mounted Military Policeman on duty on each of the following places.
    These police will be given written instructions by him as to the route to direct the 1st Northern Brigade Lorry Column and Transport.

   (a) Western end of NEUE Bridge.
   (b) Junction of DEUTZER FREIHEIT and MULHEIMER STRASSE.
   (c) Junction of DANZIER STRASSE and MULHEIMER STRASSE.
   (d) Junction of DANZIER STRASSE, FRANKFURTER STRASSE and BERGISHE GLADBACHER STRASSE.
   (e) Western end of MULHEIMER Bridge on S. FREIHEIT.
       (This man is on duty to direct the transport of "A" Company, 3rd Bn. M.G.C. along the DEUTZER STRASSE to its junction with the DANZIER STRASSE.)

4. The above police will fall in in rear of the 1st Northern Bde. Transport column, after No. 3 Coy. of the Divisional Train is past.

18th June 1919.

Major,
Brigade Major, 1st Northern Brigade.

Distribution:-
   1. 51st Northd. Fus.
   2. 52nd Northd. Fus.
   3. 53rd Northd. Fus.
   4. Lieut. Pilling.
   5. Brigade Headqrs.
   6. No. 3 Coy. Train.
   7. 231st Field Coy. R.E.
   8. 142nd Field Ambulance.
   9. VI Corps Cyclists. (S.D.R.)
  10. "A" Coy. 3rd Bn. M.G.C. (S.D.R.)
20&11. Northern Division. "G" and "Q".
  12. Staff Captain.
  13. D.A.P.M. 1st Northern Brigade.
  14. Capt. S. Milloy, M.C., Bde. Transport Officer.
15/17. File.
18/19. War Diary.
  21. No. 3 M.T. Coy., G.H.Q.

Appendix 2

S E C R E T.

1st Northern Brigade.
G.130/14.

1ST NORTHERN BRIGADE

Instructions for Advance No. 3.

(A). INTELLIGENCE ARRANGEMENTS.

(B). Arrangements for Control over German Railways.

Reference 1/200,000 COLOGNE. Sheet 59.

A. INTELLIGENCE ARRANGEMENTS.

1. Prisoners, taken by the advanced troops will be disarmed and collected at the following places, a guard not exceeding 10% of the number of prisoners being left at these places by the mounted troops or leading Battalion, whichever has captured them. In the case of mounted men these will be relieved by Infantry of 53rd Nor&hd. Fus. when they come up
    (a) Main Cross Roads WIPPERFURTH.
    (b) Junction of Roads just north of H in HUCKESWAGEN.
    (c) Junction roads just south of W in RADEVORMWALD.
    (d) Road junction just N.E. of R in HALVER.

    These Infantry guards will remain in these positions until the arrival of the Brigade Headquarters lorries, when arrangements will be made by the D.A.P.M. attached 1st Northern Brigade to deal with the prisoners and the dismounted personnel left behind will be brought on by lorry under Brigade arrangements. The D.A.P.M. has a certain number of personnel of Military Foot Police and Traffic Control men; these will be used for convoying prisoners to the Divisional Cage at Advanced Divisional Headqrs.
    Owing to the distance it may be necessary for the D.A.P.M. to use one of the lorries at his disposal to pass back the prisoners when the numbers captured warrant this course.

2. Disposal of Documents. Prisoners will not be searched until arrival at the Divisional Cage. If however there is any sign of prisoners attempting to destroy or throw away letters, documents etc., they will be searched on the spot and all documents, maps etc., removed made into bundles, labelled with the prisoners name, and delivered to the Intelligence Officer on arrival at the cage.

-2-

3. **Intelligence Police.**

(A) Sergeant R.A.B.YOUNG will report to the 1st Northern Brigade for duty on J-1 day before 16.00 hours, he will then be despatched to report to O.C. 53rd Northumberland Fusiliers and will be attached to this Battalion for the advance. Sergeant ORNSTEIN will report to D.A.P.M. 1st Northern Brigade at 16.00 hours on J-2 day. This N.C.O. will be attached to Brigade Headquarters until LUDENSCHEID is reached when he will remain at this place.

(b) The duties of the above will be :-
(i) To obtain information as to active Spartacists and to report their hideouts to the D.A.P.M. 1st Northern Brigade or in his absence to the Commander of the Unit to which he is attached.
(ii) To assist in searching houses of important people and to forward all incriminating documents to I (b) Office.
(iii) To deliver to any Burgomaster copies of Marshal FOCH'S "Order to Civil Population" and other orders.
(iv) To report any matters affecting the safety of the troops which may come to their knowledge to the Unit Commander to whom they are attached.

4. **Intelligence Reports.** Will be sent in each evening by O.C. Mounted Troops and Leading Battalion, also by other Units when they have matters of interest to report, to reach Brigade Headqrs. at 14.30 hours, in accordance with 1st Northern Brigade Instructions No. 2 para. 11 (ii). It is thought that in many cases very useful information will be gleaned from inhabitants of villages by individuals.
The chief points upon which information is required are as follows
(a) Enemy intentions and orders issued.
(b) Location of Formations and Units, approximate strength and organisation.
(c) What defensive measures, if any, have been taken by him.
(d) Moral.
(e) Location of Military Stores and Depots.
(f) Whether any evacuation of Stores and Rolling Stock has taken place and their destination.
(g) Have any demolitions been prepared, if so, where.
(h) Concealment of Arms and Ammunition.
(j) Have any orders for mobilisation been issued.
(k) Opinion of prisoners on the situation which has arisen.

5. **TRAFFIC CONTROL.** The D.A.P.M. 1st Northern Brigade will arrange for the necessary traffic control in the vicinity of the NEUE Bridge and through MULHEIM. Posts to be found by the Mounted Military Police on J-1 day to be in position by 0700 hours.
These M.M.P. will follow on later with the Brigade Group Transport.
Detailed instructions on this are being given to the D.A.P.M.

B. **ESTABLISHMENT of CONTROL OVER GERMAN RAILWAYS.**

1. One of the principal objectives, as laid down in para. 1. 1st Northern Brigade Instructions No.1 is to secure complete control over the German Railway systems that are considered essential to our advance.

2. The essential measures to be taken by Unit Commanders to carry this out are as follows:-
   (a) To occupy and guard stations and bridges in the area in which they are billetted.
   (b) To put up notices, copies of which will be sent to Units.
   (c) To occupy head Railway Offices of any German systems in their area.
   (d) To compel German personnel to remain at their posts.
   (e) To stop all movements of trains until control of the General Management has been taken over by the Sous Commission.
   Guards placed over stations etc. for these purposes must be given definite orders in writing.

3. Damage to Lines. In case of a withdrawal only, in order to prevent circulation of German trains whilst awaiting the resumption of the advance, it may be necessary to damage the permanent way. If this should be necessary, the damage must be only purely temporary (e.g. the breaking of a rail in one or two places).

4. Sous Commission. Once the Sous Commission has taken over, it will be the duty of Unit Commanders to ensure that
   (a) No railway working is interfered with and no Railway Officials are molested or interfered with in their work. In the first instance these Railway Officials will have no passes but the Sous Commission will provide these as soon as practicable.
   (b) No railway lines or telegraphs are interfered with; they are vital to the continued working of the railway.
   (c) No railway buildings or premises are commandeered without reference to Brigade Headquarters.

5. ACKNOWLEDGE.

18th June 1919.

Major,
Brigade Major, 1st Northern Brigade.

Copies to:-
Recipients of 1st Northern Brigade Instructions No. 1
+ Civil Staff Captain.

Appendix 3.

S E C R E T.

1st Northern Brigade.
G.100/2/5.

1. Reference 1st Northern Brigade G.100/2 dated 27th May 1919 (1st Northern Brigade Instructions No. 1).

2. June 17th was J-3 day and movements laid down for J-1 day will be carried out on June 19th, and all necessary steps will be taken to undertake the operations laid down for "J" day on June 20th.
   No action, however, on June 20th is to be taken, nor is the present perimeter to be crossed, until definite orders to that effect are issued from Brigade Headquarters.

3. Consequent on the above, the position of the Brigade at midnight June 19th/20th will be as follows:-
   (a) Mounted Troops at DELLING with patrols on the perimeter from LINDLAR to WIPPERFELD.
   (b) Brigade Headquarters, KURTEN.
   (c) Remainder of Brigade Group along the road from road junction just south of the N in KURTEN to DURSCHEID.
   (d) 1st Northern Infantry Brigade Transport, KURTEN.

4. When the date for "J" day is notified, the advance will be continued on the general lines laid down in G.100/2/1 of the 30th May 1919.

5. ACKNOWLEDGE.

19th June 1919.

Major,
Brigade Major, 1st Northern Brigade.

Copies to all recipients of G.100/2 dated 27th May 1919.

Appendix 4

1st Northern Brigade.
G.100/21.

Northern Division.

LOCATION LIST.

Reference Germany, Sheet 59. 1/200,000.

Unit.	Headquarters.
1st Northern Bde. H.Q.	KURTEN, on KURTEN - WIPPERFURTH Road just north of its junction with KURTEN -DHIUM Rd.
8th T. M. Battery.	Restaurant, BROICH. KURTEN.
O.C. Mounted Troops.	DELLING CHURCH with troops at WIPPERFELD and Pt. 279 on BIESFELD - HARTEGASSE Road.
51st Northd. Fus.	On East side of BIESFELD - KURTEN Road 1½ miles South of N in KURTEN.
52nd Northd. Fus.	On West side of BIESFELD - KURTEN Road, 1 mile S.W. of E in KURTEN.
53rd Northd. Fus.	On West side of BIESFELD - KURTEN Road just S.W. of the junction with KURTEN -WIPPERFURTH Road.
M.G. Coy.	Do. Do. Do.
Cyclists.	¼ Mile North of E in DELLING.
231st Fld. Coy. R.E.	On west of BIESFELD - KURTEN Road south of N in KURTEN.

A sketch shewing the disposition of the various Units is attached.

Lieut.Colonel,
Commanding 1st Northern Brigade.

20th June 1919.

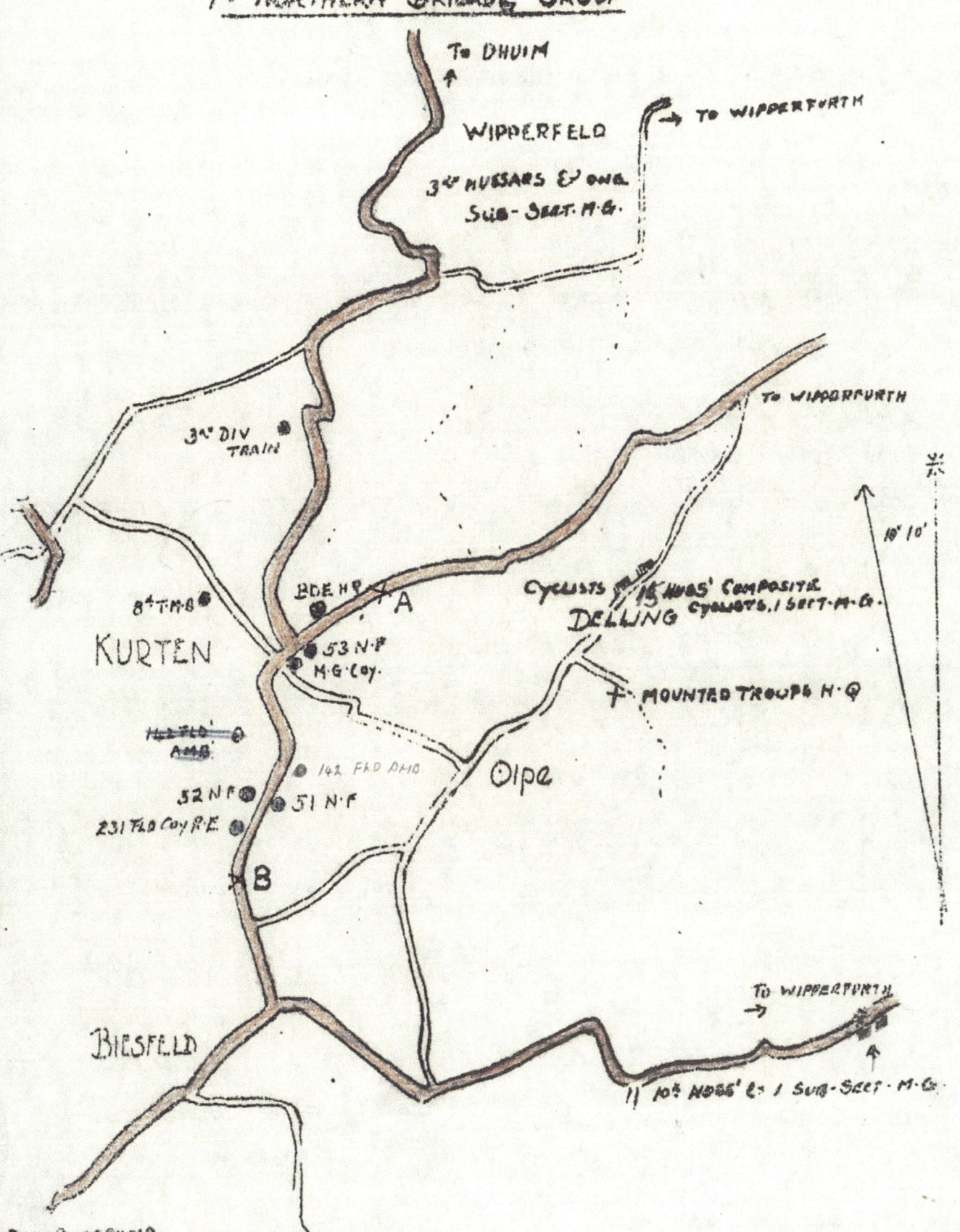

Appendix 5.   War Diary.

SECRET.   1st Northern Brigade.
                                                    G.136/87.

ADDENDUM No. 2 to 1st Northern Brigade Instructions No. 3.

To para. 6 CONTACT AEROPLANES.
Add new sub-para. as follows:-

6.(d) For all inter-communication between aeroplanes and troops on the ground (artillery and infantry) the following system of identifying points will be used with the 1/100,000 and 1/200,000 maps. Both of those maps are squared, though on the 1/100,000 maps the squares are not perfect where the sheets join.

(i) A point will be identified on the map as follows:-

   First. The sheet Number, e.g. 59 in case of 1/200,000 or 3K in case of 1/100,000.

   Second. Break Signal "X".

   Third. The square, identified by the number and letter shown on left margin and top margin of the sheet, the number being placed first, i.e. 2H.

   Fourth. The co-ordinates of the point in the square (or rectangle in some cases on 1/100,000 map), each side being considered as divided into ten spaces in the usual old British system.

   For example:-
     (i) OSTHEIM on the 1/100,000 map would be described as 3LX 2 D 40.30.
     (ii) Cross roads three miles S.E. of LUDENSCHEID on the 1/200,000 map would be 59 X 3 H 40.35.

(ii) In the case of zone calls a square of 5,000 metres on the 100,000 and 1,500 metres on the 200,000 maps will be considered as a zone and the zone call will be repeated three times, e.g. the zone call of the zone containing OSTHEIM would be 3 LX 2 D repeated 3 times followed by the definite description of the points as explained in the 1st para.

(iii) Co-ordinate cards for use with both the 1/100,000 and 1/200,000 will be issued as soon as possible, meanwhile cards can be easily constructed for use where great accuracy is required.

ACKNOWLEDGE.

24th June 1919.

                                                    Major,
                                                    Brigade Major,
                                                    1st Northern Brigade.

Distribution.

1. 51st Bn. Northd. Fus.   7. Northern Division "G".
2. 52nd Bn. Northd. Fus.   8. O.C. Northern Div. Sig. Coy.
3. 53rd Bn. Northd. Fus.   9. 13th Squadron, R.A.F.

Appendix 5.

Amendment No.1 to 1st Northern Brigade Instructions for Advance No.2
Signal Arrangements.

In Para.6 (a) 3rd line.

For " A black streamer" substitute " A coloured streamer ".

- - - - - - - * * * - - - - - - - - -

Addendum No.1 to 1st Northern Brigade Instructions No.3 (A).
Intelligence Arrangements.

Add new Para.

Para.1 (a). METHOD OF DEALING WITH RUSSIAN PRISONERS.

The following instructions have been received from Marshal FOCH :-

(i) A considerable number of Russian Prisoners of War are actually located in the German territory which the Allied Armies may reach in the event of military operations being resumed.

(ii) It is expected that the Germans will attempt as they did after the signature of the Armistice, to rid themselves of such prisoners by releasing them, or sending them into the Allied lines.

(iii) The sudden influx of these prisoners would be likely to cause considerable inconvenience to our Armies. Their transportation outside the zone of operations and the provision of the necessary guards would necessitate the employment elsewhere of transport and personnel which could be more usefully employed.

(iv) The Allies will therefore only take over and assume responsibility for those Russian Prisoners of War who remain under discipline in their camps. All others will be turned back into the German lines.

Major,

Brigade Major, 1st Northern Brigade.

25/6/19.

Copies to all recipients of 1st Northern Brigade Instructions for
Advance Nos. 2 and 3.

SECRET.

Copy No.   1st Northern Brigade.
            G.100/33.

Appendix 6.

1st Northern Brigade Order No. 1.
==*=*=*=*=*=*=*=*=*=*=*

Reference Germany, Sheet 59, 1/200,000.

1.   In the event of Peace being signed without any further advance taking place, the Northern Division is withdrawing to the dispositions as they existed prior to J-3 day.

2.   The 1st Northern Brigade Group will move back to their previous billets on A-1 and A day.
    Personnel proceeding by lorry in accordance with Table A. attached. by road
    The Transport in accordance with Table B. attached, halting for A/B night at BERG GLADBACH.

3.   Attention is directed to G.H.Q. "Notes on March Discipline" dated 22nd May 1919, issued to all Officers.

4. TENTS AND BLANKETS.

(a)   If the tents are dry they will be struck and with the blankets will be conveyed to the billets of Units by lorries.
    Units will therefore make arrangements to close up their personnel in the lorries at present at their disposal in order to leave the necessary lorries for their tents and blankets. No further lorries will be issued for this purpose with the exception of one which will be placed at the disposal of O.C. Mounted Troops for the conveyance of tents and blankets of the Hussar Squadron and Machine Gun Squadron.

(b)   If the tents are still wet and orders are issued from Bde. Headquarters that these shall be left standing the following Guards will be detailed by Units to take charge of these until such time as they are collected.
    51st Bn. Northumberland Fusiliers.
    1 Officer, 2 N.C.Os. and 12 men to guard the tents of the Battalion and those of 142nd Field Ambulance.
    52nd Bn. Northumberland Fusiliers.
    1 Officer, 2 N.C.Os. and 12 men to guard the tents of the Battalion and those of 231st Field Coy. R.E.
    53rd Bn. Northumberland Fusiliers.
    1 Officer, 3 N.C.Os. and 18 men to find Guards to look after the tents of the Battalion, "A" Coy. 3rd Bn, M.G.C. and 3rd Hussars.
    O.C. Mounted Troops.
    1 or 2 N.C.Os. and 8 or 10 men to guard the tents remaining at DELLING. These men will be dismounted and their horses will accompany the Squadron to COLOGNE.
    Arrangements will be made to collect these later by lorry and convey them to rejoin their Regiment.

    Officers Commanding Infantry Battalions taking over tents of other Units will obtain from the Officer Commanding the Unit whose tents they are taking charge of, a signed certificate stating the number of tents, mallets, pegs, etc., which have been handed into their charge. A duplicate of this certificate will be forwarded to Brigade Headquarters.

    Details as regards the rationing of the men so left behind will be issued as occasion arises.

- 2 -

5. LEWIS GUNS AND MOBILE RESERVE.

Lewis Guns and Magazines will be carried on the lorries with the teams.

Boxed Lewis Gun Reserve Ammunition previously carried on the lorries, will, for this move, be carried on the limbers, thus giving more room for blankets, tents, etc.

6. INSPECTIONS AND CERTIFICATES.

Before any Unit/leaves the ground on which they have been encamped, an inspection will be carried out by a Senior Officer of that Unit.

A certificate signed by the Officer making the inspection to the effect that the camp was left in a thoroughly clean condition will be forwarded to Brigade Headquarters.

7. GUARDS IN COLOGNE.

The 51st Bn. Northumberland Fusiliers will take over the guards as detailed on attached list from 2nd Light Brigade on the day after arrival at the barracks in COLOGNE.

The strength of these guards will be as detailed in G.1000/30 of 7/5/19 and amendments thereto.

All details of relief of these guards will be arranged direct between O.C. 51st Bn. Northumberland Fusiliers, and Officer Commanding Battalion 2nd Light Brigade at present furnishing the guards.

The usual taking over certificates will be forwarded to Bde. Headquarters.

8. ACKNOWLEDGE.

Major,
27th June 1919.   Brigade Major, 1st Northern Brigade.

Issued through No.3 Sect.Div.Sig.Coy. at _1300 hours_

Copy No.1. 51st Bn.Northd.Fus.
"   No.2. 52nd Bn.Northd.Fus.
"   No.3. 53rd Bn.Northd.Fus.
"   No.4. O.C. 1st Northern T.M.B.
"   No.5. O.C. No.3 Sect.Div.Sig.Coy.
"   No.6. Lieut.Pilling, Bde.H.Q.
"   No.7. O.C. Mounted Troops.
"   No.8. Detachment Cyclists.
"   No.9. O.C. "A" Coy. 3rd Bn.M.G.C.
"   No.10 231st Field Coy.R.E.
"   No.11 142nd Field Ambulance.
"   No.12 O.C. "J" Sect. M.T.
"   No.13 Bde. Transport Officer.(Capt.Milloy).
"   No.14 C.R.A.
"   No.15.D.A.P.M. 1st Northern Bde.
"   No.16 Northern Division "G".
"   No.17 Northern Division "A".
"   No.18 2nd Northern Brigade.
"   No.19 3rd Northern Brigade.
"   No.20 D.A.P.M. Northern Divn.
"   No.21 Major-General

TABLE A.

Move of 1st Northern Brigade Personnel by Lorry.   To accompany 1st Northern Brigade Order No.1 dated 27/3/19.

1. Serial No.	2. Date.	3. Unit.	4. Starting Point.	5. Time of passing S.P.	6. Destination.	7. Route.	8. REMARKS.
1.	A-1	51st Northd. Fus.	Junction of road & Track 1½ miles S. of N — in KURTEN.	09.00	RELWITZ STRASSE School.	BERG GLADBACH – NEUE BRIDGE – BAYEN Str. via the Walls to LUXEMBURGER Str.	This move may be ordered to take place on A. day in which case an amendment will be issued.
2.	A day.	251st Field Coy. R.E.	Do.	12.15	VINCENZ STATZ.	BERG GLADBACH – NEUE BRIDGE – BAYEN Str. via the Walls – AACHENER Str.	
3.	A day.	52nd Northd. Fus. with 18 Pdr. and detachment.	Do.	12.30	SCHWENATHER STR. School.	As in Serial No. 1	On arrival at COLOGNE, 18 Pdr. & detachment will rejoin Div. Arty.
4.	A day.	Detachment Cyclists.	Road junction just S. of E in DURRING.	12.10	Fort V. HUNGERSDORF.	Road junction just W. of Pt.150 on BIESFELD – LINDE Rd. – Road junction just N.E. pass junction of O in BIESFELD LINDE – BIESFELD & KURTEN-BIESFELD BERG GLADBACH – NEUE BRIDGE – BAYEN STR. UHER – SACHEN SALIER – HOHENSTAUFEN – HAPSBURGER Ringe – AACHENER STRASSE.	1 hour is allowed between the time that 52nd N.F. pass junction of roads and the hour at which Cyclists are due to pass this point.

TABLE A. (Continued).

3. Unit.	4. Starting Point.	5. Time of passing S.P.	6. Destination.	7. Route.	8. REMARKS.
Cy. 3rd Bn. M.G.C.	Point where track crosses the road just S. of N in KURTEN.	12.25	RIEHL Barracks.	BERG GLADBACH – NEUE BRIDGE – KAISER FRIEDRICH STRASSE – FROHN GASSE – RIEHLER Str.	Cyclists Follow from junction of LINDE – BIESFELD KURTEN – BIESFELD Roads.
rthern Bde x L.T.M.B.	Do.	12.30	GEIBEL Strasse.	BERG GLADBACH – NEUE BRIDGE – Bayen Str. – WALLS – BACHEMER STRASSE.	
ed Troops (Cyclists).			COLOGNE Area.	BERG GLADBACH – MULHEIM Bridge.	To be clear of junction of LINDE – BIESFELD and KURTEN – BIESFELD Roads by 08.00 hours.
Northd.Fus.	Junction of OLPE – KURTEN and KURTEN – BIESFELD Roads just S of N in KURTEN.	08.15	Artillery Barracks, BONNER STRASSE.	BERG GLADBACH – NEUE BRIDGE – BAYEN STRASSE – WALLS – BONNER STRASSE.	Timed to cross NEUE BRIDGE at 10.30 not before.

...er will ride in the front of the Lorry Column of each Unit. This Officer is responsible for the Route are maintained. – ½ Mile is allowed between each Unit's column and 2 Miles between 52nd Bn.Northd.Fus. ...lists.
...ng at their destinations, Unit Commanders will give instructions to the N.C.O. i/c of their Unit Lorry ... No. 3 M.T. Coy. G.H.Q. at AMSTERDAMMER STRASSE, NIPPES, where they will report to the O.C. No. 3 Coy.

TABLE B.

To accompany 1st Northern Bde. Order No.1.

Serial No.	Unit	Starting Point.	Time of passing S.P.	Destination.	REMARKS.
1.	59 Bde. Transport.				
2.	" " "				
3.	" " "				
4.	Units Transport.				
5.	1st Northd. Fus.	Junction of OLPE – BIESFELD and KURTEN roads N.E. of Pt. 285.	09.20	BERG GLADBACH.	
6.	2nd Northd. Fus.	Do.	09.25	Do.	
7.	3rd Northd. Fus.	Point where OLPE – KURTEN Road joins KURTEN – BIESFELD Road just So. of N in KURTEN.	09.00	Do.	Follows 2nd Northd. Fus. from junction of OLPE – BIESFELD and KURTEN BIESFELD Roads.
8.	Northern. Headqrs.	Do.	09.05	Do.	
9.	Coy. 3rd Dn. M.G.C.	Do.	09.08	Do.	
10.	4th Field Coy. As in Serial No.4. R.E.		09.42	Do.	Follow "A" Coy. 3rd Bn. M.G.C. from junction OLPE – BIESFELD and KURTEN BIESFELD Road.
11.	3 Coy. Div. Train. As in Serial No.3.		09.15.	Do.	

TABLE B. (continued).

1. Serial No.	2. Date.	3. Units Transport.	4. Starting Point.	5. Time of Passing S.P.	6. Destination.	7. Route.	8. REMARKS.
8.	E day.	51st Northd. Fus.	Point where Railway crosses road ½ mile S. of H in BERG GLADBACH.	07.10	CASINO, Transport lines.	NEUE BRIDGE – KAISER FRIEDRICH STR. – KOMMODIEN STR. – ZEUGHAUS STR. – FRIESEN STR. – HOHENZOLLERN RING – AACHENER STR.	Head of Column timed to arrive NEUE BRIDGE at 10.30 hours
9.	Do.	52nd Northd. Fus.	Do.	07.14	Do.	Do.	
10.	Do.	1st Northern Bde. H.Q.	Do.	07.18	Do.	Do.	
11.	Do.	53rd Northd. Fus.	Do.	07.21	Artillery Barracks, BONNER STR.	NEUE BRIDGE – BAYEN STR. – UBIER RING – BONNER STR.	
12.	Do.	"A" Coy. 3rd Bn. M.G.C.	Do.	07.25	RIEHL Barracks.	NEUE BRIDGE – KAISER FRIEDRICH STR. – RIEHLER STR.	
13.	Do.	231st Field Coy. R.E.	Do.	07.30	VINCENZ STATZ.	As in Serial No. 8.	
14.	Do.	No. 5 Coy. Div. Train.	Do.	07.35	WEISSHAUS.	NEUE BRIDGE – BAYEN STR. – AFILZEN GRAB. – MÜHLEMBACH – ROTHGERBER BACH – WEYER STR.	

TABLE B. (Continued).   Sheet 2.

[...]ptain S. [M]ILOY, M.C., Brigade Transport Officer will be in command of all the Transport of the [...]roup during the whole march.

[Fo]llowing distances will be maintained in accordance with G.H.Q. "Notes on March Discipline".

   Between Transport of Units, 100 yards.

[T]he normal halts at 10 minutes to each clock hour will be maintained after passing the Starting [Point].

[Uni]ts will, as far as possible, keep their Transport clear of the road until the transport of the [un]it it is to follow has passed.

[Th]e times laid down in the above table for passing the various starting points will be strictly [kept]to. Officers are reminded that it is an equally bad mistake to pass the starting point before [the] laid down as to be late in passing.

[The] O.C. 142nd Field Ambulance has been ordered to detail one Ambulance Car with the necessary medical [staff] to proceed along the road after the Transport Column remaining with the Transport until their [arrival] in COLOGNE.

COLOGNE Guards to be taken over by 51st Battalion
Northumberland Fusiliers, in accordance with para.
7 of 1st Northern Brigade Order No. 1.

Reference 1st Northern Brigade G.1000/30 of 7/5/19 and amendments.

Serial No.	Details of Guard.
1.	DOCKS.
11.	Train Guards. Docks to EIFEL TOR etc.
3.	SCHNUR GASSE. (Detention Barracks).
5.	Powder Magazine, RADENBERG.
6.	FORT VII.
14.	COTTON SPINNERY, 25 BAYEN Strasse.
13.	44 C.C.S., UBIER RING.
13.(G.1000/30/3)	EIFEL TOR Goods Station. EIFEL TOR Power Station.
14.(G.1000/30/3)	ALTENBURG Browery, MARIENBURG.
15.	MILITAR LAZARETT, KARTHAUSER Wall.

Railway Patrols between SUD BRUCKE and EIFEL TOR Goods Station.

APPENDIX "A"

A. LORRIES.

Units will be allotted Lorries for the move to COLOGNE as follows :-

A - 1 day.   51st Bn.Northd.Fus   33 Lorries.

A day.   1st Northern T.M.B.   5 Lorries.
1st Northern Bde. H.Q.   3 Lorries.
52nd Bn.Northd.Fus.   33 Lorries.
B.Sect. 142nd Field Amboe.   3 Lorries.
Detachment Cyclists.   4 Lorries.
18 Pdr. Detachment.   2 Lorries.
231st Field Coy. R.E.   9 Lorries.
"A" Coy. 3rd Bn.M.G.C.   8 Lorries.
Mounted Troops.(for tents).   1 Lorry.

B. day.   53rd Bn.Northd.Fus.   34 Lorries.

B. SUPPLY ARRANGEMENTS.

1. Supplies for consumption A. day will be issued in normal way on A-1 day.
2. Supplies for consumption B. day will be issued on afternoon of A-1 day.
3. Supplies for consumption C & D days will be issued on B. day.
4. Iron Rations will be withdrawn from the men by Units and consumed as part of normal ration, corresponding underdrawals being effected.
5. All guards left in present area will be provided with 2 days rations.

C. BAGGAGE WAGGONS.

Baggage Waggons will report as under:-

51st Bn. Northd.Fus. at 10.00 hours on A-1 day.
1st Northern Bde. H.Q. & L.T.M.B.)
52nd Bn. Northd. Fus.   )
) at 11.00 hours on A-1
Detachment Cyclists.   ) day, rejoining Train
18 Pdr. Detachment.   ) by 08.00 hours A. day.
231st Field Coy. R.E.   )
"A" Coy. 3rd Bn.M.G.C.   )

53rd Bn. Northd. Fus. are allotted 1 extra lorry to carry baggage as their baggage wagons will march a day before the Battn. marches.

D. PERSONNEL.

Personnel from Divisional Reception Camp will rejoin their Units on the day of return to COLOGNE.

E. ORDNANCE.

Units are responsible for bringing in their tents into their former billets where they will be stored until further instructions are received.

Blankets will be taken back and will be returned to Store on C day under orders which will be issued later.

G.100/33/1.

ADDENDUM No. 1 to 1st Northern Brigade Order No. 1, dated 27/6/19. (G.100/33)

To TABLE A, Move of 1st Northern Brigade Personnel by lorry. ADD the following :-

Serial No.	Date.	Unit.	Starting Point.	Time of passing S.P.	Route.	Destination.	REMARKS.
9.	A day.	"B" Section, 142nd Field Ambulance.	As in serial No. 1	12.45	VOGELSANGER STR. — BERG GLADBACH — NEUE BRIDGE — KAISER FRIEDRICH STR. — ZEUGHAUS STR. — VENLOER STR.	"	Follow Brigade Headquarters from S.P. mentioned in serial No. 1.

[signature] Major,
Brigade Major, 1st Northern Brigade.

28/3/19.

Copies to all recipients of G.100/33 of 27/6/19.

War Diary

1st Northern Brigade.
G.100/33/2.

APPENDIX NO.2 to 1st NORTHERN BRIGADE ORDER NO.1 of 27/6/19.

Reference Appendix "A" to 1st Northern Brigade Order No.1 dated 27/6/19.
The following readjustment of lorries will take place.

1. (a) O.C. "J" Sect M.T.Company will detail 2 lorries to report at once to 51st Bn Northumberland Fusiliers.
   (b) Units will detail lorries as follows to report to Staff Captain at the Road Junction just South West of Brigade Headquarters at 10.00 hours tomorrow 29/6/19.

Brigade Headquarters	3 lorries.
O.C. "J" Section, M.T.Coy.	2 lorries.
Sect.142 Field Ambulance.	1 lorry.
53rd Bn Northd Fus.	1 lorry.

   (c) O.C. Detachment Cyclists will detail 1 lorry to report to O.C.Mounted Troops, DELLING, at 10.00 hours Tomorrow, 29th inst. If tents are to be struck, O.C.Mounted Troops will load his tents on the early morning of "A" day and send a representative with the lorry to Brigade Headquarters to hand over the tents to the Staff Captain.

   (1) 7 of the above lorries are required to report to O.C. 529 Field Company.R.E. at HOHKEPPEL and 1 lorry for tents of Hussar Squadron.
   Details of these journeys will be given by the Staff Captain on reporting.
   Lorry drivers will be given rations by Units for 29th and 30th instant.
   (2) After conveying 51st Bn. Northumberland Fusiliers to their destination the 3 lorries detailed to these will be ordered to report to the H.Q. 2nd Northern Brigade at HILGON.
   (3) 53rd Northumberland Fusiliers will ration the lorry drivers for the 29th and 30th instant.
   (4) After the above readjustments have taken place Units will be in possession of lorries as detailed in Appendix A mentioned above
   (5) All petrol tins issued will be taken by Units in their lorries and handed over to Officers i/c Supplies the next time refilling takes place on return.
   When this is done a report will be made to 1st Northern Brigade Headquarters stating number of petrol tins handed over.

   Lieut. A/Staff Captain
   1st Northern Brigade.

28/6/19.

Distribution :-
51st Northumberland Fusiliers.
52nd Northumberland Fusiliers.
53rd Northumberland Fusiliers.
1st Northern T.M.B.
Lt. Pilling, Bde. H.Q.
O.C. Mounted Troops.
O.C. Detachment Cyclists.
"A" Coy. 3rd Bn.M.G.C.
231st Field Coy. R.E.
142nd Field Ambulance.
O.C. "J" Sect. M.T.Coy.

Army Form C. 2118.

WAR DIARY

INTELLIGENCE SUMMARY

(Erase heading not required.)

1st Northern Brigade. Sheet 1.

Instructions regarding War Diaries and Intelligence Summaries are contained in F.S. Regs., Part II. and the Staff Manual respectively. Title Pages will be prepared in manuscript.

Place	Date	Hour	Summary of Events and Information	Remarks and references to Appendices
Cologne	July 1st		Location of Units of 1st Northern Brigade:— 1st Northern Brigade Headquarters. 107 Bachemer Strasse, LINDENTHAL. 51st Bn. Northd. Fus. VOLKS SCHOOL, REDWITZ STR., SULZ, COLOGNE. 52nd Bn. Northd. Fus. BERRENRATHER STRASSE School, " " 53rd Bn. Northd. Fus. Artillery Barracks, MARIENBURG, " 1st Northern L.T.M.B. 3 KLOSTER STRASSE, LINDENTHAL. 53rd Northumberland Fusiliers arrived in Artillery Barracks from KURTEN.	
	2nd		2 Battalions in training. 2 Companies 52nd Northumberland Fusiliers and T.M.Battery proceeded to LACHEM and RIEHL Rifle Ranges to complete firing of G.M.C.	
	3rd		General Holiday for all VI Corps troops for celebration of Peace.	
	4th		Battalions in training. Brigade Major visited 53rd Northumberland Fusiliers Sports Final. Report forwarded Division on the dirty condition billets were in when taken over by 1st Northern Brigade from Light Division. Divisional Headquarters moved to 8 VIRCHOW STRASSE, LINDENTHAL.	
	5th.		53rd Northumberland Fusiliers took over all Guards found by the Brigade. 8 Officers and 339 N.C.Os. and Men of the Brigade on guard duties. Fighting Strength of the Brigade, 84 Officers, 2212 Other Ranks.	
	6th		Divine Services. Brigadier-General J.W. SANDILANDS, C.B.,C.M.G.,D.S.O., took over command of the Brigade.	
	7th		Battalions in training.	
	8th		Battalions in training. Casuals of 51st and 52nd Northumberland Fusiliers proceeded to RIEHL and LACHEM Rifle Ranges to complete firing of G.M.C.	
	9th		Battalions in training. Lieut.Col. GIRDWOOD, C.M.G.,D.S.O., and Capt. N.B.PIGG, D.S.O.,M.C., 51st Northumberland Fusiliers and 4 men per Battalion proceeded to PARIS for Victory March.	
	10th		Battalions in training.	
	11th		Battalions in training.	
	12th		52nd Northumberland Fusiliers took over all Guards found by the Brigade. 8 Officers, 275 N.C.Os. and Men of the Brigade on guard duties. Fighting Strength of the Brigade, 77 Officers 2091 O.R.	
	13th		Divine Services.	
	14th		Battalions in training. Lecture by Mr. J. BURNS, M.A.; in VI Corps School on "An hour in the National Gallery". 51st and 52nd Northumberland Fusiliers attended.	
	15th		Battalions in training.	

2449 Wt. W14957/M90 750,000 1/16 J.B.C. & A. Forms/C.2118/12.

Army Form C. 2118.

WAR DIARY
INTELLIGENCE SUMMARY
(Erase heading not required.) Sheet 2.

Instructions regarding War Diaries and Intelligence Summaries are contained in F. S. Regs., Part II. and the Staff Manual respectively. Title pages will be prepared in manuscript.

Place	Date	Hour	Summary of Events and Information	Remarks and references to Appendices
Cologne	July 16th		Battalions in training. 2 Companies 53rd Northumberland Fusiliers proceeded to RIEHL and LACHEM Rifle Ranges to fire G.M.C.	
	17th		Battalions in training.	
	18th		Battalions in training. 51st Northumberland Fusiliers sports.	
	19th		51st Northumberland Fusiliers took over all Guards found by the Brigade. 8 Officers, 275 O.R. on guard duties. Fighting Strength of the Brigade. 74 Officers, 1997 O.R. Today observed as a holiday for all ranks, for the celebration of Peace in common with the people of the British Empire.	
	20th		Divine Services.	
	21st		Battalions in training. Major A. E. SANDERSON, D.S.O. proceeded to U.K. on leave. Lieut. A.J.PARSLOW assumed duties of Brigade Major.	
	22nd		Battalions in training. Brigade H.Q., 51st & 52nd Northd. Fus. Transport moved to new billets at EIFEL TOR.	
	23rd		Battalions in training.	
	24th		Battalions in training. Casuals of the Brigade proceeded to LACHEM to complete firing G.M.C.	
	25th		Battalions in training.	
	26th		Battalions in training. 53rd Northumberland Fusiliers took over all guards found by the Brigade. 7 Officers, 338 O.R. on guard duties. Fighting strength of the Brigade, 73 Officers, 2005 O.R.	
	27th		Divine Services.	
	28th		Battalions in training.	
	29th		Battalions in training.	
	30th		Battalions in training.	
	31st		Battalions in training.	

A/Brigade Major, 1st Northern Brigade.

WAR DIARY

INTELLIGENCE SUMMARY

(Erase heading not required.)

Army Form C. 2118.

Location.
Headquarters.1st Northern Brigade.
15 GEIBEL STRASSE.LINDENTHAL.COLN.

51st Bn.Northd.Fus. REDWITZ STR. SCHOOLS. SULZ.COLN.
52nd.Bn.Northd.Fus. BERRENRATHER SCHOOL. SULZ.COLN.
53rd.Bn.Northd.Fus. Artillery Barracks. MARIENBURG.COLN

Instructions regarding War Diaries and Intelligence Summaries are contained in F.S. Regs., Part II. and the Staff Manual respectively. Title pages will be prepared in manuscript.

Place	Date	Hour	Summary of Events and Information	Remarks and references to Appendices
	AUGUST 1919.			
COLOGNE.	1st.		Battalions in Training.	
	2nd.		52nd.Bn.Northumberland Fusiliers took over all Guards found by the Brigade. 9 Off. 266 O.Rs. on Guard. Fighting strength of Brigade 71 Off. 1991 O.Rs..	
	3rd.		Divine Services.	
	4th. August Bank Holiday.		Observed as a holiday for all ranks. VIth Corps TORCHLIGHT TATTOO.	
	5th.		Battalions in Training. VIth Corps TORCHLIGHT TATTOO.	
	6th.		Battalions in Training.	
	7th.	11.30	Practice Ceremonial Parade, EXERZIER PLATZ. MERHEIM. COLOGNE. Wire received from Division ordering Brigadier General J.W.Sandilands. CB. CMG. DSO.. to report to 2nd Highland Brigade which is proceeding to England to-morrow. Bt.Major. A.E.Sanderson.DSO. returned from Leave U.K., and resumed duties as Brigade Major.	
	8th.		Battalions in Training. Brigadier General J.W.Sandilands CB. CMG. DSO.. departed to take over command of 2nd Highland Brigade. Division wires Col. C.D.Hamilton Moore CMG. DSO. Indian Army Commanding 1st Royal Warwickshire Regiment will assume the duty of Brigadier General vice Brigadier General J.W.Sandilands CB. CMG. DSO..	
	9th.		51st.Bn.Northumberland Fusiliers took over all Guards found by the Brigade. 7 Off. 307 O.Rs. on Guard. Fighting strength of the Brigade 65 Offs. 1965 O.Rs. Lieut. Colonel W.P.S.Foord. DSO., took over temporary command of the Brigade.	
	10th.		Divine Services.	
	11th.		Battalions in Training.	

Army Form C. 2118.

WAR DIARY
or
INTELLIGENCE SUMMARY.

(Erase heading not required.)

Instructions regarding War Diaries and Intelligence Summaries are contained in F.S. Regs., Part II. and the Staff Manual respectively. Title pages will be prepared in manuscript.

Place	Date	Hour	Summary of Events and Information	Remarks and references to Appendices
COLOGNE.	12th		Battalions in Training. Lecture on "Through the Balkans" by Captain De Windt at the Brigade Area School to 500 N.C.Os. and Men of the Brigade.	
	13th		Battalions in Training.	
	14th		Battalions in Training.	
	15th		Battalions in Training. Practice Parade by 52nd and 53rd Bn. Northumberland Fusiliers for Ceremonial Review.	
	16th		Battalions in Training.	
	17th		Divine Services.	
	18th		VIth Corps Ceremonial Parade. Troops inspected by Army Council. Brigadier General C.D.Hamilton Moore CMG. DSO. assumed Command of the Brigade.	App. No. 1.
	19th		Battalions in Training. 53rd.Bn.Northumberland Fusiliers took over all Guards found by the Brigade. 6 Off. 265 O.Rs. on Guard. Fighting strength of the Brigade 67 Off. 1850 O.Rs.	
		22.00	Repetition of VIth Corps TORCHLIGHT TATTOO.	
	20th		Battalions in Training. Casuals of the Brigade proceeded to LACHEM Range to fire General Musketry Course. Scheme for holding courses within the Battalions for the purpose of Training Lewis Gunners.	
	21st		Battalions in Training.	
	22nd.		Battalions in Training. Examinations for 2nd and 3rd Class Army Education Certificates.	
	23rd.		Battalions in Training. 52nd.Bn.Northumberland Fusiliers took over all Guards found by the Brigade. 4 Off. 225 O.Rs. on Guard. Fighting strength of the Brigade 66 Off. 1807 O.Rs.	

3.

Army Form C. 2118.

WAR DIARY
or
INTELLIGENCE SUMMARY.
(Erase heading not required)

Summary of Events and Information	Remarks and references to Appendices
Divine Services.	
Battalions in Training.	
Battalions in Training. Wire received from Division ordering Bt. Major A.E.Sanderson, DSO. to report to War Office forthwith for duty as Brigade Major at Wellington Barracks, ALDERSHOT.	
Battalions in Training. Brigade Major attended a meeting of Brigade Majors at Division. Amendment to Defence Scheme issued.	App. No. 2
Battalions in Training. Conference at Brigade Headquarters. Attended by Commanding Officers and Adjutants of Battalions.	
Battalions in Training. Notes of Conference forwarded Battalions re Brigadier's Training Scheme etc. Firing of Casuals at LACHEM suspended. Division team events for ARMY RIFLE MEETING being fired.	
Battalions in Training. 51st.Bn.Northumberland Fusiliers took over all Guards found by the Brigade 5 Off. 240 O.Rs. on Guard. Fighting Strength of Brigade 75 Off. 1744 O.R..	
Divine Services. Brigade Major (Bt.Major A.E.Sanderson, DSO.) leaves to take up new appointment as Brigade Major at ALDERSHOT.	

[signature]
Captain.
for Brigade Major, 1st Northern Brigade.

1st Northern Brigade.
G.500/88

51st.Bn.Northumberland Fusiliers.
52nd.Bn.Northumberland Fusiliers.
53rd.Bn.Northumberland Fusiliers.
- - - - - - - -

Subject:- Training of Lewis Gunners.

1. The Brigadier does not consider that the present system of training Lewis Gunners under Company arrangements in vogue in some battalions of the Brigade is satisfactory.

    The course which the men undergo in these circumstances is not continuous as it is interrupted by Guards; and the instruction thus given cannot be as good as would be the case in battalion classes under thoroughly trained instructors.

2. The Brigadier wishes Commanders to organise classes under the Battalion Lewis Gun Officer at once, each course to be of 14 days duration.

    Each course may be sub-divided into classes, the number of such classes to be held within the Battalion at one time will depend on the number of really efficient Lewis Gun N.C.O. Instructors available. No one class should, however, consist of more than 10 Officers, N.C.O's and men.

    The Battalion Lewis Gun Officer should supervise these classes and deliver lectures on the weapon itself and on its tactical handling.

3. The Brigadier wishes also to point out that a Company or Platoon Commander cannot possibly command his unit efficiently unless he thoroughly understands the use of each weapon with which the men of his command are armed.

    He therefore wishes all officers who have not passed through a school of Lewis Gunnery to attend a Battalion Course, as many officers as can be spared attending each course held.

4. The Battalion Lewis Gun Classes should be struck off all other training and Guard duties during the 14 days they are under instruction.

5. Battalions will please forward the following information to reach Brigade Headquarters by 18.00 hours 23rd August:-

    (a) The date on which the 1st. Battalion Course will start.
    (b) The number of classes to be held, at one time, and the number of men in each class.
    (c) The number of officers attending the 1st course.

(Sgd) A.E.SANDERSON.   Major,

Brigade Major, 1st Northern Brigade.

20th August 1918.

G.1600/8/3

AMENDMENT AND ADDENDUM No. 1 to 1st Northern Brigade Defence Scheme dated 27/4/19.

----

1. **ACTION TO BE TAKEN IN THE EVENT OF MINOR CIVIL DISTURBANCES.**

    Para. 2 (b) delete the words " reinforce the Guard at" and delete from "This Company" to " "A" Battalion".

    NOTE:- There is now no permanent Guard at the DOCKS; this duty having now been taken over by Police.

2. **DEFENCE SCHEME IN THE EVENT OF CIVIL DISTURBANCES IN COLOGNE G.1600/8.**

    (a) Para. 4   Delete the whole of Para 4. and substitute the following:-

    ORDER TO MOVE.

    In the event of Orders being received for the Brigade to move the Code Word "RHINE" will be sent from Brigade Headquarters. On receipt of this Code Message Units of the 1st Northern Brigade (less Guards and Detachments) will take the following action.

    (a) "A" Battalion.

    (i) Headquarters will move to ARTILLERIE CASERNE (if not already there).

    (b) "B" Battalion.

    (i) One Company will be sent to the Supply Depot of the HANSA WERFT and AGGRIPPA WERFT (Docks) and will picquet all approaches thereto.
    (ii) Half Company will be sent to Guard the Cold Store at No. 229 SEVERIN STRASSE (LINDESEIS FABRIK) and will picquet all approaches thereto.
    (iii) Send One Company to the Packing Base, A.S.D., EIFEL TOR.
    (iv) On reaching these positions the Officer Commanding each of the above detachments will send two orderlies to report to O.C. "B" Battalion at ARTILLERIE CASERNE.

    (c) The 51st and 52nd.Bn.Northumberland Fusiliers will each detail one Platoon to remain behind when the remainder of the Battalion marches off.
    These Platoons will guard the Barracks and Stores of their respective Battalions during the absence of these Units.

    (d) "C" Battalion and "B" Battalion (less detachments mentioned in para 4 (b) and 1st Northern Light Trench Mortar Battery will move to ARTILLERIE CASERNE and come into Brigade Reserve.

    (e) Brigade Headquarters will be established at the ARTILLERIE CASERNE.

    (b) Para. 7. Delete the word "CASINO" in each case and substitute EIFEL TOR.

    (c) Para. 7.(a) For 52nd and 53rd. Northumberland Fusiliers substitute 51st and 52nd. Northumberland Fusiliers respectively.

    .... Major.
    Brigade Major, 1st Northern Brigade.

28/8/19.
Distribution as for G.1600/8.

1st Northern Brigade. G.1000/143.

ORDERS OF GUARDS to be furnished by "A" Battalion, 1st Northern Brigade.
=*=*=*=*=*=*=*=*=*=*=*=*=*=*=*=*=*

Dated 1st July 1919, and all amendments thereto, except those orders issued from time to time with guards mentioned below, are hereby cancelled.

	Minimum strength.				Details as regards Guards.
	Offs.	N.C.Os.	Men.	L.Gs.	
(Barracks)	—	2	8	—	Finds one sentry by day and a double sentry by night.
MAGAZINE.					
Company.	2	10	70	4	These Guards find six sentries by day, doubled by night.
...	2	3	22	2	Garrison and Defence of Fort VII responsible for Guarding all Arms and Ammunition stored there, also for the defence of the Fort in case of disturbances. Finds main Guard 1 N.C.O. and 6 men (one sentry by day doubled at night)
Goods	—	2	8	1	Responsible that no unauthorised person removes stores from Warehouse. By night responsible that seals of trucks are unbroken and patrols warehouse. Finds single sentry by day. Double by night.
C.S.	—	2	10	—	Works under orders of O.C. No. 44 C.C.S. Duty to guard prisoners admitted to C.C.S..
M.T.: BREWERY.	—	2	15	—	Finds 4 posts nightly. (a) Main Gate. (b) Back Gate. (c) Army Vehicle pool. (d) Workshop., also 1 patrol.
BARETT WALL.	—	2	8	—	Finds 2 sentries from 12.00 to 14.00 hours and from 18.00 to 07.00 hours.

Sheet 2.

Minimum Strength.

	Offrs.	N.C.Os.	Men.	L.Gs.	Details as regards Guards.
...ard.					
...ON.					
...	1	4	24	—	Finds 4 sentries by day and 5 by night, also extra sentries when prisoners are being exercised.
...OTHING DEPOT.					
...RASSE.	—	2	8	—	
...DQUARTER GUARD.	—	2	8	—	Finds a double sentry over Brigade Headquarters.
...DQUARTER ...ARD.	—	1	4	—	Remains on for one week under N.C.O. i/c Brigade H.Q.. Guard. Finds 1 sentry over Garage. Remainder being off duty.
...IVISION ...ER GARAGE.	—	1	3	—	Comes on duty nightly.

...ETS found by "A" Battalion, 1st Northern Brigade.

Strength.

	Offrs.	N.C.Os.	Men.		Details as regards Picquets.
Picquet.					
...	1	2	2		Report to A.P.M.. COLOGNE. at DOM HOTEL AT 19.00 hours daily.
...L.	—	2	2		Report to A.P.M.. at Police Billet behind MONOPOL HOTEL at 19.00 hours daily.
STATION Patrol.	—	1	5		Report to D.A.P.M.. Main Station daily at 21.30 hours. Only required on Saturdays and Sundays. Report Police Substation No. 8 NEUMARKT for Police Guide.
...O GASSE and ...STRASSE.	1	1	6		Duty, patrol THIEBOLD GASSE and AGRIPPA STRASSE from 20.00 to 24.00 hours.
... TOR.	1	2	2		This picquet will be taken over from 2nd Northern Brigade from 30th August inclusive.

[signature] Major.

Brigade Major, 1st Northern Brigade.

...s for G.1000/76.

Diaries and Intelligence
[...] in F.S. Regs., Part II
respectively. Title pages
manuscript.

Locations:- Hdqrs. 1st Northern Brigade.
107 Bachemer Str. Lindenthal
REDWITZ STRASSE.
BONNER STRASSE.
BRUHL.

Army Form C. 2118.

WAR DIARY
1st.Bn.N.F.,
52nd.Bn.N.F.,
53rd.Bn.N.F.,

or

INTELLIGENCE SUMMARY
xxxxxxxxxxxxxxxxxxxxxxxxxxxx
(Erase heading not required.)

Summary of Events and Information	Remarks and references to Appendices
Battalions in Training.	
Battalions in Training. Letter received from Division re selection of Units for Mixed Brigade in Germany. 51st N.F. selected.	
Battalions in Training.	
Fort 11. and LACHEM RANGES taken over from Brigade Casuals by 9th Durham Light Infantry, the former having completed firing G.M.C..	
Battalions in Training.	
53rd.Bn.Northd.Fus., took over all Guards furnished by the Brigade at present found by 51st Bn.Northd.Fus.. 5 Offs. 194 O.Rs. of Brigade on Guard. Fighting strength of Brigade 66 Offs. 1610 O.Rs..	
Divine Services. Parties from each Battalion proceeded by Lorry to KREUZAN to fire in competitions at ARMY RIFLE MEETING.	
Battalions in Training.	
Battalions in Training.	
Battalions in Training.	
Battalions in Training. Brigadier General C.D.Hamilton Moore. CMG. DSO.. proceeded on leave to U.K.. Lieut. Colonel. W.P.S.Foord. DSO.. assumed command of the Brigade.	
Battalions in Training. 52nd.Bn.Northd.Fus. took over Brigade Guards from 53rd.Bn.Northd.Fus.. 5 Offs. and 214 O.Rs. of the Brigade on Guard. Fighting Strength of Brigade 69 Offs. 1549 O.Rs.	

Army Form C. 2118.

WAR DIARY

INTELLIGENCE SUMMARY.

(Erase heading not required.)

Instructions regarding War Diaries and Intelligence Summaries are contained in F. S. Regs., Part II. and the Staff Manual respectively. Title pages will be prepared in manuscript.

Place	Date	Hour	Summary of Events and Information	Remarks and references to Appendices
COLOGNE.	14th.		Divine Services.	
	15th.		Battalions in Training. Conference of Brigade Majors held at Division.	
	16th.		Battalions in Training. Conference at Brigade Headquarters of Commanding Officers and Adjutants to discuss reorganization of Brigade when demobilization under A.O. 321. has been effected.	
	17th.		Battalions in Training. G. in C. visited Brigade and Battalions Commanders assembled at Artillery Barracks, MARIENBURG. (H.Q. 53rd.Bn.Northd.Fus). Brigade Education Officer lectured Brigade H.Q. Company and 1st Northern L.T.M.B., on "Future Life in the workshop."	
	18th.		Battalions in Training. Orders received from Northern Division for one battalion to be detailed to relieve 16th Bn. Lancashire Fusiliers at BRUHL.	
	19th.		Battalions in Training. Further orders received from Northern Division that move will be carried out by route march on 22nd Sept.. Advanced party to be sent on 21st instant to take over Ammunition Dump Guard at BRUHL. 1st Northern Brigade instructions for relief by 53rd.Bn.Northd.Fus. of 16th Lancashire Fus. BRUHL issued. Instructions for taking over Artillery Barracks, BONNER STRASSE, MARIENBURG by 52nd.Bn.N.F.. issued.	App. 1. App. 2.
	20th.		Battalions in Training. 51st.Bn.Northd.Fus. relieved 52nd.Bn.Northd.Fus. of Brigade Guards. Total number on Guard duties 4 Offs. 207 O.Rs. Fighting Strength. 72 Offs. 1572 O.Rs.	
	21st.		Divine Services. One Company 53rd.Bn.Northd.Fus. proceeded by lorry to BRUHL to take over billets and Q.V. Ammunition Dump Guard from 16th Lancashire Fus. 5 Offs. and 160 O.Rs of 53rd.Bn.Northd.Fus. on guard duties.	
	22nd.		Remainder of 53rd.Bn.Northd.Fus. proceeded by route march to BRUHL and arrived and move completed by 12.00 hours. Advanced party 52nd.Bn.Northd.Fus. proceeded to Artillery Barracks, MARIENBURG to take over Barrack Stores and quarters.	

Army Form C. 2118.

WAR DIARY

~~INTELLIGENCE SUMMARY~~

(Erase heading not required.)

Instructions regarding War Diaries and Intelligence Summaries are contained in F.S. Regs., Part II. and the Staff Manual respectively. Title pages will be prepared in manuscript.

Place	Date	Hour	Summary of Events and Information	Remarks and references to Appendices
COLOGNE.	23rd.		Battalions in Training. 52nd.Bn.Northd.Fus. proceeded by route march to Artillery Barracks, move completed by 12.00 hours.	
	24th.		Battalions in Training.	
	25th.		Battalions in Training.	
	26th.		Battalions in Training.	
	27th.		Battalions in Training. 52nd.Bn.Northd.Fus. relieved 51st.Bn.Northd.Fus. of Brigade Guards. Total number on Guard Duties 9 Offs. 414 O.Rs.. Fighting Strength of Brigade 73 Offs. 1596 O.Rs.	
	28th.		Divine Services.	
	29th.		Battalions in Training. Conference at Division H.Q.. of Brigade Majors. Subject. "Revision of Defence Scheme".	
	30th.		Battalions in Training. Information received from Rhine Army H.Q. that Brigadier General C.D.Hamilton Moore CMG.. DSO.. would not return from leave.	

Captain.

Brigade Major, 1st Northern Brigade.

Appendix 1.

1st Northern Brigade. Q.32/1191.

Instructions for
Relief of the 16th Bn. Lancashire Fusiliers, BRUHL.
by 53rd Bn. Northumberland Fus.

MOVE. 1. The 53rd.Bn.Northumberland Fusiliers is detailed to relieve the 16th Bn. Lancashire Fusiliers at BRUHL. The relief will take place on 22nd September 1919.

ADVANCED PARTY. 2. An advanced party will proceed by lorry to BRUHL on the morning of the 21st September to take over all barrack stores and billets at BRUHL. A lorry to convey this party will report to the Artillery Barracks BONNER STRASSE at 08.00 hours.

Q.V.DUMP GUARD. 3. One Company 53rd.Bn.Northumberland Fusiliers will proceed on the morning of the 21st September by lorry to BRUHL and will take over the Guard at the Q.V. Ammunition Dump from the company of 16th Bn. Lancashire Fusiliers. Company Commander of this company will carry out a reconnaissance of the Guard and billets on the 20th September.

10 lorries to convey this company will report at the Artillery Barracks at 07.30 hours on 21st September.

MAIN BODY. 4. 53rd.Bn.Northumberland Fusiliers (less 1 company) will proceed to BRUHL by march route on 22nd September to arrive at BRUHL before 12.00 hours. 15 lorries will be provided for carriage of baggage and will report at 07.00 hours on 22nd September at Artillery Barracks.

SUPPLY. 5. Arrangements have been made for a lorry to be attached 53rd.Bn.Northumberland Fusiliers for the drawing of supplies from the present re-filling point.

MEDICAL. 6. Sick will be evacuated daily by an Ambulance reporting from the 142nd Field Ambulance.

CIVIL DISTURBANCE. 7. Copy of Orders for Battalion in the event of Civil Disturbance is attached.

8. Attention is directed to Rhine Army A.5590.F.S.1., a copy of which is attached. This order must be strictly observed.

ACKNOWLEDGE.

JMWoods
Captain.

19th Sept. 1919.   Staff Captain, 1st Northern Brigade.

Distribution:— 53rd.Bn.Northumberland Fusiliers.
16th Bn. Lancashire Fusiliers.
Supply Officer, 1st Northern Brigade.
142nd Field Ambulance.
Northern Division "Q"
Northern Division "A".
52nd.Bn.Northumberland Fusiliers.
British Administrator. LINDENTHAL.

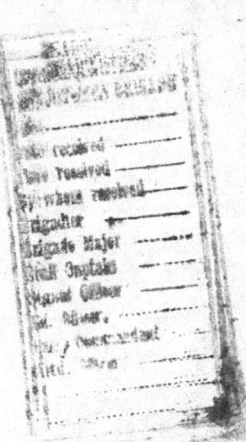

Appendix 2.

1st Northern Brigade.

Q.32/1192.

Instructions for

Taking over Artillery Barracks, BONNER STRASSE

by 52nd. Bn. Northumberland Fus.

52nd. Bn. Northd. Fus. Move to BONNER STRASSE.	1. Consequent on the move of 53rd. Bn. Northumberland Fusiliers detailed in this office No. Q.32/1191 of even date, the 52nd Bn. Northumberland Fusiliers will take over the Artillery Barracks, BONNER STRASSE on 23rd September 1919. The move will be carried out by march route and will be completed by 12.00 hours 23rd September.
Advanced Party	2. An advanced party of 52nd. Bn. Northumberland Fusiliers will proceed to Artillery Barracks on the 22nd September and will take over the Barracks complete with all barrack stores.
Lorries for Baggage.	3. 12 lorries will be provided for the move of baggage and will report at BERRENRATHER STRASSE at 07.00 hours 23rd September.
Barrack Stores.	4. 52nd. Bn. Northumberland Fusiliers will notify the Area Administrator LINDENTHAL by 18.00 hours 20th September the buildings and billets which will be vacated by them with a list of all barrack stores to be handed over to him. These must be handed and a receipt obtained on 23rd. September. A certificate will also be obtained at the same time that they have been handed over thoroughly clean and in good repair.
1st Line Transport.	6. 1st Line Transport will accompany battalion.

Captain.

19th Sept. 1919.   Staff Captain, 1st Northern Brigade.

Distribution:-
    52nd. Bn. Northumberland Fusiliers.
    53rd. Bn. Northumberland Fusiliers.
    British Administrator, LINDENTHAL.
    Supply Officer, 1st Northern Brigade.
    Northern Division "G".
    Northern Division "A".

BEF

Northern Div, formerly 3 Div

2 Northern Inf Bde

1/5 W. Yorks

1919 Feb to 1919 Oct

From 49 Div 146 Bde

Vol 48.

3.X.
11 sheets

1/5th Battalion Prince of Wales's Own (WEST YORKSHIRE) Regt.

WAR   DIARY.

Period: From 28th February 1919   to 31st March 1919.

February - March 1919

WAR DIARY
or
INTELLIGENCE SUMMARY.
(Erase heading not required.)

Army Form C. 2118.

Instructions regarding War Diaries and Intelligence Summaries are contained in F. S. Regs., Part II. and the Staff Manual respectively. Title pages will be prepared in manuscript.

Place	Date	Hour	Summary of Events and Information	Remarks and references to Appendices
MONCHEAUX	FEB 28	ALL DAY	Education 0900 to 1000. A check of arms/walks order proceeded to EVIN 10 to join the 1/7 Bn WYORK R. 3 Officers & 80 O.R. under LT. J.W. RUSHFORTH M.C. proceeded to EVIN to attend a lecture on "Woman's Part in the War".	REF MAP Sh 44 A 1/40000
do	MAR 1	ALL DAY	Companies were at the disposal of Company Commanders for cleaning up equipment & harness. 10 to 11.00. The Commanding Officer inspected the Battalion on the Battalion Football Ground at 11.15 Riano.	2/0
do	2	UNTIL 0645	The Battalion moved to COLOGNE. The Battalion paraded at the Cross roads MONCHEAUX CHURCH at 0645 & proceeded by march route to DOUAI where it entrained leaving DOUAI at 1220 Riano.	2/0
IN THE TRAIN	3	ALL DAY	The remainder of the day was spent in the train.	2/0
			The day was spent in the train	2/0
COLOGNE	4	FROM 0220	The Battalion arrived at NIPPES SIDING at 0220 hours & remained in the train until 0900 when it detrained & proceeded by march route to its billet in VENLOER STR. EHRENFELD. The Battalion was accommodated in a factory with Bn. H.Q., Mess & Married Quarters.	2/0
do	5	ALL DAY	Companies were at the disposal of Company Commanders for interior economy.	2/0
do	6	ALL DAY	Companies were at the disposal of Company Commanders for interior economy & arms drill.	2/0
do	7	ALL DAY	A lecture was given by the Medical Officer to the Battalion at 0900. Companies were at the disposal of	2/0

WAR DIARY or INTELLIGENCE SUMMARY

Army Form C. 2118.

March 1919.

Place	Date	Hour	Summary of Events and Information	Remarks and references to Appendices
COLOGNE	7	(con'd)	Company Commanders for guard mounting & close order drill from 1500 to 1245 hours	REF MAP, PLAN DER STADT COLN 1:15000 500.
do	8	ALL DAY	The Divisional General inspected the Battalion at 0930 in BLUCHER PARK at 1500 the Battalion marched to the NEW SCHOOL BICKENDORF.	200.
do	9	ALL DAY	The Commanding Officer inspected the Battalion on the Barrack Square, after which he inspected the Barracks. R.C. Parade Service was held in the R.C. Church MECHTERN STRASSE, at 1030.	200.
do	10	ALL DAY	The Battalion bathed at the NEPTUN BATHS, NEPTUN STRASSE. The Barrack Commander inspected the Billets, Mess, Canteen, Cook house & c.	200.
do	11	ALL DAY	Education 0900 to 1000. The Battalion paraded on the Barrack Square at 1030 for Co's inspection, after which Companies carried out Coys. P.T. Close order & arms drill until 1245 hours on 11 to close order drill & Pass, of the 3rd Class Army Cert. A.	200.
do	12	ALL DAY	Education & training as yesterday, 23 O.R. of the Battalion were awarded the 3rd Class Army Cert. A.	200.
do	13	ALL DAY	Education 0900 to 1000. The Battalion paraded on the Barrack Square at 1030 hours and marched to BLUCHER PARK & carried out ceremonial drill.	200.
do	14	ALL DAY	Education & training as yesterday.	200.
do	15	ALL DAY	The Battalion paraded on the Barrack Square at 0900 & marched to BLUCHER PARK to see a demonstration guard after which it returned to Barracks & Companies were at the disposal of Company Commanders for interior economy.	200.

Army Form C. 2118.

WAR DIARY
or
INTELLIGENCE SUMMARY.
(Erase heading not required.)

Summary of Events and Information	Remarks and references to Appendices
	REF MAP PLAN DER STADT 1:15,000.
Parade Services were held as under: C. of E. in the Theatre at 1100 hours, R.C. in the	2910
NECHTERN STRASSE, EHRENFELD at 1015 hours.	
The Battalion bathed in the NEPTUN BATHS NEPTUN STRASSE	2910
the Range at LACHEM was at the disposal of the Battalion	
2 Officers and 40 Other Ranks firing Application Practice Having	
had tea the remainder of the Battalion were at	
the disposal of Coy Comdrs. Inspections for internal Economy	
also things of equipment etc. The Commanding Officer	
inspected the draft found the Mr. Jn. but those who	
were warned the 13th on the previous day LIEUT	
C.J.B. SMITH and 2/LIEUT C.R.C. HARISON joined the Bn by	
Mtr from Bn Wkshops. 16.3.19 Leave Allotted to	
A & D Coy Serjeants & Capt. & A/Adjt. B.E. ABLITT M.C.	
16 %??	
Leaving proceeded to U.K. on leave #7 3. 19 Capt. HENRY	
1 SHRIEVE assumed duties as Acting Adjutant Capt.	
Q.M. F. VEAL having proceeded to U.K. on leave 14.3.19	

WAR DIARY
or
INTELLIGENCE SUMMARY.

Army Form C. 2118.

March 1919

Place	Date	Hour	Summary of Events and Information	Remarks and references to Appendices
COLOGNE	(March) 18	ALL DAY	LIEUT. B.T. CUSSONS attended the Test of Quartermasters on that date. The Exercise of which the Bn. were Spectators went will to Schedule. Rendezvous at "NORTHERN DIVISION" Road. "3rd Divisions" had also taken share.	
do	19	ALL DAY	Education 0900-1000. The Bn. paraded at 10.30 hours for route march. The following officers joined the Bn. via Base. Capt. A.C. ROOTH M.C. posted to "C" Coy. Lieut. T.D. GRIFFITHS. posted to "D" Coy. Lieut. R.W. ROBINSON. posted to "A" Coy. 2Lieut. W. COOK posted to "D" Coy.	
do	20	ALL DAY	Education 0900-1000. The Bn. less No.1 Coy an Brigade Guard paraded at 10.30 hours & marched to BLUCHER PARK for ceremonial drill. The Brigadier paraded an inspection from 1000 to 1200 hours.	
do	21	ALL DAY	The Range at LAHEM was at the disposal of the Bn. & 4 officers & 40 O.R. fired application & rapid practices.	

March 1919

Army Form C. 2118.

WAR DIARY
or
INTELLIGENCE SUMMARY
(Erase heading not required.)

Place	Date	Hour	Summary of Events and Information	Remarks and references to Appendices
COLOGNE	21 (Cont'd)	ALL DAY	The remainder of the Bn. not on duty were at the disposal of Company Commanders for interior economy.	
do	22	ALL DAY	Classes were held from 0900–1000 from 1000 to 1245. The remainder were at the disposal of Company Commanders for interior economy.	
do	23	ALL DAY	Church of England Church Parade at 1100 hours in the Roth Krona Kirche. Roman Catholic Church Parade in MECHTERN STRASSE, EHRENFELD at 1015 hours. Wesleyan Church Parade (including those Church of Scotland) in the Garrison Church at 1100 hours. Bn. Col. (T/Brig Gen.) G.G.S. CAREY C.B., A.M.G. had reviewed numerous at 9.30 am by Brigade and Bn. Col. (T/Brig Gen.) H.C. Potter C.M.G., D.S.O.	
do	24	ALL DAY	The Battalion bathed in the NEPTUN BATHS. When not at the BATHS men were at the disposal of Coy.	

WAR DIARY
or
INTELLIGENCE SUMMARY.

Army Form C. 2118.

Summary of Events and Information	Remarks and references to Appendices

Onward to the inspection of 1 B.Rs. GasDrill & kit inventory.

On the 11th there was a lecture in the Mess tent by the Rev T. HUNTER BOYD at 1930 hrs entitled "The Slavs in BOHEMIA and the BALKANS"

A Church parade 0900 to 1000 hours held by the Brigade was held at LEATHER PARK, the training under Coy arrangements at the 1130 hrs and the Battalion returned to Camp.

An occasional stand at 1230 hrs. Remainder of the morning of the inspection of the men and kit having in the afternoon.

Church parade 0910 to 1000 hrs of the B Bn. Parade of the Revrd Personnel at 1030 hrs at 6.45 in the evening. All Coys were detailed in the disposal of any Observer and officers to be on to deal with any arms dust short marching of Platoon Bn Staff. Twenty Officers + 518 O.R. of the 5 Bn (T.D.) Battalion paraded through the Bank and were to hear at the

Army Form C. 2118.

...es and Intelligence
...F. S. Regs., Part II.
...tively. Title pages
...ipt.

WAR DIARY
or
INTELLIGENCE SUMMARY.
(Erase heading not required.)

Summary of Events and Information	Remarks and references to Appendices
strength & posted to Companies.	
Education 0900 to 1000 hours. Companies at the disposal of Coy Commanders for interior economy. The readjustment of billets necessary owing to the large increase in the strength of the Bn was carried out. "B" & "D" Coys moving to new billets in the Transport lines. The following is an extract from list No 231 "Appointments, Commissions etc" approved by the Field Marshal Commander in Chief of the British Armies in France dated 11.3.19:-	
INFANTRY (Territorial Force) 5th Bn. W. York Regt. Capt. B.E. ABLITT, M.C. to be Adjutant (vice Capt. D.S.H. FREEMAN M.C. to Regimental duties) 21st October 1918.	
Church Services were held as follows:- C of E in Battalion Theatre at 1100 hours. R.C. in MECHTERN STRASSE, EHRENFELD at 1025 hours. Wesleyans & other Free Churches in the GYMNASIUM (Y.M.C.A.) NUSSBAUMER STRASSE at 1100 hrs.	

(A9175) Wt W2355/P361 600,000 12/17 D. D. & L. Sch. 52a. Forms/C2118/15

WAR DIARY or INTELLIGENCE SUMMARY.

Army Form C. 2118.

March 1919

Place	Date	Hour	Summary of Events and Information	Remarks and references to Appendices
COLOGNE	31	ALL DAY	The Bn. received reinforcements from the 53rd Yok. Regt. billeted at the NEPTUN BATHS. The Commanding Officer inspected the reinforcements from the 53rd Yok. Regt. at 14.30 hours. Medical inspection each day held Monday and at billets of these new joined men were at the disposal of their Commanders down for fitness for training, instruction. SF.

March 1919.

WAR DIARY
or
INTELLIGENCE SUMMARY.

(Erase heading not required.)

1/5th. Bn. P.W.O. (W YORK) Regt.
Army Form C. 2118.

Place	Date	Hour	Summary of Events and Information			Remarks and references to Appendices
				Offs.	O.R.	
			Effective Strength at the end of February	31	465	
			INCREASE during March 1919	Offs.	O.R.	
			Cross-posted from 1/7th. W York. R.	10	219	
			Lieut. C.P.O. Nanson - Lieut. T.V. Riley			
			Lts. C.J.R. Smith - R.W. Robinson - A.B. Mortimer			
			Cpts. T.D. Griffiths - G.L. Booth 2/Lts. D. Steele - W.Cook		5	
			Evacuated Sick to duty	20	518	
			Reinforcements 53rd (Y.S) York & Lancs Rgt.			
			T.W. Motram - N. Parrington - J.P. Brown - E. Plummer			
			Capts. E. Ford			
			L.St.J. Reeve Lts. R.M. Evans - C. Deucher - J.H. Palin - V.B. Briggs			
			A.T. Edwards J.E. Hartshorn - T. Allen 2/Lts. R.V. Wildsmith - G.G. Burman			
			R. Blacker - J. Dunnington - T.H. Lowe - J. Gill - S.B. Mardon	30	742	
				61	1207	
			DECREASE during March 1919	4	77	
			Cross-poster to 1/7th. W York Rgt.			
			Lts. D.N. Spankie - R.G. Harrowing. 2/Lts. H.A. INGRAM - G.N. Elliott			
			U.K. Re-enlistment furlough		5	
			Posted to Truck Kitchen Coy.		3	
			Demobilized - Lt. H. Berghoff - 2/Lt. J.A. Goslyn	3	41	
			Demobilized whilst on leave Lt. C.G. Maufe ...		8	
			To E.F.C. H.Q. Clerk.		1	
			2nd. Army Headquarters		2	
			Taken on 146th. Brigade Establishment		2	
			Posted to K.O.Y.L.I.		1	
			Ordered to Depot. whilst on leave ...(det. Sick)		1	
			Evacuated Sick		10	
			To A.S.C. - Capt. (Chaplain) H. Waterworth	1	1	
			To 146th. B.M.R. Cadre Establishment			
				8	152	
				53	1055	

W Oates
Lieut-Col.
Commanding 1/5th. Bn. P.W.O. (W YORK) Regt.

1/5th.Bn.P.W.O.(WEST YORKSHIRE).REGT.

WAR DIARY.

APRIL.1919.

WAR DIARY
or
INTELLIGENCE SUMMARY.
(Erase heading not required.)

1/5th Bn. P.W.O.(W.York) Regt
Army Form C. 2118.

Place	Date	Hour	Summary of Events and Information				Remarks and references to Appendices
				Offs.	O.R.	Offs.	O.R.
			Effective Strength at the end of March			53	1055
			Increase during April 1919				
			Cross posted from III Corps Con. Camp.	1	4		
			from 1/7th W.York.R. Lt.W.KERR-MORGAN		5		
			VIIIth Corps Con. Camp		10		
			Evacuated Sick to duty		10		
			Cross posted from 10th W.York.R.		4		
			Reinforcements 52nd.Bn. W.York.R.				
			Capt. J.F.Spencer, H.W. Cowling, Capt. B.Hutchinson, Capt. G.H.Segar				
			A.R Speight, Capt. P.G.Alexandre, Lieut. H.F.Thompson,				
			Lieut. T.Pilgrim, Lieut.S. H. Evans, Lieut. N.W.Gibbons, F.White,				
			R.G.Hickton, J.E.Featherstone, J.H.Clegg, H.W.A.Young,				
			A.Broomfield, J.E.Tillotson, 2/Lt.H.Retburg, W.Smith				
			2/Lt. W.P.Robinson, H.C.Dawn, S.Bennett, W.Broadley, M.J.Quill,				
			E.McGuire, G.A.Broadbent, E.Bays, H.Gash, J.W.Meskimmon,				
			T.W.Parker, W.R. Ormiston.	31	422		
			Cross posted from 1/4th York & Lanc Regt.				
			Lieut. J.R.Allett, 2/Lt. A. Cameron	2			
			Cross posted from 52nd. N.F.				
			Lieut. P. Brookes	1		35	455
						88	1510

WAR DIARY
or
INTELLIGENCE SUMMARY.

(Erase heading not required.)

Army Form C. 2118.

Place	Date	Hour	Summary of Events and Information			Remarks and references to Appendices
				Offs.	O.R.	
			Brought forward.	88	1510	
			DECREASE during April 1919. .... Offs. O.R.			
			To U.K. for Service in Russia Capt. G.L.Booth, Capt. T.B.Griffiths	2		
			Cross posted to 52nd. N.F. Lieut. C.Deucher	1	21	
			Evacuated sick			
			Cross Posted to 1/6th Bn. W.YorkR. 2/Lt. H.Retberg	1	1	
			Demobilized whilst on leave Capt. A.P.O'Reilly, Capt. E.Ford, Capt. J.D Barrett, 2/Lt.A. Lapish, Lieut. F. White, P.G. Alexandre, Capt. N. Parrington, T.W. Mottram, Lieut. J.E. Hartshorn, 2/Lt. L.H. Reeve, J.A. Brough, C.G. Burman, Lieut. T. Allen, 2/Lt. J.W Meskimmon	14	48	
			To Home establishment	1		
			Discharged to Re-enlist		1	
				18	72	
				70	1438	

W^y Cordes
Lieut-Col.
Commanding 1/5th Bn. P.W.O.(W.York) Regt.

WAR DIARY
or
INTELLIGENCE SUMMARY.

Army Form C. 2118.

(Erase heading not required.)

Summary of Events and Information	Remarks and references to Appendices
The Battalion bathed at the NEPTUN & the SCHOOL BATHS. A Lecture under the auspices of the Royal Army Temperance Association was given by CAPT WEEKS R.A.M.C. in the Theater at 14.30 Hours	REF MAP PLAN DER STADT COLN 1/15,000 Etc.
Boys were at the disposal of Company Commanders for Regton Scouting. The N.C.O's Class was continued. A Scouts Class was formed under LT T.E. DICKERSON M.S. Scout Officer.	Etc
Education 0900-1000. The Battalion fell in in Coys in the Barrack Square at 10.30 hours & marched to BLUCHER PARK for Platoon training Return-Quick. B Coy Battn was employed in in the afternoon. The Platoon Officer gave a Lecture to the Non-commrd. Com. the 53rd York & Lancaster Regt at 14.30. The N.C.O's Class & the Scouting Class were continued.	Etc
Education as yesterday. The Battalion less 'D Coy' Assaulting went on a Cruise at The N.C.O's Contind. Education Classes were continued. B Coy Bn T Coy Bn Scouting Volunteers was active in in the afternoon. 'D Coy' was at the disposal of as Company Com manders to represent the Regton Guard.	Etc
'D Coy' Relieved 'E' Company A the Bn for Y YORK on Baggage Guard at the ARTILLERY	

Army Form C. 2118.

WAR DIARY
or
INTELLIGENCE SUMMARY.
(Erase heading not required.)

Instructions regarding War Diaries and Intelligence Summaries are contained in F. S. Regs., Part II. and the Staff Manual respectively. Title pages will be prepared in manuscript.

Place	Date	Hour	Summary of Events and Information	Remarks and references to Appendices
COLOGNE	5	CONT'D	DEPOT NIPPES. The remainder of the Battalion was at the disposal of Company Commander Bensonsen	REF MAP PLAN DER STADT. COLN 1:15000
			In interior economy.	
do	6	ALL DAY	Church Parade services were held as under:- C. of E. In the Theatre at 1100 hours.	do
			Wesleyans: In the Gymnasium, NUSBAUMER STRASSE at 1150 hours. ROMAN CATHOLICS	
			In the Church MECHTERN STRASSE at 0730. The Commanding Officer inspected	
			Barracks commencing at 1145 hours	do
do	7	ALL DAY	'A' & 'C' Coys paraded at the NEPTUN & SCHOOL BATHS respectively. 'B' Coy	
			fired everything — Off Rifles practice on the Formative Range near the School	
			Baths. Pt of the Boys 'A' & 'C' Coys were at the disposal of Coy Commanders	
			In Coy Training. Sewing Drill — Lecture Drill — Lewis Gun — Bombing instruction	
			was carried out in the afternoon. During the afternoon the Lecture given instructed	
			the Battalion. 31 Officers & 422 O.R. from the 52nd Br. W. York Regt. Joined	
			the Battalion as reinforcements. CAPT. B.E. ABLITT M.C. joined the Battalion again	
			Coore & assumed the Duties of Adjutant.	do
do	8	ALL DAY	Education 0900 to 1150. The Remainder of the Battalion bathed at the NEPTUN	
			& SCHOOL BATHS. 'C' Coy was at the disposal of its Company Commander for Beloum	

WAR DIARY
or
INTELLIGENCE SUMMARY.
(Erase heading not required.)

Army Form C. 2118.

Place	Date	Hour	Summary of Events and Information	Remarks and references to Appendices
COLOGNE	8	CONT.	Training. A Coy fired Grouping & Application on the Miniature Range near the School. The Second Army Defeated Us again again to that of "ARMY OF THE RHINE"	REF MAP PLAN DER STADT COLN 1:15,000
do	9	ALL DAY	Education 0900 to 1000. Coys were at the disposal of Company Commanders for Minor Economy & Organization	do
do	10	ALL DAY	Education 0900 to 1100. 'D' Coy fired Grouping & Application practices on the RANGE at LACHEM. The remainder of the Battalion were at the disposal of Coy Commanders for Platoon, Lewis Gun & Bombing Training	do
do	11	ALL DAY	Education 0900 to 1100. All Coys with the exception of 'B' Coy were at the disposal of Company Commanders for Platoon Training from 1100 to 1245. From 1400 to 1600 Lewis Gun & Bombing instruction was carried out. 'B' Coy fired Bombing & Application practices on the Range at LACHEM. A Lecture was given by Rev. Gadsden F.J. ATKINS at 1830 hours on "What Belgium means to us".	do
do	12	ALL DAY	Education 0900 to 1000. In the remainder of the morning HQ & Coys were at the disposal of Company Commanders for various economy	do
do	13	ALL DAY	Parade services were held as under: C of E. @ Ja the Theatre at 1000 R.C. HQ 'A''C' Coys (?) Ja the Theatre at 1045 'B' + 'D' Coys. WESLEYANS. Ja the Y.M.C.A.	

Army Form C. 2118.

WAR DIARY
or
INTELLIGENCE SUMMARY.
(Erase heading not required.)

Place	Date	Hour	Summary of Events and Information	Remarks and references to Appendices
COLOGNE	13	CONTD	NUSSBAUMER STRASSE SCHOOL at 1000 hrs. ROMAN CATHOLICS to the CHURCH in METCHERN STRASSE at 0820. The Commanding Officer inspected Billets.	REF MAP. PLAN DER STADT COLN 1/5000 do.
do	14	ALL DAY	Bouillon 0845 to 1045. H.Q. Jaeghin & "B" Coy baths at the NEPTUN BATHS. "A" Coy baths at the school baths. Parades as follows – 0830 to 0700 Physical Training, 1100 to 1245 "D" Coy was at the disposal of its Company Commander in Mushetry, Bayonet Training, Arms Drill & Section Training. 1400 to 1545. All Coys Rifle Gun, Bombing & Mushetry Instruction. "C" Coy Wire Bombing and Application Practice on the Miniature Range. The Medical Officer inspected all O.R.'s of the Bn in the Parade Commencing at 1400. A Class of N.C.O's for the Malaysian was formed under the Bn. Sgt. Major N.C.O. The Scouting & Snooping Classes were resumed.	do
do	15	ALL DAY	Bouillon 0845 to 1045. D Coy bathed at the NEPTUN BATHS. C Coy bathed at the school baths. Parades as follows – 0630 to 0700 Physical Training, 1100 to 1245. A Coy was at the disposal of its Company Commander for Musketry, Bayonet Training, Arms Drill & Section Training. B Coy Lewis Bombfact & Application Practice on the Miniature Range. The Bn. Scouting and Sig Scallers Classes were continued.	do

WAR DIARY
or
INTELLIGENCE SUMMARY.
(Erase heading not required.)

Army Form C. 2118.

Instructions regarding War Diaries and Intelligence Summaries are contained in F. S. Regs., Part II. and the Staff Manual respectively. Title pages will be prepared in manuscript.

Place	Date	Hour	Summary of Events and Information	Remarks and references to Appendices
COLOGNE	16	ALL DAY	Education 0845 to 1045. Parades 0630 to 0700 & Rifle Exercises 1150 to 1300. "D" Coy. Coys (except "D" Coy) proceeded on a Route march. "D" Coy were carrying out Application practice on the Miniature Range. 1400 to 1515 hours. Lewis gun training. The Coy Scouting & Signalling Classes were continued.	Ref. Col. PLAN DER STADT COLN 1:15000
do	17	ALL DAY	Education 0845 to 0945. Parades 0630 to 0700. Physical Training 1000 to 1300. All Companies except "C" Coy were at the disposal of Company Commanders for Platoon & Company Training. 1400 to 1515. Lewis gun training. "C" Coy been carrying out Application practice at the Range at LACHEM. Coy Scouting Class & Company Classes were continued. The change in the arm inclusive of "K" Company "Copies" to "2nd Parade" was notified from this date. The Signalling Class were continued.	no
do	18	ALL DAY	GOOD FRIDAY. Church parade was held as follows: C of E, St the Theatre at 1000 & 1045 hours. Wesleyans. 01 NUSSBAUMER STRASSE SCHOOLS 01 1025. Roman Catholics. at the Church NECHTERN STRASSE 01 0850.	no
do	19	ALL DAY	Education 0845 to 0945. Parades 0630-0700 P.T. & Running drill 1000 to 1200. Coys THQ were at the disposal of Company Commanders to whom economy.	no
do	20	ALL DAY	Church parades were held as follows: Church of Eng. Com. St the Theatre at 0945 +	no

Army Form C. 2118.

WAR DIARY
or
INTELLIGENCE SUMMARY.
(Erase heading not required.)

Summary of Events and Information	Remarks and references to Appendices

Red Shop
PLAN DER STADT
COLM. 1.15 000

1100 Rons. Headquarters at Nussbaumer Str. School at 1100. Roman Catholics, Sa.
The Church Mechtern Str. at 0820 hours. The Commanding Officer worked in Billets. DRO
Education 0845 to 0945 'D' Coy bathed at the School Baths. Parades 0630-0700
Physical Training. 1200-1300 General training for 'A' & 'B' Coys. S.B.R. Inspection.
Courses Drill & Musketry for 'C' Coy & 'D' Coy. The rest of the Battn. The Battalion
N.C.O. Inspected by the Medical Officer in the afternoon. The Coml. of the Battalion
"Battere" & Stone Russe. "Camp kellner" was published. The Battalion against the General DRO
house.
Education 0845 to 0945. HQ Company & 'C' Coy bathed at the Neptune Baths.
'B' Coy bathed at the School Baths. Parades 0630 to 0700 . 1000 to 1300 'A'
Company Platoon training & Musketry. 1100 to 1300 'D' Coy Platoon training & Musketry
'B' & 'C' Coys when not at the Baths Platoon drill, Musketry & Bayonet Training.
General Sir. W.R. Robertson, G.C.B., K.C.V.O., D.S.O., A.D.C. assumed command of the
Rhine Army. Vice General Sir Herbert C.O. Plumer, G.C.B. G.C.M.G. G.C.V.O. A.D.C. DRO
A lecture on Venereal Disease was given to the Battalion in the Theatre at 0930 hours
by the Rev. G.H. Heaslett, B.A. 'A' Coy bathed at the School Baths. Parade as yesterday. DLE

Army Form C. 2118.

WAR DIARY
or
INTELLIGENCE SUMMARY.
(Erase heading not required.)

Place	Date	Hour	Summary of Events and Information	Remarks and references to Appendices
COLOGNE.	24	ALL DAY	Battalion 0845 to 1045. Parade. 1100 to 1300. ROUTE MARCH. 1445 to 1515. Lewis Gun Company & Smoking Instruction. The Junior N.C.O's class was examined by their Officer. Lewis Gun Class at 1730.	do.
do	25	ALL DAY	Battalion 0845 to 0945. "A", "B" & "D" Coys. carried out Company training in the Zeppelin Shed area. 1000 to 1200. At 1200 from the Battalion area "C" Coy turned up a march to Battalion Drill. Specialist Coys. held Ordinary & Machine Gun, Bombing, Musketry instruction. Officers Parade. 1430 to 1515. Lewis Gun Instruction in each Coy. "C" Coy. was at the disposal of its Company Commanders to introduce to Battalion Guards in the Village.	do.
do	26	ALL DAY	Battalion 0845 - 0945. The Battalion took over the Barrack Guards in the week ending May 3rd. "C" Coy proceeded to the ARTILLERY DEPOT NIPPES and one platoon of "B" Coy. to No 4 Col BROCKELMUND. From 1000 to 1200 the Remainder of the Battalion was at the disposal of unit Commanders in Minor economy.	do
do	27	ALL DAY	C. of E. In the Theatre at 1030. Roman Catholic Church parade were held as follows:- at 1015. Mincumformis at the Y.M.C.A. NUSSBAUMER Mass at the CHURCH MECHTERN STRASSE at 1100. The Commanding Officer inspected Barracks after Church parade.	do

Army Form C. 2118.

WAR DIARY
or
INTELLIGENCE SUMMARY.
(Erase heading not required.)

Instructions regarding War Diaries and Intelligence Summaries are contained in F. S. Regs., Part II. and the Staff Manual respectively. Title pages will be prepared in manuscript.

Place	Date	Hour	Summary of Events and Information	Remarks and references to Appendices
				REF MAP PLAN DER STADT COLN. 1:15,000.
COLOGNE	28	ALL DAY	The Battalion took over Dublin Brigade Guards. Education 0845 to 0945. "D" Company bathed at the NEPTUN BATHS. Details of "A" "B" & "C" Coys bathed at the SCHOOL BATHS. The Commanding Sergeant inspected the Duties of the H.Q.	200
do	29	ALL DAY	Education 0845 to 0945. H.Q. bathed at the NEPTUN BATHS. Scanned bathed at the SCHOOL BATHS. Details of "A" "B" & "C" Coys cleaned up equipment in preparation for BRIGADE CEREMONIAL tomorrow. "D" Coy was at the disposal of the Company Commander. The Commanding Sergeant inspected the Duties of "D" Coy.	200
do	30	ALL DAY	The Battalion paraded at 0900 hours and marched to EXERCIER PLATZ NIEL for Practice Brigade Ceremony, returning to BARRACKS at 1345 hours.	200

5 X.
10 sheets

15th Bn: PWO (W.R.) Regt.

War Diary

May 1919

Army Form C. 2118.

WAR DIARY
or
INTELLIGENCE SUMMARY.
(Erase heading not required.)

Summary of Events and Information			Remarks and references to Appendices
	Offs.	O.R.	
EFFECTIVE STRENGTH as the end of April 1919:-	70	1438.	
Increase during May 1919:-	Offs.	O.R.	
From Hospital		18	
From Base		45	
Struck off strength in error :-			
Capt. A.P.O. Riley and Capt J.D. Barrett ...	2		
Lt-Col V.T.R. Ford D.S.O. ...	1		
From 51st. Royal West Sussex		1	
From No. 3. Military Prison...		1	
	3	65	
	73	1503.	
DECREASE during May 1919:-			
Demobilized - Lt B.A. King, Lt A.B. Mortimer and Lt E.E. Briggs	3	55	
To U.K. (Auth.A.G.8658 (o) 21/1/19 - Lt J.H. Palin. ...	1		
Died in 44th. C.C.S.		1	
Cross posted to 9th. T.M.B. ... Capt G.H. Segar and Lt N.W. Gibbons.	2	15	
Cross posted to VIth. Corps Headquarters		1	
Demobilized whilst on leave in U.K.		3	
Cross posted to the 20th. Bn. D.L.I. Regt.		150	
Cross posted to the 51st. Bn. Northumberland Fus. Regt. ...		100	
	6	325.	
	67	1178.	

1/6/19.

[signature] Lieut-Col.
Commanding 1/5th. Bn. P.W.O. (W YORKSHIRE) Regt.

Army Form C. 2118.

WAR DIARY
or
INTELLIGENCE SUMMARY.
(Erase heading not required.)

Instructions regarding War Diaries and Intelligence Summaries are contained in F. S. Regs., Part II. and the Staff Manual respectively. Title pages will be prepared in manuscript.

Place	Date	Hour	Summary of Events and Information	Remarks and references to Appendices
				PLAN DER STADT COLN 1/15000
COLOGNE	MAY 1	ALL DAY	Companies were at the disposal of Company Commanders for Saluting drill, S.B.R. inspection + Close order drill.	dto
do	2	ALL DAY	Education 0845 to 0945. The Battalion paraded on the Barrack Square at 1015 hours and proceeded to the ZEPPELIN AREA for parade ceremonial. Winning 'C' Company at 1230 hours. From 1400 to 1600 hours Companies were at the disposal of Company Commanders for Lewis gun, Bombing + Musketry Instruction.	dto
do	3	ALL DAY	Education 0845 to 0945, after which Companies were at the disposal of Company Commanders for Interior Economy until dinner. The Coy Officers during which time Aor Coy Lucenoril Coy A, B & C Coys. were relieved by detachments of the 1/4 Bn York + Lancaster Regt.	dto
do	4	ALL DAY	Church parades were held as follows:— C.of E. In the Theater at 1000 hours. Roman Catholic MECHTERN STRASSE. Nonconformists. In the Y.M.C.A. NUSSBAUMER STRASSE. The Commanding Officer inspected parades after Church parade.	dto
do	5	ALL DAY	The Battalion (less Scanchon) attended a Divisional Ceremonial Parade at the EXERCIER PLATZ. Companies paraded separately + marched to the Battalion starting point via PLATEN STRASSE + SUBBEL RATHER STRASSE which was passed at 0740 hours.	

Army Form C. 2118.

WAR DIARY
or
INTELLIGENCE SUMMARY.
(Erase heading not required.)

Instructions regarding War Diaries and Intelligence Summaries are contained in F. S. Regs., Part II. and the Staff Manual respectively. Title pages will be prepared in manuscript.

Place	Date	Hour	Summary of Events and Information	Remarks and references to Appendices
				PLAN DER STADT CÖLN 1:15000
COLOGNE	5	CONTD.	Battalion returned to Barracks at 1530 hours. The Battalion were commd by Lieut A.P.R. NEESHAM & J.E. TILLOTSON D.S.O. M.C.	270
do	6	ALL DAY	The Band & Drums, The Companies H.Q. and B Coy. bathed at the NEPTUN STRASSE BATHS. 'D' Coy bathed at the SCHOOL BATHS. The Bishop of Lichfield gave a Lecture in The Theatre at 1030 hours. Subject. The Earliest Democracy. After A + C Coys proceeded to the ZEPPELIN AREA A + C Coys attended. After the Lecture A + C Coys proceeded to the ZEPPELIN AREA for Branch and Section Drill. B + D Coys carried out Gas + Box Resp. Drill. Bath day at the Coln. B + D Coys carried out Gas + Box Resp.	
				270
do	7	ALL DAY	Education 0845 - 1045. Parade 1045 to 1300 Battalion Ceremonial practice in the ZEPPELIN AREA. 1450 to 1600 B'C + 'D' Coys Lewis Gun + Musketry instruction. A Coy bathed at the SCHOOL BATHS commencing at 1330 Pm	270
do	8	ALL DAY	The Battalion took part in a Review by Field Marshal H.R.H. THE DUKE OF CONNAUGHT K.G., K.T., K.P. etc. The Battalion marched to Barracks to the Wilhelm Saurwal EXERCIER PLATZ at 0750. Returning to Barracks at 1500 hours	270
do	9	ALL DAY	Education 0930 - 1030. 'A' Coy field gunnery + Officers practice on the Range	

(39473) Wt W4358/P366 600,000 12/7 D.D.&L. Sch.52a- Form/C2118/15

WAR DIARY or INTELLIGENCE SUMMARY

Army Form C. 2118.

Summary of Events and Information	Remarks and references to Appendices
LACHEM "AACHEN" The Battalion carried out Physical Training from 7	PLAN DER STADT CÖLN 1/15000
Company Drill 1045 to 1130. Lewis Gun Training & Battalion Schemes 1430-1630	do.
Education 0930 to 1030. The Battalion bathed at the NEPTUN BATHS & subsequently	do.
the S.D. clothing was passed through the delouser, together with the Blankets of the Battalion	
Church Parade Services were held as follows :- C.f.B. 9a. The Office of 4550 Home	
Roman Catholics, 9am in the Church MECHTERN STRASSE, 0930 Presbyterians 9a. the	
Y.M.C.A. NUSSBAUMER STRASSE at 1100 hours. The Commanding Officer inspected Billets	
after Church Parade. 'D' Coy took over Guard & Piquet duties at LONGERICH from	do.
the Right Flank.	
Education 0930 to 1130. H.Q. & 'C' Coy bathed at the NEPTUN STRASSE BATHS	
'A' Coy bathed at the SCHOOL BATHS. 'B' Coy Lewis Gun Training + Physical Training	
on the Miniature Range. At the end of the Books on the Range, 'A' 'B' + 'C' Coys	
carried out S.B.R. & Respirator Drill. Squad Drill when arms. Guard duties were	
given to Musketry instruction. The Divisional Staff Captain inspected the Rifles + C.E.I.	
The Guards & Piquets supplied by 'D' Coy at LONGERICH were sniffed numbered 62 NCOs + 1401	do.
Coy. I/Co. to 6 Officers + 150 O.R.	

WAR DIARY
or
INTELLIGENCE SUMMARY.

(Erase heading not required.)

Army Form C. 2118.

Summary of Events and Information	Remarks and references to Appendices
Education as usual early. 'B' Coy bathed at the NEPTUN STRASSE BATHS. The Rifle	PLAN DER STADT COLN 1:15,000
of 'A' Coy were inspected by the Armourer Staff Sergeant. 'C' Coy fired on the Miniature	
Range. 'A' Coy carried out Company training in the ZEPPELIN AREA. The WORK)	
N.C.O's Class was run by 2 Lieut V.T.R. FORD, anciently commanded the Battalion during the absence of Lt. Col. ODDIE D.S.O. in France	2/6
Education 0930 to 1030. Training: 'C' Coy fired on the Open Range at LACHEM	
'B' Coy carried out Musketry exercises in the Miniature Range. 'A' Coy carried out Bayonet fighting	
in the ZEPPELIN AREA. 1230. 2 i/c - Inspection was carried out in the afternoon. The N.C.O's	2/6
Class was continued.	
Education in afternoon. 'A' Coy fired on the Open Range at LACHEM. 'C' Coy fired	
on the Miniature Range. 'B' Coy carried out Company training in the ZEPPELIN AREA	2/6
The N.C.O's Class was continued.	
The Battalion paraded at 0900 hours + marched to COLOGNE to take part in the	
Reception of MARSHAL FOCH.	
Education 0930 to 1030. 'C' Coy fired 13 "Sheets" on the Open Range at LACHEM	2/6
The remainder of the Battalion were at the disposal of Company Commanders.	
Weather been fine.	2/6

Army Form C. 2118.

WAR DIARY
or
INTELLIGENCE SUMMARY.
(Erase heading not required.)

Instructions regarding War Diaries and Intelligence Summaries are contained in F.S. Regs., Part II. and the Staff Manual respectively. Title pages will be prepared in manuscript.

Place	Date	Hour	Summary of Events and Information	Remarks and references to Appendices
COLOGNE	18	ALL DAY	Church parades were held as under: C Purch & Coy paraded in the Theatre at 1030. Run on Bakstrice. One coy at MECHTERN STR. CHURCH at 0930. W/Coy one Son Br's after Church parade.	PLAN DER STADT CÖLN 1-1:15.000 200
	19		Education for C & details of A Coy 0930-1030. A Coy 0930-1130. Physical training from 0845-0915. Coy training for A & B Coys on the Hopelm area. B Coy on the LACHEM Range firing Part 1 of the GMC. Lt &Lt TYSHAM lectured on the "Fallacies of Bolshevism" at 1500. The Lecture was very much appreciated.	
	20		Training as for yesterday. A Coy had visit of N/Lt H Strong Falls from 1000-1200. 2/Lt H.C. FAWN proceeded on Educational Course at Army School.	RM RAK
	21		Education 0930-1030. Physical training 0845-0915. 1030-1200 Lieut-Col A/Capt H.I. SHAFTOE proceeds on leave to U.K.	
	22		Training as before except that C Coy were firing on LACHEM Range before lunch Part 1. Owing to difficulties with repair	

WAR DIARY or INTELLIGENCE SUMMARY

Army Form C. 2118.

Tennis leave to cultivate MT & ORDIE PIO T.D. to received training is intensified with by orders received to despatch 150 men to the 20th D.L.I. & 100 men to the 51st N.F. These men paraded at 1100 were despatched at 1100 hours. BMD

Specialist training continued

Coys on interior economy with exception of those men who had failed to qualify on Pak Ri & G.M.C. These men were sent up under 2/Lt L. McGuire to repeat at the LA CHEM Range. RST

The Preliminary Heats of the Battn Sports were run in the afternoon.

Church parade as usual. The Battn Sports were held in the afternoon were very successful. 2 by both PS?
the Battn took over duties of the Brigade. 2 by both
over the Guards at NEUMARKT. & 16 Coy plus 2 platoons of
'A' Coy went to the Artillery depot at NIPPES. D coy RSB
returned from LONGERICH

Army Form C. 2118.

WAR DIARY
or
INTELLIGENCE SUMMARY.
(Erase heading not required.)

Place	Date	Hour	Summary of Events and Information	Remarks and references to Appendices
COLOGNE	27th	ALL DAY	No training parade owing to number of duties. A Coy furnished bathing the Corps Commander Sir AYLMER HALDANE inspected billets & stated that they were in first condition well looked after. Early during morning a fire took place at the artillery depot Nippes & two sheds were burnt down	RSM
do	28th	do	Men of D Coy + transport billeted at School Bachs. No training parade owing to all men being on duties	RSM
	29th		No training parade possible. Total of from savings certificates for 15 weeks amount to £ 80.14/-	RSM
	30th		No training parade. Nothing to report from the parade. The Battn are relieved from R.M. Guards by the 14th	RSM
	31st		Bn York thanks in Regt. trops at disposal of Coy commander for interior economy	RSM

1/5th Bn. P.W.O. (W. York Regt)

WAR DIARY

JUNE 1919

6.X.
9 shets

WAR DIARY
or
INTELLIGENCE SUMMARY.

(Erase heading not required.)

Army Form C. 2118.

Summary of Events and Information

Effective strength at the end of May 1918.

	Offs.	O.R.	Offs.	O.R.
			67	1178

Increase during June 1918:-

	Offs.	O.R.
From 1/4th. York & Lanc R. — Capt R.J. Riley.		
" 2nd. Nthn. T.M.B. — Lt. N.W. Gibbons.	3	5.
" R.A.M.C. — Capt R.G. Ackland.		
" 1st Army Animal Collecting Camp.		2.
" Hospital		
	3	7.
	70	1185

Decrease during June 1918:-

	Offs.	O.R.
To 2nd. Nthrn T.M.B. — Lt. S.R. Mardon	1	3.
" 83rd Gen. Hospital — Capt.L.W. Batten		
" 1/4th. York & Lanc R. — Lt-Col. V.T.R. Ford	3	
" U.K. Cashiered — Lt. H.W.A. Young.		
Transferred to M.M.P.		2.
Demobilized — Capt R.J. Riley	1	6.
Demobilized to re-enlist.		1.
Transferred to VIth Corps Schools		1.
" " A.P.O		2.
	5	15.
	65	1170

JULY 1st. 1918.

[signature]

Commanding 1/5th. Bn. P.W.O. (W YORK REGT.)
Lieut-Col.

WAR DIARY
or
INTELLIGENCE SUMMARY.

(Erase heading not required.)

Army Form C. 2118.

Summary of Events and Information	Remarks and references to Appendices
The usual church parades. B & S in the to School theatre at 1030. Non-	
conformists at 1100 in Nuestsaeur St annex, Roman Catholics in the McKellen St annex	
Church. The bill inspected billets after church parades. Lt Col V.T.R	BPA
FORD DSO assumes duties & Revd in command and Major N H Freeman takes	
command of D Coy.	
Education for A & D Coys 0930 - 1030; B & D Coys 0930 - 1130.	
A & C Coys billed B & D carried out Company training	BSA
Medical Inspection in the afternoon.	
Ceremonial parade - March past "Royal Salute" - carried out at 0900	BSA
on the Hippodrome Area on the occasion of the King's Birthday.	
Remainder of the day was kept as a holiday.	
Education 0930 - 1130. Training under Coy commanders on Coy parade	BSA
grounds. Specialist training under Specialist Officers. Board held	
to examine Shoeing Smiths.	
The Range at LACHE M was at the disposal of B & D Coys from 0800	
onwards for firing of G.M.C. Junior officers class under LtCol TORA.	

WAR DIARY
or
INTELLIGENCE SUMMARY.
(Erase heading not required.)

Army Form C. 2118.

Summary of Events and Information	Remarks and references to Appendices
Lecture by Professor R.J. WILDEN-HART M.A on "POLAND" at 0930.	
The Battalion route marched for remainder of morning - VENLOER STRASSE	PSI
MILITAR RING STRASSE -	
Junior Officers under Lt Col FORD for tactical scheme	
LT. S.R. MARRON is posted to the T.M.B. & LT N.W. GIBBONS returned to duty	
300 of the Battalion proceeded on trip up the Rhine. Haversack	
rations were taken the trip was a success	PSI
O.C.M. convened to try LT T H W A YOUNG for shooting enemy civilian	
Junior Officers under LtCol FORD for tactical scheme	
Parade service as usual. C of E church parade held in the	
School theatre at 1000	
No training carried out, the day being Whit Monday. Bathing	PSI
and Interior Economy under Coy Commanders. Medical Inspection	
carried out during the morning.	
Education P+D Cup 0915 - 1015. The Range at LACHEN at	PSI
disposal of 'A' & 'E' Coys for firing of Part I, S of the GMC Specialist	
Training Continued	

WAR DIARY
or
INTELLIGENCE SUMMARY

Army Form C. 2118.

Place	Date	Hour	Summary of Events and Information	Remarks and references to Appendices
RICKENDORF	11th	All Day	Education 0915-1015. Training under Coy Commanders carried out in Zeppelin area 1030-1245. Junior Officers class + specialist training continued	A/A
	12th		Education 0915-1115. Training under Coy Commanders in Rosentale Square continued. 1130-1300 Officers class + Specialist training continued. B + D Coy have LACHEM Range from 1300 hours onwards. War Savings Certificate subscriptions amount to £205. 0.6 ft/d the month of May. The Battalion takes over Brigade Guards. A Coy takes over the NEUMARKT	A/A
	13th		Guard + D Coy the NIPPES GUARD. Inspected by the Bell at 1000 hours	A/A
	13th		Education 0830-0930. 0945-1300 Training under Coy Commanders in Zeppelin area. D Coy have the use of the miniature range	P/A
	14th		Specialist training continues. The Battalion takes over Brigade Guards. A Coy take over the NEUMARKT GUARD + D Coy the NIPPES GUARD. Inspection by the C.O. at 1050 hours before mounting.	A/A
	15th		Owing to the Battalion being on duty, no men are available for church parades.	P/A

Army Form C. 2118.

WAR DIARY
or
INTELLIGENCE SUMMARY.
(Erase heading not required.)

Instructions regarding War Diaries and Intelligence Summaries are contained in F.S. Regs., Part II. and the Staff Manual respectively. Title pages will be prepared in manuscript.

Place	Date	Hour	Summary of Events and Information	Remarks and references to Appendices
BICKENDORF	16	ALL DAY.	The Battalion being in Brigade duty, N.O. Info. were available for learning	270
do	17	do	The Divisional horsing crossed over 18 cross roads to the RUHR VALLEY all Brigade Guards funnelled on the Battalion were relieved and the day was spent in preparation for the advance tomorrow.	270
do	18	UNTIL 0700.	The Battalion moved forward towards the RUHR VALLEY marching out of Barracks at 0700 hours in Rifle Coy to the 101 to 300 Bayonets. The Battalion was detailed to furnish the advance guard to the Brigade. The guard was found by 'C' 'B' 'D' Coys with HQ. 'A' + 'C' Coys under Bde Command & Major VANDERZEE followed with the BRIGADE MAIN BODY. The Battalion moved by march route COLN - MULHEIM- to DÜNNWALD reaching the billets in BONN at 1015 hours where it remained for the remainder of the day.	REF. MAPS. COLN 1:20,000 COLSCHEID 1:15000 K 270
DÜNNWALD	19	until 0727	The march forward was resumed at 0727 Hours. The Battalion was Adv. Guard furnishing the advance guard and march forward in the following order "HQ" "D" "C" "A" Coys on march route DÜNNWALD - SCHLEBUSCH - BURSCHEID arriving at the billets in place at 0950 hours and remaining for the remainder of the day.	270
BÜRSCHEID	20	ALL DAY	Companies were at the disposal of Company Commanders for interior economy and training.	270

Army Form C. 2118.

WAR DIARY
or
INTELLIGENCE SUMMARY.
(Erase heading not required.)

Instructions regarding War Diaries and Intelligence Summaries are contained in F. S. Regs., Part II. and the Staff Manual respectively. Title pages will be prepared in manuscript.

Place	Date	Hour	Summary of Events and Information	Remarks and references to Appendices
BÜRSCHEID	21	ALL DAY	Specialist training was carried on under Specialist Officers. Remainder of the Battalion was at the disposal of Company Commanders for work in Billets.	do
do	22	ALL DAY	Dress was formed. Church parades were held as under. C. of E. at 1030 hours. Remainder at 0930 hours. Both services were held in the Orchard adjoining "C" Coys Billet.	do
do	23	ALL DAY	Companies were at the disposal of Company Commanders for Bloss training and Musketry. Specialist training under Specialist Officers & N.C.O. was carried on	do
do	24	ALL DAY	The Battalion paraded at 0900 hours for S.B.R and boot inspection after which Company and Specialist training was carried out until 1230 hours. A photograph close to Officers was arranged of Officers Specialist training.	do
do	25	ALL DAY	Companies were at the disposal of Company Commanders of training. The Officers Class was continued under Specialist Officers.	do
do	26	ALL DAY	Training as yesterday.	do
do	27	ALL DAY	Company and Specialist training as yesterday	do
do	28	ALL DAY	Companies were at the disposal of Company Commanders for training from 0900 to 1045. Specialist training was from under Specialist Officers. At 1145 hours a Battalion parade was held when a tactical scheme was carried out. Pass was again	do

Army Form C. 2118.

WAR DIARY
or
INTELLIGENCE SUMMARY.
(Erase heading not required.)

Place	Date	Hour	Summary of Events and Information	Remarks and references to Appendices
BÜRSCHEID	29	UNTIL 0845	The Battalion returned to COLOGNE taking up its original dispositions in the BICKENDORF area. The Battalion was conveyed by Motor Lorry leaving BÜRSCHEID at 0845 hours + arriving at NEW SCHOOLS BICKENDORF at 1045 hours	APP
COLOGNE	30.	ALL DAY	The Battalion took over Brigade guards. 'D' Coy + 2 Platoons of 'C' Coy proceeding to the Artillery Depot NIPPES. 'A' + 'B' Coys furnishing the Remainder of the guards. The Remainder of the Battalion were at the disposal of Company Commanders to retrain economy & bathing	AB

7. X.
2 sheets

1/5th Battalion Prince of Wales's Own.
(West Yorkshire Regt.)

War Diary. July
1919.

Army Form C. 2118.

WAR DIARY
or
INTELLIGENCE SUMMARY.

(Erase heading not required.)

Diaries and Intelligence in F. S. Regs., Part II respectively. Title pages manuscript.

Summary of Events and Information | | | Remarks and references to Appendices

EFFECTIVE STRENGTH at the end of JUNE 1918. :-

	Officers	Other Ranks.
	65	1170

INCREASE during JULY 1918. :-

	Officers	Other Ranks.
From 1st. Batn. W. Yorks. Regt.		11
" 3rd. " -do-		1
" Details " -do-		1
	65	1183

DECREASE during JULY 1918. :-

To Own Unit — Capt. R. G. Ackland R. A. M. C.	1	
U. K. for Demobilization		10
Posted to Home Depot		1
" Command H. Qrs. MONS.		1
" Details Batn. W. Yorks. Regt.		29
Evacuated to U. K. (Sick)		4
Transferred to Signal Section R. E.		8
-do- No. 2 Sanitary Section		1
-do- Royal Army Service Corps.		38
-do- Corps of Royal Engineers.		8
-do- Corps of Military Police.	1	1
	64	89
		1094

August 1st. 1918.

W. J. Cade
Lieut-Col.
Commanding 1/5th Bn. P.W.O. (West Yorkshire Regiment)

WAR DIARY
or
INTELLIGENCE SUMMARY.
(Erase heading not required.)

Army Form C. 2118.

Summary of Events and Information	Remarks and references to Appendices
	PLAN DER STADT CÖLN 1:15.000
Bavarian 0845 to 0945 'B' Coy carried out Musketry Practices on the Immolene Range	220
'C' Coy Bombing training on the ZEPPELIN area.	
'B' Coy took with the Brigade guard at the Buch; COLOGNE. Shore run of 'A' + 'C' Coys were at the disposal of Coy Commanders for Route ma training. MAJOR GENERAL	220
A.A. KENNEDY C.M.G. assumed command the Irish Division 30-6-19	220
To commemorate the Signing of Peace this day was observed as a Holiday	220
Details of Companies carried out Route gun training - where economy	200
Training in Details on Holiday	220
'A' Coy proceeded to LONGERICH to take over Brigade guards there	220
'B' Coy + 'D' Coy + the two platoons of 'C' Coy who relieved the Brigade guards Coys of the 1/4 Bn York + Lancaster Regt. JP. Bolson + a party consisting of	
LIEUTS DUNNINGTON + BLACKER and H.D.R. proceeded to RIEHL BARRACKS how to taking part in the Victory March in PARIS. LT COL ODDIE D.S.O. T.D. was in charge of the Brigade party.	220
'D' + 'B' Coys bathed at the SCHOOL BATHS. The Battalion was medically inspected. An inoculation for the 2nd + 3rd Class Boxly were held in the Ishoter.	220

Army Form C. 2118.

WAR DIARY
or
INTELLIGENCE SUMMARY.
(Erase heading not required.)

Instructions regarding War Diaries and Intelligence Summaries are contained in F. S. Regs., Part II. and the Staff Manual respectively. Title pages will be prepared in manuscript.

Place	Date	Hour	Summary of Events and Information	Remarks and references to Appendices
COLOGNE	8	COMTD	MAJOR W. H. FREEMAN M.C. assumed command of the Battalion vice LT. COL. W. ODDIE D.S.O. M.C. to PARIS for Victory March.	REF MAP PLAN DER STADT COLN. 1/15 000
do	9	ALL DAY	Battalion 0845 to 0945. "D" Coy carried out Musketry practice on the open range LACHEM. Remainder of Battalion carried out Company training on the ZEPPELIN AREA 1500 to 1300.	200
do	10	ALL DAY	The Barrack Commandant inspected the Battalion and Reported on the ZEPPELIN AREA after which Companies were at the disposal of Company Commanders for Company training.	200
do	11	ALL DAY	The Battalion (less two Platoons of "A" Coy) proceeded up the RHINE by steamer for a days trip. The Battalion entrained at COLN EHRENFELD and proceeded to BONN where it joined the steamer at 1030 hours returning to BONN at 1700 hours & arriving at Brussels at 2145 hours.	200
do	12	ALL DAY	Battalion 0930 to 1130. "B" Coy fired on the Range at LACHEM. "A" Coy trained at the SCHOOL BATHS. Remainder of the Battalion were at the disposal of Company commanders for interior economy. 1130 to 1300.	200
do	13	ALL DAY	Church Parade were held as under. Church of England in the Theatre at 1000 hours	200

Army Form C. 2118.

WAR DIARY
or
INTELLIGENCE SUMMARY.
(Erase heading not required.)

Instructions regarding War Diaries and Intelligence Summaries are contained in F. S. Regs., Part II. and the Staff Manual respectively. Title pages will be prepared in manuscript.

Place	Date	Hour	Summary of Events and Information	Remarks and references to Appendices
COLOGNE	13	CONT.D	Non commissioned. At Thurn Baumen Strasse at 1100 hours. Roman Catholics at the Church FELTEN STRASSE at 0900 hours.	REF MAP PLAN DER STADT COLN. 1:15,000 200
do	14	ALL DAY	At the Church parade the C.O. inspected Barracks. Education 0845 to 0945. "B" + "D" carried out Company & musketry training in the ZEPPELIN AREA 1015 – 1800. "C" Coy fired on the Ren Range LACHEM.	200
do	15	ALL DAY	Education 0845 to 1045. The Commanding Officer inspected "D" Coy on the Barrack Square at 1145 hours. Details of "B" Coy fired on the Miniature Range. "C" Coy carried out Musketry & Company training on the Barrack Square.	200
do	16	ALL DAY	Education 0845 to 0945. The Commanding Officer inspected "B" Coy at 1030 hrs. + "C" Coy at 1045 hours. "D" Coy fired on the Rifle Range at LACHEM. So the attention the Battalion was medically inspected.	200
do	17	ALL DAY	Education 0845 to 0945. O 1045 The Battalion turned up in Marching Order on the ZEPPELIN AREA Whereing to Barracks at 1300 hours.	200
do	18	ALL DAY	Education 0845 to 0945. "B" + "D" Coys were at the ZEPPELIN AREA. "C" Coy fired commencing from 1030 hours in the ZEPPELIN AREA. Lt. Col W. ODDIE D.S.O. T.D. and party returned from PARIS on the Miniature Range. Lt. Col Oddie resumed command of the Battalion with the return. Lt. Col ODDIE	200

WAR DIARY
or
INTELLIGENCE SUMMARY.
(Erase heading not required.)

Army Form C. 2118.

Place	Date	Hour	Summary of Events and Information	Remarks and references to Appendices
COLOGNE	19	ALL DAY	This day having been fixed by Parliament as the day of National Wroning it was observed as a holiday.	do
do	20	ALL DAY	Church parades were held as follows:- C.I.E. at 10.50 a.m. in the Theatre. Roman Catholics at 10.30 a.m. in the Church MECHTERN STRASSE. Nonconformists at 11.00 a.m. in Y.M.C.A. NUSSBAUMER STRASSE. After Church parade the Commanding Officer inspected billets.	do
do	21	ALL DAY	The Battalion took over Bayard Guards. 'A' Coy and one Platoon of 'B' Coy went to the Docks T EIFELTOR. 'C' Coy remained at LONGERICH.	do
do	22	ALL DAY	Education in 'B' Coy + H.Q. 0845 to 0945 after which 'D' Coy was at the disposal of Company Commanders in cleaning up and drills.	do
do	23	ALL DAY	Education in 'B' Coy + H.Q. 0845 to 0945. after which 'B' Coy was at the disposal of Company Commanders to clean up and Guard Mounting drills.	do
do	24	ALL DAY	Education in 'D' Coy + H.Q. 0845 to 0945. From 1000 to 1300 'D' Coy carried out Company training.	do
do	25	ALL DAY	Education in 'B' Coy + H.Q. 0845 to 0945. Three cheers + 150 O.R. from 'D' Coy the Band + Drums proceeded to RIEHL BARRACKS to welcome the 2nd Batt Gordons	do

Army Form C. 2118.

WAR DIARY
or
INTELLIGENCE SUMMARY.
(Erase heading not required.)

Instructions regarding War Diaries and Intelligence Summaries are contained in F. S. Regs., Part II. and the Staff Manual respectively. Title pages will be prepared in manuscript.

Place	Date	Hour	Summary of Events and Information	Remarks and references to Appendices
COLOGNE	26	ALL DAY	Education in "D" Coy & HQ 0845-0945. The Drums proceeded to BLUCHER PARK to practice Bugle Band practice. From 1030 to 1300 hours HQ "B" & "D" Coys were at the disposal of Company Commanders for intensive economy	
do	27	ALL DAY	Church Parades were held as under. C of E in the Church ROTHEHAUS STR. at 1130 hours. R.C's & Non-conformists proceeded to respective services independently.	280
do	28	ALL DAY	The Battalion was relieved of Barrack Guards by the 1/4th Bn York & Lancaster Regt. The Band & Drums & The Special Guard from "D" Coy proceeded to the STADT WALD Barrack Ground to practice parade for the Torchlight Tattoo.	280
do	29	ALL DAY	The Band & Drums & Guard of "D" Coy paraded as yesterday for Torchlight Tattoo practice. "A" "B" & "C" Coys were at the disposal of Company Commanders for training. From 1150 to 1245. Education 0845 to 1045 hours.	280
do	30	ALL DAY	Education 0845 to 1045. After which the Commanding Officer inspected "B" & "C" Coys in full Marching Order. The Band & Drums & the Special Guard from "D" Coy proceeded to the STADT WALD for Tattoo practice. The Battalion was otherwise employed in the afternoon.	280
do	31	ALL DAY	Education 0845 to 0945. Companies were at the disposal of the Company Commanders for training. "C" Coy had the use of the Miniature Range	280

1/5th Bn. P.W.O. (West Yorkshire) Regt.

——: War Diary :——

1 to 31st August. 1919.

WAR DIARY
or
INTELLIGENCE SUMMARY.
(Erase heading not required.)

Army Form C. 2118.

Instructions regarding War Diaries and Intelligence Summaries are contained in F. S. Regs., Part II. and the Staff Manual respectively. Title pages will be prepared in manuscript.

Place	Date	Hour	Summary of Events and Information	Remarks and references to Appendices
COLOGNE	August 1	ALL DAY	Education 0845 to 0945 after which 'A' 'B' & 'C' Coys proceeded to the ZEPPELIN AREA. In practice march past & ceremonial. The Band, Drums & the Special Guard of 'D' Coy attended torchlight tattoo practice.	PLAN DER STADT COLN 1/5000 APO
do	2	ALL DAY	Education 0845 to 0945. At 1130 the Battalion formed up in close column of Companies on the ZEPPELIN AREA for practice ceremonial march past.	APO
do	3	ALL DAY	Church Parades were held as under. C. d. & E. in practice at 1000 hours. Wesleyans in SANATORIUM NUSSBAUMER STRASSE at 1100 hours. R.C. in the Church MECHTERN STRASSE at 0900 hours. After Church parade the Commanding Officer inspected Barracks.	APO
do	4	ALL DAY	Except for billeting the day was devoted to a Holiday. The Band & Drums and Special Guard of 'D' Coy. took part in the VI Corps Tech Light Tattoo at the STADTWALD CRICKET GROUND.	APO
do	5	ALL DAY	School and H.Q. billed. Education 0845 to 1045. Companies were at the disposal of Company Commanders from 1100 hrs. 1100 to 1245 'A' Coy furnished a Guard of Honour to 3 Officers & 150 O.R. to GENERAL GOURAUD on his arrival at the HOTEL CHATEAU. At 1745 hours. The same parade as yesterday took part in the VI Corps Torch Light Tattoo.	APO

Army Form C. 2118.

WAR DIARY
or
INTELLIGENCE SUMMARY.
(Erase heading not required.)

Place	Date	Hour	Summary of Events and Information	Remarks and references to Appendices PLAN DER STADT COLN 1:15000
COLOGNE	6	ALL DAY	Battalion 0845 to 0945. After which Companies were at the disposal of Company Commanders in Quarters in the ZEPPELIN AREA until 1130 hours when the Battalion paraded for Service Ceremonial. Of the Personnel & Companies lucia to the Army Horse Show in the best (1) Battalion (2) Limb (3) Coton. the Battalion Occupied the Council in the Post Boxes.	do
do	7	ALL DAY	The Battalion took part in the Bnghs Packet Cadent on the EXERCIER PLATZ.	do
do	8	ALL DAY	Battalion 0845 to 0945. From 1015 to 1130 Companies were at the disposal of Company Commanders to company training when the Battalion turned up for ceremonial until 1245 hours. So the afternoon the Medical Officer unspected the Battalion.	do
do	9	ALL DAY	Battalion 0845 to 1045. After which Companies were at the disposal of Company Commanders to interior economy. The Battalion scored "Pack Drill" were elected (at Army Hq) the assumed alumnumy loans	do
do	10	ALL DAY	Church Parades were held as under. B.C.J.E at 1045 hour in the Church ROTHEHAUS STRASSE. Rumm Battalion at 0930 hours in the Church MECHTERN STRASSE. Wesledowng at 1110 hours in the GYMNASIUM NUSSBAUMER STR.	do
do	11	ALL DAY	The Battalion took over Garrison Guards. 'A' Coy going to the Barracks at "B" Coy to LONGERICH	do

Army Form C. 2118.

WAR DIARY
or
INTELLIGENCE SUMMARY.
(Erase heading not required.)

Place	Date	Hour	Summary of Events and Information	Remarks and references to Appendices
Cologne	12	ALL DAY	Details of Companies as on Guards were at the disposal of Company Commanders for practice guard mounting. Cleaning up. MAJOR W.H. FREEMAN M.C. assumed command of the Battalion during the absence of Lt Col W. ODDIE in England on leave.	PLAN DER STADT COLN 1:5000 8No 8No
do	13	ALL DAY	Cleaning up & inspection	
do	14	ALL DAY	The Battalion less 'A' Coy and 2 Platoons of 'B' Coy) took part in a Brigade practice advance on the EXERCIER PLATZ. CAPT H.I. SHAFTOE assumed the duties of acting Adjutant during the absence of CAPT B.E. ABLITT MC in England on leave.	8No 8No
do	15	ALL DAY	Cleaning up in the 13 K ind	8No
do	16	ALL DAY	The Battalion were relieved of Brigade guards. The Band & Drums own Special guard from 'D' Coy attended the dismissal & opening of the Zoch Picht Schoo on the STADT WALD Bickel Gasse	8No
do	17	ALL DAY	Church Parades were held as under :- C.of.E in the Church ROTHEHAUS STR at 1130 hours, Nonconformists in the GYMNASIUM MUNIZBAUMER STR at 1100 hours. R.C. in the CHURCH MECHTERN STR at 0930 hours.	8No

Army Form C. 2118.

WAR DIARY
or
INTELLIGENCE SUMMARY.
(Erase heading not required.)

Instructions regarding War Diaries and Intelligence Summaries are contained in F. S. Regs., Part II. and the Staff Manual respectively. Title pages will be prepared in manuscript.

Place	Date	Hour	Summary of Events and Information	Remarks and references to Appendices
COLOGNE	18	ALL DAY	The Battalion attended a review of the VI Corps by the Army Council at the EXERCIER PLATZ.	PLAN DER STADT COLN 1:15 000
do	19	ALL DAY	Education 0845 - 1045. Again 1100 to 1245 Companies were at the disposal of Company Commanders for training in Company Garrison Games. The return N.C.O's & Coys were examined. The Bomb and Lewis & the Special guard L'D'Coy took part in the VI Corps Torch light Tattoo commencing at 9200 hours.	200
do	20	ALL DAY	Education 0845 - 0945. 158 O.R. of the Battalion were put through the Gas Chamber. The remainder of the Battalion were at the disposal of Company Commanders for Platoon & Company Training on the ZEPPELIN AREA. 'A' + 'B' Coys bathed in the afternoon.	200
do	21	ALL DAY	Education 0845 to 0945. A further 150. O.R of the Battalion were put through the Gas Chamber. The remainder of the Battalion carried out Company training until 1130 hours when they paraded on the ZEPPELIN AREA. In Battalion Drill. At the Open Arms Show in the evening the Battalion secured First Prize in the Best Cook House.	200
do	22	ALL DAY	Education 0845 to 0945. A further 150 O.R. were put through the Gas Chamber. The remainder of the Battalion carried out Company training in the ZEPPELIN AREA.	200

WAR DIARY or INTELLIGENCE SUMMARY

Army Form C. 2118

(Erase heading not required.)

Summary of Events and Information	Remarks and references to Appendices
	PLAN DER STADT. COLN 1:15,000
Evacuation 0845 to 1045. The Commands of the Battalion was put forward the Divisional Commander to which economy.	No
8.00 Chambers. Coys were at the disposal of Company Commanders to which economy.	
Church parade. Service were held as under: C. of E. At the church Rothehaus Strasse	
at 1130 hours. Roman Catholics: In the Gymnasium Nussbaumer Strasse at 1100 hours	
Roman Catholics: At the Mechtern Str Church 0/0930 hours	No
Education 0845 to 0945. From 1000 to 1300 Companies were at the disposal of	
Company Commanders for platoon + company training. HQ + "C" Company bathed	No
Education 0845 to 1045. From 1100 to 1245 Companies were at the disposal of Company	
Commanders for Company training. "B" Company Medical Records	No
Education 0845 to 0945. From 1000 hours to 1245 hours training in platoon in	
ZEPPELIN AREA.	No
Education 0845 to 0945. Training as yesterday. Lt Col W ODDIE D.S.O. T.D. returned	
to the Battalion from leave + assumed command.	No
The Battalion ordered to Kall + Soetenich has to relieving the 1/5 Bn Kings (R.L.)	
Regiment in these + other duties under the Central Marshall of Rhine army. The	
Battalion started at 0730 hours + proceeded by March route to NIPPES where

Army Form C. 2118.

WAR DIARY
or
INTELLIGENCE SUMMARY.
(Erase heading not required.)

Place	Date	Hour	Summary of Events and Information	Remarks and references to Appendices
RHINE ARMY TROOPS				REF MAP. GERMANY 1 L. 1:100,000.
KALL	29 (CONT.)		Unit continued arriving at Kall at 14:50 hours. Companies were located with right at Kall. Battalion HQ marched to Soetenich where it took up its quarters.	$\frac{A}{1}$
SOETENICH	30	ALL DAY	The relief of the 1/5th Bn Kings (R.L.) Regt commenced. Companies carried to their new localities, 6th coy to Bonn. "A" Coy took over the Zimmerath area. "B" Coy the Schleiden area (Company HQ at Hellenthal) "C" Coy the Mountjoi area + "D" Coy took over duties under the area Commandant Hellenthal (with Company HQ at Mechnerich.)	do.
do	31	ALL DAY	Daily routine.	do.

Army Form C. 2118.

WAR DIARY
or
INTELLIGENCE SUMMARY.
(Erase heading not required.)

Instructions regarding War Diaries and Intelligence Summaries are contained in F. S. Regs., Part II. and the Staff Manual respectively. Title pages will be prepared in manuscript.

Place	Date	Hour	Summary of Events and Information			Remarks and references to Appendices
				Officers.	Other Ranks.	
			EFFECTIVE STRENGTH at the end of JULY 1919.	64	1094	
			INCREASE during AUGUST 1919. :-	NIL.	NIL.	
				Officers.	Other Ranks.	
			DECREASE during AUGUST 1919. :-	NIL	NIL	
			Evacuated to U.K. (sick) Lieut. E. Bays.	1	-	
			To U.K. under instructions from Rhin Army., Lieut. T. Pilgrim.	1	-	
			CHINESE LABOUR CORPS. NOYELLES. Lieut. R.M. Evans.	1	2	
			Transferred to Signal Section, Royal Engineers.		33	
			—do— to Corps of Royal Engineers.		16	
			—do— to Royal Army Service Corps.		47	
			—do— to Medical ...		9	
			—do— to Ordnance ...		1	
			Taken on Establishment of 206 Employment Company.		20	
			To U.K. for Demobilization.	3	128	
				3	128	
				61	966.	
			2nd. September, 1919			

[signature]
Commanding 1/5th Bn. P.W.O. (West Yorkshire Regiment) Lieut-Col.

2nd Northern Infantry Brigade.

Northern Division "A"

           Herewith War Diaries for the month of September.

20th October, 1919.

Lieut.
A/Staff Captain, for G.O.C.
2nd Northern Infantry Brigade.

Army Form C. 2118.

WAR DIARY
or
INTELLIGENCE SUMMARY.
(Erase heading not required.)

Instructions regarding War Diaries and Intelligence Summaries are contained in F.S. Regs., Part II. and the Staff Manual respectively. Title pages will be prepared in manuscript.

Place	Date	Hour	Summary of Events and Information					Remarks and references to Appendices
				Officers	Other Ranks.	Officers	Other Ranks.	
			EFFECTIVE STRENGTH at the end of AUGUST 1919.			61	966.	
			INCREASE during September 1919 :-					
			From R.A.M.C. for duty as Medical Officer, Capt. H.A. Hill, R.A.M.C.	1				
			From. Details Battn. W.York. Regt.		1			
						62	967.	
			DECREASE during September 1919 :-					
			To U.K. for Demob. (Lieut. H.F. Thompson.)	1	30			
			To U.K. (sick) (Lieut. M.J. Quill.)	1	3			
			Disembodied in U.K. Lieut. F.W. Edwards.	1				
						3	33	
						59	934	

W. Golder
Lieut-Col.,
Commanding 16th Battn. P.W.O. (West Yorkshire Regiment)

1st October 1919.

1/5th Bn. Prince of Wales's Own.
(West Yorkshire Regt.

War Diary.

for Period from 1st to 30th
September 1919.

Army Form C. 2118.

WAR DIARY
or
INTELLIGENCE SUMMARY.
(Erase heading not required.)

Summary of Events and Information	Officers	Other Ranks	Officers	Other Ranks	Remarks and references to Appendices
EFFECTIVE STRENGTH at the end of AUGUST 1919.			61	966.	
INCREASE during September 1919 :-					
From R.A.M.C. for duty as Medical Officer, Capt. H.A. Hill. R.A.M.C.	1				
From Details Battn. W.York. Regt.		1			
			62	967.	
DECREASE during September 1919 :-					
To U.K. for Demob. (Lieut. H.F. Thompson.)	1	30			
To U.K. (sick) (Lieut. M.J. Quill.)	1	3			
Disembodied in U.K. Lieut. F.W. Edwards.	1	–			
			3	33	
			59	934.	

1st October 1919.

W.S. Came
Lieut-Col.,
Commanding 16 th Battn. P.W.O. (West Yorkshire Regiment)

Army Form C. 2118.

WAR DIARY
or
INTELLIGENCE SUMMARY.
(Erase heading not required.)

Instructions regarding War Diaries and Intelligence Summaries are contained in F.S. Regs., Part II. and the Staff Manual respectively. Title pages will be prepared in manuscript.

Place	Date	Hour	Summary of Events and Information	Remarks and references to Appendices
				REF MAP GERMANY 1:100 000
SOETENICH	SEPT 1	ALL DAY	All Companies daily routine under Regtl routine under Rhine Army. Bond + Dawes to all available O.R. H.Q. paraded at 0915 hrs under Lt JE TILLOTSON DSO	
			M.C. to Rhl Hero Pvt R.T.	200
do	2	ALL DAY	Daily routine	200
do	3	ALL DAY	Battalion H.Q. moved to URFT. Coomejul armed of SOETENICH. Reveille Companies daily routine. CAPT & ADJT BE ABLITT M.C. assumed duties of Officers on return from leave	200
URFT.	4	ALL DAY	Daily Routine.	200
do	5	ALL DAY	Daily routine. Somelun was issued to the formation of a Lkh Company called	200
			H.Q. Company	200
do	6	ALL DAY	Daily routine	200
do	7	ALL DAY	Daily routine	200
do	8	ALL DAY	Daily routine	200
do	9	ALL DAY	Daily routine	200
do	10	ALL DAY	Daily routine. 2 Bn Others + 3 other Others all moved to advance House 21 Cdr Bopn CCo Bn BOLOGNE	200

Army Form C. 2118.

WAR DIARY
or
INTELLIGENCE SUMMARY.
(Erase heading not required.)

Summary of Events and Information	Remarks and references to Appendices
Daily Routine	2/10
Daily Routine	2/10
Daily Routine	2/10
Daily Routine	2/10
Daily Routine	1/10
Daily Routine	2/10
Daily Routine. 1 Officer + 50 O.R. "D" Coy moved to EUSKIRCHEN on Guard Duty	2/10
Daily Routine	2/10
A + C Coys moved to Botzone and assumed Police duties under P.M. G.H.Q.	8/10
Otherwise daily Routine.	4/10
Daily Routine.	5/10
Daily Routine	6/10
Daily Routine	7/10
Daily Routine	9/10
Daily Routine	9/10

Army Form C. 2118.

WAR DIARY
or
INTELLIGENCE SUMMARY.
(Erase heading not required.)

Instructions regarding War Diaries and Intelligence Summaries are contained in F. S. Regs., Part II. and the Staff Manual respectively. Title pages will be prepared in manuscript.

Place	Date	Hour	Summary of Events and Information	Remarks and references to Appendices
URFT	26	ALL DAY	Daily Routine.	do
do	27	ALL DAY	Daily Routine	do
do	28	ALL DAY	Daily Routine. C of E Church parade was held in the H.Q Dining hall URFT	do
do	29	ALL DAY	Daily Routine	do
do	30	ALL DAY	Daily Routine. On audit Board consisting of CAPT. J.P. BROWN & LT B. CUSSONS assembled at MECHERNICH to audit the accounts of the Battalion Mess Catering Association for the period 29th April to 30 September 1919. The accounts shewed that there some £450 on embro of the Association and that during the above period £1699-16-2 had been subscribed. The accounts were passed by the Board	do

1/5th Bn. P.W.O (West Yorkshire Regiment).

War Diary.

October, 1919.

Army Form C. 2118.

WAR DIARY
or
INTELLIGENCE SUMMARY.
(Erase heading not required)

Instructions regarding War Diaries and Intelligence Summaries are contained in F.S. Regs., Part II. and the Staff Manual respectively. Title pages will be prepared in manuscript.

Place	Date	Hour	Summary of Events and Information				Remarks and references to Appendices
				Off.	U.R.	Off.	U.R.
			Effective strength at the end of September, 1918.			50	984
			Increase during October, 1918.	NIL.			
			Decrease during October, 1918.				
			To U.K. (sick) ...(Capt. F. Veal)	1			
			Posted to R.A.S.C. from 27.9.18 as per Northern Division letter A 4377/151 dated 27.9.18. Lieut. E.W. Plummer				
			Lieut. H. Dawn, Lieut. W. Kerr-Morgan and Lieut. C.J.B. Smith	4			
			Transferred R.A.M.C.		2		
			R.A.S.C.		11		
			Proceed for dispersal				
			Lieut. Gash H. Lieut. Jones S.L.				
			,, Clegg J.H. ,, Edwards A.T.				
			,, Broadbent G.A. 2/Lt. Briggs V.H.				
			2/Lt. Steele B. ,, Gill J.				
			,, Cameron A.	9	120		
			Cross posted to 1/6th West York. Regt.		11		
						14	483
						45	501

signature Lieut-Col.

Commanding 1/5th Bn. P.W.O. (West York) Regt.

NOVEMBER 1ST, 1918.

WAR DIARY
or
INTELLIGENCE SUMMARY.

(Erase heading not required.)

Army Form C. 2118.

Summary of Events and Information	Remarks and references to Appendices
Daily Routine	REF MAP GERMANY 1. L. 1/100,000
Daily Routine	do
Daily Routine	do
Daily Routine	do
Daily Routine	do
Daily Routine	do
Daily Routine	do
Daily Routine	do
Daily Routine	do
Daily Routine	do
Daily Routine. The HQ of "D" Coy was moved from MELMENICH to SCHLEIDEN.	do
Daily Routine	do
Daily Routine	do
Daily Routine	do
Daily Routine	do
Daily Routine	do

Army Form C. 2118.

WAR DIARY
or
INTELLIGENCE SUMMARY.
(Erase heading not required)

Place	Date	Hour	Summary of Events and Information	Remarks and references to Appendices
URFT	OCT 17	ALL DAY	Daily routine. MAJOR W.H FREEMAN M.C. assumed command of the Battalion Vice LT. COL. W. ODDIE D.S.O. T.D. in temporary command of 2nd Yorkshire Infantry Brigade	P/o
do	18	ALL DAY	Daily routine	P/o
do	19	ALL DAY	Daily routine. The 'B' + 'D' Coy personnel on Leave horses were withdrawn to KALL	P/o
do	20	ALL DAY	Daily routine. 2 N.C.O's + 16 O.R. reinforced the D Coy detachment at EUSKIRCHEN.	P/o
do	21	ALL DAY	Daily routine	P/o
do	22	ALL DAY	Daily routine	P/o
do	23	ALL DAY	Daily routine. 39 O.R. from 'B' + 'D' Coys were enrolled to the 1/6th Bn W. YORK R and joined that Battalion. LT. COL ODDIE D.S.O. T.D. resumed command of the Battalion	P/o
do	24	ALL DAY	Daily routine	P/o
do	25	ALL DAY	Daily routine	P/o
do	26	ALL DAY	Daily routine	P/o
do	27	ALL DAY	Daily routine	P/o

Army Form C. 2118.

WAR DIARY
or
INTELLIGENCE SUMMARY.
(Erase heading not required.)

Instructions regarding War Diaries and Intelligence Summaries are contained in F. S. Regs., Part II. and the Staff Manual respectively. Title pages will be prepared in manuscript.

Place	Date	Hour	Summary of Events and Information	Remarks and references to Appendices
URFT	28	ALL DAY	Daily Routine	P/O.
do	29	UNTIL 0945	Headquarters & details of B & D Coys arrived to COLOGNE, entraining at CALL, & detraining at NIPPES. On arrival they proceeded to BICKENDORF where they were accommodated at the NEW SCHOOL BUBBLERATHER STRASSE	880
COLOGNE	30	ALL DAY	Companies were at the disposal of Company Commanders.	880
do.	31	ALL DAY	92 Other Ranks paraded on the Barrack Square at 0930 hours & proceeded to join the 1/6 Bn W YORK R to which Battalion they were transferred. The remainder of the O R in Barracks were inspected by the Medical Officer.	880

BEF

Northern Div
formerly 3 Div

2 Northern Inf Bde

13 K. L'POOL

1919 APR. to 1919 OCT

FROM 9 BDE 3 DIV

Army Form C. 2118.

WAR DIARY
or
INTELLIGENCE SUMMARY.   13th.(S).Bn.The King's(Liverpool Regt)
(Erase heading not required.)

APRIL 1919

Summary of Events and Information	Remarks and references to Appendices

River-trip. Lecture "Transport" & "Canada". Ceremonial Drill. Football. Officers soccer 13th.Kings. 2. 52nd. Kings. 3
Drill. P.T. Lewis Gun & Musketry Instruction. Interior Economy. Education Classes. Football competition Regtl. XI v. 14th.Bde for Bde League King's won. 3..1. C.Coy 13th.King's..0 v. 51st.King's..3.
Drill, Musketry. Lewis Gun Instruction. Recreational Training Rugby. Officers v. 52nd.Kings officers 13th.King's Officers 13th.Kings 2tries (6pts) 52nd.Kings 3 tries (9pts).
Drill, education, Lewis Gun, Musketry, Baths, Recreational Training. "B" Coy..13. v. Transport..0
"D" Coy. 13th.Kings..0 v. "C/ Coy 52nd.Kings..0
Kit inspection, Interior economy, Lecture by Medical Officer, Recreational Training, Regtl. XI..1 v. 168.Bde.R.F.A....0
Divine Services. Football. Rugby results. 52nd.Welsh..12.pts. v.13th.Kings..0
P.T., Musketry, Ceremonial & Guard Duties. Lewis Gun Instruction, Signalling classes. Educational training Recreational Training Football "A" Coy 13th.Kings..3 v. "C" Coy. 52nd.Kings...3.
B.F., Lewis Gun Instruction. Baths. Platoons in attack and defence. Signalling classes.Educational training Recreational training Football Bde Ass.League. 13th.Kings..3. v. 52nd.Kings..1
Lt.Col. G.L.Torrens. assumed command.
P.T., Musketry. Ceremonial & Guard Duties. Interior economy. B.F. Signalling. class. Education & Recreational training. Football "B" Coy..1 v. "D" Bty.168.Bde.R.F.A..2.
P.T., B.F., L.G., Ceremonial. Construction of Range. Educational training. Recreational Training Football. "D" Coy. 1 v. "D" Bty.168.Bde.R.F.A...1. Divnl.Soccer Comptn.Regtl.XI..2. v. 1/5 Borders../3
P.T., L.G., Musketry.Drill.Educational training, range construction. Recreational training.
Educational training, Drill. Interior economy. Recreational training.
Divine services.
Educational Training, Drill, Platoon in attack and defence. P.T.,L.G.,Musketry.Range Construction Baths.Medical Inspection. Recreational training. Semi.final Inter-platoon comptn.
Drill. P.T., B.F., L.G., Musketry. Educational training, Baths, Medical Inspection Recreational training. Final Interplatoon competition No.10 plat..3.pts. v. No.4.plat..1.pt.
P.T., Gas drill. Musketry. Platoons in attack and defence. L.G.,rifle bombing. Education. Recreational training. Bde. League match 13th.Kings..6. v.52nd.Kings...2.
Range Construction. P.T., L.G., Education, Drill, musketry. Interior economy. Continuous wearing of s.b.r. Recreational training. "B" Coy..2. v. "C" Coy..1.

Army Form C. 2118.

(SECRET)
Instructions regarding War Diaries and Intelligence Summaries are contained in F.S. Regs., Part II. and the Staff Manual respectively. Title pages will be prepared in manuscript.

WAR DIARY continued.
or 13th.(S) Bn. The King's (Liverpool Regt.)
INTELLIGENCE SUMMARY. APRIL 1919

(Erase heading not required.)

Place	Date	Hour	Summary of Events and Information	Remarks and references to Appendices
BEUEL.	18th.		Divine services. Football. 13th.Kings..3. v. 53rd. Kings..0	
	19th.		Work on defence scheme. Range construction. Recreational training.	
	20th.		Divine Services.	
	21st.		Work on defence scheme. Range construction. Baths recreational training.	
	22nd.		Baths. Work on defence scheme. Range construction. Football.Bde.League.13th.Kings..0 v. 1st.Kings Bde.H.Q.0	
	23rd.		Platoon training. Education training. Recreational training Arrival of draft from 53rd.Kings	
	24th.		Platoon training, Range Construction, Recreational training.	
	25th.		Platoon training. Inter-company relief. "B" Coy relieved "D" in outpost line. Football. Bde League 13th.Kings..2. v. 51st. Kings..1.	
	26th.		Platoon training. Inspection of billets by C.O.. Recreational training. "H.Q." 2. v. Band 2. Football "C" & "D" officers..2. v. "C"&"D".N.C.Os...2.	
	27th.		Divine Services. Football. Route March. Tactical scheme. One coy on range. Education.Recreational training.	
	28th.		Platoon training. Range firing. Recreational training. Football "C". 2. v. "D". 2.	
	29th.		Platoon training. Education. Range firing, Education Recreational Training.	
	30th.		Platoon training. Lecture. "Naval Subjects". Range firing, Education Recreational Training.	

1st. May. 1919

JK Tower MAJOR.
COMMANDING 13th BATTALION THE KING'S (LIVERPOOL REGT)

Army Form C. 2118

WAR DIARY of 13th. (S). Bn. THE KING'S (LIVERPOOL REGIMENT)

~~INTELLIGENCE SUMMARY~~

(Erase heading not required.)

MAY. 1919

SECRET

Instructions regarding War Diaries and Intelligence Summaries are contained in F.S. Regs., Part II. and the Staff Manual respectively. Title Pages will be prepared in manuscript.

Place	Date	Hour	Summary of Events and Information	Remarks and references to Appendices
BEUEL.	1/5/19.		Tactical Scheme - Manning of Defence Positions.	
	2nd.		Platoon Training. Education. Range Firing. Recreational Training.	
	3rd.		Interior Economy. Medical Inspection. Medical Lecture. Lectures by Company Commanders. Recreational Training. - Football - "H.Q." 7 v. Transport..1.	
	4th.		Divine Services. Football - "H.Q." ..9 v. 1st.King's T.M.B..0.	
	5th.		Platoon Training. Baths. Company Route Marches, combined with tactical scheme. Baths. Education. Recreational Training.	
	6th.		Platoon Training. Baths. Range Firing. Lecture by Canon Mayrick at OBERCASSEL. Education. Lecture. Recreational Training. Football Bde League - 52nd.King's 2. v 13th.King's..1.	
	7th.		Platoon Training, Coy Route March. Lecture by Commander Everard on "Naval Subjects". Education Recreational Training. Football "C" Coy..O v. "H.Q."..0	
	8th.		Platoon Training. Education. Lecture. Route March. Recreational Training.	
	9th.		Platoon Training. Lecture by ~~Canon~~ Bishop of Lichfield on "Imperialism". Education. Recreational Training.	
	10th.		Interior Economy. Kit Inspections. Lecture by M.O. Recreational Training - "C" Coy..1 v. "D" Coy..3	
	11th.		Divine Services.	
	12th.		Platoon Training. Baths. L.G.Classes. Route Marches. Education. Range Firing. Bombing Classes. Recreational Training.	
	13th.		Platoon Training. Baths. Range Firing. Education. Recreational Training.	
	14th.		Platoon Training. Education. Range Firing. ~~Recreational Training~~ - ~~Hockey Match~~) ~~Officers~~ - ~~Hockey~~ - ~~13th.King's.~~ ~~5xx~~ ~~51st. King's.~~ ~~X~~ Route March. Recreational Training. Football - "A" Coy..1. v. 51st. Manchester.Regt..0	
	15th.		Platoon Training. Education. Range Firing. Recreational Training.- Hockey Match - Officers - Hockey. 13th. King's..O. v. 51st. King's..7.	
	16th.		Platoon Training. Education. Range Firing. Recreational Training.	

SECRET

Army Form C. 2118

WAR DIARY (continued-)
or
INTELLIGENCE/SUMMARY 13th.(S).Bn. The KING'S (LIVERPOOL REGIMENT)
MAY. 1919

(Erase heading not required.)

Instructions regarding War Diaries and Intelligence Summaries are contained in F.S. Regs., Part II. and the Staff Manual respectively. Title Pages will be prepared in manuscript.

Place	Date	Hour	Summary of Events and Information	Remarks and references to Appendices
BEUEL	17.5.19.		Platoon Training. Interior Economy. Medical Lecture. Recreational Training – Hockey– "D" Coy. 1 v. "C" Coy. 0.	
	18th.		Divine Services.	
	19th.		Company Training. Lewis Gun & Bombing Classes. Route Marches, with tactical schemes. Baths. Inspection of "A" Coy Platoon scheme by G.O.C. Brigade. Education. Recreational Training. Hockey. "D" Coy. 4. v. "H.Q.". 0	
	20th.		Company Training. Baths. Range Firing. Gas Chamber. Education. Lecture by Archdeacon Jones on "British Character Builders". Recreational Training. Hockey "D" Coy. 4. "H.Q.". 0.	
	21st.		Company Training. Lecture by Lt.Col. Tysham., on "Bolshevism". Route March and Tactical Scheme. Range Firing. Education. Recreational Training.	
	22nd.		Company Training. Inspection of Platoon Tactical Scheme by G.O.C. Brigade. Education Recreational Training. Hockey – Officers v. 52nd. King's exixxx 5 v 0. Officers. –lost 5 – 0.	
	23rd.		Company Training. Range firing. Lecture. Education. Recreational Training.	
	24th.		Kit Inspections. Interior Economy. Lecture by M.O. Lecture by Rev. T.Knight "Are the Gospels Reliable"?	
	25th.		Divine Services.	
	26th.		Company Training. Route Marches, combined with Small Tactical Schemes. Brigade 200x Range – "D" Coy. Education. Lewis Gun Classes. Baths. Recreational Training – Battn Boxing Tournament.	
	27th.		Company Training. Baths. Gas Chamber. Platoon Demonstration witnessed by Divisional Commander. Education. Recreational Training. Cricket Practice.	
	28th.		Company Training. Lecture by Rev. T.Heaslett – Subject "Venereal Disease". Education. Recreational Training.	
	29th.		Company Training. Brigade Range. Education. Recreational Training. Cricket Practice.– "Probables" v "Possibles"	
	30th.		Company Training. Inter-Coy.Relief.– "C" Coy relieved "B" Company in the Outpost Line. Education. Recreational Training. Hockey Practice.	
	31st.		Company Training. Inter Company Relief. "D" Coy relieved "A" Coy at NDR. HOLTORF. Education. M.O's Inspection. Recreational Training.	
	1st. June. 1919.			

COMMANDING 13th. BATTALION THE KING'S (LIVERPOOL REGIMENT)
COLONEL.

SECRET

WAR DIARY
or
INTELLIGENCE SUMMARY

(Erase heading not required.)

Army Form C. 2118

13th. (S) Bn. The King's (Liverpool Regiment)

JUNE. 1919.

Place	Date	Hour	Summary of Events and Information	Remarks and references to Appendices
BEUEL.	JUNE 1st.		Divine Services. "A" Coy Training "as strong as possible", Range Firing, Route March,	
	2nd.		Coy Training. Recreational Training. Cricket Match v. 51st. King's (L.R.)	
	3rd.		KING'S Birthday. Brigade Ceremonial Parade, saluting the King. Rest of the day a holiday.	
	4th.		Coy Training, Firing on RAMMERSDORF Range. Cricket Match.	
	5th.		Coy Training, Maxx Range. Education.	
	6th.		Coy Training, 30yds.Range. Education.	
	7th.		Brigade Range. Kit Inspections, Cleaning, etc. Education.	
	8th.		Divine Services.	
	9th.		Brigade Range. - 30 yds. Range.	
	10th.		Coy. Training. Education.	
	11th.		Route March & Tactical Scheme. 30yds. Range. Education.	
	12th.		Coy Training. Brigade Range.	
	13th.		Coy Training. Education.	
	14th.		Kit Inspections. Lectures by Company Commanders & Medical Officer. Medical Inspection, Education.	
	15th.		Divine Services.	
	16th.		Practice Parade and cleaning for Commander-in-Chief's Inspection.	
	17th.		C in C's Inspection cancelled. J-3 day, Stores dumped etc.	
	18th.		J-2 day. Preparations for move completed.	
	19th.		Move to SIEGBURG-MULLDORF. "C" Coy remained at Outpost Positions.	
	20th.		Coys at disposal of Coy Commanders. Education.	
	21st.		Coys at disposal of Coy Commanders. Education. Battalion Concert.	
	22nd.		Divine Services. Hockey - Officers 4 v. Rest of Battn. 2.	
	23rd.		Battalion Parade (Less "C" Coy). Education.	
	24th.		Battalion Parade. Education.	
	25th.		Battalion Parade. Education. Hockey. "D" Coy 4 v Rest of Battn 1	
	26th.		Battalion Parade. Education.	
	27th.		Battalion Parade for Route March. Education. Hockey. "B" Coy.O. v. "H.Q." 6.	
	28th.		Coys at disposal of Coy Commanders., for kit inspections, lectures etc.	
			Medical Inspection. Hockey "A" Coy. 2. v. "H.Q." 2.	
	29th.		Divine Service.	
	30th.		Return to former billetting area. "A" & "B" Coys to BEUEL. "D" Coy to NIEDER-HOLTORF.	

A. Cecil Pettit
COLONEL
COMMANDING 13th. BATTALION THE KING'S (LIVERPOOL REGT)

Army Form C. 2118

SECRET

WAR DIARY

or **13th. (S). Bn. The King's (Liverpool Regiment).**

INTELLIGENCE SUMMARY JULY. 1919.

(Erase heading not required.)

Summary of Events and Information

Inter-Company Relief.
A. Company relieve C. Company on Outpost Line.
B. Company relieve D. Company on Support Line.
Brigade Rifle Meeting - Lewis Gun Competition.
Brigade Rifle Meeting - Evelyn Wood Competition,
 Battalion Competition.
 Officers' Revolver Competition.
General Holiday in Commemoration Signing of Peace.
Brigade Rifle Meeting.- Falling Plate Competition,
 Officers' Rifle Competition.
Total No. of Points scored 13th. King's. - 18½ - 51st. King's. = 3. = 52nd. King's. =14½.
Training = Kit Inspection = Education.
Running of Heats for Battalion Sports.
Divine Services.
Company Training = /D. Company 30 yards Range - Education. = Battalion Sports.
B. Company 30 yards Range - C. Company Brigade Range - Training - Education.
Brigade Boxing Points 52nd. King's = 3.- 13th. King's. = 2. - 51st. King's. = 1.
Hill Climbing Exercise - Cricket (Cologne Post Cup) 13th. King's V No. 2. Coy.
Western Div. R.A.S.C. - Result = No. 2. Coy.25 rounds - 13th. 70. Runs for 5. 2 Wickets.
Training - C. Company 30 yards Range - Education - Battalion Cross-Country Run =Winning Team C. Coy
B. Company Brigade Range - Training - D. Company 30 yards Range - Education.
Kit Inspection - Billet Inspection - Lecture by Company Commanders - Lecture by M.O.
Medical Inspection. Cricket (Cologne Post Cup). 13thKings v. 1st Western Gen. B H.
Divine Services.
Company Training. - 2nd. Class Army Certificate Examination.
Company Training. - 3rd. Class Army Certificate Examination.
Swimming - Brigade Competition.
Major Torrens: D.S.O. left for England.
Cricket (Cologne Post Cup) v. Lancashire Fusiliers.
Hill Climbing Exercise - Education - Hockey Match - H.Q. 2. V. C. Company 2.
River Trip.
Company Training - C. Company Tactical Scheme in conjunction with 1st. King's. Bde. T.M.B.
Education - Cricket (Cologne Post Cup) V 39- SIEGE BATTY R.G.A.

Remarks and references to Appendices

Army Form C. 2118

SECRET.

WAR DIARY
or
INTELLIGENCE SUMMARY

of 13th (S). Battalion The King's (Liverpool Regiment).

(Erase heading not required.)

Place	Date	Hour	Summary of Events and Information	Remarks and references to Appendices
	JULY.			
	19th.		Kit Inspection. – Cleaning of Billets – Lecture by Company Commander – Lecture by M.O. Education.	
	20th.		Divine Services.	
	21st.		Company Training. – C. Company 30, yards Range – D. Company Brigade Range. – Education.	
	22nd.		Company Traing. – B. Company 30 yards Range – Education (1st. Class Army Certificate Examination).	
	23rd.		Company Training. – (1st. Class Ary Certificate Examination) – Brigade Sports (1st) 52nd, King's (wnd. 2nd). 13th. King's (3rd.) 51st, King's.	
	24th.		Company Training. – B, Company Brigade Range – D. Company 30 yards Range – Education. (1st, Class Army Certificate).	
	25th.		Company Training = C. Company 30. yards Range – D. Company Tactical Scheme with 1st, King's L.T.M.B. – Education. – Divisional Sports (Heats).	
	26th.		Kit Inspection – Cleaning of Billets – Lecture by Company Commanders – Lecture by M.O. Lecture to Officers on Military Law – Medical Inspection – Education – Divisional Sports.	
	27th.		Divine Service.	
	28th.		Platoon Traing. – B. Company 30 yards Range – D. Company Brigade Range – Education – Cricket V. 15th. Lancashire Fusiliers – King's Won.	
	29th.		Company Training. – Education – Cricket – Inter-Battalion.	
	30th.		Hill Climbing Exercise. – Education – Cricket V. 4th. Suffolks – King's won. B. Company. Relieved from NDR. HOLTORF by 51st. King's and returned to BEUEL.	
	31st.		D, Company Brigade Range. – Education.	

V.Bilnahn

LIEUT. COLONEL.
COMMANDING 13TH. BATTALION THE KING'S (LIVERPOOL REGIMENT).

SECRET.

WAR DIARY 13th.Bn.The King's (Liverpool Regt.)

INTELLIGENCE/SUMMARY AUGUST 1919.

(Erase heading not required.)

Instructions regarding War Diaries and Intelligence Summaries are contained in F.S. Regs., Part II. and the Staff Manual respectively. Title pages will be prepared in manuscript.

Place	Date	Hour	Summary of Events and Information	Remarks and references to Appendices
BEUEL. GERMANY.	AUGUST. 1st.		"C" Coy. 30yds. Bombing Range. "B" & "D" Coy. Scheme in conjunction with 1st.Kings Bde T.M.B Education. Cricket 13th. K.L.R. v 10. R.W.Kent. King's won.	
	2nd.		Kit Inspection. Cleaning up of billet. Lecture by Coy.Comdrs. Lecture by Medical Officer Medical Inspection. Lecture to officers by C.O. Education. Cricket 13th.King's v 92nd. Field Ambulance. King's Won.	
	3rd.		Divine Services.	
	4th.		General Holiday. Cricket Match "C" Coy v "D" Coy., "C" Coy won. Soccer Match "C" v "D" - Extra. Draw. Rugby practice. - Officers.	
	5th.		Platoon Training. "C" Coy. Brigade Range. (morning)	
	6th.		Coy. Training. "C" Coy. 30 yds. Bombing Range Education. Cricket 13th.Kings v 207 R.A.F. King's Won.	
	7th.		Coy. Training. "B" Coy. Early Brigade Range (morning) "C" Coy. Brigade Range (afternoon) Education. Cricket. 13th. King's. v 52nd. Royal Sussex.	
	8th.		Coy. Training. "B""C" Coy. Brigade Range (morning) Education. Hockey Match. 13th.King's V. 92nd. Field Ambulance. King's won.	
	9th.		Disenfection entire Battalion. Major Gen. RICHIE. C.B. C.M.G. assumes Command of the Divn.	
	10th.		Divine Services.	
	11th.		Battalion Tactical Scheme. B. and C. Coys.	
	12th.		C. Coy. relieve A. on Outpost Line. Platoon Training. Education. Cricket. 13th. King's V. 52nd. Bedfords. - King's won. Hockey. 13th. King's V. 52nd. King's - 13th won.	
	13th.		Kit Inspection - Medical Inspection - B. Coy. 30yds. Bombing Range - Education - Cricket. 13th. King's V. Lancs. Div. Sig. Coy. - King's won.	
	14th.		Rhine Trip.	
	15th.		B.Coy. Brigade Range (morning) - A Coy. Brigade Range (afternoon) - Education. Hockey H.Q. V. D.Coy. - D.Coy. won.	
	16th.		A.Coy. Brigade Range. - Kit Inspection - Cleaning of Billets - Lecture by Coy.Commrs. Lecture by Medical Officer - Medical Inspection - Education - Cricket 13th. King's V. 121 Batty. R.H.A. - King's won.	
	17th.		Divine Services.	
	18th.		Battalion Exercise.	
	19th.		Company Training. A. Coy. Brigade Range (afternoon) C.Coy. 30yds. L.G. and Bombing Range. Education. Cricket 13th. King's. V 10Corps. Sigs. - King's won.	
	20th.		Bombing. Lewis Gun - Education - Sport. Cricket Match V. Royal Fus.	
	21st.		Education - Musketry - Coy.Training. Sport. Cricket.	

SECRET.

WAR DIARY

13th. Bn. The King's (Liverpool Regt).

or

INTELLIGENCE/SUMMARY. AUGUST.1919.

Army Form C. 2118.

(Erase heading not required.)

Place	Date	Hour	Summary of Events and Information	Remarks and references to Appendices
BEUEL GERMANY.	AUGUST.			
	22nd.		Education - Musketry - Coy.Training - Sport. Cricket.	
	23rd.		Education - Coy. Training - Musketry -	
	24th.		Divine Services.	
	25th.		Brigade Range. (Musketry) Education. Medical Inspection.	
	26th.		Commanding Officers' Lecture. Coy. Training.	
	27th.		Coy. Training. Brigade Range - Education -	
	28th.		Field Day.	
	29th.		Brigade Range. - Educational Trng. Coy.Training. L.G. Practice.	
	30th.		Bombing on the BEUEL Range - Musketry on the RAMERSDORF RANGE - 2.Coys.	
	31st.		Divine Services.	

V.B.Thurston LT. COLONEL.
COMMANDING. 13th. BATTALION THE KING'S (LIVERPOOL REGIMENT).

Secret

Instructions regarding War Diaries and Intelligence Summaries are contained in F. S. Regs., Part II. and the Staff Manual respectively. Title pages will be prepared in manuscript.

WAR DIARY
or
INTELLIGENCE/SUMMARY
(Erase heading not required.)

13th. (S) Bn. The King's (Liverpool Regt) Sept. 1919

Place	Date	Hour	Summary of Events and Information	Remarks and references to Appendices
BEUEL GERMANY	Sept.			
	1st.		Musketry on Bde Range. Bombing. Education. Sport (Cricket).	
	2nd.		2/1 Battalion Field Day.	
	3rd.		Brigade Range. Education. 30yds.L.G.&.Bombing Ranges.	
	4th.		Battalion Parade. Brigadier General's Inspection.	
	5th.		Company Tactical Scheme. Brigade Range at RAMERSDORF.	
	6th.		Brigade Range. 30yds.L.G.&.Bombing Ranges.	
	7th.		Divine Services.	
	8th.		Education. ⁄ Coy. Training.	
	9th.		Battalion Exercise.(Field Day.)	
	10th.		Education. 30yds.L.G.&.Bombing Ranges. Platoon Training.	
	11th.		Battalion Parade. RAMERSDORF Range (Musketry)	
	12th.		Coy. Scheme. Bombing Range. Education	
	13th.		Kit Inspection. Education.	
	14th.		Divine Services.	
	15th.		Casuals firing on Brigade Range. Education and Coy Training.	
	16th.		Battalion Parade (including complete Transport) Education.	
	17th.		Coy. Scheme. 30yds.L.G.and Bombing Ranges. Education. Interior Economy. Medical Inspection.	
	18th.		Battalion Exercise.	
	19th.		30yds. Range. Coy. Tactical Scheme. Interior Economy Casuals on RAMERSDORF Range.	
	20th.		Kit Inspection. C.O.'s Inspection of Billets. Interior Economy.	
	21st.		Divine Services.	
	22nd.		Brigade Range. Coy.Tactical Scheme. 30yds.L.G.&.Bombing Ranges. Close order drill. Army Educational Certificate Examination 2nd and 3rd. Class.	
	23rd.		Battalion Parade./Parade for General Lambert's Farewell. Interior Economy.	
	24th.		RAMERSDORF Range. Education.	
	25th.		Intx Battalion Route March.	
	26th.		RAMERSDORF. Range 30yds. L.G.and Bombing Range. Coy. Tactical Scheme.	
	27th.		Kit Inspection. K Interior Economy. Battalion= reduced to two companies "A" & "C" Coys. with effect from Octr. 1st,	
	28th.		Divine Services. Individual Training. Medical Inspection. Education.	
	29th.		Interior Economy.	
	30 th.		Battalion Route March. Advance and Rearguards.	
30/9/19				

Comdg 13th.Bn.TheKing's (Liverpool Regt)

Major.

SECRET

WAR DIARY
~~INTELLIGENCE/SUMMARY~~ 13th (S) Bn. The King's (Liverpool Regt).

SEPTEMBER 1919

Instructions regarding War Diaries and Intelligence Summaries are contained in F.S. Regs. Part II and the Staff Manual respectively. Title pages will be prepared in manuscript.

(Erase heading not required).

Place	Date	Hour	Summary of Events and Information	Remarks and references to Appendices
BEUEL Germany	Sept. 1st		Musketry on Brigade Range. Bombing. Education. Sport (Cricket)	
	2nd		Battalion Field Day.	
	3rd		Brigade Range. Education. 30x.L.G and Bombing Ranges.	
	4th		Battalion Parade. Brigadier General's Inspection.	
	5th		Company Tactical Scheme. Brigade Range at RAMERSDOFF	
	6th		Brigade Range, 30x yds. L.G. and B Bombing Ranges.	
	7th		Divine Services.	
	8th		Education. Company Training.	
	9th		Battalion Exercise. (Field Day).	
	10th		Education 30yds. L.G.. Platoon Training.	
	11th		Battalion Parade. RAMERSDORF Range (Musketry)	
	12th		Company Scheme. Bombing Range. B Education..	
	13th		Kit Inspection. Education.	
	14th		Divine Services.	
	15th		Casuals firing on Brigade Range. Education. Company Training.	
	16th		Battalion Parade. (including complete Transport) Education.	
	17th		Company Scheme. 30yds. L.G. and Bombing Ranges. Education. Interior Economy. Medical Inspection.	
	18th		Battalion Exercise.	
	19th		30yds. Range. Coy Tactical Scheme. Interior Economy. Casuals on RAMERSDORF Range.	
	20th		Kit Inspection. G.O's Inspection of Billets. Interior Economy.	
	21st		Divine Services.	
	22nd		Brigade Range. Coy Tactical Scheme. 30yds. L.G. and Bombing Ranges. Closed order drill. Army Educational Certificate Examination. 2nd and 3rd Class.	
	23rd		Battalion Parade. Education.	
	24th		RAMERSDORF Range. Battalion Parade for General Lambert's Farewell. Interior Economy.	
	25th		Battalion Route March.	
	26th		RAMERSDORF Range. 30yds. L.G.and Bombing Range. Coy. Tactical Scheme.	
	27th		Kit Inspection. Interior Economy. ~~Companies~~ Battalion reduced to two Coys "A" & "C" Coys with effect from Octr. 1st.	
	28th		Divine Services.	
	29th		Interior Economy. Individual Training. Medical Inspection. Education.	
	30th		Battalion Route March. Advance and Rearguards.	

Hammersmith Major.
Commanding 13th. Battalion The King's (Liverpool Regt)

Army Form C. 2118.

WAR DIARY 13th Liverpool Regt.
or
INTELLIGENCE SUMMARY. October 1919.
(Erase heading not required.)

Summary of Events and Information	Remarks and references to Appendices
Ramersdorf Range. Individual & Platoon Training. Education.	
Battalion Parade. Education.	
Ramersdorf Range. Individual & Platoon Training. Education.	
Kit Inspection. Interior economy. C.O.'s Inspection of billets. Education	
Divine Services.	
Interior Economy. Section Training. Medical Inspection. Education.	
Battalion Route March. Advance & Rearguards.	
Section training. Platoon Training. Close Order drill. Ramersdorf Range.	
Companies at disposal of Company Commanders.	
Ramersdorf Range. Section Training. Ceremonial Drill. Medical Inspection. Education.	
Kit Inspection. Interior Economy. C.O.'s Inspection of billets. Education.	
Divine Services.	
Company Training. Interior Economy. Section Training. Medical Inspection.	
Section Training, Platoon Training. Close Order Drill. Education.	
Companies at disposal of company commanders. Education.	
Close Order drill. Section Training. xxxxxxxxxxxxxx Education.	
Close Order drill. Section Training . Ceremonial Drill. Medical Inspection.	
Ml.iv.igadumotion. vinimbewxin Inspection of Billets. Education.	

WAR DIARY
13th Liverpool Regt.
October 1919.

or

INTELLIGENCE SUMMARY.

(Erase heading not required.)

Army Form C. 2118.

Summary of Events and Information	Remarks and references to Appendices
Divine Services	
Interior Economy. Section Training. Education.	
187 o.r. proceeded to join 52nd Kings. Company Training. Education.	
144 o.r. transferred to 51st Kings. Education.	
Lts. Newling, Smith & Potter & 2/Lts Jones, Clegg, Christian & Brearley left for U.K. demobilized. 52 o.r. proceeded to join 51st Kings.	
Captain Redhead, Lt. Pope, Captain Richard, Lt. Lewtes, Lt. Milton proceeded to join 52nd K.L.R. and Lt. Baldwin to 51st K.L.R.	
Lts. Ready, Cox and 2nd Lts. Costello, Reminson, Hogg & Williams proceeded for demobilisation, but did not leave KOLN owing to congestion.	
Sunday. No Divine Service. Strength of Bn. 48.	
Lt. Rogers demobilised. Remaining men kept as detachment from 51st K.L.R. under 2nd Lt. Baldwin M.O. D.C.M.	
Board held on Regt. Documents. 14th Infantry Brigade Shield won by 13th K.L.R. passed to 51st K.L.R. to be used in their Brigade of the Independent Division.	
Remaining details of Battalion proceeded for demobilisation.	

BEF

Northern Div
formerly 3 Div

2 Northern Inf Bde.

1919 Mar to 1919 Oct

Northern Division "A".   2nd Nthn. Inf. Bde. G.213.

Herewith War Diaries for the month of March 1919.

[signature] Major.
Brigade Major for Colonel.
Commanding 2nd Northern Infantry Brigade.

5th May 1919.

Army Form C. 2118.

WAR DIARY
or
INTELLIGENCE SUMMARY.
(Erase heading not required.)

Headquarters,
2ND NORTHERN INFANTRY BRIGADE.
MARCH 1919.

Summary of Events and Information	Remarks and references to Appendices
13th K.L.R. drew with the 1st R.S.F. at MERZENICH in the first round of competition "B". 1st N.F. were presented with the Cup for winning the competition "A" by the Army Commander at DUREN.	
Final of inter-company competition within the group between 13th K.L.R. and 1st N.F. played at Blucher Park. "Z" Coy., 1st N.F. won by 2 goals to 1.	
Brigade Commander inspected 1/6th W.York.R. and transport. Army Commander inspected 4th York & Lanc.Regt., prior to transfer to this Brigade.	
1/5th W.York.R., and 1/4th York & Lanc.R., arrived.On Brigade.strength. H.Q.established. 13th K.L.R., beat the 1st R.S.F., at MERZENICH by 16 points to 0. 1st N.F., were beaten by the 2nd R.Scots., by 15 points to 0 at BLUCHER PARK.	
Div.General inspected 4th York & Lanc.R. and 6th W.York.R. at BLUCHER PARK. Capt.James, Brigade Major, reported for duty. Div.Commander inspected 6th W.York.R.	
Div.Commander inspected 1st N.F., and 4th R.F., to say "GOODBYE". Final, Regimental Football, 1st Gordon Highlanders beat 2nd Royal Scots 5 - 3 at BLUCHER PARK. Army Commander presented cups and medals.	
Brigade Commander inspected billets, R.F.	
Div.Commander inspected 1/5th W.York.R. Brigade Commander visited Lachem Range. "Z" Coy., N.F., beat "B" Coy., 2nd Royal Scots 5 - 2 Semi-final inter-Coy., football.	

------ CONTINUED ------

Army Form C. 2118.

WAR DIARY
or
INTELLIGENCE SUMMARY.

Headquarters,
2ND NORTHERN INFANTRY BRIGADE.
MARCH 1919.

(Erase heading not required.)

Summary of Events and Information

Brigade Commander visited 1st Bn. Kings with Gen. Harrington.
Brigade Major visited LACHEM RANGE.

Brigade Commander inspected billets and transport of 5th W. York. R.
Capt. J. J. Houlton lectured to 4th York & Lanc. R. on "Colonial Expansion"

Final Div. Rugby Comp. - BLUCHER PARK 1430. Royal Scots beat 13th Kings (26 - Nil).
Final inter-Coy. Football BLUCHER PARK. 1st Royal Scots beat No.1.Coy., D.A.C. (3 - Nil).

Brigade Commander visited LACHEM RANGE with Divisional Commander.
Final inter-platoon football BLUCHER PARK. Draw.

Brigade Trial Match (Rugby)
Mr. D. F. Holmes lectured to 4th York & Lanc. R. on the "League of Nations".

Training.

Guard from Divisional H. Qrs. demonstrated to three Battalions at BLUCHER PARK.
Div. & Bde. Commanders were present. Div. adopted name of "Northern Division".

Final Corps Football BLUCHER PARK. 3rd Div. beat 2nd Div. draw = 1 - 1.

Brigade Commander inspected 5th W. York. R. and 4th York & Lanc. R. BLUCHER PARK.
Replay Final Corps Football BLUCHER PARK 3rd Div.

Conference C.O's. 1300 hours. H. Qrs. 6th W. York. R.

Brigade Commander visited 6th W. York. R.

Training.

Div. Commander visited Brigade Guards with Brigade Commander.

----- CONTINUED -----

Army Form C. 2118.

WAR DIARY
or
INTELLIGENCE SUMMARY.
(Erase heading not required.)

Headquarters,
2ND NORTHERN INFANTRY BRIGADE.
MARCH 1919.

Instructions regarding War Diaries and Intelligence Summaries are contained in F.S. Regs., Part II. and the Staff Manual respectively. Title pages will be prepared in manuscript.

Place	Date	Hour	Summary of Events and Information	Remarks and references to Appendices
COLOGNE.	22.		Bvt.Col.(T) Brig-Genl.) G.G.S.Carey C.B., C.M.G., assumed Command of Brigade vice Bvt.Col.(T. Brig-Genl.) H.C.Potter C.M.G., D.S.O.	
"	23.		Training.	
"	24.		Rev.T.Hunter Boyd lectured to 5th W.York.R., on "The Slavs in Bohemia and the Balkans."	
"	25.		2.0.pm. phone message from Div.Commander. All troops to be confined to barracks, in anticipation of Sparticist troubles. All clear 5.0.pm.	
"	26.		Training.	
"	27.		Training.	
"	28.		Commander-in-Chief visted Army area.	
"	29.		53rd York & Lanc.(Y.S. Bn) arrived and joined 5th W.York.R.	
"	30.		Training.	
"	31.		51st and 52nd (Y.S.) Bns, W.York.R., arrived at COLOGNE to be split up among Brigades. Lieut.Bodimeade joined the Brigade H.Qrs., for duty.	

2nd NORTHERN INFANTRY BRIGADE.

Army Form C. 2118.

WAR DIARY
or
INTELLIGENCE SUMMARY.
(Erase heading not required.)

Summary of Events and Information	Remarks and references to Appendices

1st August 1919.

The Bde. less 6th W.York.R. moved to COLOGNE by Bus. Transport by road staging at DUNWALD Units took over billets previously occupied by them prior to the move. Brig.-Genl.RAMSAY CB.CMG.DS.O. left the Bde. to assume command of the 30th Divn. in France. Col.T.M.HOWARD DSO, 6th W.Yor.k.R. took over command of the Brigade.
6th W.York.R. moved to COLOGNE from HILGEN by Bus. Transport rejoined the Bde. from DUNWALD.
Col. HEADLAM, CMG, DSO, assumed Command of the Bde.
5th W.York.R. took over Bde.Guards at NIPPES Depot, Ehrenfeld etc. 4th York & Lancs. found Guard of one Company for LONGERICH, ARMY AMMUNITION DUMP.
Brig-General POTTER CMG, DSO, took over command of the Brigade.
Brigadier inspected 5th W.York.R. on Zeppelin Area Ground. Battalion paraded with transport under Major A.E.FREEMAN, MC.
6th W.York.R. Regimental Sports held in BLUCHER PARK.
Brigadier inspected 6th W.York.R. under command of Bvt.Colonel T.M.HOWARD, DSO, in BLUCHER PARK.
Brig-General POTTER CMG, DSO, departed on leave and Bvt.Colonel.HEADLAM, CMG, DSO, 4th York & Lancs.R. took over command of the Brigade. Orders received from the Division to stop all Musketry in the Brigade as the range was required for other troops. Orders issued accordingly.
6th W.York.R. found Guard of Honour in DOM PLATZ, for American C-in-C. 4th York & Lancs.R. held their Regimental Sports in BLUCHER PARK in the afternoon.

During the month Company training as far as the ground permitted was carried out by Battalions. One Battalion and one Company were required weekly to find the guards allotted to the Brigade. Musketry was carried out on the LACHEM RANGE up to 16th, when orders to discontinue the General Musketry Course were received as the range could no longer be allotted to the Brigade. Practices were carried out on Battalion 30 yards ranges. Weather was very hot but a considerable amount of rain fell during the month which did not greatly interfere with training.

Major.
Brigade Major, 2nd Northern Infantry Brigade.

WAR DIARY
or
INTELLIGENCE SUMMARY

(Erase heading not required.)

Army Form C. 2118.

HEADQUARTERS,
2nd NORTHERN INFANTRY BRIGADE

No. A/328?
Date.........

Original

Summary of Events and Information

Brig-General POTTER, C.M.G., D.S.O. returned from leave and assumed command of Brigade.

100 O.R's of the Brigade took part in the VI Corp TORCHLIGHT TATTOO in STADTWALD, LINDENTHAL.

5th.W.York.R. provided Guard of Honour for General GOURARD who visited COLOGNE.

4th. York & Lanc.R. formed a Guard of Honour for General GOURARD in DOMPLATZ.

Divisional Eliminating Competition for Army Horse Show held. Brigade very successful.

Practice parade held for Review of VI Corps by Army Council on EXERCIER PLATZ N.W. of MERHEIM.

Brigade practice parade for the Review held on EXERCIER PLATZ.

Review of VI Corps held by Army Council held on EXERCIER PLATZ at 11-00 hours.

Army Horse Show took place in the afternoon, 5th. W.York.Regt. won stripped mule class, and 4th. York & Lanc.Regt. won 3rd. Prize in Mule-drawn limber class.

5th. W.York.Regt. moved to URFT district to do Control Post duty under the orders of P.M. RHINE ARMY in relief of 1/5th. King's Own Royal Lancaster Regt.(IX Corps). Move was carried out by Rail and Route March.

Docks Guard of one company was taken over by 45 O.R's from the Brigade trained as Military Police by VI Corps.

Army Form C. 2118.

WAR DIARY
or
INTELLIGENCE SUMMARY.

(Erase heading not required.)

Original

Instructions regarding War Diaries and Intelligence Summaries are contained in F. S. Regs., Part II. and the Staff Manual respectively. Title pages will be prepared in manuscript.

Place	Date	Hour	Summary of Events and Information	Remarks and references to Appendices
COLOGNE.	AUG. 1919. 1st.-31st.		During the month the usual training was carried out but owing to the congestion on the Ranges the Brigade ceased firing the General Musketry Course. The usual Guards were found by one Battalion each week. Owing to departure of 5th. W.York.Regt. Guards found by the Brigade were reduced to 16 N.C.O's. and 84 men at the end of the month.	

COLOGNE,
1/10/19.

G. Garton, Major,
Brigade Major, 2nd. Northern Infantry Brigade.

Army Form C. 2118.

2nd. NORTHERN INFANTRY BRIGADE.

WAR DIARY

or

INTELLIGENCE SUMMARY.

(Erase heading not required.)

Place	Date	Hour	Summary of Events and Information	Remarks and references to Appendices
COLOGNE.	1st. to 30th.		Usual training carried out during the month. Battalions carried out Range Practices at LACHEM RANGE. 1/5th. West Yorkshire Regiment remained at URFT and carried out police duties under the orders of P.M., G.H.Q. Weather variable. 21 Officers 428 Other Ranks demobilized during the month. Total since July 23 Officers 517 Other Ranks. VI Corps Horse Show held on September 30th. Corps Commander presented 1/6th. West Yorks. Regt. with Cup won by them in the Corps Basket Ball Competition.	
	23rd.		30 Candidates sat for 3rd. Class Certificate examination and 17 were awarded certificates.	

COLOGNE,
3/11/19.

J.J.Garth
Major,
Brigade Major, 2nd. Northern Infantry Brigade.

Northern Division 'A' Details

Herewith War Diaries for the
month of October 1919.

[Stamp: HEADQUARTERS, 2nd NORTHERN INFANTRY BRIGADE. A.3452 Date 4.11.19]

[Stamp: A. & Q.M.G., NORTHERN DIVISION. 5/11/19]

4/11/19.

Staff Capt. for G.O.C. 2nd Nthn Inf. Bde

Captain

Army Form C. 2118.

2nd. NORTHERN INFANTRY BRIGADE.
WAR DIARY
or
INTELLIGENCE SUMMARY.
(Erase heading not required.)

OCTOBER.

Instructions regarding War Diaries and Intelligence Summaries are contained in F. S. Regs., Part II. and the Staff Manual respectively. Title pages will be prepared in manuscript.

Place	Date	Hour	Summary of Events and Information	Remarks and references to Appendices
COLOGNE.			Usual training and musketry practices on LACHEM RANGE carried out during the month.	
"	6th.		Conference held at Divisional Headquarters and Battalions warned that they would have to proceed to ENGLAND at short notice for strike duty, orders subsequently cancelled.	
	12th.		6th. West Yorks.Regt. won KALK Association Football Cup final and were presented with a Shield.	
	15th.		Brig-Genl. H.C.POTTER, C.M.G., D.S.O. proceeded on leave and Col.ODDIE, D.S.O., took over command of the Brigade.	
	17th.		Orders received that 1st. and 2nd.Northern Brigades were to be amalgamated.	
	20th.		Units of 1st. Northern Brigade/ ~~Units of 1st. Northern Brigade~~ came under orders of Brigade Commander 2nd.Northern Brigade. ~~following Battalions taken over~~ Following Battalions taken over:- 51st. and 52nd.North'd. Fus. and 19th. Middlesex Regt. at BRUHL, for purposes of the Defence Scheme.	
	22nd.		Brig-Genl. H.C.POTTER, C.M.G., D.S.O., returned from leave and re-assumed command of the Brigade.	
	23rd.		New Defence Scheme issued (see appendix) Amendment to Defence Scheme issued.	I
	28th.		Practice of VI Corps Defence Scheme carried out in the morning	
			One Company 52nd.North'd. Fus. (strength 6 Offrs. and 200 O.R's.) proceed to ANTWERP by train to do police duties.	
	29th.		5th. W.Yorks.Regt. (less 2 Companies) returned to COLOGNE from URFT and came under the orders of G.O.C., 2nd.Northern Brigade, and moved into billets in BICKENDORF. 4 Officers and 100 O.R's 52nd.North'd Fus. came under the orders of Rhine Police /and

WAR DIARY or **INTELLIGENCE SUMMARY**

Army Form C. 2118.

Place	Date	Hour	Summary of Events and Information	Remarks and references to Appendices
COLOGNE	30th.		and assumed Police Duties on the RHINE.	
			100 O.R's. 52nd.North'd. Fus. placed at disposal of P.M., COLOGNE for police duties.	
			Issued amendment to Defence Scheme (Appendix)	2
			During the month two candidates sat for A.S.A.S. Elementary Exam. and both gained "Passes"	
			12 Officers and 841 O.R's. were demobilized during the month.	
			Total since 1st. July 1919 :- 35 Officers and 1358 O.R's.	
COLOGNE, 4/11/19.				

J.J. Garlan
Major,
Brigade Major, 2nd.Northern Infantry Brigade.

1. Herewith copies, numbered as under of 2nd Northern Infantry Brigade "Action to be taken in the event of Civil Disturbances in COLOGNE Area".

2. All previous orders and instructions are cancelled and will be destroyed.

3. Acknowledge.

    Copy No. 1.   G.O.C..
               2.   51st.Bn.Northumberland Fusiliers.
               3.   52nd.Bn.Northumberland Fusiliers.
               4.   5th.Bn.West Yorks.
               5.   6th.Bn.West Yorks.
               6.   4th.Bn.York and Lancs.
               7.   2nd Northern L.T.M.B..
               8.   19th.Bn.Middlesex Regt.
               9.   41st.M.G.Battalion.
              10.   RHINE ARMY CONCENTRATION CAMP.
              11.   No. 24 Remount Hospital.
              12.   VIth Corps School.
              13.   Staff Captain.
              14.   Northern Division "G".
              15.)
              16.)   File.
              17   *War Diary*
              18   *" "*

                                                Major.,
Brigade Major, 2nd Northern Infantry Brigade.

28th October 1919.

Copy No 18.

HEADQUARTERS,
2nd NORTHERN
INFANTRY BRIGADE.
No. 4/28
28/10/19

SECRET.

2nd Northern Infantry Brigade.

ACTION TO BE TAKEN IN THE EVENT OF MAJOR CIVIL DISTURBANCES IN COLOGNE.

1. **CODE OF ORDERS.**

    In the event of serious Civil Disturbances being apprehended the following code messages will be sent from Brigade Headquarters.

    WARNING ORDER.   "MOSELLE"
    ORDER TO MOVE.   "RHINE"

2. (a) On receipt of code message "MOSELLE".

    (i) All troops will be confined to barracks and prepared to move at one hours notice.

    (ii) All officers will rejoin and remain with their troops.

    (iii) A company M.G.Battalion will come under the orders of G.O.C. 2nd Northern Brigade and will send an officer to Brigade Headquarters, SCHILLER GYMNASIUM. PIUS STRASSE. for orders.

    NOTE. One section M.Gs. from another company will proceed to the DOCKS and one section to EIFEL TOR.

    (iv) The SCHNUR GASSE Guard will be doubled by 51st.Bn.Northumberland Fusiliers.

    (v) The 52nd.Bn.Northumberland Fusiliers will send one section to re-inforce the Police at BONN TOR Goods Station.

    (vi) Guards on the following places will be withdrawn and rejoin their Battalion.

    (a) No. 44. C.C.S.. (UBIER RING).
    (b) MILITAR LAZARET. KARTHAUSER WALL (Ordnance Depot).
    (c) BICKENDORF BAKERY. EHRENFELD.
    (d) No. 2 WATER TANK COMPANY.

    (vii) Guard at RHINE ARMY VEHICLE RECEPTION PARK. AACHENER TOR will be mounted by 6th.Bn.West Yorkshire Regiment, if not already there.

    (viii) Two extra orderlies, cyclists if possible, will be sent by 51st.Bn.Northumberland Fusiliers, 52nd.Bn.Northumberland Fusiliers and 6th.Bn.West Yorkshire Regiment, to Brigade Headquarters,   SCHILLER GYMNASIUM.

    (ix) Transport will stand by in their Transport Lines ready to move. (Men will be armed and supplied with 60 S.A.A.)

    (x) Demobilizable personnel at RHINE ARMY CONCENTRATION CAMP will be formed into armed companies as far as rifles available permit, the remainder into un-armed companies, and officers detailed to each company. Ammunition will be issued to each man in possession of a rifle at the rate of 60 rounds per man.

Sheet 2.

(b) On receipt of code message "RHINE" the following additional steps will be taken.

(i) 51st.Bn.Northumberland Fusiliers will send

    (a) One company to EIFEL TOR Goods Station
    (b) One company to the DOCKS (HANSA WERFT and AGRIPPA WERFT)
    (c) Two platoons to ELECTRIC POWER STATION, BONNER WALL. (near BONN TOR).
    (d) Remainder of battalion with Transport will move to ARTILLERIE KASERNE, BONNER STRASSE, where they will be in Brigade Reserve.

(ii) 52nd.Bn.Northumberland Fusiliers

will be in Brigade Reserve in ARTILLERIE KASERNE. BONNER STRASSE.

(iii) 6th.Bn.West Yorkshire Regiment will send

    (a) Two platoons to the COLD STORE (LINDESEIS FABRICK) NO. 229 SEVERIN STRASSE.
    (b) Two platoons to the Telephone Exchange CACILIEN STRASSE.
    (c) One platoon under an officer to SCHLACHT UND VIER HOF, LIEBIG STRASSE, to guard Brigade Transport.
    (d) Remainder of battalion will be in Brigade Reserve at SCHILLER GYMNASIUM. PIUS STRASSE.

(iv) 4th.Bn.Yorks and Lancs.

will come under the orders of G.O.C. 3rd.Northern Brigade.

(v) 19th.Bn.Middlesex Regiment (London Division)

    (a) will send one company to reinforce the Guard at VOCHEM DUMP.
    (b) Remainder of battalion, less any Patrols considered necessary, will remain in present billets in Brigade Reserve, prepared to move to COLOGNE if required.
    (c) As communication between Brigade Headquarters and 19th.Bn.Middlesex Headquarters will be difficult, O.C. 19th. Middlesex will act according to the situation round BRUHL demands, and may use the companies in Brigade Reserve if required locally, reporting any action taken to Brigade Headquarters.

    NOTE. 6th Corps Cyclists are responsible for guarding KNAPSACK Electric Power Station.

(vi) M.G.Company

will assemble at SCHILLER GYMNASIUM. PIUS STRASSE.

(vii) 2nd.Northern T.M.B..

will remain at OVERBECK STRASSE School.

Sheet 3.

    (viii) Rhine Army Concentration Camp.
            No. 24 Remount Hospital.
            VIth Corps School.

        (a) All available men will be held in readiness in Brigade Reserve, in their billets prepared to move where ordered.

        (b) Will each send 1 officer and 2 orderlies, cyclists if possible, to report to Brigade Headquarters at ARTILLERIE KASERNE. BONNER STRASSE.
            These officers will bring states shewing
            (1) Strength of unit.
            (2) Number of rifles available.
            (3) Number of O.Rs. available as a reserve after necessary guards have been detailed to safeguard billets etc..

    (ix) Brigade Headquarters.

        will be established at ARTILLERIE KASERNE. BONNER STRASSE.

3. RESPONSIBILITY FOR repeating WARNING ORDER and ORDER TO MOVE.

    (a) Battalions will be responsible for forwarding code messages "THAMES" "MOSELLE" etc., as under:-

UNIT.	TO WARN.	LOCATION.
51st.Bn.Northd.Fus..	VIth Corps School.	GYRHOF STRASSE.
52nd.Bn.Northd.Fus..	RHINE ARMY CONCENTRATION CAMP.	ULRICH GASSE.
do.	No. 24 Remount Hospital.	MARIENBURG.
6th.Bn.West Yorks.	RHINE ARMY RECEPTION PARK.	

    (b) In addition to above, battalions will be responsible for warning all Guards found by them.

4. DRESS. Fighting Order.

                                                    Major.

28/10/19.   Brigade Major, 2nd Northern Infantry Brigade.

[HEADQUARTERS, 2nd NORTHERN INFANTRY BRIGADE.]

SECRET. No. 4/28/1   2nd Northern Infantry Brigade.
Date 28/10/19.

ACTION to be taken in the event of Minor Civil Disturbances or threatened disturbances in COLOGNE.

---

1. In the event of Minor Civil Disturbance or threatened disturbance in COLOGNE, action will be taken in accordance with para. 2. (below)., on receipt of the Code Word "THAMES" or on the "ALARM" being given by Maroon or sounded on the bugle.

2. (i) 51st.Bn.Northumberland Fusiliers will send
    (a) One company to EIFEL TOR Goods Station.
    (b) One company to the DOCKS (HANSA WERFT and AGRIPPA WERFT).

   (ii) 6th.Bn.West Yorkshire Regiment will send
    (a) Two platoons to the Telephone Exchange CACILIEN STRASSE.
    (b) Two platoons to COLD STORE (LINDESEIS FABRICK) No. 229 SEVERIN STRASSE.

3. To indicate that a Civil Disturbance is occurring an order to sound the "ALARM" on the bugle will be given by any Staff Officer of the Army or Corps Headquarters, or the Military Governor's Staff.

4. The object of sounding the "ALARM" is to inform men in the streets and billets quickly that a Civil Disturbance is taking place.

5. On the "ALARM" being sounded by any Bugler on Guard, the other Buglers within hearing distances will pick up the call and repeat it.
   Guards which have been provided with Maroons will fire Maroons.
   Buglers will step forward clear of the guard post, and sound the call in various directions.

6. All ranks, on hearing the call, will proceed to their unit parade ground as quickly as possible.

7. It is necessary to sound the "ALARM" as well as to endeavour to telephone the various centres, as th since the rioters would probably cut telephone lines before causing the disturbance.

8. Unit Commanders will ensure that all ranks are thoroughly acquaint with the "ALARM" sounded on the bugle, and that Buglers are able to sound the call quickly and well.
   They will be careful to prevent practice calls being taken for the genuine "ALARM".

9. All men will be continually warned on parades that in the case of disturbance, or of crowds assembling, they must keep clear and must not move in the direction of the crowds.

                                    J.S.Gartlan   Major.
                        Brigade Major, 2nd Northern Infantry Brigade.

Copies to:-
51st.Bn.Northd.Fus.   RHINE ARMY CONCENTRATION CAMP.
52nd.Bn.Northd.Fus.   No. 24 Remount Depot. Hospital.
 6th.Bn.W.Yorks.   VIth Corps School.
 4th.Bn.York & Lancs.   Northern Division "G".
 2nd.Northern T.M.B..   Staff Captain.
 File. (3)

2nd.Northern Infy.Bde.,
G.728/2.

To:- All recipients of 2nd.Nthn.Infy.Bde. G.728/ of
28/10/19.

Following amendments will be made to above letter:-

1. Para.2(a)(viii) Amend to read "Battalions will send 2 extra orderlies, cyclists if possible, to Brigade Headquarters, SCHILLER GYMNASIUM."

2. Para.2(b)(v) amend to read:- 19th.Middlesex Regt.

   (a) 19th.Middlesex Regt.(less 1 Company) will be in Brigade Reserve at ARTILLERI KASERNE, BONNER STRASSE.

   (b) 1 Company will guard VOCHEM Ammunition Dump."

3. Add new para.:-

   "2b(x) 5th. W.Yorks.Regt. will move into Brigade Reserve in SCHILLER GYMNASIUM.

4. Para.3(a) Amend as follows:-

   6th. W.Yorks.   RHINE ARMY
                    RECEPTION PARK.   AACHENER TOR.
        "   "   142 FIELD AMBLCE.   VOGELSANGER
                                                STRASSE.

Major.

BEF

Northern Div
formerly 3 Div

1 Northern Bde

53 North'd Fus

1919 Mar. to 1919 Sept

53 North'd Inf. Bde.

Army Form C. 2118.

WAR DIARY
or
INTELLIGENCE SUMMARY.

(Erase heading not required.)

Instructions regarding War Diaries and Intelligence Summaries are contained in F. S. Regs., Part II. and the Staff Manual respectively. Title pages will be prepared in manuscript.

Place	Date 1919 MARCH	Hour	Summary of Events and Information	Remarks and references to Appendices
CATTERICK	1/6		General preparations prior to Battalion proceeding Overseas to join the Northern Division in the Army of Occupation GERMANY. Drafts were being received daily. All ranks during this period passed through the gas chamber. Steel helmets were taken fitted. The rear party under LIEUT. S.A.T. KERR was organised to hand over barracks, stores re. Demobilisation of eligibles was in progress and all ranks not proceeding Overseas or for demobilisation were despatched to the 3rd Bn. NORTH'd FUS:	A⁴
	7		During the morning stores were loaded on to trucks. Final preparations before leaving Camp.	
		2130.	H.Q. B & C Coys and one platoon of D Coy entrained on camp railway at CENTRAL STATION.	
		2220	Remainder of Battalion entrained at same place. On detraining from Camp railway, parties proceeded to CATTERICK BRIDGE station & entrained in "specials". During the march from camp to station snow was falling very heavy. Consequently before the train moved off all ranks were very wet.	A⁴
		2315	Train moved off 10 minutes late with 38 officers and 602 O.R. APPENDIX "A"	
	8/11		The train stopped for half an hour at PETERBOROUGH at 0500 hours where hot tea was supplied.	

Army Form C. 2118.

WAR DIARY
or
INTELLIGENCE SUMMARY.
(Erase heading not required.)

Place	Date	Hour	Summary of Events and Information	Remarks and references to Appendices
	MARCH 1919 8/11		On arrival at DOVER at 1030 hours the Battalion detrained and marched to REST CAMP No 2. where dinner was provided. Officers had lunch at Officers' rest house. At 1245 hours embarked on the S.S "QUEEN ELIZABETH" which moved off at 1310 hours on a very calm sea. The crossing was smooth, but cold. The Bn. disembarked at DUNKERQUE at 1630 hours and marched through town to No. 3 REST CAMP arriving here at 1830 hours. Coy had hot meal and spent the night in tents.	Coy
DUNKERQUE		0830	The next day at 08.30 hours the battalion paraded and marched to SANDS SIDING. Battalion entrained at 11.15 hours in trucks, the train moving off one hour & 9 minutes late. On arriving at MERRIS at 13.55 hours the train stopped for an hour where dinner was provided. The next "Halte" depot was BAISIEUX where tea was provided at 2010 hours. The next hot meal was supplied at GHISHENGHAM at 0405 hours on 10th inst. The train at this point was nine hours late. At CHARLEROI the train stopped for nearly two hours, where a meal was again provided. We were then 11½ hours late. We reached HUY at 1725 hours on the 10th Inst. Tea.	Coy

Army Form C. 2118.

WAR DIARY
or
INTELLIGENCE SUMMARY.
(Erase heading not required.)

Instructions regarding War Diaries and Intelligence Summaries are contained in F. S. Regs., Part II. and the Staff Manual respectively. Title pages will be prepared in manuscript.

Place	Date	Hour	Summary of Events and Information	Remarks and references to Appendices
	MARCH 1919			
	10		A considerable amount of interest was taken during the journey, more especially from BAILLEUL to LILLE, where a number of Officers & N.C.O.s had previously fought, throughout the journey the weather was splendid.	Coy
COLOGNE	11	0400	Arrived outskirts of City. Proceeded slowly to station. Detrained, unloaded, & stores loaded on to lorries, tea provided. Bn. joined up & marched off by march route to EFFEREN. Sec.Lieut C.J.A. MOSES went to hospital from train.	Coy
EFFEREN		0730	Bn. joined up & marched off by march route to EFFEREN. H.Q. A, C, & D Coys in the village. B. Coy. attacked at HERMULHEIM Strength of B.H. 81 O.R. received from 1st Bn. NORTHd. FUS. Capt. E.G. PEASE. M.C. Lieut D. PILLING, 2/Lieut E. COPPICK, 2/Lieut. R. SKEY reported for duty from 1st.Bn. NORTHd. Fus. Rev. W.H.S. WOOD returned from 1st Bn. NORTHd. Fus.	Coy Coy
		0930		
	12		Nothing of interest	
	13		Capt. W.M. STEWART R.A.M.C. returned to ENGLAND being relieved by Capt. A.S. WESTMORELAND R.A.M.C. from 1st. Bn. R.S.F.	Coy
		1400	The Bn. had the honor of being inspected by Gen. Sir HERBERT PLUMER, the Batta being formed up in line. After the inspection the Bn. marched past at a slow and S. of Saluters (Bn. H.Q.) The General Officer Commanding in Chief expressed his appreciation of the turn out of the men, and spoke to several of the Officers and N.C.O.s.	Coy

WAR DIARY
or
INTELLIGENCE SUMMARY.

Army Form C. 2118.

Place	Date	Hour	Summary of Events and Information	Remarks and references to Appendices
EFFEREN	1919 March 14		Sec. Lieuts. T.A.C. HOLMES & J.J. SIMPSON reported for duty from 1st Bn. NORTH^d FUS:	
	15	1100	Route march to VOLKGARTEN. The Bn: had been previously warned that the VOLKGARTEN would be their position of rendezvous in case of riots or trouble of any description, + it was therefore necessary that all ranks should know as much as possible about the approaches, + the general situation. The Officers + N.C.O.s spent about half an hour studying the position. Re-organization of Bn. to make up 'B' Coy, which was only 38 strong. Drafts had been promised but they failed to report, consequently it was necessary to bring this Coy. up to the approximate strength of the other Coys. Nothing of interest to report.	
	16			
	17		See Lieut A.H. APPLEBY reported from 1st Bn. NORTH^d FUS for duty on returning from leave. 2/Lieut C.J.A. MOSES returned from Hospital. Officers + N.C.O.s Tactical Guard mounting Demonstration at 51st Bn. NORTH^d FUS. Parade ground VOLMSCHULE HEDWITZ STRASSE. Nothing of interest to report.	O$_y$ O$_y$ O$_y$ O$_y$
	19/21	1100		

Army Form C. 2118.

WAR DIARY
~~INTELLIGENCE SUMMARY.~~
(Erase heading not required.)

Instructions regarding War Diaries and Intelligence Summaries are contained in F. S. Regs., Part II. and the Staff Manual respectively. Title pages will be prepared in manuscript.

Place	Date 1919 MARCH	Hour	Summary of Events and Information	Remarks and references to Appendices
EFFEREN	22	13.30	Battalion proceeded by march route to SÜLZ AREA. To occupy new billets.	
			H.Q. A & B Coys. in MANDERSCHNEIDER SCHOOL. C & D Coys. in MÜNSTEREIFELER SCHOOL.	Coy Coy
			Officers in billets in close proximity.	
SÜLZ	23		Church parade. 2/Lieut. H. RIGBY reported for duty from 1st Bn. North'd Fus. on returning from leave.	
	24		Commenced Guard duties. Advance party went to PULLHEIM GIVEN HINTHERN to arrange billets but away to other arrangements the Bn. never moved to that AREA.	Appendices 3. Coy
	25	1400	Orders received from 6th H.Q. that a Bolshevist meeting was to be held at the STADTWALDT. The Bn. was ordered to stand by in case of trouble. All guards to were doubled, + the remainder of the Bn. were organised into two Companies under the command of Major M.G. WEST. Lewis gun teams of 1 NCO + 6 men were despatched to transport lorries, but nothing happened & "stand down" was ordered at 1946 hours. Normal conditions to be resumed.	Coy

Army Form C. 2118.

WAR DIARY
INTELLIGENCE SUMMARY.
(Erase heading not required.)

Place	Date	Hour	Summary of Events and Information	Remarks and references to Appendices
SÜLZ	March 1919 26		Lieut. D.S. ROWE reported for duty from 1st Bn. NORTHd FUS. on returning from leave. Officers Rugger match with 51st Bn. NORTHd FUS. Score 5 points to nil for 53rd Bn. The ground was very wet, & it made the handling of the ball very difficult. It was a very evenly contested game, the 51st scoring within a few minutes from time.	
	27/28		Nothing of interest to report.	
	29		2/Lieuts P.M. NEASHAM, R.W.T. SPELMAN & G.S. WORTHINGTON reported for duty from 9th Bn. NORTHd FUS.	ay
	30		Lieut. S. PEARSON M.C reported on returning from leave from 1st NORTHd FUS. Capt. A.L. SCAIFE M.C reported for duty from 36th Bn NORTHd FUS.	ay
	31		2/Lieuts A.H. APPLEBY & H. RIGBY proceeded to No. I. CAMP for transfer to ENGLAND for demobilization.	ay

AWood
Lieut.-Colonel
Commanding 53rd Bn. Northd. Fusiliers.

Guards provided by
53rd. Bn. North'd. Fusiliers,
24th. March 1919.

	GUARD.	N.C.Os.	MEN.
D.	Schür Gasse	2	8
E.	Military Police Guard under A.P.M.	2	8
F.	R. E. Dump	1	3
G.	Luxemberger Wall	1	3
H.	Headquarters 8th Inf. Bde.	2	8
I.	VI Corps Guard	4	17

Appendix "B"

Lieut.-Colonel
Commanding 53rd Bn. Northd. Fusiliers.

Appendix "A"

Lieut. Colonel	G. A. Yool.
Major	W. C. West.
Captain	H. M. Carrick.
"	J. W. Crake.
"	J. W. James.
"	G. A. McPherson.
"	W. McCall.
"	F. R. Peirson.
"	O. G. Platt.
"	W. N. M. Stewart. RAMC
Lieut.	F. Airey.
"	C. V. Alder.
"	C. A. Balden.
"	J. C. Brown.
"	F. W. Clay.
"	J. W. Cockburn.
"	A. F. Dence.
"	H. S. Fotherby.
"	V. C. Gray.
"	S. Hall.
"	T. J. Hooper.
"	B. Peacock.
"	A. T. Pitcher.
"	J. W. C. Read.
"	E. Rose.
"	A. Rowe.
"	A. E. Saw.
"	L. G. Skey.
"	J. B. Wilson.
2/Lieut	A. Branker.
"	G. T. B. Colbourne.
"	H. N. Hopper.
"	H. C. Jamieson.
"	J. Musgrove.
"	C. J. A. Moses.
"	B. T. G. Pringle.
"	P. J. Simms.
"	~~H. J. Simpson.~~
"	E. J. Webb

Lieut.-Colonel
Commanding 53rd Bn. Northd. Fusiliers.

NOMINAL ROLL
OF
53RD BN. NORTHUMBERLAND FUSILIERS,
PROCEEDING OVERSEAS.

Regtl.No.	Rank & Name.
9188	R.S.M. Sykes J.
93957	C.S.M. Hornby W.
93960	C.Q.M.S. Reece A.K.
93963	A/Sgt.(O.R.Sgt) Rawdin H.
94078	Sgt. Smithson M.
58277	A/Sgt. Clarkson J.W.
93449	A/Sgt. Hayward B.S.E.
38919	A/Sgt. Pearce F.
41519	Cpl. Binks A.
93903	L/Cpl. Yielder R.
93848	L/Cpl. Lindsay W.E.
93888	L/Cpl. Firth L.
93940	L/Cpl. Dorman J.W.
93859	Pte. Armstrong J.
93860049	Pte. Atkinson J.G.
93891	" Anderson T.
93898	" Airey J.S.
93952	" Anderson T.
93825	" Bancroft S.
93832	" Bennions W.
93861	" Bradley J.P.
93862	" Bradbury G.G.
93874	" Brogden J.
93884	" Buckley H.S.
93885	" Buckley W.
93904	" Bakewell B.
93923	" Brown J.
93937	" Bell T.
93938	" Bellerby R.W.
93470	" Bell T.
93819	" Chaplin F.A.
93833	" Cambridge B.Y.
93838	" Convery D.
93842	" Cook J.G.
93843	" Crowther T.W.
93844	" Curnock P.A.
93850	" Cooper B.R.B.
93887	" Cooper H.
93892	" Conway J.
93907	" Cyples J.M.
93917	" Clarkson W.H.
93918	" Colebourne C.A.
93943	" Calow J.L.
93455	" Collard G.
93863	" Davison A.
93864	" Donnelly F.
93919	" Dickinson T.W.
93931	" Day W.
93944	" Denton S.
93924	" Basby H.
93827	" Feather H.
93865	" Flower H.
93869	" Farrage S.
93908	" Ford A.H.
93920	" Fletcher A.
93491	" Farrar W.
93851	" Grant J.
93852	" Gray F.
93925	" Gibson H.
93953	" Giggal L.
93840	" Hendrey T.J.
93845	" Hodgson F.
93846	" Holland H.
93866	" Havis F.
93876	" Hardy A.R.

NOMINAL ROLL OF 53RD BN. NORTH'D FUSILIERS PROCEEDING OVERSEAS.

SHEET 2.

Regtl.No.	Rank & Name.
93877	Pte. Hobson J.
93889	" Holdsworth W.
93909	" Hackett C.J.
93926	" Haigh J.W.
93941	" Hutchinson G.W.
93932	" Heal H.F.
93820	" Jagger W.
93870	" Jenner W.B.
~~93949~~	" ~~Jobling J.~~
93955	" Jackson H.
93921	" Kirk C.H.
93853	" Longthorne J.
93871	" Lemon M.T.
93878	" Lumb F.R.
93893	" Leightly J.E.
93901	" Laverick A.
93911	" Lister N.B.
93912	" Lund W.A.
93835	" McGill J.J.
93867	" McGough T.
93868	" McGravey P.
93879	" McCormac H.
93910	" Murray J.M.
93945	" Maughan R.
93890	" Newsome T.L.
93745	" Nicholls J.A.
93821	" Priestly G.A.
93841	" Proud H.
93880	" Pepper H.
93914	" Parkinson S.B.
93927	" Patterson G.E.
~~93946~~	" ~~Parker W.~~
93922	" Price C.F.
93828	" Ratcliffe R.
93895	" Robertson J.W.
93929	" Robinson G.W.
93822	" Sheridan J.T.
93855	" Skellett W.
93873	" Straugheir K.
93881	" Shaw H.
93896	" Smith J.
93936	" Selby H.
93951	" Sinclair F.
93836	" Tunstall R.
93818	" White N.
93823	" West F.E.
93824	" Wilkinson R.O.
93830	" Waddington D.
93831	" White R.H.
93856	" Webster H.
93883	" Wildman G.
93897	" Wilson H.C.C.
93916	" Willows H.
93930	" Walker J.J.
93956	" Willis G.
93857	" Yarrow G.C.
93853	" Younger E.
93948	" Tiplady W.
93894	" Quickmire S.
93928	" Peterson J.
93826	Collins S.

NOMINAL ROLL OF 53RD BN. NORTH'D FUSILIERS PROCEEDING OVERSEAS.

SHEET 3.

Regtl.No.	Rank & Name.
94001	Pte. Adams R.W.W.
94002	" Appleton D.
94003	" Betts H.
94004	" Bradford W.C.S.
94005	" Bowerbank F.G.
94006	" Brown J.
94007	" Beaver W.
94008	" Bescoby A.W.
94009	" Brammer H.G.
94010	" Carter T.
94011	" Cockerill E.
94012	" Creese E.T.B.
94013	" Clark W.
94014	" Chapman H.
94015	" Cowall W.
94016	" Campbell D.
94017	" Duncanson C.
94018	" Dent H.
94019	" Dickinson F.S.
94020	" De Groat D.G.
94022	" Dalton W.S.
94023	" Eyre J.T.
94024	" Evans E.
94025	" Evans G.
94026	" Emmett C.R.
94027	" Fenny T.
94028	" Fairlamb R.
94029	" Fountain J.E.
94030	" Feetham A.
94031	" Flowers W.W.
94032	" Fairburn H.
94033	" Boyes J.
94034	" Corr F.
94035	" Emery C.P.
94036	" Fields R.
94037	" Gomersall E.H.
94038	" Brindley H.
94039	" Holt B.S.
94040	" Hartley J.H.
94041	" Mulvenna D.
94042	" Makin W.
94043	" Marshall G.
94044	" Phillips C.J.Z
94045	" Schofield F.J.
~~94046~~	" ~~Rhodes C.~~ 94046 Pte Rhodes.C.
94047	" Wraith T.

"B" Coy.

46148	A/C.S.M. Head W.J.
11	A/Sgt. Hart W.
203045	A/Sgt. Johnson J.
93450	A/Cpl. Henshaw R.
93482	Pte. Springall J.A.
93469	" Massey G.
93463	" Wright A.
94048	" Argyle G.
94049	" Adamson C.
94050	" Archer J.
94051	" Atkinson I.
94052	" Brown D.
94053	" Brown H.
94054	" Barker C.
94055	" Bingley G.H.
94056	" Bedford J.
94057	" Bartlette G.
94058	" Birdsall A.E.
94059	" Blackburn F.
94060	" Castledine B.
94061	" Crammon W.
94062	" Harmer H.

NOMINAL ROLL OF 53RD BN. NORTH'D FUSILIERS PROCEEDING OVERSEAS.

SHEET 4.

Regtl.No.	Rank & Name
94063	Pte. Hart H.
94064	" Holmes T.
94065	" Hinde J.W.
94066	" Jones R.E.
94067	" Jacobs A.
94068	" Lawson E.
94069	" Rigby J.
94070	" Smith G.
94071	" Shepherd C.
94072	" Sparkes S.B.
94073	" Sheldon W.
94074	" Thornton V.
94075	" Tolley J.
94076	" Willett J.
94077	" Wetherill H.

"C" Coy.

29 93959	A/C.S.M.	Wright G.
93961	A/C.Q.M.S.	West F.E.
539	Sgt.	Ford G.W.
93962	Sgt.	McCrae J.B.
93964	A/Sgt.	Johnson E.H.
45178	A/Cpl.	Napper H.
29500	Cpl.	Shann SS
93557	A/Cpl.	Robson J.W.
93559	L/Cpl.	Bone R.H.
93576	A/Cpl.	Allanson W.F.
56296	L/Sgt.	Davies F.W.
92006	Pte.	Gooder P.
92002	"	Shore T.
93479	"	Alberts W.
93519	"	Ashington W.
93547	"	Ackroyd O.
93598	"	Addison J.G.
92010	"	Auckland G.R.
93487	"	Barker A.R.
93505	"	Burns W.H.
93520	"	Beaumont G.
93544	"	Bareham F.G.
93549	"	Bowron C.
93555	"	Buckland G.
93569	"	Bewley D.G.
93570	"	Bickley W.
93571	"	Buckton A.
93577	"	Batty A.
93591	"	Barraclough S.
93609	"	Brunton L.
93624	"	Bainbridge T.W.
93638	"	Balmforth S.
93639	"	Blackenbury C.
93647	"	Batty C.J.
93657	"	Bates T.
93680	"	Brown S.
92016	"	Ball C.G.
93481	"	Cockbain T.
93490	"	Collins C.W.
93511	"	Carter A.P.
93521	"	Carter H.S.
93522	"	Clough A.
93560	"	Campbell W.N.
93579	"	Cherry W.M.
93592	"	Conlon H.S.
93625	"	Collins H.M.

NOMINAL ROLL OF 53RD BN. NORTH'D FUSILIERS PROCEEDING OVERSEAS.

SHEET 5.

Regtl.No.	Rank & Name.
93632	Pte. Collins J.
93640	" Carter J.
93649	" Coates P.
93648	" Cellina A.
93660	" Close H.L.
93687	" Clark H.W.
92038	" Close C.C.
92047	" Child T.
93482	" Darbyshire A.
93550	" Darrell F.R.
93561	" Dennis B.
93573	" Dobbie J.
93580	" Dunn F.
93600	" Davies T.F.
93611	" Dibbs F.W.
93612	" Dixon G.
92051	" Dowson G.
51781	" Dixon J.
93523	" Ely C.A.
93524	" Fisher F.
93556	" Forster M
93601	" Forster T.E.
93504	" Ghiotti M
93525	" Gough W.J.
93527	" Gummery J.
93551	" Greaves R.H.L.
93562	" Ginnever A.
93602	" Greaves R.
93613	" Green D.
93618	" Grieves J.T.
93641	" Gray A.F.
93662	" Gibson W.
92072	" Gains J.M.
92081	" Gibbs T.W.
93492	" Hill A.
93499	" Hargreaves F.A.
93507	" Holmes R.H.
93548	" Hoyle J.O.
93563	" Howland J.
93603	" Hendry P.A.
93614	" Hamilton C.E.H.
93634	" Hetherington F.S.
93635	" Holt J.
93644	" Hindle D.G.
93643	" Hewitt R.
93642	" Heaps F.
93689	" Hiscock A.
93715	" Hodgson J.E.
92087	" Holles H.C.
92090	" Hay C.G.
92099	" Harrison A.E.
92101	" Hope J.
92104	" Houston J.
93575	" Irving R.G.
93619	" James A.E.
93564	" Judson A.
93464	" Johnson W.E.D.
93493	" Jones A.E.
92112	" Jenkins A.
92114	" Jenkinson S.
93528	" Kenzie T.R.
93664	" Knox A.H.
92122	" Kinder J.R.
93494	" Leek J.W.
93508	" Lloyd G.M.
93545	" Limley W.E.
93620	" Lindo H.
93636	" Leigh J.McD
93462	" Leary S.C.

NOMINAL ROLL OF 53RD BN. NORTH'D FUSILIERS PROCEEDING OVERSEAS.

SHEET 6.

Regtl.No.   Rank & Name.

Regtl.No.	Rank & Name
92124	Pte. Lee A.
92131	" Lomas J.
92132	" Luty C.
93513	" Mooney E.
93529	" Moye M.
93568	" Miller A.A.
93554	" Mondinalli V.
93654	" Metcalfe F.B.
92141	" Marley M.
66955	" Marley R.
92145	" Mennell C.R.
92144	" Mellor H.B.
92146	" McHale J.
92147	" Mason W.
92150	" Mallon G.
93495	" Nalton E.
93581	" Needler C.R.
93582	" Newton G.
93530	" O'Conner J.
93531	" Ormondroyd F.
93595	" Outhwaite T.
93483	" Paulin T.
93501	" Procter M.
93565	" Pilling A.
93615	" Parkinson J.T.
93622	" Pond F.W.
93465	" Phillips P.
93583	" Priestly W.
92159	" Pickering M.D.
92167	" Pearson C.
93514	" Riley C.E.
93532	" Randerson C.L.
93533	" Rothwell S.
93553	" Robson J.A.
93584	" Reid F.R.
93585	" Rennison A.
93586	" Robinson T.W.
~~93616~~	" ~~Ress B.~~ 93616 B. Rees.
92173	" Robinson H.
92176	" Roper C.
92177	" Ryder E.
93484	" Sibbald J.S.
93534	" Shaw N.
93535	" Simpson A.
93536	" Swift C.R.
93558	" Storey E.T.
93566	" Simpson N.
93587	" Starkey C.
93605	" Southern L.R.
93650	" Smith J.H.
93503	" Stobart T.
92183	" Stephenson J.C.
92186	" Stirk P.
92188	" Smith F.
92189	" Smith C.B.
92190	" Smith D.T.
92191	" Smith W.
92199	" Sharp W.
92200	" Squirrell B.J.
93515	" Thackeray A.
93516	" Thornton F.
93538	" Tennant W.

NOMINAL ROLL OF 53RD BN. NORTH'D FUSILIERS PROCEEDING OVERSEAS.

SHEET 7.

Regtl.No. Rank & Name.

93588	Pte.	Thornton C.
93596	"	Tickle V.B.
92209	"	Traves A.
92211	"	Tait A.
92217	"	Toft F.J.
92219	"	Thorpe A.
92221	"	Taylor J.W.
~~93589~~	"	~~Uttley T.W.~~
93485	"	Wilson W.J.D.
93486	"	Wylie J.W.
93498	"	Watson C.
93510	"	Wombwell T.H.
93517	"	Walker J.
93518	"	Walsh J.
93539	"	Wetherill G.
93540	"	Wells H.
93541	"	Western L.
93542	"	Whitwam G.W.
93546	"	Williamson R.
93567	"	Wardell T.C.
93590	"	Walker W.
93608	"	Wylie E.B.
93497	"	Waterhouse J.
92225	"	Wilson J.E.
92232	"	Withycombe H.
92236	"	Walker C.W.
92237	"	Watts E.C.
92241	"	Yeoman J.R.
93509	L/Cpl.	Tomlinson T.D.
3228	A/St/Sgt.	Jones A.E. R.A.O.C.
~~93708~~	Pte.	~~Collinson J.H.~~
92034	"	Carruthers R.H.

"D" Coy.

93958	C.S.M.	White W.A.
204262	A/Sgt.	Walker A.
9528	Sgt.	Porteous W.
291907	A/Sgt.	Audus S.N?
93656	Pte.	Allison J.H.
93685	"	Breeze G.
93707	A/L/Cpl.	Bailey A.
93742	Pte.	Blakey W.
93768	"	Bennington F.W.
93775	A/L/Cpl.	Burnop J.T.
93776	Pte.	Burrell C.
93787	"	Bearpark H.L.
93788	"	Beverley A.R.
93789	"	Blythe A.
93790	"	Brown J.H.
93810	"	Brown W.
93702	A/L/Cpl.	Cebley W.C.
93700	Pte.	Calvert J.W.
93701	"	Clarke J.C.
93725	A/L/Cpl.	Croucher T.G.
93730	Pte.	Cowgill F.
93738	"	Collingwood G.
93617	"	Clemitus J.
93599	A/L/Cpl.	Charlton J.G.
93762	Pte.	Cordingley C.E.
93763	"	Crabtree A.
93769	"	Connor J.
93777	"	Cosgrove J.
93811	"	Cross B.S.

NOMINAL ROLL OF 53RD BN. NORTH'D FUSILIERS PROCEEDING OVERSEAS.

SHEET 8.

Regtl.No.	Rank & Name.
93652	Pte. Dowson T.
93681	" Driver E.W.
93739	" Douglas T.G.
93626	A/L/Cpl. Davison J.P.
93743	Pte. De Vere T.T.
93778	" Denkin A.
93791	" Duffield G.S.
93661	" Edminson J.J.
93713	" Fothergill R.
93593	" Fletcher E.D.
93779	" Farrar A.
93780	" Ferguson R.I.
93791	" Flynn J.P.
93663	" Gray R.
93695	" Greenwood L.G.
93693	" Geldard H.
93731	" Green L.
93744	" Green C.A.
93758	" Galbraith A.
93759	" Gowing A.
93782	" Griffin A.C.
93792	" Gott F.
93716	" Hunter W.
93717	" Hurworth R.W.
93732	" Hallowell H.
93733	" Hitchen J.D.
93750	" Hurst G.D.
93794	" Hall C.
93795	" Hutty A.E.
93740	" Ingram H.
93709	" Johnson C.
93729	" Johnson L.H.
93783	" Johnson W.
93456	A/L/Cpl. Johnson G.W.
93665	" Logan G.E.
93666	Pte. Lumsden N.
93719	" Leonard R.P.
93627	" Liddell G.
93751	" Lazenby J.
93752	" Lees F.
93673	" Meltham G.F.
93682	" Moon W.J.
93690	" McIntosh T.
93696	" Miller A.H.
93703	" Moles F.
93710	" May H.
93771	" McKee E.
93772	" Muirx G.E.
93628	" McGee J.
93655	" Newton J.
93704	" North F.
93799	" Newton W.T.
93668	" O'Loughlin M.
93726	A/L/Cpl. Oakley H.E.
93675	Pte. Patchett E.
93735	" Pepper W.
93604	" Peebles J.H.
93746	" Peacock T.G.
93764	" Parker H.
93784	" Patterson J.S.W.
93800	" Park S.
93801	" Pashby A.

NOMINAL ROLL OF 53RD BN. NORTHUMBERLAND FUSILIERS
PROCEEDING OVERSEAS.

SHEET 9.

Regtl.No.	Rank & Name.
93813	Pte. Porter J.J.
93814	" Prior J.
93676	" Robinson W.
93677	" Rushforth W.
93747	" Richardson J. 93749 Pte. Robson J.S.
93748	" Robinson W.R.
93760	" Rogerson T.R.V.
93765	" Robinson A.
93785	" Robinson W.
93802	" Ridsdale E.
93651	A/L/Cpl.Stewart R.
93711	Pte. Squire H.
93722	" Stoves R.
93723	" Swift C.W.
93766 93466	" ~~Swift W.~~ Smith W. 93466
93606	A/L/Cpl.Sutcliffe T.
93623	Pte. Scott T.B.
93754	" Slinger E.
93755	" Stork J.
93766	" Sykes J.H.
93774	A/L/Cpl.Stewart J.L.
93786	Pte. Smith T.W.
93803	" Sandiforth E.
93804	" Skelton G.
93805	" Sisson J.W.
93806	" Straw A.E.
93815	" Skillings H.G.
93645	" Turner E.
93670	" Thompson J.
93671	" Thompson R.
93684	" Temperley M.
93712	" Toole G.
93741	" Thompson M.M.
93646	" Willis D.C.
93691	" Walker T.M.
93809	" Wood J.W.
93736	A/L/Cpl. Weatherall J.
93757	Pte. Whitehead M.
93761	" Ward J.W.
93767	" Ward T.
93816	" Wilkinson T.F.
93729	" Young R.
93793	" Graham G.
93698	" Sykes R.W.
93706	" Scott T.
93683	" Stoddart R.L.S.
93727	" Robson C.
93773	A/L/Cpl. Steel A.C.
93667	Pte. Nicholson J.T.
93753	" Mitchell L.
92041	" Cartwright W.R.
92044	" Crawshaw C.
92L64	" Fletcher A.
92066	" Francis J.E.
92009	" Anderson G.
92111	" Ireland H.
92091	" Hunt H.
92143	" Miller T.W.
92019	" Bates W.H.
92130	" Lazzeri G.
92096	" Hall P.D.
92192	" Stout C.E.
92059	" Everingham A.
92045	" Cannon P.
92025	" Braid L.

NOMINAL ROLL OF 53RD BN. NORTHUMBERLAND FUSILIERS PROCEEDING OVERSEAS.

SHEET 10.

Regtl.No. Rank & Name.

Regtl.No.	Rank & Name
92102	Pte. Howard F.W.
92017	" Baskerville J.
92133	" Loohey J.
92020	" Bower E.
92154	" Nertney B.
92218	" Thorpe T.E.
92175	" Redfern J.
92155	" Ord W.
92223	" Wood J.W.
92178	" Rogers P.
92054	" Downes A.
92007	" Allen A.
92026	" Buttery R.W.
92046	" Colton F.
92103	" Hird G.
92222	" Twineham W.
92008	" Allen J.J.
92042	" Clarke F.W.
92065	" Fairweather H.
92149	" Marsh F.
92238	" Williams B.
92021	" Brown W.
92040	" Creaser R.
92244	" Farr L.
92195	" Sanderson R.E.
92235	" Wright J.
58987	" Callighan J.
127389	" Preston B.
93261	" Lunn B.
93253	" Dighton F.J.
58986	" Mole R.
93257	" Vertigan H.
93678	" Smith H.

Lieut.Colonel.
Commanding 53rd Bn. Northumberland Fusiliers.

Scotton Camp,
Catterick.
7.3.1919.

53rd Bn. Northumberland Fusiliers.

Army Form C. 2118.

WAR DIARY
or
INTELLIGENCE SUMMARY.
(Erase heading not required.)

Instructions regarding War Diaries and Intelligence Summaries are contained in F. S. Regs., Part II. and the Staff Manual respectively. Title pages will be prepared in manuscript.

1 Northern

Place	Date 1919	Hour	Summary of Events and Information	Remarks and references to Appendices
SULZ.	APRIL 1		Bn under R.S.M. Officers under Adj.	SF
			G.O.C. 8th INF Brigade spent 1½ hours during training and expressed satisfaction at improvement on Bn.	
		14.30	Col Cox lectured at 14.30 hours in the Gymnasium MANDERSCHNIEDER SCHOOL on "Temperance" Approx 50 men signed the pledge.	SF
	2	11.00	100 OR attended lecture in the Gymnasium, REDWITZ STRASSE. by Mr T.E.KING on "How the Navy helped the Army to win the war".	
			The Bn Football team played the 51st Bn N Fus on the SPORTS PLATZ. Very even game and finished with no score.	SF
	3		Inspection of transport by G.O.C. 8th INF. BDE.	
			Battalion Route march.	SF
	4		Nothing of interest to report	SF
	6		Bn "Rugger" and "Soccer" teams played the 51st and 52nd Bn N Fus teams respectively in both matches 53rd Bn were victors. The Rugger match was very strenuously played result 3 points to Nil. In the Soccer the 53rd Bn were much superior winning by 5 goals to 2	SF

51st Bn. Northumberland Fusiliers.

WAR DIARY
or
INTELLIGENCE SUMMARY.
(Erase heading not required.)

Army Form C. 2118.

Place	Date 1919	Hour	Summary of Events and Information	Remarks and references to Appendices
SULZ.	APRIL 6/8		Nothing of Interest to report.	
	9		Guard Mounting Competition won by "A" Coy with "D" "C" "B" Coys 2nd, 3rd & 4th respectively. JUDGES. L.O.C. 8th INF. B.DE. and Divl Staff Captain.	O.F
			The Bn Soccer team were visitors to the 52nd N.F.uo and lost by 2 goals to 1.	
	10		Bn Route March. Nothing further of interest to report.	O.F
	11		"B" Coy and part of "C" Coy went for a pleasure trip up the Rhine. The weather was dull and threatening. The boat moved off about 0930 hours and Proceeded slowly up the river and arrived at ANDERNACH at 1400 hours where the Bn disembarked and strolled about for an hour and a half. The party returned to COLOGNE at 1800 hours. A most enjoyable day was spent and was very much appreciated and much interest taken.	25
	12/13		Nothing of interest to report.	2F
	14		2/Lt. Holmes left for employment with the Civil Staff Captain.	2F
	15		The Divisional Commander inspected the cooking arrangements of the Bn.	
			RQMS Rouse and 2/Lt E Coppick left Bn on transfer to P.B. W. Bn.	25

53rd Bn. Northumberland Fusiliers.

WAR DIARY
or
INTELLIGENCE SUMMARY.
(Erase heading not required.)

Army Form C. 2118.

Place	Date 1919	Hour	Summary of Events and Information	Remarks and references to Appendices
SOLZ	APRIL 16		Lt. Col. W.P.S. FOORD. DSO. and Major PERRY. DSO. MC. arrived and took over command and 2nd in command of the Bn. respectively. Mess feeding told.	SF
	17		Battalion Route march.	SF
			2/Lt. R. Story left to join no 2 P.B.W. Coy.	
	18		Received preliminary orders re moving to ARTILLERY BARRACKS. BONNERSTRASSE.	SF
			Nothing of interest to report.	.
	19		Assistant Adjutant proceeds to MARIENBURG to arrange Officers billets	SF
	20		Signal Officer visited ARTILLERY BARRACKS in BONNERSTRASSE. to make signal arrangements.	SF
			Guard Commanders reconnoitre routes from MANDERSCHNIEDER School to guards to be taken over.	
	21		Bn. took over guards from the 52nd SHERWOOD FORESTERS. whom we relieve tomorrow.	SF
			8 Officers and 163 other ranks mounted.	
	22		Bn. moved to BONNERSTRASSE BARRACKS. moved out 1000 hours arriving 1115 hours	SF
	23		St Georges day. Bn Parade at 1030 for a lecture in Church by Bn. Chaplin. re "St Georges Day."	SF
MARIENBURG	24/25		Nothing of interest to report.	SF
	26		Bn. played Veterinary Hospital at Soccer. Result we won 6-0	SF

53rd Bn. Northumberland Fusiliers.

WAR DIARY
or
INTELLIGENCE SUMMARY.
(Erase heading not required.)

Army Form C. 2118.

Place	Date 1919	Hour	Summary of Events and Information	Remarks and references to Appendices
MARIENBURG	APRIL 27		Nothing of interest to report.	
	28		The following officers and proceeded to Dieppe to join the 9th Bn N. Fus. 2/Lt W.J. Webb. Lieut Colbourne Lieut Hooper.	87
			Bn marched to VI Corps Cinema for a lecture by Lord Morris. Subject "The Growth of the British Empire."	87
	29		A Coy Headquarters moved into quarters along with the Door Guard. O.C. J Coy taking over the command of the guard which now consists of all his Coy.	87
	30		93928. Pte Peterson "A" Coy entered today at SUDFRIED HOF GENNETRY at 1430 hours.	87
			D Coy provide firing party. Lieut. Fotherby and Coy represented A Coy officers. Capt O. C. Platt M.B.E. MC. proceeded to A.D.R.T. Cologne on one months probation for appointment of R.T.O.	

C.S. Ford
Lieut.-Colonel
Commanding 53rd Bn. Northd. Fusiliers.

Army Form C. 2118.

WAR DIARY
or
INTELLIGENCE SUMMARY.
(Erase heading not required.)

Instructions regarding War Diaries and Intelligence Summaries are contained in F. S. Regs., Part II. and the Staff Manual respectively. Title pages will be prepared in manuscript.

Place	Date	Hour	Summary of Events and Information	Remarks and references to Appendices
Marienburg	1919 May			
	1st.		Capt. E.G.Bease. M.C. assumed command of "C" Coy vice Capt. O.G.Platt. O.B.E. M.C. on 1 Months probation as R.T.O.	
	2nd.		Preparing for Inspection by Commander in Chief.	
	3rd.		The Commander in Chief's Inspection cancelled at 1315 hours All Guards found by the Bn were relieved today.	
	4th.		Nothing of Interest to report.	
	5th.		Battalion embussed at 0730 hours and Debussed at 0900 hours at NIEHL. Paraded at 1000 hours on Divisional Parade Ground and rehearsed Divisional March Past. At 1220 hours marched back to debussing point where Battalion fell out and pick-niched. Returned to Barracks at 1500 hours The day was warm and sunny.	
	6th.		The Battalion practised the March Past on Barrack Square. Football Match between Officer's and Sergts ended in a victory of 3 goals to one for the Officer's.	
	7th.		Nothing of interest to report.	
	8th.		Inspection of Northern Division by the Duke of Connaught at EXERCIER PLATZ, MERHIEM. Battalion paraded at 0645 hours on Battalion Parade Ground and were conveyed by Lorry to NIEHL.	
	9th.		Nothing of interest to report.	
	10th.		Battalion Firing on Range at LONGSRICH. "D" Coy on short Range. "A" "B" "C" Companies on LACHEM Ranges - Paraded at 0815 hours., conveyed by lorries at 0830 hours. Returned between 1600 and 1700 hours.	
	11th.		Church Parade in Barrack Church at 1000 hours. Battalion Parade at 0945 hours.	
	12th.		Nothing of interest to report.	
	13th.		Battalion practiseing Ceremonial Order. Weather beautifully warm and sunny.	
	14th.		Football Match between the Battalion and the Signal Coy of the Royal Engineers. After an exciting game in which both sides showed very excellent form the match ended in a draw.	
	15th.		Nothing of interest to report.	
	16th.		Marshal Foch's visit to Cologne, escorted down the Rhine by Motor Launches from Coblentz. The Battalion Paraded at 0900 hours in clean walking out dress and side arms. They lined the route and the neighborhood of the NEUE BRUCKE at 1030 hours and formed the Gaurd of Honour.	
	17th.		The Battalion took over Brigade Guard Duties from the 52nd. Bn. Northumberland Fusiliers at 1000 hours "B" Company of this Battalion proceeded to the Docks under Capt Crake.	
	18th.		Return match between the R.E. Signal Coy and the Battalion, owing to being on guard we could not raise a strong team and were finally beaten by three goals to one.	
	19th.		Nothing of interest to report.	
	20th.		Hot weather still continues. Very dry.	

(A7192) W. W2659/M1293 75,000 4/17. D.D. & L. Ltd. Forms/C.2118/14.

Army Form C. 2118.

WAR DIARY
or
INTELLIGENCE SUMMARY.
(Erase heading not required.)

Instructions regarding War Diaries and Intelligence Summaries are contained in F. S. Regs., Part II. and the Staff Manual respectively. Title pages will be prepared in manuscript.

Place	Date	Hour	Summary of Events and Information	Remarks and references to Appendices
MARIENBURG	1919. May. 21st.		Nothing of interest to report.	
	22nd.		Nothing of interest to report.	
	23rd.		180 Men transferred to this Battalion from the 1/6th West Yorks Regt. 126 Reported, the remainder being on leave, in hospital and on courses etc, etc. These men were divided between the Four Compys.	
	24th.		Battalion were relieved of all Guard Duties by the 51st Battalion Northumberland Fusiliers. SUD BRUCKE Guard was taken over by the 7th Middlesex Regt. All Companies reported everything correct and nothing of importance had occurred during the week.	
	25th.		Battalion Photograph in Mass. Full parade including all Officer's. W.Os. Sergts taken in groups with the Commanding Officer, 2nd in Command and the Adjutant. Corporals and L/Cpls were also taken.	
	26th.		Barracks inspected by the Corps Commander and the Brigadier. "A" and "B" Coys proceed to Rifle Range at LACHEM for one week. "B" Coy at RIEHL Barracks. All troops were confined to Barracks owing to Civil disturbances at 1600 hours Tramways in Cologne on strike. Confinement raised at 2100 hours.	
	27th.		"C" Coy firing on short range at Fort Vll. Much cooler.	
	28th.		"D" Coy on short range at Fort Vll. Nothing further to report.	
	29th.		"D" Coy still on short range at Fort Vll.	
	30th.		"C" Coy on Fort Vll. range for the second time. Each of these Coys had two days firing on the short range.	
	31st.		Battalion paraded at 0730 hours and proceeded down to the DUSSELDORFER WHARF where they embarked for a trip up the Rhine at 0900 hours. It was a beautiful day and the trip was a great success. The boat took us as far as REMARGEN. A great deal of bathing amongst the German people on the river bank which caused much amusement. Battalion arrived back about 1730 hours. The Trip was commanded by Major. D.H.H.Perry. 2nd. in Command of the Battalion.	

ARMY OF THE RHINE.
31.5.1919.

W.W.Cee Capt. Adjt. for
Lieut-Colonel.
Commanding. 53rd. Bn. Northumberland Fusiliers.

Sheet. 1.

Army Form C. 2118.

WAR DIARY
or
INTELLIGENCE SUMMARY.
(Erase heading not required.)

Place	Date	Hour	Summary of Events and Information	Remarks and references to Appendices
Cologne.	1919 June 1.	1000	Church Parade.	
			Nothing further of interest to report.	
	2.		92819 Pte Bates W.H. & 84789 Pte Frost. W. of "D" Coy. tried by D. G. O. M. Weather very much cooler.	
	3.		His Majesty King George V Birthday. After a parade at 0900 hours at which three cheers were given for His Majesty, the Battalion was dismissed, and the rest of the day was spent as a holiday.	
			Heavy showers of rain.	
	4.		Nothing of interest to report.	
	5.		Weather continues cold and very wet.	
	6.		"A" and "B" Coys. returned from Lechem and Rhiel Ranges. 1st Northern Brigade Cinematograph arrived, and remains with this Battalion for a week. First performance was given to-night and was very much appreciated by the men.	
	7.	1000	Battalion took over all Brigade Guards for one week.	
		1430	A cricket match was held at Exercier Platz Rhiel against "G" Battery R.H.A. The game provided a certain amount of excitement and the scores were:- 53rd Battn. Northd Fus. 115 . R.H.A. 144 . A win for the Battery of 29 Runs.	

Army Form C. 2118.

Sheet. 2.

WAR DIARY
or
INTELLIGENCE SUMMARY.
(Erase heading not required.)

Instructions regarding War Diaries and Intelligence Summaries are contained in F. S. Regs., Part II. and the Staff Manual respectively. Title pages will be prepared in manuscript.

Place	Date	Hour	Summary of Events and Information	Remarks and references to Appendices
	1919			
Cologne.	June.8.	1000	Church parade in Barrack Church.	
			The weather has become very hot and sultry.	
	9.		Whole holiday granted to the troops on the occasion of it being Whit-Monday. "D" Coy. on Powder Magazine Guard were complimented by the G.O.C. on their general efficiency.	
	10.		Nothing of interest to report.	
	11.		A cricket match had been arranged with 11 Squadron R.A.F., but this had to be postponed owing to this Squadron not being located in Cologne.	
	12.		Weather continues very hot.	
			A friendly Cricket Match was arranged with No. 7 F.A. at Rhiel Barracks. The score was 53rd Northd Fus. 23 runs, whilst the F.A. made a total of 90 runs for 6 wickets.	
	13.		Nothing of interest to report.	
	14.		Nothing of interest to report.	
	15.		Church Parade in Barrack Square at Fort VIII. "D" coy., doing small schemes on the Golf Links near the Barracks.	
	16.	1000	"C" Coy. on short Range at Fort VIII. "D" coy., doing small schemes on the Golf Links near the Barracks.	
			Very fine hot weather still continues.	
	17.		Q.V.Rs arrived to take over Brigade Guards.	
			Preparations made for forward move into Germany.	
	18.		Q.V.Rs took over Brigade Guards.	
			Battalion busily engaged in packing prepatory to move forward.	
	19.		Lorries arrived at 1300 hours.	
			Moved from Cologne by lorry to Kurten 30 miles east of Rhine, via Deutz Gladbach.	
			Left Cologne at 0750 hours.	
Kurten.		1300	Arrived Kurten at about 1200 hours. Troops bivouacked for the night.	
			Communication established with Brigade. Situation normal.	
			This is the leading Battalion. 51st and 52nd. Northd. Fusiliers following in rear.	
			3rd Hussars immediately in front.	
			93753 Pte G.Elreath. died at 36th C.C.S. with meningitis.	

Army Form C. 2118.

Sheet. 3.

Instructions regarding War Diaries and Intelligence
Summaries are contained in F.S. Regs., Part II.
and the Staff Manual respectively. Title pages
will be prepared in manuscript.

WAR DIARY
or
INTELLIGENCE SUMMARY.
(Erase heading not required.)

Place	Date	Hour	Summary of Events and Information	Remarks and references to Appendices
Kurten.	1919. Jun. 20.		Carried on with training and out-door schemes. No one allowed outside the boundaries of the Camp. Extra Police mounted, and bathing restricted to the lower reaches of stream. Weather hot, but turned to rain during evening. Good bathing facilities for the Men.	
		1300	Transport arrived from Gladbach.	
		1400	3rd Divisional Train arrived.	
	21.		Weather cooler, but otherwise fine. No orders yet to move. German Government designs, and a Specialised Government takes its place. They promise to sign the Peace Terms.	
		2100	72 tents arrived for the Men. Rain set in. We carried on with Sports, two companies held Sports, "A" & "B" Coys. Wet drill drawn Tent and Instruction.	
	22.	1000	Church Parade in the Camp. Sports amalgamated "B" & "D" Coys. Some very good entries.	
		1730	Hot weather again.	
	23.		General Sir William Robertson C.in.C. Rhine Army paid us a surprise visit, and stated we might be boot or mufti any time in 24th.	
			Much rain falling, and owing to this factor "C" Coys Sports had to be cancelled. Weather b.d.	
	24.		Owing to bad weather Tactical Scheme had to be postponed.	
	25.		Tactical Scheme March.	
	26.		Afternoon Scheme sent on Reconnaissance Scheme of Mount ???	
	27.		Battalion Route March.	
	28.	1800	Message from Brigade. Peace had been Officially signed.	
	29.	1000	Church Parade. 2/Lieuts Hooper and Pringle went to England prior to going out to India.	
	30.	0900	Transport left Kurten for Berg Gladbach, where they bivouaced for the night. Lieut. Colonel W.P.S. Foord. DSO took over command of 1st Northern Brigade. Major. B.H.H. Perry DSO.MC. assumed command of the Battalion.	

Army of the Rhine.

WMcCrae Capt William Bart
Lieut-Colonel
Commanding 53rd Bn. Northd. Fusiliers.

Army Form C. 2118.

WAR DIARY
or
INTELLIGENCE SUMMARY.
(Erase heading not required.)

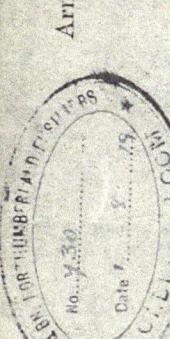

Place	Date	Hour	Summary of Events and Information	Remarks and references to Appendices
Kurten.	1919 July. 1.		"B" Day. Moved back to Cologne by Lorries. Left Kurten 0815 hours. Transport arrived Barracks 1100 hours. Left Kurten 0815 hours. Took over Barracks from K.R.R. 2/Lt.Neasham and 26 Men were left at Kurten as Rear Party.	
Marienburg.	2.		Cleaning up and settling down after return from Kurten.	
	3.		General Holiday for Peace Celebrations.	
	4.		Heats of Battalion Sports run in afternoon. Weather Fine.	
	5.		Sports in afternoon.	
	6.		Trip up the Rhine.	
	7.		Started from Cologne by special train to Bonn. Left Bonn by Boat at 1000 hours. Turned back on outskirts of Coblenz. Arrived back at Bonn at 1745 hours, returning to Barracks at 2000 hours. Weather very fine. Took over Brigade Guards.	
	9.		Church Service at 1000 hours.	
	12.		New Brigadier General visited Barracks.	
	13.		Colonel Foord went on leave. Major B.H.H. Perry D.S.O., M.C. assumes command of the Battalion.	
	16.		Battalion returns from Guards.	
	18.		Church Parades 1000 hours.	
	19.		"C" Coy proceeded to Fort 11. and "D" Coy. to Rhiel to fire G.M.C. Trip up the Rhine. Church Parades 1100 hours. Major B.H.H. Perry D.S.O., M.C. leaves for England. Major J.Walsh D.S.O. assumes command of the Battalion.	
	25.		Lieut.Colonel Foord D.S.O. returned from leave, and re-assumes command of Battalion. "C" and "D" Companies returned from Ranges.	
	26.		Battalion took over Brigade Guards. Musketry Casuals left for Fort 11. to fire G.M.C.	
Cologne. 31.7.19.				

W.S.Foord
Lieut. Colonel.
Commanding 53rd Northumberland Fusiliers.

WAR DIARY
or
INTELLIGENCE SUMMARY.
(Erase heading not required.)

Army Form C. 2118.

Instructions regarding War Diaries and Intelligence Summaries are contained in F.S. Regs., Part II. and the Staff Manual respectively. Title pages will be prepared in manuscript.

Place	Date	Hour	Summary of Events and Information	Remarks and references to Appendices
Marienburg, COLOGNE.	1919 Aug. 4.		Bank Holiday. No Military Training.	
	5.		Torch Light Tattoo at Lindenthal.	
	6.		Practice of Ceremonial Parade. The G.O.C. attended and expressed his appreciation of the Parade.	
	7.		Practice Parade on Barrack Square for the Review at Merheim.	
	8.		Brigadier General Sandilands C.B. C.M.G. D.S.O. left the Brigade. Lieut. Colonel W.P.S. Foord. DSO. assumed command of the Brigade.	
	11.		Lecture by the Brigade Education Officer.	
	12.		Lecture by Capt H. De Windt.	
	12. 13. 14.	14.30	Lecture on Civics at VI Corps School. Capt J.W. Croke, 2/Lieut. J. Musgrove, and 2/Lieut. J. G. Carris attended	
	15.		Practice Review Parade at Stadt Spiel Platz by G.O.C. Northern Division.	
	18.		Review by Army Council at Merheim. Lieut. Col. W.P.S. Foord. DSO assumes command of the Battalion. Brigadier General Hamilton-Moore CMG DSO. took over Command of Brigade.	
	19.	21.30.	Torch Light Tattoo at Lindenthal. Took over Brigade Guards.	
	20.		Casuals proceeded to Fort 11, Lachem, Merheim to fire G.M.C.	

WAR DIARY
or
INTELLIGENCE SUMMARY.
(Erase heading not required.)

Army Form C. 2118.

Place	Date	Hour	Summary of Events and Information	Remarks and references to Appendices
Marienburg. COLOGNE.	1919. Aug. 23.		Company Commanders Conference.	
	25.		Sports Officer attended Conference 282 Duren Strasse.	
	27.		Battalion Route March.	
	28.		Major. J. Walsh. DsO. to Hospital as result of Motor Cycle accident.	
	29.		Battalion Rifle team fired at Lochem Ranges. Preliminary Contest for Rhine Army Rifle Championship.	
	30.		Rhine Trip. Capt. G. A. Macpherson in charge.	
Marienburg. 31.8.19				

Lieut.-Colonel.
Commanding 53rd Bn. Northumberland Fusiliers.

Army Form C. 2118.

WAR DIARY
or
INTELLIGENCE SUMMARY.
(Erase heading not required.)

Summary of Events and Information	Remarks and references to Appendices
Lecture to the Warrant Officers and N.C.Os. by the Commanding Officer in the Cinema.	
Route March at 0800 hours. Firing re-commenced at Lachem Range for Casuals.	
Casuals returned from Fort.8.	
The Battalion became "A" battalion and took over the Brigade Guards.	
The Rifle Team leaves for Drove for the Army Rifle Meeting.	
Church of England service at 1000 hours.	
Rifle Team secured the 4th.Prize in Event No.7.Gas Competition.	
Rifle Team secured the 4th.Prize in Event No.2. at the Army Rifle Meeting.	
Route March at 0900 hours. Route:- Bonner Strasse-Rondorff-Neuenhof-Kalscheuren-Militar Ring Strasse.	
Officer's Conference.	
Preparing for Move.	
"C" and "D" Companies moved to Q.V. Dump, VOCHEN.	
"A" and "B" Companies moved out to BRUEHL.	
Concert in Cinema by Y.M.C.A. Party.	
Leave and Demobilisation was suspended on account of Railway strike in England.	

Sheet. 2.

Army Form C. 2118.

WAR DIARY
or
INTELLIGENCE SUMMARY.
(Erase heading not required.)

Instructions regarding War Diaries and Intelligence Summaries are contained in F. S. Regs., Part II. and the Staff Manual respectively. Title pages will be prepared in manuscript.

Place	Date	Hour	Summary of Events and Information	Remarks and references to Appendices
BRUHL.	1919. Sept			
	26.		Cinema opened in Bruhl.	
	28.		Delousing of Clothing and Blankets.	
	29.		Football Match against 25th. Bgde. R.G.A. in second Round Y.M.C.A. Shield. Won. 3 - 2.	

Army of the Rhine.
30.9.19.

Erab
Major.
Commanding 53rd. Bn. Northumberland Fusiliers.

BEF

Northern Div
formerly 3 Div

2 Northern Inf Bde

1/6 W. Yorks

1915 Mar to 1919 Oct

From 49 Div 146 Bde

1/6 W York Reg. A.F.O

WAR DIARY
or
INTELLIGENCE SUMMARY.
(Erase heading not required.)

Army Form C. 2118.

17.

Place	Date 1919	Hour	Summary of Events and Information	Remarks and references to Appendices
COLOGNE	MARCH 1		Parades according to Programme	
	2		Church Parades	
	3		Education & Training - Brigade Commander's Inspection also billets	
	4		Education & Training - Rate of exchange s/mks = 1/11 5 frs = 3/10 warning to all ranks. German pamphlets seized - warning to all ranks	
	5		Inspection by the Divisional Commander - Training afterwards. Football (Assoc.) 1/6 West York Regt 3 goals - 9th Brigade H.Q one.	
	6		Education & training - Officers posted as follows:- A. Coy. 2.Lt. Richardson (E) 2.Lt Jacques - 2.Lt Pale - 2.Lt Marshall - B. Coy. Capt. Pikes M.C. 2.Lt Todd 2.Lt Shrewsmith - C.Coy G. Gregory 2/Lt Dalton - 2.Lt Harrison 2.Lt Richardson (F.B) - D. Coy. 2.Lt Rumney - 2.Lt Ruskin 2.Lt Wilkinson (w). - 2.Lt E Wilkinson to receive pay of appointment as Education officer - 2.B. 2/Lt Pinkerton relinquishes the appointment & Education Off. on transfer to 1/7th West Yorks Regt.	
	7		A & B Coys take over Brigade Guards of German Artillery & Ammunition stores C & D Coys Training	
	8		A & B Coys Guards - C & D Coys Training	

Army Form C. 2118.

WAR DIARY
or
INTELLIGENCE SUMMARY.
(Erase heading not required.)

Instructions regarding War Diaries and Intelligence Summaries are contained in F. S. Regs., Part II. and the Staff Manual respectively. Title pages will be prepared in manuscript.

Place	Date	Hour	Summary of Events and Information	Remarks and references to Appendices
COLOGNE	MARCH 9		C & D Coys relieve A & B Coys. Discipline all ranks warned against fraternising with inhabitants.	
	10		A & B Coys Training. C & D Coys Guards. Lt. W Rennison relinquishes the acting adjt of Capt. on ceasing to be employed as actg adjt. C. 13.2.19.	
	11		Education — Parades as per programme.	
	12		Baths for battalion — KAMMERCHERGASSE — COLOGNE placed "out of Bounds"	
	13		Training Range duties & Range Practices — Eleven representatives of this batt. play in trial match for Brigade (Rugby).	
	14		Parades as per programme. Lt. Jacques transferred to C Coy. from A. Coy.	
	15		Parades as per programme. Lecture by Archdeacon WAKEFORD on Social & Industrial questions. 2 Lt Rumney transferred from D Coy to A Coy. Draft of 263 arrived from 1st Bn West York Regt. Officers posted as follows:— A. Coy. — Lt. R.A. Russell — 2 Lt. G.R. Taylor MM. 2 Lt. G.A. Hunter — B. Coy. — Lt. B. H.L. Pearson — Lt. F. de B. Price — Lt. G.E. Fowler — 2 Lt. Th. Buckitt. C. Coy. 2 Lt. F. Bird 2 Lt. G. Oglesby — D. Coy — A/Capt. B.C.V.K. Peabody DSO. MC. Lt. H.W. Brown — 2 Lt. L.T. Murray — 2 Lt. T.F. Bridges — Lt. L.P. Dobson.	

Army Form C. 2118.

WAR DIARY
or
INTELLIGENCE SUMMARY.
(Erase heading not required.)

Place	Date	Hour	Summary of Events and Information	Remarks and references to Appendices
COLOGNE	MARCH 16		Divine Services & Kit Inspection.	
	17		Brigadier General inspects battalion. Rifles & ammunition to be carried on all parades away from billets.	
	18		Education & Bn Drill – no officer, NCO or man will be allowed to boat or yacht on the Rhine unless he has passed a test – i.e. swim 200 yards.	
	19		Brigadier's Inspection.	
	20		Parades as per programme.	
	21		Batt. Route March. A draft of 296 arrived from 51/Y "B" West York Rgt. Officers posted as follows:– A. Coy. 2Lt Burnard. B. Coy. Lt Powell. C. Coy. 2Lt Stansfield, 2Lt Henderson M.C., D.Coy. 2Lt Jameson. The following officers are to report here from 1/5th Bn. W.Y.R. A/Capt Crabtree M.C. 2Lt Lockerby, 2Lt Jobson, 2Lt Hammerton, 2Lt Garlick, 2Lt Unwison M.C., 2Lt Raisbeck, 2Lt Thompson, 2Lt Webb, 2Lt Fletcher.	
	22		Parades as per programme.	
	23		Divine Services – C.O.'s inspection of billets	
	24		Batt. Route March – The following officers arrived: Lt. E. 2Lt. Smyth-Pigott (WYR)	

Army Form C. 2118.

WAR DIARY
or
INTELLIGENCE SUMMARY.
(Erase heading not required.)

Instructions regarding War Diaries and Intelligence Summaries are contained in F.S. Regs., Part II. and the Staff Manual respectively. Title pages will be prepared in manuscript.

Place	Date	Hour	Summary of Events and Information	Remarks and references to Appendices
			from 93rd L.T.M. Battery - Lt.(a/Capt.) Montgomery M.O. from 92nd L.T.M. Battery. Lt.(a/Capt.) Montgomery relinquishes rank of a/Capt. on ceasing to Command 93rd L.T.M. Battery.	
			7.9. C.P.M. No 263030 Cpl. Byers J.E. found "not guilty" in charge of striking a superior officer.	
	25		Education – Training	
	26		Education – Baths for Battalion.	
	27		Parades as per programme, having a lecture on German propaganda.	
	28		Parades as per programme, having of Commander-in-Chief visiting this area.	
	29		D.Coy. Take over Brigade Guards. 2 Lt. A. Henderson posted to A Coy having arrived from England.	
	30		Divine Services. The following officers arrived from 52nd (YS) Bn York & Lancs. 1/Capt C.P. Grant. D.R. Hayett, Lt. J.R. Rolin, 2 Lt. E.W. Colebrook, 2Lt. H.D. Walmsley, 2 Lt. E.O. Pauling.	
	31		Education – Training instead of Route march owing to weather.	

R.J. Mowat Lt. Col.
Commanding 1/6 Bn. W. York R

Army Form C. 2118.

1/6 W York Regt

2.Z.
5 sheets

WAR DIARY
or
INTELLIGENCE SUMMARY.
(Erase heading not required.)

Place	Date	Hour	Summary of Events and Information	Remarks and references to Appendices
Cologne	1919 April 1		Parade as Bn Programme – Brigade Commander's Parade – Lecture in Y.M.C.A. Lieut J.P. WADE proceeded to U.K. for demobilisation 31.3.19.	
	2		Parade as Bn Programme – Baths – 2/Lieut W. GARLICK + 2/Lieut C. THOMPSON returning from leave + is taken on our strength being transferred from the 5th Bn W. YORK Regt.	
	3		Parade as Bn Programme.	
	4		Inspection Parade – Bn Ceremonial Parade – Pay + Coys at O.C. Coys disposal. Inspections – Baths – Lieut G.N. BISATT to be a/capt with pay + allowances of Lt whilst employed as a/Adjt. 6.3.19.	
	5			
	6		Divine Services – Inspections by C.O. etc.	
	7		Inspection – Education Batn Route March – Retreat sounded at 18.35 hrs. Complaint of misconduct of troops travelling by rail. Battn move from NAUSSBAUMER Str. SCHOOLS & PLATEN Str. SCHOOLS to SCHILLER GYM. LINDENBORN SCHOOLS. BRAVENRAUTH SCHOOLS. Received draft of 33 officers & 530 O.R. from 51st & 52nd Bns W. YORK Regt. Officers – 51st W. YORK Regt – Capt. BURNE wal, Capt R. SINCLAIR me mn	

(39175) Wt W355/P360 Gap20 12/7 D.D.&L. Sch 53a. Forms/C.2118/15

Army Form C. 2118.

WAR DIARY
OR
INTELLIGENCE SUMMARY.
(Erase heading not required.)

Place	Date	Hour	Summary of Events and Information	Remarks and references to Appendices
Cologne	April 4 (cont)		Lieut. B.R. TROUGHTON-DEAN. Lieut. F.H. BIRCH. 3/Lieut. W.K.D. M.M. 2/Lt. A. CURRIE. 2/Lt.	
			Cpl. CARTLIDGE. 2/Lt. R.M. DAVIDSON. 2/Lt. D.R. AUTY. R.D. & HODGE. 2/Lt. J.C. HAZELIP.	
			2/Lt. E.V. DOBSON. 2/Lt. H. SCOTT. 2/Lt. W.H. de VOIL. 2/Lt. R.V.H. SETTLE. 2/Lt. F.B. SMITH.	
			R.D.F.L. RACE —— 52nd Bn W. YORKS Rgt.: - BREVET MAJOR O.R.B. CHIESMAN.	
			CAPT S. WILLIAMS, CAPT. H.S. BUCKELL. CAPT. O. ILLINGWORTH CAPT BRIGHT,	
			Lieut. F.C. KING. Lt. F.O. LANCASTER M.C. 2/Lt. G.W. ARNOLD. 2/Lt. F.T. EVANS, 2/Lt.	
			(W. BURKE) W. BARFITT. 2/Lt. T. GARVEY, 2/Lt. M.N. ORM ROD. 2/Lt. F. PRITCHFORD	
			2/Lt. R.N. BATTYE.	
	6.		Re-organization. LACHEM RANGE at disposal of Bn.	
	7.		Coys at disposal of Coy Commanders — LACHEM RANGE	
			Parades — Squadron Physical Drill Platoon + Arms Drill, Guard Mounting.	
	10		Half Holiday	
	11.		Parades as Bn. programme Heads of Range Practices	
			"A" Coy. average yearly 10.56. "B" Nil "C" 10.34. "D" 11.31. Lieut. F. BIRD U.K. for demobilization	
	12.		Coys at disposal of Company Commanders — BATHS.	
	13.		Results of Inter-March A.9.BK F. H.A. MG. Battn. NIL	
			DIVINE SERVICES.	

Army Form C. 2118.

WAR DIARY
or
INTELLIGENCE SUMMARY.
(Erase heading not required.)

Place	Date	Hour	Summary of Events and Information	Remarks and references to Appendices
Cologne	14/4/19		Parades as Bn Programme. ROUTE MARCH. Retreat sounded at 1840 hrs.	
	15.		Parades as Bn Programme. 2 Lt. G. Osgerby to U.K. for demobilization	
	16.		Parades as Bn Programme. - BATHS. Lt. W. Garlick, Lt. G.M. Puckrin	
			2 Lt. H.B. Webber, 2 Lt. A. Henderson, 2 Lt. D.Y. Fletcher to U.K. for demobilization	
	17		Parades as Bn Programme. - LACHEM RANGE.	
	18		DIVINE SERVICES. Bt. Lt. Col. T.N.S.H. Howard, D.S.O. assumes command	
			of the Battalion. Lt. Col. F.G. Horshaw M.C. relinquishes the acting handling	
			Lt. Col., on ceasing to command a Battalion	
			MAJOR E.D. STANSFIELD M.C. to U.K. for demobilization	
			CAPT. C.E.K.K. PEBERDY D.S.O. M.C. transferred to 1/5th Bn WEST YORKSHIRE Regt.	
			1/Lt. COL. F.C. BOUSFIELD (WEST YORK Regt) taken on strength of this unit from	
			17th MARCH	
	19.		Parades as Bn Programme - NEPTUNE BATHS. FOOTBALL Bn O/R's RHA O/R's	
	20		Divine Services.	
	21		Parades as per Bn Programme.	
	22		Education - Bn Ceremonial Drill at BLUCHER PARK. Retreat sounded at 1845 hrs	

WAR DIARY
or
INTELLIGENCE SUMMARY.
(Erase heading not required.)

Army Form C. 2118.

Place	Date	Hour	Summary of Events and Information	Remarks and references to Appendices
Clayn	April 22 (cont.)		Lieut E.G. GREGORY, Lieut W.D. MONTGOMERY M.C. 2 Lt RAISTRICK, 2 Lt E.V. HARRISON, 2 Lt W. BARFITT, 2 Lt O.W. COLEBROOK, 2 Lt C. THOMPSON to U.K. for demobilization.	
	23		Bn (less A Coy) BATHS. A Coy Kit Inspection by Commanding Officers. Lecture in Gymnasium.	
	24.		Parades as per Bn Programme in BUCHER PARK.	
	25.		Inspections - Education - Bn ROUTE MARCH. Officers posted to this Bn from 23.4.19 :- T/Capt (A/major) T.H. RUSSELL, 2 Lt E.A. PETCH, 2 Lt H.D. FITZPATRICK, 2 Lt M.G. YEATES. Officers transferred to 9th Bn D.L.I.- Capt R. HAYLETT M.C. Lt C.P. GRANT M.S.	
	26		Parades as Bn Programme. 2 Lt H. RETBURG transferred from 1/5th Bn to this unit. 2 Lt T.W. BURKITT proceeded to 231 P.O.W. Camp & is struck off strength of this unit.	
	27		Divine Services. Officers struck of Strength :- To 61st DIV. H.Q. Capt H.S. BUCKLE. Capt W.L. BURNE. To 1/3th WEST RIDING. Lieut H.W. JACQUES, G. FOWLE, F.L. GRICE.	

Army Form C. 2118.

WAR DIARY
or
INTELLIGENCE SUMMARY.
(Erase heading not required.)

Place	Date	Hour	Summary of Events and Information	Remarks and references to Appendices
Cologne	27		2/Lieuts J.C. HAZELIP, Q.B. SMITH, D. AUTY, A. CURRIE, M.G. YEATES, F.D. FITZPATRICK. To UNITED KINGDOM. Lt. G.R. TROUGHTON-DEAN, Lieuts E.V.K. SETTLE, M.V. ORMROD, Br. LITCHFORD.	
	28		First Post 21.15 hrs. Last Post 21.45 hrs. Lights Out 22.00 hrs.	
	29		Parades as per Bn Programme - BLÜCHER PARK.	
	30		Parades as per Bn Programme - LA CHEM RANGE. Baths as per firing Parade as per Programme - EXERCIER PLATZ. 2ND NORTHERN BRIGADE RANGES First Post 21.30 hrs, Last Post 22.00 hrs. Lights out 22.15 hrs. Officer struck off the strength from 28.4.19. Lieuts H.L. PEARSON to 220 P.O.W. Company. 2/Lt LT MURRAY to 232 P.O.W. Company. 2/Lt A.R. JEBSON to 237 P.O.W. Company.	

T.N. Howard
Lt Col
commanding 1/6 Bn. (P.W.O.) W. York R.

2nd Nthm. Inf. Bde.

G465

Northern Division "A".

Herewith War Diaries for the month

of May, 1919.

[signature]
Captain.
Staff Captain for G.O.C.
2nd Northern Infantry Brigade.

3rd July 1919.

Army Form C. 2118.

WAR DIARY
or
INTELLIGENCE SUMMARY.
(Erase heading not required.)

5-7.
5 sheets

Place	Date	Hour	Summary of Events and Information	Remarks and references to Appendices
COLOGNE.	1919 May 1st		Parades as per Bn. Programme. GUARD OF HONOUR of Officers 50 men to receive GENERAL PETAIN at Commander-in-Chief's House.	
	2nd		Parades as per Bn. Programme; 2 hours devoted to cleaning billets; A & D Coys - Baths; 3 O. Ranks despatched for demobilization.	
	3rd		Divine Services	
	4th		Ceremonial Parade on EXERCIER PLATZ at LACHEM. (Practice for the Review by H.R.H. The DUKE OF CONNAUGHT)	
	5th		"C", "D", & H.Q. Coys, and Transport at Baths. "A" & "B" Companies carried on Miniature Range.	
	6th		Parades as per Bn. Programme. Lt. Smyth-Pigott M.C. & 15 O ranks posted to 9th L.T.M BATTERY, & struck off the strength.	
	7th		NORTHERN DIVISION REVIEW. All arms of the Northern Division paraded in Review Order on EXERCIER PLATZ at LACHEM and were reviewed by FIELD MARSHAL H.R.H. The DUKE OF CONNAUGHT K.G. Genl. Sir Wm. ROBERTSON, G.C.B., H.R.H. expressed his satisfaction with the parade, and complimented all ranks of the division.	

WAR DIARY
or
INTELLIGENCE SUMMARY.
(Erase heading not required.)

Army Form C. 2118.

	Summary of Events and Information	Remarks and references to Appendices
	2/Lt BURNARD appointed SPORTS OFFICER, Bn LEWIS GUN Class commenced.	
	2/Lt PETCH, GARVEY, RICHARDSON and SCOTT proceeded to P.O.W. Compys.	
	Parades:- 1 hours Education. Whole Battn. bathed & clothes fumigated.	
	2/Lt BRIDGES appointed Musketry Officer. Bn relieved the 4th YORK and	
	LANCS REGT on Brigade Duties.	
	2nd Lt MARSHALL posted to the 231st PRISONER OF WAR COY., y.O.Ranks	
	despatched for demobilization.	
	Parades:- as per Battalion Programme.	
	Officers' classes under the 2nd in Command commenced.	
	Major C.G. BOUSFIELD posted to 15th PRISONER OF WAR COY and LT A FOSTER M.C	
	to the 237th P.O.W COY. 4 O Ranks despatched for demobilization and	
	14 O Ranks received from 1st Bn W. YORK REGT.	
	Parades as per Battalion Programme.	
	2/Lt FOTHERBY posted to the 237th and 2/Lt STANSFIELD to 241st P.O. WAR COYS	
	PARADES as per Battalion Programme. Lt/Col E.J. POLLARD and	
	PARADES as per Battalion Programme.	

WAR DIARY
or
INTELLIGENCE SUMMARY.
(Erase heading not required.)

Army Form C. 2118.

Place	Date 1919	Hour	Summary of Events and Information	Remarks and references to Appendices
Sobagne	May 15	(cont)	10 other ranks proceeded to England for demobilization.	
			T/CAPT WHITE appointed T/MAJOR	
	16		PARADES as per Battalion Programme. "B" & "C" Coys and H.Q. Transport and 2 M. Stores at Baths.	
	17th		PARADES as per Battalion Programme. 1 Other Rank despatched for demobilization.	
	18th		Battalion relieved from Brigade Duties by 4th Bn YORK and LANCS REGT.	
			2/LT E PEARSON posted to 231st PRISONER OF WAR COY.	
	19th		PARADES as per Batt. Programme. CAPT R SINCLAIR ML, MM taken over Command of "C" Coy. 3 Other Ranks joined from 1st Bn W YORK REGT. and 1 O.R from BASE. 3 O.Rs posted to VI CORPS H.Q and struck off strength. 2 Other Ranks despatched for demobilization.	
	20th		Parades as per Battn. Programme. Baths for "B" & "D" Coys and also for H.Q, R.M Stores and Transport. 2 Other ranks reported from Hospital and one other rank from Base.	
	21st		C.O's Ceremonial Parade.	
	22nd		Parades as per Battalion Programme. Baths for "A" & "B" Coys	

WAR DIARY
or
INTELLIGENCE SUMMARY.

(Erase heading not required.)

Army Form C. 2118.

Place	Date	Hour	Summary of Events and Information	Remarks and references to Appendices
Cologne	May 1919 23		Capt. C.E. Peterdy, D.S.O, M.C. De-taken on the strength 2 Other ranks reported from 1/5th W. York. Regt. The Batln. embarked on the Rhine Steamer "Loreley" at 08.30 hours and proceeded down the RHINE to a point near REMAGEN. Meals were taken on board and a canteen arranged. The trip was much appreciated by all ranks.	
	24		6 a.m. Lt. Brook proceeded to U.K. for demobilization. Divine Services.	
	25		"C" Coy proceeded to LONGRICH to relieve Guard of the 1/5 W. York. Regt. "B" and "D" Coys practised on miniature RANGE at LACHEM 2 other ranks despatched for demobilization and 3 other ranks posted to HOME DEPOTS	
	26		Coy Commander inspected Battle Posts. Party of Lt. Foster to 237 P.O.W. Coy cancelled. Shortened card distributions on bologne.	
	27		Parades as for Battalion programme. Normal conditions resumed at 22.00 hrs.	
	28		Guards re-informed and "alarm" action taken. Medical inspection by Medical Officer 2 Canteens held at LACHEM range. No distant trances. Parades as Battalion programme	
	29		Ascension day. General German holiday.	
	30		Parades as for Battalion programme. "B" Coy exercised on miniature Range.	
	31		Parades as per Battalion programme. Successful Cricket Match against 3/R Warwick Regt. W.York R = 259 for 5 wickets. R.Warwick Regt 39 all out.	

Army Form C. 2118.

WAR DIARY
or
INTELLIGENCE SUMMARY.
(Erase heading not required.)

Place	Date	Hour	Summary of Events and Information	Remarks and references to Appendices
Cologne	1919 June 1st		Divine Service:- C.of.E. at 11.30 hours in Protestant Church in ROTHESHAUS STRASSE. R.C. @ 09.30 hours in MECHTERN STRASSE CHURCH. Nonconformists at NUSSBAUMER STRASSE SCHOOL at 11.00 hours.	H.T. Habute
	2nd		Parades as per Battalion Programme. "B" Coy practised on Miniature range. Conference of Company Commanders and Specialist Officers. Court of enquiry held under presidency of Major E.P.V.K. PEBERDY, DSO MC to enquire into four cases of illegal absence. G.R.O. against interrogation republished. Training to comprise 4 hours only each day. This period to include compulsory education. 1 Other rank detailed for demobilization.	
	3rd		King's Birthday. Ceremonial parade of the Battalion in BLÜCHER PARK. ROYAL Salute, March past and three cheers for His Majesty given. Remainder of day observed as a holiday.	
	4th		Parades as per Battalion programme. Summary of Evidence taken against three other ranks.	
	5th		Parades as per Battalion Programme. "B" Company bathed at LINDENBORN Schools. "A" Company escorted on the Miniature Range. Weather dull.	

WAR DIARY
or
INTELLIGENCE SUMMARY.
(Erase heading not required.)

Army Form C. 2118.

Place	Date	Hour	Summary of Events and Information	Remarks and references to Appendices
Cologne	1919 June 6th		Parades as per Battalion Programme. Field General Court Martial assembled at SCHILLER GYMNASIUM (Bn. H.Q.) under presidency of Major T.H. Russell. Two other ranks of this unit tried and convicted. Weather wet. Lewis Gun demonstration in BLUCHER PARK.	
	June 7th		Battalion takes over Brigade Guard duties of 2nd Northern Brigade. Special classes arranged for Battalion stretcher bearers and sanitary men.	
	June 8th		Divine Services. R.C.s at MECHTERN STRASSE Church. C of E at ROTHESHAUS STRASSE Protestant Church, and Non-conformists at NUSSBAUMER STRASSE Schools. Lieut MOCATTA, W.E. taken on the strength.	
	June 9th		WHIT MONDAY, observed as a holiday by order of the Corps Commander. Officers' conference at 09.00 hours at B.O.R. 1 Other rank arrived from Base. 1 other rank posted to 9th Trench Mortar Battery and struck off the strength.	
	June 10th		Parades as per Battalion Programme. Miniature range allotted to "C" Compy. 1 Other rank arrived from No 5 Military Prison.	
	June 11th		Demonstration to Companies in Guard Mounting. Field General Court Martial on three other ranks at BICKENDORF SCHOOLS.	

WAR DIARY
OR
INTELLIGENCE SUMMARY.

(Erase heading not required.)

Army Form C. 2118.

Summary of Events and Information

Parades as per Battalion Programme. Corps Commander inspected Brigade Guards found by this unit. Miniature Range allotted for "C" Coy "B" Company bathed.

Parades as per Battalion Programme. Demonstration in Guard Mounting. 3 other ranks despatched for demobilization. 1 O.R. evacuated to United Kingdom, sick.

Battalion relieved from Brigade guards by 1/5 Bn W. Yorks Regt. "D" Coy & Transport bathed.

Divine Services. Lieut King and 30 other ranks struck off the strength. 1 Other rank rejoined from Hospital. Picquet found at AACHENER TOR of 1 Officer, 2 N.C.Os. and two men.

Parades as per Bn Programme. Instructions received that a new advance party of Brigade is imminent. The advance party of rehearsing unit arrive. All surplus stores of Brigade sent to 137 Sheffield Quartd. Canal found over this Brigade Dump by this unit.

Army Form C. 2118.

WAR DIARY
or
INTELLIGENCE SUMMARY.
(Erase heading not required.)

Instructions regarding War Diaries and Intelligence Summaries are contained in F. S. Regs., Part II. and the Staff Manual respectively. Title pages will be prepared in manuscript.

Place	Date 1919	Hour	Summary of Events and Information	Remarks and references to Appendices
Cologne & Dunwald	June 18th		Advance party under Lt WH DE VOIL move off at 07.00 hours by bycycle. Battalion move by route march for DÜNNWALD, and bivouacs in a wood erected. At 20.00 hours owing to rain all other ranks were put into very close billets in Barn, Kitchens, living rooms, etc.	
Dunwald Hilgen	19th		Battalion continue advance and Billet in HILGEN.	
HILGEN	20th		Foot inspection of Battalion carried out. Parades under Company Commanders. Bullets cleaned, Equipment fitted and general smartening-up parades. Capt. Bright and one other rank struck off the strength.	
"	21st		Parades under Company Commanders. Instructors issued necessary outpost duties	
"	22nd		Divine Services. Lewis Gun Demonstration under Capt. L. Reed M.C. Brevet-Major Sherman struck of strength. Capt. /Hon. R.A.M.C attached as Medical Officer.	
"	23rd		Battalion practised in Outpost operators. 4 other ranks struck off the strength	

Army Form C. 2118.

WAR DIARY
or
INTELLIGENCE SUMMARY.
(Erase heading not required.)

Instructions regarding War Diaries and Intelligence Summaries are contained in F. S. Regs., Part II. and the Staff Manual respectively. Title pages will be prepared in manuscript.

Place	Date	Hour	Summary of Events and Information	Remarks and references to Appendices
HILGEN	June 1919	24th	Parades under Company Commanders. As many men bathed as possible in tubs by a Stream. Concert given to Battalion in Hall at "C Coy's" Billet.	
"		25th	Parades under Company Commanders. Officers and Scouts practised in exercises on Marching on Compass bearings.	
"		26th	Outpost scheme practised by the Battalion, A & B Companies acting as defenders and C & D as attacking enemy.	
"		27th	Parades under Company Commanders. Mess Tin Cooking Competition carried out. Head Quarter Company winning.	
"		28th	Demonstration Parade. (Swords Drill etc.) PEACE SIGNED at Versailles. Salute of 101 guns fired from left Bank of the Rhine at COLOGNE.	
"		29th	Divine Services (Peace thanksgiving service) for all denominations. Cross Country runs, "B" Company winning.	
"		30th	Advance party move by motor-buses to COLOGNE to take over billets formerly occupied by the Battalion.	

Lt. Colonel
Comdg 1/6 Bn West York Regt.

Army Form C. 2118.

WAR DIARY
or
INTELLIGENCE SUMMARY.
(Erase heading not required.)

Place	Date	Hour	Summary of Events and Information	Remarks and references to Appendices
	1919			5.7
COLOGNE	1st July		Battalion moved by "Bus" from HILGEN and proceeded to former billets in EHRENFELD, COLOGNE. "A" Coy occupy the GRAVENREUTH STRASSE SCHOOLS, "B" Coy, the LINDENBORN SCHOOLS, and "C" "D" Coys with Headquarters the SCHILLER GYMNASIUM, PIUS STRASSE.	4 sheets
-.-	2nd		Whole Bn. rested. Day devoted to general cleaning of quarters, clothing and equipment.	
-.-	3rd		General Holiday in celebration of the signing of PEACE.	
-.-	4th		Parades:- Education, "A" + "B" Coys on range at LACHEM. "C" "D" Coys, Guards Drill and training and Platoon commanders. MAJOR HORNSHAW, MC struck off the strength.	
-.-	5th		1 Other rank joined from BASE. Parades as per Company Commanders	
-.-	6th		Divine services for all denominations. All rifles of the Battalion inspected by Staff Sgt Armorer. One Other Rank demobilised.	
-.-	7th		Parades as per Battalion Programme. "C" "D" Companies hereon on range at LACHEM.	
-.-	8th		Field General Court Martial assembled at Headquarters of the	

Army Form C. 2118.

WAR DIARY
or
INTELLIGENCE SUMMARY
(Erase heading not required.)

Instructions regarding War Diaries and Intelligence Summaries are contained in F. S. Regs., Part II. and the Staff Manual respectively. Title pages will be prepared in manuscript.

Place	Date	Hour	Summary of Events and Information	Remarks and references to Appendices
	1919			
COLOGNE	July 8th		1/5th W. YORK REGT. One other rank of then unit convicted. Miniature Range allotted to "C" Coy. "A" Coy and Lewis Gunners of "B" Coy exercised on range at LACHEM. Demonstration to all Officers and NCOs in Guard mounting and Saluting.	
-:-	July 9th		Parades:- Education, "A" Coy Miniature range. Remainder of Battalion under Company Commanders. In the afternoon Battalion Sports held in BLUCHER PARK.	
-:-	July 10th		Parades as per Battalion Programme. Runners Competition (excluding all batmen) held. Court of enquiry assembled to enquire into four cases of illegal absence.	
-:-	July 11th		Battalion inspected in BLUCHER PARK by G.O.C. 2nd Northern Infantry Brigade. Inspection of kits of "A" & "B" Coys by C.O. "C" & "D" Coys bathed at NEPTUNE BATHS. H.Q. Coy bathed at LINDENBORN SCHOOLS.	
-:-	July 12th		Parades as per Battalion Programme. Medals won in Competitions presented to winners by C.O. Field General Court-martial assembled at Battalion Head Quarters. 1 Other Rank taken on strength from BASE.	

Army Form C. 2118.

WAR DIARY
or
INTELLIGENCE SUMMARY.
(Erase heading not required.)

Instructions regarding War Diaries and Intelligence Summaries are contained in F. S. Regs., Part II. and the Staff Manual respectively. Title pages will be prepared in manuscript.

Place	Date	Hour	Summary of Events and Information	Remarks and references to Appendices
COLOGNE	July 13 1919		Divine Services for all denominations. Retreat for week ending 19-7-19 sounded at 19.10 hours	
"	July 14th		Battalion takes over Brigade Guards of the 2nd Northern Infantry Brigade. "B" Coy detached at NIPPES and "E" Coy at COLOGNE DOCKS. VICTORY MARCH in PARIS. Bn Colours carried in procession by Lts BRIDGES & WILD.	
"	July 15th		MINIATURE Range allotted to "D" Coy. 1 other rank taken on strength from BASE. Inspection of Transport by C.O.	
"	July 16th		Parades as for Battalion Programme. Battalion bathed at OVERBECK STRASSE Schools and LINDENBORN Schools	
	" 17th		Education. Training. Firing on range	
	" 18		Education Training. Firing on range. 27.O.R. struck off strength	
	" 19.		Holiday.	
	" 20.		Divine service	
	" 21.		Education Training. Firing on miniature range	
	" 22.		Education Training. Firing on miniature range	
	" 23.		Education Training. Firing on miniature range	

WAR DIARY or INTELLIGENCE SUMMARY

Army Form C. 2118.

(Erase heading not required.)

Summary of Events and Information

Leather equipment changed for web.
Education. Ceremonial drill. War Medal ribbons issued.
Education. Provided Guard of Honour to receive American Commander in Chief of American Rhine Army. (Major General Allen)
Divine Service.
Education. Training under Coy. Commanders. Firing on miniature range.
Education. Ceremonial drill. Firing on miniature range.
Education. Provided Guard of Honour to receive General FAYOLLE, FRENCH ARMY.
Education. Training. Firing on miniature range.

J. S. Knox
Colonel.
Commanding 1/6 Bn. W. York R.

Northern Division "A".　　　2nd Northern Infantry Brigade.
------------------------   A/3177.

             Forwarded.

                                         Captain.
                                Staff Capt: for G.O.C.
                         Commanding 2nd Northern Infantry Bde.

Northern Division "A"   2nd Northern Infantry Brigade.
                              A/3177.

Forwarded.

                                                Captain.
                                    Staff Capt: for G.O.C.
                            Commanding 2nd Northern Infantry Bde.

WAR DIARY
or
INTELLIGENCE SUMMARY.
(Erase heading not required.)

Army Form C. 2118.

Summary of Events and Information

Parades – Education & Training under Company Commanders in BÜCHERPARK

Miniature range allotted to "D" Coy. "A", "B", "C" and "D" Coy bathed.

Parades as per Battalion Programme.

Divine Service, for Church of England Wesleyans and Roman Catholics.

Battalion strike over guards of 2nd Northern Infantry Brigade
"A" Coy on guard at LONGERICH, "D" Coy = DOCKS Guard
"B" Coy = BICKENDORF Guard and HOHENZOLLERN BRIDGE Picquet.
"C" Coy – Battalion Guard.

Paraded as for Battalion Programme. Lewis Gunners exercised on Miniature Range
2 Other ranks struck off the strength.
Parades as per Battalion Programme. "B" & "A" Companies bathed at LINDENBORN
Schools and Transport at OVERBECK STRASSE SCHOOLS.

Battalion paraded as strong as possible and proceeded to LACHEN for practice of Divisional Review on EXERCIER PLATZ under Company Commanders. Baths allotted to "A","D" & Companies.

Remarks and references to Appendices

G.2.
errata

Army Form C. 2118.

WAR DIARY
or
INTELLIGENCE SUMMARY.
(Erase heading not required.)

Instructions regarding War Diaries and Intelligence Summaries are contained in F. S. Regs., Part II. and the Staff Manual respectively. Title pages will be prepared in manuscript.

Place	Date	Hour	Summary of Events and Information	Remarks and references to Appendices
Cologne	1919 Aug 9th		Training under Company Commanders. Battalion distinguishing mark worn on tunic jackets by Regimental Tailors. 3 Companies bathed. 13 Other ranks struck off the strength.	
—	Aug 10th		Divine Services:— Church of England at 11.30 hrs at ROTHE HAUS STRASSE CHURCH; Roman Catholics at 09.30 at MECHTERN STRASSE CHURCH and Nonconformists at NUSS BAUMER STRASSE SCHOOLS at 11.00 hrs.	
—	Aug 11		Parades under Company Commanders. Special parades for fitting and exchanging clothing. 3 extra guards taken over by Battalion from No 2 Water Tank Company.	
—	Aug 12		Officers' Conference held at 11.00 hrs. 2 Other ranks struck off the strength.	
—	13		Parades as per Battalion programme. "D" Coy. medically inspected. "C" Company Anti Gas drill through Gas Chamber. 1 Subaltern Gas Officer & 2 Companies bathed. 36 Other ranks transferred to R.E.	
—	14		Brigade Practice on EXERCIER PLATZ of Percent.	
—	15th		Parades as for Battalion programme. H.Q. and two companies bathed. 1 other rank demobilized.	

WAR DIARY
or
INTELLIGENCE SUMMARY.

(Erase heading not required.)

Army Form C. 2118.

	Summary of Events and Information	Remarks and references to Appendices

Parades:- 0800 to 0900 hours Education 0900 to 1200 hours Battalion training and Recreational Drill in BLUCHER PARK

Divine Service for Church of England, Roman Catholics, and Wesleyans

LIEUT W.E. MOCATTA affiliates Tent Battalion

Battalion paraded with NORTHERN DIVISION on EXERCIER PLATZ at LACHEM and was reviewed by Rt Hon WINSTON CHURCHILL M.P. (Chief of the Army General) and other members of the Army General. Capt M.B. CONSTANT M.C. (Yorkshire Regt) reported for duty.

Parades as per Battalion programme. Lieut A. FOSTER M.C. reported for duty.

Parades as per Battalion Programme. 2 Companies tested.

Officers Conference at 10.15 hours, 7 other ranks struck off strength

Parades as laid down in Battalion Programme. "B" & "D" Coys tested

Lt Col N.F. BARWELL MC assumed command of the Battalion in succession to Brt Col T.W.S.M. HOWARD DSO appointed G.O.C. 3rd London Brigade

Battalion Parade as strong as people in BLUCHER PARK for instruction by the Commanding Officer

WAR DIARY
or
INTELLIGENCE SUMMARY

Army Form C. 2118.

Place	Date	Hour	Summary of Events and Information	Remarks and references to Appendices
Cologne	1919 Aug 23		Parades as laid down in Battalion Orders. Medical inspection of Headquarter Coys. 1 Other rank struck off strength, 1 other rank attached from 16th Bn. Gloucester Regt.	
-	24		Divine services as laid down in Battalion Orders. Medical Inspection of "B" Coy at 09.15 hour	
-	25		Battalion takes over guards of the 2nd Northern Infantry Brigade	
-	26		Special musketry Parade under Lieut F.G. Lancaster M.C. Two other ranks struck off the strength.	
-	27th		Parades as laid down in Battalion Orders. Medical Inspection of "A" Coy	
-	28th		The Battalion relieved of the following guards by 3rd Northern Brigade. HOHENZOLLERN BRIDGE, flugpart G, MALL RAF PLATZ flugpart. LONGERICH guard.	
-	29		Parades as laid down in Battalion Orders	
-	30		Parades as laid down in Battalion Orders	
-	31		Divine Services as laid down in Battalion Orders.	

A. Burnett Lt Col
Comdg 1/6 Bn. W. York R

Army Form C. 2118.

WAR DIARY
or
INTELLIGENCE SUMMARY.
(Erase heading not required.)

7.Z
Archives

Place	Date	Hour	Summary of Events and Information	Remarks and references to Appendices
Cologne	Sept 1919 1st		Commanding Officer's lecture on "The Introduction to the study of modern War."	
	2nd		Commanding Officer's lecture to all Officers on Modern War. Lecture by him on W.O.'s Lecture on "From Pyramid to Skyscraper."	
	3rd		The Battalion with Transport concentrated at BLUCHER PARK to be photographed.	
	4th		Bathing of all Coys from 2 p.m. Coy. Officers Parade at BLUCHER PARK. Musketry Party firing at LACHEM RANGE	
	5th		The Batt. moved to RODENKIRCHEN and bivouacked returning on the 6. 2/Lt Jamieson drowned	
	6th		Batt. returning to Barracks. Divine Service.	
	7th		Funeral of Pte TURTON. W. "B" Coy takes place at SUDERIEDHOF. Battalion Parade at BLUCHER PARK.	
	8th			
	9th		Battalion takes over Brigade Guards.	
	10th		The Burial of 2/Lt JAMIESON takes place today at SUDERIEDHOF. Bathing of Coys from 2 p.m. today.	

Army Form C. 2118.

WAR DIARY
or
INTELLIGENCE SUMMARY.
(Erase heading not required.)

Place	Date	Hour	Summary of Events and Information	Remarks and references to Appendices
Cologne	Sept. 1919 11th		Commanding Officers Lecture to all officers. Parades as per Battn. Programme	
"			The Battalion Basket Ball Team won the VI Corps' Basket Ball Team Championship defeating the 7th Middlesex Regt. 10 points to 1 in the Semi-final and 190th Brigade R.F.A. 12 points to 2 in the Final.	
"	12		Training as per Coy. Commdrs. Coy. Parade States.	
"	13		Parades as per Battn. Training Programme	
"	14		0700 & 0800 'C' and 'D' Coys Double Company Run in shorts and shoes. Divine Services. The Batt. Musketry Teams have scored the following prizes at the Rhine Army meeting. 1st Prize Team Event No 8. 3rd " " " No 2. " " " No 5.	
"	15		From 1015/1215 hours paraded at SCHILLER GYMNASIUM for	

WAR DIARY or INTELLIGENCE SUMMARY.

Army Form C. 2118.

(Continue) Class Instruction in P.T. & B.F.
Baths handing over Brigade friends to 1/4th York & Lanc. Regt.
Battalion Drill.
1 Billion handed to NEPTUNE BATHS & interior Bath. Apparatus
Sports. Prizes given away by Mrs. Potter.
Commanding Officers Parade.
Bath as strong as possible moved to LACHEM Exercise Platz for Training.
0900 - 1800 Instruction
1000 - 1200 Interior Economy.
Divine Services.
Baths taken over Brigade Guard. Thorough delousing of all khaki.
Details available fired on Range at Lachem.
Parades as laid down in Battalion Orders.
Parades as laid down in Battalion Orders.
Details available fired on range at Lachem.

Army Form C. 2118.

WAR DIARY
or
INTELLIGENCE SUMMARY.
(Erase heading not required.)

Place	Date 1919	Hour	Summary of Events and Information	Remarks and references to Appendices
Cologne	Sept. 27		Parades as laid down in Battalion Orders.	
"	" 28		Divine Service. Collection at C. of E service for Church Memorial to fallen at YPRES. Amount collected 530 Mark.	
"	" 29		One Company fired on Lackem Range, Battalion relieved of Brigade Guards by 4th York. Lancs Regt.	
"	" 30		One Company fired on Lackem range. Training as laid down in Battalion Orders.	

Walter Adcock Lieut
Col
for OC
1/6 Bn W. York Regt.

MEMORANDUM.

From 1/6 W. York Regt

To 2nd N. Inf Bde

Cologne
1 - 11 - 1919

Herewith War Diary for month of October 1919

p. H de Vort Lt
a/Adj

WAR DIARY
or
INTELLIGENCE SUMMARY
(Erase heading not required.)

Army Form C. 2118.

Place	Date	Hour	Summary of Events and Information	Remarks and references to Appendices
Bologne	1919 October 1st		Parades as laid down in Battn Orders. 1 Boy. Fired on LACHEM RANGE=	
-do-	2nd		Details of all boys fired on Lachem Range. Rifles of Battalion inspected by Armourer Sergeant. 26 ORs awarded 2nd class Army certificates and 18 OR 3rd class certificates	
-do-	3rd		Battalion Route March. Audit of Officers mess accounts.	
-do-	4th		Details of all boys fired on LACHEM RANGE. BATTALION reorganised into 3 boys as follows. "C" boy renamed No "1" boy. "D" boy renamed No "2" boy. "B" boy renamed No "3" boy. Nos 1 & "D" boys comprised of retainable men. No "3" boy of releasable. Nos 1, 2 & "A" boys first all releasable personnel to No 3 boy. No 3 boy first all retainables to No 1 Boy. ("A" boy wastes out) Command of boys as follows :- No 1 boy Capt R. Sinclair MB. MM.; No 2 boy Capt Rn Crabtree MB; No 3 Boy. Capt G Read MB. ⟨Capt L.E.V.R⟩ Peabody relinquishes acting rank of Capt on ceasing to command a company	

WAR DIARY
OR
INTELLIGENCE SUMMARY.
(Erase heading not required.)

Army Form C. 2118.

Summary of Events and Information | Remarks and references to Appendices

Divine Service. Muster parade & roll call of Battalion.
Battalion relieved 1/4th York & Lancs Regt of Brigade Guards of 2nd Northern Infantry Brigade.
Training under Coy Commanders. Reorganization of Platoons.
Lecture to all Officers by Lt W H DE VEIL. Subject "Pay Mess Books"
Training under Coy Commanders. Medical Inspection of Battalion.
2 Coys Bathed. Lt ALBISTON lectured to all Officers Subject "Transport"
Parades as laid down in Battalion Orders
No 1 Coy fired on LACHEM RANGE. No 3 Coy Bathed
No 2 Coy fired on LACHEM RANGE. Lecture to all Officers by O.C.
During Service as laid down in Battalion Orders. Watches & Clocks put back one hour at midnight (Summer Time ends)
Battalion relieved of Brigade Guards. General cleaning up of Quarters
Capt G Rees M.C. demobilized. Command of No 3 Coy taken over by
2/Lieut E E RICHARDSON

WAR DIARY
or
INTELLIGENCE SUMMARY
(Erase heading not required.)

Army Form C. 2118.

Summary of Events and Information	Remarks and references to Appendices

Rhine Trip. Battalion entrained at WEST BAHNHOF COLN. & proceeded by train to BONN. Thence by steamer to a point near COBLENZ, returning by river to COLOGNE.

No 2 Coy fired on range at LACHEM. Parades as laid down in Battalion Orders.

No 1 Coy fired on range at LACHEM. Parades as laid down in Battalion Orders. Transport and No 7 Coy fired.

Coys at disposal of Company Commanders.

Divine Service as laid down in Battalion Orders.

Battalion takes over Brigade Guards of 2nd Northern Infantry Bde. Parades as laid down in Battalion Orders.

2nd Northern Infantry Brigade Officers move into Schiller Gymnasium. Parades as laid down in Battalion Orders.

N.C.O. class under Regimental Sgt. Major. Officers class under the Commanding Officer.

Army Form C. 2118.

WAR DIARY
or
INTELLIGENCE SUMMARY.
(Erase heading not required.)

Summary of Events and Information	Remarks and references to Appendices

Parades as laid down in Battalion Orders. Details of all boys bathed.
Medical Inspection of the Battalion; N.C.Os class under R.S.M.
Other parade as laid down in Battalion Orders.
Divine Service as laid down in Battalion Orders.
Companies at disposal of Coy Commanders. Civil disturbance.
Defence Scheme practised.
Parades as laid down in Battalion Orders. N.C.Os class under R.S.M.
Parades as laid down in Battalion Orders. 2 Companies bathed.
Parades as laid down in Battalion Orders. Medical Inspection of Battn.
N.t. Coy formed under command of LIEUT F.G. LANCASTER M.C. from draft
received from 1/5 W. Yorks Regt. LIEUTS BROWN H.W. PRICE F de B. J. Bull
GALE F. and 2/LT HUNTER posted to N.t. Coy. J. Brunt
and H. Holt
2/Lt
1/6 W Yorks Regt
from 1/6 W Yorks Regt.

BEF

Northern Div
formerly 3 Div

2 Northern Bde

1/4 Y & L Regt

1919 Mar to 1919 Oct

From 49 Div 148 Bde

1/4th (H) Bn. YORK & LANCASTER REGIMENT.

v   W A R   D I A R Y
         From
    1st. to 31st. MARCH.
         1 9 1 9

                                        LIEUT.COLONEL.
2nd. April. 1919.   Comndg. 1/4th (H) Bn. York & Lancaster Regiment.

WAR DIARY
or
INTELLIGENCE SUMMARY.

(Erase heading not required.)

Army Form C. 2118.

4TH (HALLAMSHIRE) BN YORK & LANCASTER REG.

Place	Date	Hour	Summary of Events and Information	Remarks and references to Appendices
KERPEN	1-3-19		Marched from KERPEN to COLOGNE (14 miles) - Billeted in RIEHL BARRACKS and took over from 1st Bn Coldstream Guards. March discipline was good and none fell out.	
COLOGNE	2-3-19		Day spent in cleaning up Barracks and settling down.	
	3-3-19		Inspected by General Sir H. Plumer GCB etc - Guard and Arms Drill - orders for transfer to 9th I.B. received	
	4-3-19		Moved from RIEHL Barracks to 9th I.B. at EHRENFELD - very crowded.	
	5-3-19		Inspected by Divisional Cmdr, Major General Dinwall CB, in BLUCHER PARK at 10·00 hours	
	6-3-19		Commanding Officer's Parade for all Officers - Squad and Guard Drill - Physical Training in Blucher Park.	
	7-3-19		Close Order Drill - Arms Drill and Physical Training - Lecture in Rio Paradise at 17·30 hrs.	
	8-3-19		Baths in NEPTUN Baths and Medical Inspection.	

SPECIAL ORDER OF THE DAY.

by

Major General N.J.G. Cameron, C.B., C.M.G.,

Commanding 49th (West Riding) Division..

-:-:-:-:-:-:-:-:-:-:-:-:-:-:-:-:-:-

Headquarters,
49th (W.R.) Division,
20th February, 1919.

Officers, Non-commissioned Officers and men of the 49th

(West Riding) Division,

The 1/5th and 1/6th Battalions of the West Yorkshire Regt. and the 1/4th Battalion York & Lancaster Rgt. (Hallamshires) are under orders to relieve Battalions in the 3rd Division of the Army of the Rhine. The 245th, 246th and 311th Royal Field Artillery Brigades are under orders to join the 2nd Division, also in the Army of the Rhine.

Therefore it seems certain that before long the 49th (West Riding) Division will cease to exist as an intact community in this country.

Before any Units begin to leave the Division I desire to tell you one and all how intensely I appreciate the honour of having commanded the 49th (West Riding) Division for the past sixteen months. It has indeed been a proud part of my life as a soldier.

I deeply admire the spirit which has animated the Division at all times. In this short message to you I will not attempt to review the share the Division has taken in the Great War. Suffice it for the moment to say that the YPRES SALIENT, THIEPVAL (including the LIEPZIG SALIENT and the SCHWABEN REDOUBT), NIEUPORT, PASSCHENDAELE, NIEPPE, BAILLEUL, NEUVE EGLISE, WYTCHAETE, KEMMEL, LA CLYTTE, CAMBRAI and VALENCIENNES are all names which will figure prominently in the history of the Great War, and at each of those places some considerable portion of the Division performed noble service.

To all Commanders of Units and formations within the Division, and to all Staffs, I owe my unstinted thanks for their ever loyal support.

All Regimental Officers and Other Ranks command my warm admiration, for their cheerful patience through all difficulties and hardships and for the courage and determination with which they have fought.

of
All units   all arms and departments have played their parts and played them nobly well, and there have been striking examples of that spirit of mutual co-operation which is so essential to Military Efficiency.

There seems to be a fair chance that the Division may continue to exist as such in the Post Bellum Army. If that happy state of things should come to pass I earnestly appeal to all of you to help the Division in every way you can.

4TH (HALLAMSHIRE) B YORK & LANCASTER REGT.   / I

I earnestly trust that the Divisional and Regimental Old Comrades' Associations established or about to be established will be successful in fostering Territorial interest in and affection for the Division, and in keeping alive the spirit of the 49th (West Riding) Division. It is a spirit well worth keeping alive, for it has animated you to great things in the Great War. It is something clean and unselfish for us to live up to after we cease to be soldiers.

I wish you God-speed, happiness and success wherever you go.

N. Cameron
Major General,
Commanding 49th (W.R.) Division.

Army Form C. 2118.

WAR DIARY 4TH (HALLAMSHIRE) BN YORK & LANCASTER REGT
or
INTELLIGENCE SUMMARY.
(Erase heading not required.)

Place	Date	Hour	Summary of Events and Information	Remarks and references to Appendices
COLOGNE	9-3-19		Good supply of new clothing drawn. Coys inspected for same and issued with new. Coy drill Books re-introduced. R.C. service at 1030 hrs. Strict orders issued against Fraternising.	
	10-3-19		Lecture at 0900 hrs by Capt J.S. Houlton - Subject - Colonial Expansion. Grand drill etc in Blucher Park.	
	11-3-19		Rfour into Area "C" - NIPPES. took over from 4th Bn Royal Fus. A.T.S. Coys in HARTWICH Schools, C+D in OSSENDORFER Schools - much more comfortable billets.	
	12-3-19		Cleaning up of billets - Lewis Gun Training and Drill. Coy football in afternoon. Brigade Rugger Practice.	
	13-3-19		Drill - L. Gun training etc. Lecture by Mr D.F. Holmes. Subject "League of Nations."	
	14-3-19		Musketry, Drill etc in morning - Draft of 12 officers and 265 o.rs from 2nd Bn Yorkshire Regt. and a draft of 15 officers and 312 o.rs from 2/4th (H) Bn Yorkshire Regt. arrived at 1700 hrs. All ranks of draft posted to corresponding coys to which they previously belonged. Battalion Baths in working order - Coys bathed + had clean change.	
	15-3-19		60 rounds S.A.A. only to be carried on parade (per man.) 100 rounds per man left at Coy HQ. Demonstration in Blucher Park at 1000 hrs of divisional method of carrying out guard duties.	

WAR DIARY 4TH (HALLAMSHIRE) BN YORK & LANCASTER REGT

INTELLIGENCE SUMMARY.

Army Form C. 2118.

Place	Date	Hour	Summary of Events and Information	Remarks and references to Appendices
COLOGNE	16-3-19		Divine Services - C of E. 0900 hrs - Holy Communion - 0945 hrs. Parade Service -	Corps Football Final in Blucher Park -
	17-3-19		Inspection in Blucher Park by Brig. Gen. C.H. Potter CMG. DSO cmdg 9th Inf Bde - Platoon Football in afternoon. 2 men demobilized.	
	18-3-19		Training of drafts in arms drill and guard duties - F.G.C.M held in Hackwerkschule - Maj Reichelmnc, President - 2 officers attended for instruction - Rifles and ammunition also coys this carried a parades a day from billets - Competition for Northern Division Sign - Prize 100 marks	
	19-3-19		Coys at disposal of Coy cmdrs. The Drums re-formed again - shortage of side drummers - 2 men discharged hostilities - becoming rather available in morning.	
	20-3-19		Coys at disposal of coy cmdrs - Re-organising into platoons and sections - Platoon Football "Blades" Concert Party re-started - 3 ORs joined -	
	21-3-19		Coys at disposal of Coy cmdrs - Lt Seagrave, 2/Lt Hoylewood and Hannibal, and 4 ORs demobilized - Brigade Band monthly started daily.	
	22-3-19		Battalion Baths for all coys - 3 ORs joined from 2/4th Bn - Coy football -	
	23-3-19		Divine Services in Victoria Saal - 2 ORs from 2nd Bn. 3 ORs from 4/4th joined -	

WAR DIARY 4TH (HALLAMSHIRE) BN YORK & LANCASTER REGT.

INTELLIGENCE SUMMARY

Army Form C. 2118.

Place	Date	Hour	Summary of Events and Information	Remarks and references to Appendices
COLOGNE (NIPPES)	24-3-19	0900-1000 - Education. 1015-1230 - Drill etc. in Blucher Park.	1400 hrs. officers and NCO's classes for Musketry Lt. Gun instruction.	
	25-3-19	Conference of all officers at 0930 hrs. - Drill - Snap Duties etc -	Cup football in afternoon.	
	26-3-19	0900-1000 - Education. 1015-1230 - Drill etc in Blucher Park - 2 officers and 20 ORs joined from 2/4th - 1 officer and 1 OR demobilised - 10 men and 11 ORs joined from 2nd Bn -		
	27-3-19	Battalion Route March - Officers & NCO's classes at 1400 hrs - Platoon Football -		
	28-3-19	0900-1000 - Education. 1015-1230 - Drill etc. A.B.C. Battns - 1515 hrs - Lecture in Victoria Saal by Major P. Wood - formerly of York & Lancaster Regt. - subject - "The Regiment and The Hunt" - Capts Bowman, Johnson MC, Hulton, Bailey MC and 2/Lt Scott demobilised.		
	29-3-19	Coy Cmdrs Conference at 1000 hrs. Battns for C, D and HQ. - Swimming Baths available in morning -		
	30-3-19	Divine Services - wearing of red patch on collar & tunic discontinued.		
	31-3-19	0900-1000 - Education. 1015-1230 - Drill etc.	1400 - officers + NCO's classes - Capts Rénie MC, Hornhagle + 2/Lts Norris, Castle + Clegg demobilised.	

D Marson Lt Col
Cmdg 4TH (HALLAMSHIRE) BN YORK & LANCASTER REGT.

1/4th (H) Bn. York & Lancaster Regt.

WAR DIARY

FOR

APRIL 1919.

1. 5. 19.

[signature]
w/Colonel.
Comndg. 1/4th (H) Bn. York & Lancaster Regt.

Army Form C. 2118.

WAR DIARY
INTELLIGENCE SUMMARY.
(Erase heading not required.)

Place	Date	Hour	Summary of Events and Information	Remarks and references to Appendices
COLOGNE	1-4-19		All Coy firing on Lackem range.	
	2d		⎫ Training –	
	3d		⎬ Recreational in afternoons –	
	4th		⎪ 6 hours work a day introduced –	
	5th		⎭ 8 hrs Education each week – All hostels placed out of bounds –	
	6th		Church Parade –	
	7th		Draft of 20 Officers and 430 ORs joined from 51st Welfords Regt –	
	8th		Re-organising of Coys – A & C Coys moved to Nussbaumer School –	
	9th		⎫ Training –	
	10th		⎬ Rate of exchange – 5 marks = 1/-d –	
	11th		⎭ 10 officers ns and 80 ORs demobilised –	
	12th		Route March through LONGERICH – 15 ORs demobilised	
	13th		Baths + 9 × Their Economy –	
			Divine Services – 3 officers and 10 ORs demobilised –	
	14th		Lt Col G.B. Vanhype took over command of battalion DSO	
			Lt Col D.S. Branson DSO MC left for demobilisation –	
	15th		Col. H.R. Hallam CMG DSO took over command of battalion –	
			All Coy and 7 ORs demobilised –	

WAR DIARY
or
INTELLIGENCE SUMMARY.
(Erase heading not required.)

Army Form C. 2118.

Place	Date	Hour	Summary of Events and Information	Remarks and references to Appendices
COLOGNE	16-4-19		Route March. 4 offs and 80 ORs demobilyst. 16 ORs discharged to res Lokomot.	
	17th		Musketry. Education. Drill.	
			1 man wounded on guard at artillery depot.	
	18th		Good Friday - Parade Service at 1100 hrs - 3 officers demobilysed -	
	19th		Batts - Interior Economy - Coy footballe in Blucher Park.	
	20th		Church Parade -	
	21st		Training	
	22nd		All Coys fired on range at Lachem - Major Rowden MC & 2/Lt Tony Dunsbligd -	
	23rd		Practice Defence Scheme - Lecture on "Venereal Disease" by RSM Tayleth.	
	24th		Firing on Lachem Range - 2 Officers and 30 ORs demobilysed -	
	25th		Lecture at 1000 hrs in Victoria Schule on "Health + Citizenship" by Dr Tyson -	
	26th		Batts - Interior Economy - C.O. inspected each Coy during the week -	
			Officers v NCO's footballe match abandoned before time owing to weather.	
	27th		Divine Service. 4 ORs demobilysed -	
	28th		Roll call at 2200 hrs in future. Last post at 2150 hrs - 2nd Army Divisional Races	
	29th		Half holiday for those attending Races - Bn ceremonial parade at 1100 hrs Col Kack	
	30th		Bde ceremonial parade at Lachem - Edward W. Offict 4th (Hallam My) Batt Y & Regt.

Col.

1/4th (H) Bn. York & Lancaster Regt.

WAR DIARY
FOR
MAY 1919

From the "operations" point of view
nothing whatever of interest has taken place

H. Headlam
Colonel.
Comndg. 1/4th (H) Bn. York & Lancaster Regt.

1. 6. 19.

Army Form C. 2118.

WAR DIARY
or
INTELLIGENCE SUMMARY
(Erase heading not required.)

Instructions regarding War Diaries and Intelligence Summaries are contained in F. S. Regs., Part II. and the Staff Manual respectively. Title pages will be prepared in manuscript.

Place	Date	Hour	Summary of Events and Information	Remarks and references to Appendices
COLOGNE	1.	5.10	ROUTE MARCH.	
	2.		MUSKETRY — TRAINING — Cleaning up for Guards to be inspected	
	3.		Inspection of billets etc by Commander in Chief	Drill + Tactics to develop to Regulat
			Battalion took part of Gen Guards. NEW MARKET NIDES ARTILLERY DEPOT ch	
	4.		No church service — voluntary services. Mr C of E = RC.	
	5.			
	6.			
	7.			
	8.			
	9.		Whole Battn on Bde Guard. 8 ORs knowledged — the officer	
			Essay competition on "The K 14 yrs 8th in Cologne" supervised the Exam	
			able to entertain. Prize by Lt Henry I.O. for best essay	
	10.		Battalion relieved from Bde Guards —	
	11.		School Parade. Low O.P. knowledges —	
			O.R.O. transferred from R.A.S.C. 2/Lieut R.E. Some	
	12.		Training — Lecture by the J. McCabe Subject "Story of Life in Persia"	
			Football cup to be taken when place.	
	13.		Batt. from to Kechin range.	
	14.		Baths. Tatting + attend at NEPTUNE BATH	
	15.		Bath. Route March. Short — Ist I was knee high snow Baniz etc.	
			— mew deaveloped.	
	16.		Took H Marshall Toch to Cologne. Baths, Cinemas, Lunch + Dinner	
			as the Magistrate based on tram afterwards by stay in motor car	

Army Form C. 2118.

Instructions regarding War Diaries and Intelligence Summaries are contained in F. S. Regs., Part II. and the Staff Manual respectively. Title pages will be prepared in manuscript.

WAR DIARY
or
~~INTELLIGENCE SUMMARY.~~
(Erase heading not required.)

Place	Date	Hour	Summary of Events and Information	Remarks and references to Appendices
Cologne	17-5-19		Rhine steamer allotted [illegible] 650 all ranks [illegible] at 8.30 [illegible] passed by BONN [illegible] landed at [illegible] march through COLOGNE back to camp	
			50 OR proceeded to RANGE on duty	
	18		[illegible]	
	19		Battalion [illegible] Bde Guard [illegible]	
	20			
	21		Scouts proceeded to the [illegible] near BRUCK for three days training under Scout Officer	
	22		1 OR demobilized.	
	23		~~[illegible] proceeded to RANGE [illegible]~~	
	24		124 OR proceeded to join 52nd Northumberland Fusiliers	
	25		[illegible] 46 OR proceeded to join 52 Northumberland Fusiliers	
	26		Relief of Quarters, bathing etc.	
	27		Training – inspection by Corps Commander of billets. 2 Coys on [illegible] Range	
	28		Inspection of [illegible] by [illegible] Officer. Sports in afternoon	
	29		1 Officer demobilized – 2 Coys on [illegible] Range	
	30		[illegible] for demobilization – Training –	
	31		HQ [illegible] on [illegible] Range	

H. J. Headlam Col.
Cmdg 4th (Hallamshire) Battn. Y. & L. Regt.

D. D. & L., London, E.C.
(10340) Wt W5300/P713 750,000 3/18 E 2688 Forms/C/2118/15

Army Form C. 2118.

WAR DIARY
INTELLIGENCE SUMMARY.
(Erase heading not required.)

Place	Date	Hour	Summary of Events and Information	Remarks and references to Appendices
Cologne	1-6-19 to 7-6-19		Battalion finding Brigade Guards.	
	8-6-19 to 17-6-19		Training.	
	18-6-19		Advance by march route to DUNWALD	
	19-6-19		Continue advance to HILGEN.	
HILGEN	20-6-19 to 29-6-19		Remained at Hilgen till signing of Peace	
	30-6-19		Return to old billets in COLOGNE by bus.	

Arthur ???
for Col.
Omg: 1/4 (H) Bn. Y. & L. Regt.

Army Form C. 2118.

WAR DIARY
INTELLIGENCE SUMMARY.
(Erase heading not required.)

Instructions regarding War Diaries and Intelligence Summaries are contained in F. S. Regs., Part II. and the Staff Manual respectively. Title pages will be prepared in manuscript.

Place	Date	Hour	Summary of Events and Information	Remarks and references to Appendices
Cologne	1/4/19 to 4/4/19		Training	
	5/4/19		Ceremonial Parade.	
	6/4/19		Battalion Guard of Honour for General GOURAUD – Cathedral Square, Cologne.	
	7/4/19		Practice Divisional Route	
	8/4/19 to 17/4/19		Training	
	18/4/19		VI Corps Review by the Army Council at MERKENICH	
	19/4/19		Battalion on Brigade Duties	
	20/4/19			
	25/4/19		Training	
	26/4/19		Battalion on a Rhine Trip from BONN to COBLENZ	
	29/4/19		Church Parade	
	30/4/19		Battalion took over Bucklendorf Area from 1/5 West York Regt.	

V.R.Dent LT. COL.

Army Form C. 2118.

PEACE
WAR DIARY
or
INTELLIGENCE SUMMARY.
(Erase heading not required.)

Instructions regarding War Diaries and Intelligence Summaries are contained in F. S. Regs., Part II. and the Staff Manual respectively. Title pages will be prepared in manuscript.

Place	Date	Hour	Summary of Events and Information	Remarks and references to Appendices
COLOGNE	1-7-19 to 31-7-19		Nothing to report.	

A. Ervington Capt
for
O.C. TR (H) Bn, Y. & L. Regt

M6945. Wt. W1422/M1160. 350,000. 12/16. D. D. & L. Forms/C./2118/14.

Army Form C. 2118.

WAR DIARY
or
INTELLIGENCE SUMMARY.
(Erase heading not required.)

Place	Date	Hour	Summary of Events and Information	Remarks and references to Appendices
Cologne	4th September 1919	12.30	Battalion remained in billets in Ehrenfeld area. Strength. 38 Officers 746 ORs - still to be demobilized, 350 ORs.	

V.T.M. Lt Col.
OC. 1/4 (H) Bn. Y. & L. Regt

WAR DIARY
or
INTELLIGENCE SUMMARY.
(Erase heading not required.)

Army Form C. 2118.

Place	Date	Hour	Summary of Events and Information	Remarks and references to Appendices
COLOGNE	1-10-19		Battalion in Villata in Nussbaumer Schule.	
	31-10-19		Strength 26 Officers 742 ors. Orders received to demobilise all Voluntarily attested men — Completed by 30% not, leaving 34 Officers 390 ors. Hand grenade found — Practices I + II of G.M.C. fired by all ranks	

M.S. Coxcroft Capt.
Comdg. 1/4 (R) Bn. Y. & L. Regt.

BEF

Northern Div
formerly 3 Div

3 Northern Inf Bde HQ.

1919 APR to 1919 JUNE

3 Northern B.E.

WAR DIARY
or
INTELLIGENCE SUMMARY

(Erase heading not required.)

Army Form C. 2118.

Page 1.
76th Infantry Brigade

VII 4 3

APRIL 1919.

Place	Date	Hour	Summary of Events and Information	Remarks and references to Appendices
COLOGNE. 59 HOHENSTAUFEN RING.	APRIL 1.		Brigade Y.M.C.A. "Durham House" opened near REIHL BARRACKS.	
"	2.		Lectures on Temperance.	
"	3.		Lecture postponed on "How the Navy assisted the Army to win the war" Lantern out of order.	
"	4.		52nd D.L.I. relieve the 51st D.L.I. on guard duties. Colonel B.J. Curling D.S.O. (60th K.R.R.C.) assumes command of 52nd D.L.I.	
"	5.		All Battns. training in guard duties.	
"	6.		Colonel Frizell D.S.O. M.C. assumes command of the 52nd D.K.O.Y.L.I.	
"	7.		Machine Gun Battn. accomodated in REIHL BARRACKS. Captn. Lumley relieves Captn. Chipperfield M.C. as Brigade Major.	
"	8.		Historical lecture by Professor Oman.	
"	9.		Brigade concentrated in Northern portion of BARRACKS. 53rd Battn. D.L.I. arrive to reinforce the Brigade.	
"	10.		76th T.M.B. formed up in the Square of Gen. McGuiness Smith M.C. Brigade assemble N of the Barracks & practice ceremonial drill for victory.	

Army Form C. 2118.

WAR DIARY
INTELLIGENCE SUMMARY
(Erase heading not required.)

APRIL 1919. Page 11. 16th Infantry Brigade

Place	Date April	Hour	Summary of Events and Information	Remarks and references to Appendices
COLOGNE	11.		Second rehearsal for Brigade parade.	
59 Wahringerstr Pg.	12.		Brigade ceremonial parade. Army Commander presents medals to U.S.A. officers.	
"	13.		Div. cinema in RIEHL BARRACKS.	
"	14.			
"	15.		Separation of Brigade transport.	
"	16.		Separation of cook house. Brigade H.Q. awarded 2nd Prize	
"	17.		51st Batt. D.L.I. third in Class IV.	
"	18.		Colonel Beaumont of the South Staffordshire Regt assumes command of the 20th D.L.S.	
"	19.		51st D.L.S. relieve the 52nd D.L.S. on guard.	
"	20.		Special services in the Barracks for all troops.	
"	21. 22.		Battns off guard do usual training programme. Very fine weather	

WAR DIARY / INTELLIGENCE SUMMARY

Army Form C. 2118.

Page III.

16th Infantry Brigade

APRIL 1919

Place	Date	Hour	Summary of Events and Information	Remarks and references to Appendices
COLOGNE Hohenzollern Ring	23		Three lectures by Rev G.H. Neaslett B.A. on Venereal Disease illustrated by Lantern Slides.	
"	24		Lecture on the navy by Commander Viscount Broome R.N. also with Lantern Slides. Very wet day training greatly handicapped.	
"	25			
"	26		Lecture with lantern slides by Mr Mastiman Smith "Alsace Lorraine".	
"	27		Brigade parade (all available men) rehearsal for Army Cmdrs inspection.	
"	28		Musketry course started on the range at REIHL.	
"	29		Capt. Fenzell appointed D.A.Q.M.G. N. Div. Capt. Bright acting as Staff Captn.	
"	30			

Total number demobilized during the month.
35 Officers 166 O.R's.

For O.C. Cmdg. 3rd rd North 16 Bgde

Army Form C. 2118.

WAR DIARY   ORIGINAL.

or

INTELLIGENCE SUMMARY.

(Erase heading not required.)

Instructions regarding War Diaries and Intelligence Summaries are contained in F. S. Regs., Part II. and the Staff Manual respectively. Title pages will be prepared in manuscript.

MAY 1919.

Place	Date	Hour	Summary of Events and Information	Remarks and references to Appendices
COLOGNE.	1st.		Weather rainy all day. 20th. Bn. Durham L.I. relieved 51st. Bn. Durham L.I. on COLOGNE Guards	
	2nd.		Weather - Very heavy showers fell during the afternoon and evening.	
	3rd.		Weather fine but dull. Commander in Chief inspected the quarters of all the Units in the Brigade in RIEHL Barracks.	
	4th.		Weather fine. 52nd. Bn. Durham L.I. relieved 20th. Bn. Durham L.I. on COLOGNE Guards.	
	5th.		Weather fine. The Brigade (less 52nd. Bn. Durham L.I.) took part in the Divisional Rehearsal Parade at MERHEIM.	
	6th.		Weather fine, with fresh wind.	
	7th.		Weather fine.	
	8th.		Weather fine. H.R.H. The Duke of Connaught K.G. etc., inspected the Northern Division on EXERCIXIER PLATZ MERHEIM. The Brigade was composed of the 20th. Bn. Durham L.I. 51st. Bn. Durham L.I. and the 5th Bn. Durham L.I. (Pioneers) on this occasion, the 52nd. Bn. Durham L.I. being on COLOGNE Guards and therefore not available.	
	9th.		Weather fine. 51st. Bn. Durham L.I. relieved 52nd. Bn. Durham L.I. on COLOGNE Guards.	
	10th.		Weather fine - Cloudy during evening. Lecture in Theatre RIEHL Barracks on the "United States of America" by Mr Sandon Perkins. In the evening Brigade Boxing Competition, in the Brigade Boxing Hall, RIEHL Barracks.	
	11th.		Weather fine during morning. Short thunderstorm during afternoon. Lecture in Theatre RIEHL Barracks on "War Savings" by Major Rayner D.S.O.	
	12th.		Weather fine.	
	13th.		Weather fine. Lecture in Theatre RIEHL Barracks on the "Panama Canal" by Mr. Sexon Mills.	

Army Form C. 2118.

WAR DIARY
or
INTELLIGENCE SUMMARY.   ORIGINAL.
(Erase heading not required.)

Instructions regarding War Diaries and Intelligence Summaries are contained in F. S. Regs., Part II. and the Staff Manual respectively. Title pages will be prepared in manuscript.

Place	Date	Hour	Summary of Events and Information	Remarks and references to Appendices
COLOGNE.	14th		Weather fine. Brigadier General W.G. BRAITHWAITE C.B., C.M.G., D.S.O., took over the Command of the Brigade from Brigadier General F.E. METCALFE C.M.G., D.S.O., who was ordered to report to the War Office.	
	15th.		Weather fine. Inspection of Transport of all Btns. by the Brigade Commander.	
	16th.		Weather fine. Marshal FOCH visited COLOGNE and the Brigade lined the route along the left bank of the RHINE from the NEU Bridge to the Landing Stage. 20th. Bn. Durham L.I. relieved the 51st. Bn. Durham L.I. on the COLOGNE guards.	
	17th.		Weather fine. Lecture in the Brigade Lecture Hall RIEHL Barracks by Mr Edgar BELLINGHAM on "HANNOVER".	
	18th.		Weather fine. All Battalions attended Divine Service in the morning.	
	19th.		Weather fine. Brigadier General F.E. METCALFE C.M.G. D.S.O. left for England. Lecture in the Brigade Lecture Hall RIEHL Barracks by Brigadier-General F.G. Stone C.M.G. on "Prussias Part in the Seven Years War"	
	20th.		Weather fine. The Brigade Commander inspected the 51st Bn. Durham L.I. and addressed all Officers.	
	23rd.		Weather fine. Northern Division letter G.8874 containing instructions for Forward Move in the eventuality of the Germans refusing to sign the Peace Terms received. 52nd. Bn. Durham L.I. relieved 20th. Bn. Durham L.I. on COLOGNE Guards.	
	25th.		Weather fine during day Showery at night. 3rd Northern Brigade 3493/issued Copy attached.	
	26th.		Weather fine. Inspection of Barracks by the Corps Commander. 3rd Northern Brigade letter A/178/5 issued (Copy attached)	
	27th.		Weather fine. Lecture in the Brigade Lecture Hall RIEHL Barracks on "Constantinople" by the Revd. J.A. DOUGLAS.	

Army Form C. 2118.

WAR DIARY
or
INTELLIGENCE SUMMARY.
(Erase heading not required.)

Instructions regarding War Diaries and Intelligence Summaries are contained in F. S. Regs., Part II. and the Staff Manual respectively. Title pages will be prepared in manuscript.

Place	Date	Hour	Summary of Events and Information	Remarks and references to Appendices
COLOGNE.	28th.		Weather fine. Inspection of 16" to" Battery Billets	
	29th.		Weather fine. 3rd Northern Brigade B.3493/1 issued (Copy attached).	
	30th.		Weather fine. 3rd. Northern Brigade B.3493/2 issued. 51st. Bn. Durham L.I. relieved 52nd. Bn. Durham L.I. on Cologne Guards.	

W.G. Braithwaite
Brigadier General,
Commanding 3rd Northern Brigade.

7th June 1919.

SECRET.

3rd Northern Brigade No. B.3493.

Ref, Maps 1/200000,
Sheets HANNOVER,
MUNSTER,
COLOGNE,
CASSELL.

Instructions for Advance,
No. 1.

1. Under certain eventualities it may be necessary for the Allied Armies to seize as rapidly as possible the RUHR basin, and to secure the Railway Communications, which are essential for a further advance, North Eastwards.

2. In seizing the Railways our object is to ensure that the German rolling stock on the lines is not evacuated on front of us and that the German personnel complete, remain at their posts, and work the Railways for us. The main Railway Communication runs :-

   COLOGNE - OHLIGS - ELBERFELD - HAGEN - UNNA -

   Important subsidiary lines are :-

   ALTENA - PLETTENBURG - KIRCHMONDEN - KROMBACH - SIEGEN and SCHWERTE - ARNSBERG - HESCHEDE.

3. The VI Corps is to advance on a two Division front, with the London Division on the right on a one Brigade front, and the Northern Division on the left on a two Brigade front on the first day, the 1st Northern Brigade being on the right, and the 3rd Northern Brigade on the left. On the second day the Northern Division is to advance on a one Brigade front, this Brigade will be the 3rd Northern. The Southern Division of the II Corps will be on the left of the Northern Division.

4. The earliest date on which the advance will be ordered (called "J" day hereinafter) will be May 26th.

5. The 3rd Northern Brigade Group will advance as detailed in March table, attached.

(- 1 -)

6. The composition of the 3rd Northern Brigade Group will be as under
   3rd Northern Infantry Brigade.
   One Squadron Dragoons.
   "G" Battery R.H.A.
   One Section M.G. Squadron.
   450th Field Company R.E.
   One Section 7th Field Ambulance.
   Detachment VI Corps Cyclists (20 strong).
   "D" Coy. 3rd M.G. Battalion.
   One 18 pdr. in Lorry.
   No.28 Siege Battery R.G.A. (Howitzer Lorry drawn.)

7. The advance on "J" day will be covered by the Mounted Troops. The Mounted Troops will be able to advance about 15 miles on this day, but the advance will be continued by the remainder of the Brigade Group in lorries and busses as rapidly as possible to the localities given in the March Table.

8. On "J" plus 1 day the Brigade Group will again push on rapidly to the posts mentioned in the March Table. The Mounted Troops following in rear on this and succeeding days until they overtake the troops carried in busses and lorries.

9. (a) On "J" day the London Division will occupy ATTENDORN and the Southern Division ELSENFELD. The 1st Northern Brigade will occupy ALTENA and LUDENSCHEID

   (b) On "J" plus 1 day the London Division will continue to advance to ARNSBERG.

10. When the advance is continued on "J" plus one day, the 3rd Northern Brigade is required to leave troops in HAGEN, SCHWERTE and DELLWIG. The Southern Division will relieve those left in HAGEN on "J" plus two days, those in SCHWERTE on "J" plus 3 days and those in DELLWIG on "J" plus 4 days.

11. Instructions will be issued later as to the attitude to be adopted in regard to the German Civil Population.

12. The 12th Squadron R.A.F. will provide Aeroplanes to reconoitre the country immediately on our front and to bring back information of the progress of the advance. These aeroplanes will be

provided with Wireless Telegraphy to communicate to Brigade Headquarters.

13. Battalions will move forward complete in personnel etc, as per War Establishment Part VII.

14. Signalling instructions are contained in appendix "A" attached. Separate Administrative instructions are being issued by the Staff Captain.

15. All Guards now detailed by the Brigade for duty in Cologne will be relieved by the 2nd Brigade, Light Division on "J" Minus Two day.

16. Acknowledge.

                                              Captain,
                          Brigade Major, 3rd Northern Brigade.

Distribution :-

No.		
1.	General Officer Commanding,	
2.	O. C., 20th Bn. D. L. I.	
3.	51st Bn. D. L. I.	
4.	52nd Bn. D. L. I.	
5.	76th T. M. B.	
6.	3rd M. G. Battn.	
7.	458th Field Coy. R. E.	
8.	7th Field Ambulance,	
9.	No. 2 Coy. Train,	
10.)	Northern Division,	
11.)		
12.	"G" Battery R. H. A.)	Through Cavalry
13.	Composite Dragoon Squadron,)	Division.
14.	No. 226 Seige Battery R. G. A.	
15.	Cavalry M. G. Squadron, (through Cav. Division)	
16.	VI Corps Cyclists,	
17.	C. R. A. Northern Division,	
18.	Brigade Signal Officer,	
19.	Staff Captain,	
20.)	War Diary,	
21.)		
22.	File.	

MARCH TABLE

Serial No.	Date.	Unit.	Destination.	Route.	Remarks.
1.	J" - 1 day.	"G" Battery R.H.A.	WEST GERGHEM	MUNKEM BRIDGE	
2.	do	Dragoon Squadron and One Section R. G. Squadron	do	ODRINGEN	
3.	do	1st Northern Infty. Bde. Group	do	SOHNECCEN	In motor buses and lorries
4.	do	Transport 3rd Northern Infty. Bde. Group	TORRINGHEM	MUNKEM BRIDGE	3rd N. G. Bde. march with the column and act as escort.
5.	"J" day.	3rd Northern Infty. Bde. Group.	SCHWEIZ and HAGEN	SCHWEIZ and HAGEN	In motor buses etc. Position of mounted troops on this night will be modified later.
6.	do	Transport, 1st Northern Infty. Bde. Group.	DABRINGHEM	OSTHEN	
7.	"J" x 1 day.	1st Northern Infty. Bde. Group.	SCOSS and GERT	ISRLHOM	In motor buses etc. Position of mounted troops on this night will be modified later.
8.	do	2nd Northern Infantry Bde. Group.	BUCKENHAGEN		
9.	"J" x 2 day.	do	OCKLINGHSE and HALVEM.		
10.	"J" x 3 day.		ALTENA.	LUDENSCHEID	
11.	"J" x 4 day.		ERNDSE	FROMBERG	

Appendix "A" to accompany 3rd Northern Brigade B. 3493.

SIGNAL ARRANGEMENTS.

The following means of communication are available in case of advance into Germany.

1. Telegraph & Telephone.
2. Visual.
3. Wireless.
4. Contact Aeroplane.
5. Cyclists and Despatch Riders.

1. TELEGRAPH & TELEPHONE.

Owing to the rapid advance on the first two or three days, it may not be possible to obtain communication by telegraph or telephone. Under no circumstances are Battalion Signallers to interfere with the permanent routes.

A signaller, experienced in permanent routes, will be attached to the advanced guard and he only will be responsible for tapping into the permanent routes in order to obtain communication with the main body. This signaller will be responsible for disconnecting lines in use in front of him (i.e. towards the enemy), in order to prevent overhearing. All such disconnections must be made good before a further advance is undertaken.

2. VISUAL.

Every effort must be made by Units to get into touch with Brigade by Visual.

3. WIRELESS.

There will be Wireless communication between Brigade Hqrs. and Division and it is hoped to obtain a Wireless set for the advanced guard. Calls will be notified later. The 12th Squadron R.A.F. have sent a W/T set, with personnel, to the Brigade for communication with contact aeroplanes.

Attention of all Officers is drawn to 3rd Northern Brigade letters, B.3423 dated 2nd May 1919, and B.3423/2 dated 24/5/19 with reference to endorsing all messages "I.B.W. Clear" or "I.B.W. Cypher".

4. CONTACT AEROPLANES.

Battalions will only make use of the Popham Panels on receipt of special orders to do so, this Order also applies to the advanced guard. As laid down in letter S.20 dated 23/5/19. Battalions will however take their ground signalling equipment with them. If the Popham Panel is used the following station calls will come into force.

Bde Headquarters.	C N
Advanced Guard.	C.N.A.
20th. D.L.I.	B.K.D.
21st. D.L.I.	M.A.D.
22nd. D.L.I.	M.B.B.

The Brigade Headquarters will put out their Popham Panel at each objective or halt.

1.

5. CYCLE ORDERLIES AND DESPATCH RIDERS.

These must be made use of to the fullest extent, a during a rapid advance when long distances are being covered daily this means of communication is the only really possible one.

All Units should pay special attention to informing all ranks before dismissing a parade on arriving in Billets, as to the whereabouts of Units and Formations Headquarters, with a view to all troops being able to assist Despatch Riders and Cycle Orderlies.

The attention of all Units is drawn to S.S. 191 Chapter III "Communication during Open Warfare.

SECRET

War Diary

3rd NORTHERN BRIGADE.

3rd N. Bde.
A/178/5.

Administrative Instructions No. 1 to accompany Instructions for Advance No. 1. (3rd Northern Brigade No. B. 3495).

1. PRESENT BILLETS.

The accomodation now occupied by the Brigade in "O" Block, RIEHL BARRACKS will be taken over by 2nd Brigade of the Light Division on our departure. O. C. Units will ensure that their portion of the buildings and Horse Lines are handed over in a clean and sanitary condition. Each Unit will obtain a Certificate to this effect from their relieving Unit and forward to this office as early as possible.

2. REAR PARTIES.

Rear Parties will be left behind at RIEHL BARRACKS as follows:-

```
20th Bn. Durham L.I.      1 Officer and 18 O.R.
51st  "     "    "        1    "     "  18  "
52nd  "     "    "        1    "     "  15  "
Brigade Headquarters,     -              7  "    (including 1 Sgt)
438 Field Coy.            -           1 N.C.O. and 3 men.
         Total 3 Officers and 63 Other Ranks.
```

The whole of the above personnel will be composed of Light Duty and Unfit men, and will be under the command of MAJOR O.B. NICHOLS, M.C., O.C. NORTHERN DIVISION RECEPTION CAMP. They will be accomodated in Barrack Rooms to be allotted by O.C. 52nd Bn. Durham L.I. Two days rations will be left behind for above personnel.

Rear Parties will be attached to the Unit of the 2nd Brigade Light Division taking over from 52nd Bn. Durham L.I. for Rations, Accomodation and Discipline from the date of relief.

3. SURPLUS STORES AND BLANKETS.

The three Battalions of the Brigade, Brigade Headquarters and 438 Field Coy., R.E., are allotted Cellars under the Orderly Room and Sergeants Mess of the 52nd Bn. Durham L.I., Block "O", RIEHL BARRACKS for the storage of all Blankets, Officers Baggage, Mens' Kit Bags, Educational and Recreational Training Stores, Office Equipment, all surplus stores in excess of authorised establishment.

All Blankets will be rolled in bundles of ten and labelled.
All Stores must be clearly labelled and an Inventory taken.
Units will arrange to send a copy of the Inventory to Brigade Headquarters as early as possible after Stores and Blankets have been dumped, together with approximate weight and cubic capacity of articles dumped. This will facilitate removal in due course.

Doors of Cellars will be locked and keys retained by the Officers in charge of Rear Parties.

A Guard composed of personnel of Units Rear Parties under the command of an officer will be responsible for the safe custody of all Stores left behind.

4. TRANSPORT.
   a. MOTOR LORRIES OR BUSES.   OR BUSSES
         All personnel will be taken forward on Lorries.
   Lewis Guns and Magazines as detailed in para 5 (d),
   necessary stationery, signal equipment as detailed in para 12,
   Medical Equipment (Para 9) will be conveyed in Lorries detailed
   for personnel. The maximum number of all ranks per Battalion who
   will be conveyed in Lorries is 650. Any surplus to these numbers
   will march with First Line Transport.

                PROVISIONAL ALLOTMENT OF LORRIES OR BUSES.

                            For personnel. For Stores. For Supplies.

   20th Bn. Durham L.I.   36
   21st "   "   "   24
   22nd "   "   "   26
   Detachment VI Corps
         Cyclists.   4   7
   D Coy. 3rd Bn. M.G.C.   7   1
   7th Field Ambulance.   4
   456 Field Coy., R.E.   7   1
   76th T.M.Battery.   2
   Brigade Headquarters.   3   3
   Spare Lorries   3

         Lorries will park in the Square of "C" Block,
   RIMHL BARRACKS on evening of J – 2 day. All personnel of
   Battalions, D Coy., M.G.C, 7th Field Ambulance, 456 Field Coy.,
   R.E., 76th T.M.Battery and Brigade Headquarters will embus in
   this Square.

         Supply Lorries and Store Lorries will be loaded
   at Refilling Point, Headquarters 456 Field Coy., R.E. and Brigade
   Headquarters and will return to the Square of "C" Block to join
   remainder of Lorries of their Units. Lorries will remain with
   units throughout the whole move.

   b. HORSE TRANSPORT.
         All First Line Transport and Baggage Wagons
   under command of Lieut. FOWLER, 22nd Bn. Durham L.I. will move
   on J – 1 day and subsequent days and with 3rd Bn. M.G.Corps as
   shown on March Table issued with instructions No. 1.
         Forage for consumption on day of move will be
   carried on First Line Transport and for the following day on
   the Supply Wagon accompanying the Column.

5. DRESS.
         Full Marching Order. Caps will be worn and Steel
   Helmets carried on the back of the Pack under the straps. Each
   man will be in possession of three pairs of Socks (1 on the man
   and 2 in the Pack). Arrangements have been made for a sufficient
   number to complete this scale to be issued from Divisional
   Laundry.
         To give the utmost freedom of action in case troops
   are required to operate out of the Lorry, all Packs will be
   removed and stacked in the front of the interior of the Lorry.

6. AMMUNITION AND GRENADES.
         (a) 120 rounds of S.A.A. will be carried on the man.
         (b) 24 rounds of P.W.A. will be carried by all
   Officers and men armed with Revolvers.
         (c) 100 rounds S.A.A. per man will be carried as
   Brigade Reserve in special Lorries which will accompany the
   Brigade Column. 1 box of Grenades will be carried on each
   Lorry conveying personnel.

         (d) All Lewis Guns in canvas carriers, 44 filled
   Drums per gun and 1 spare part bag per gun will be carried on
   the Lorries conveying the Lewis Gun personnel of Units.

5. AMMUNITION AND GRENADES (continued).

(e) O.C. 76th T.M. Battery will arrange to take 8 rounds 3" Stokes Ammunition per Gun (4 Guns only to be taken) in Lorries conveying his personnel. 99 rounds will be carried in Brigade Reserve.

7. WATER.

Four Water Lorries will travel with the Brigade Column.
Os. C. Units will ensure that all Water Bottles are full before starting each day's journey and that the water is fit for drinking. Men should be told to drink as little as possible during the day. Any spare water tins should be filled and carried as a reserve supply on the Lorries. This supply should not be used unless absolutely necessary and then only by orders of the O.C. concerned.

8. RATIONS.

All ranks will carry the unexpended portion of the day's rations in the Haversack each day, in addition to their Iron Ration. Rations for consumption the following day will be conveyed in Supply Lorries. Refilling Point at each day's destination will be notified to all Units in due course.
Iron Rations now in possession of Units in bulk will not be distributed until further notice. Iron Rations will not be consumed without permission of the Brigade Commander.

9. MEDICAL.

All ranks must be in possession of a Field Dressing.
As it is probable that the later stages of the Advance may have to be done by long marches particular care should be taken to prevent sore feet. Men should wash their feet as often as possible and Foot inspections should be held at the end of each day's march.
Two Medical Panniers per Battalion will be taken on Lorries conveying personnel.

10. BILLETS ON J - 1 DAY.

All troops will be accommodated along the Main LENNEP - WERMELSKIRCHEN Road with the head of the Column at the Neutral Zone Barrier at BORN. Units will be billeted as far as possible in the order of march for the following day, viz:-

PROTECTIVE MOUNTED TROOPS UNTIL END OF J DAY.

1 Squadron Dragoons.
"G" Battery, R.H.A.
One Section MACHINE GUN SQUADRON.

ADVANCED GUARD.

2 Sections "D" Coy., 3rd Bn. M. G. Corps.
Detachment of Cyclists.
2 Sections 458 Field Coy., R.E.
76th Light Trench Mortar Battery.
Personnel of 18 pounder in Lorry to be found by 75th Bde. R.F.A.
52nd Bn. Durham L.I.

MAIN BODY.

2 Sections "D" Coy. 3rd Bn. M.G. Corps.
1 Coy. 20th Bn. Durham L.I.
Brigade Headquarters.
Signal Section, Brigade Headquarters.
20th Bn. Durham L.I. (less 1 Coy).
458 Field Coy., R.E. (less 2 Sections).
51st Bn. Durham L.I. (less 1 Coy).

10. BILLETS ON J - 1 DAY (continued).

    MAIN BODY (continued).

        Personnel of Brigade Ammunition Lorries.
        "B" Section, 7th Field Ambulance (Two Medical Officers,
            3 Motor Ambulances and 1 Motor Cyclist).
        Personnel of Supply Lorries.

    REAR GUARD.

        2 Platoons, 51st Bn. Durham L.I.
        Personnel of 22c Siege Battery, R.G.A. and
        Escort 2 Platoons, 51st Bn. Durham L.I.

        A portion of above will be in billets and remainder will Bivouac in the Fields at the side of the Road.

11. BILLETTING PARTIES.

    of 1 Officer and 4 O.R. per Battalion and 1 Officer and 2 O.R. of all other units will meet the Staff Captain at WEMMELSKIRCHEN CHURCH at 09.00 hours on J - 1 day.
    Billeting Parties of all units starting from RIEHL BARRACKS will be conveyed in a Lorry which will leave "C" Block, RIEHL BARRACKS at 08.30 hours on that day. Each Billeting Party should, if possible, include one German speaking Officer or man.
    Billeting arrangements for the remainder of the stages of the march will be issued day by day. Billeting parties detailed for the first day should be made available for the whole of the move.

12. COOKING UTENSILS.

    All available Camp Kettles will be carried in Lorries conveying personnel of Units.

13. SIGNAL EQUIPMENT TO BE CARRIED ON LORRIES.

    Each Battalion will take on its Lorries one Signal Pannier, containing all ringing telephones in their possession, One 4 x 3 Buzzer Unit, One D 3 Telephone, Popham Panel, Ground Sign and Strips, also supply of enamel wire. Any D 3 wire which Battalions may possess must also be taken on the lorries. At least 50% of the Signal flags available will be distributed amongst Battalion Headquarter and Company Signallers. One Lucas Lamp and One D 3 (if available) will be carried by Signallers : Battalion Headquarters and each Company. Telescopes, Field Glasses and Prismatic Compasses will be distributed accordingly.

14. ACCIDENTS TO MOTOR LORRIES.

    In the event of a Motor Lorry breaking down, this is on no account to hinder the progress of the remainder of the Column. The broken down vehicle must be cleared out of the way at once and its occupants placed in empty reserve Lorries following with the Rear Guard.

    15. The two Platoons of 51st Bn. Durham L.I. who are acting as escort to the 22c Siege Battery, R.G.A. and the two Platoons forming the Rear Guard will go to the head of the column at BORN and provide the outposts.

16. All units will provide guards for their own Lorries and for their Billets or BIVOUACS.

[signature]
Captain,
Staff Captain, 3rd Northern Brigade.

Distribution:-

No. 1. General Officer Commanding.
 2. O.C. 20th Bn. Durham L.I.
 3. O.C. 51st Bn. Durham L.I.
 4. O.C. 52nd Bn. Durham L.I.
 5. O.C. 76th T.M. Battery.
 6. O.C. 3rd Bn. M.G. Corps.
 7. O.C. 458th Field Coy., R.E.
 8. O.C. 7th Field Ambulance.
 9. O.C. No. 2 Coy. N. Div. Train.
 10.)
 11.) Northern Division.
 12. "G" Battery, R.H.A.   ) Through Cavalry
 13. Composite Dragoon Squadron) Division.
 14. No. 232 Siege Battery, R.G.A.
 15. Cavalry M.G. Squadron (through Cavalry Division).
 16. VI Corps Cyclists.
 17. C.R.A., Northern Division.
 18. Brigade Signal Officer.
 19. Staff Captain.
 20.)
 21.) War Diary.
 22. File.

S E C R E T.

3rd. Northern Brigade B.3493/1.

Reference Map : Sheet COLOGNE. 1/200,000.

1. Herewith March Table for "J" day which cancels Serial Numbers 1, 2 and 3 of March Table issued with 3rd. Northern Brigade B.3493 dated May 25th.

2. Transport and surplus personnel of 3rd. Northern Infantry Brigade Group will move to TURINGERT on "J" day under orders of O.C. 3rd. M.G. Battalion.

3. Station Call for Brigade Headquarters will be W.O. and not O.N. as stated in para. 4 of Appendix "A" issued with B.3493 dated May 25th.

4. Brigade Headquarters will close at present location in COLOGNE at 11.30 hours on "J" day, and open at the CHATEAU near Bridge under Railway 200 yards from WERMELSKIRCHEN Station on arrival.

During the march Brigade Report Centre will be at the head of the main lorry column.

5. ACKNOWLEDGE.

[signature]
Captain,
Brigade Major, 3rd. Northern Brigade.

29th May 1919.

Distribution :-

1. G.O.C.
2. O.C. 20th. B. Durham L.I.
3. 21st. B. Durham L.I.
4. 22nd. Bn. Durham L.I.
5. 76th. F.A. Battery.
6. 3rd. M.G. Battn.
7. 438 Field Company R.E.
8. 7th. Field Ambulance.
9. No. 2 Coy. Train.
10.)
11.) Northern Division.
12. 1st Northern Brigade
13. 2nd. Northern Brigade.
14. "G" Battery R.H.A.
15. Composite Dragoon Squadron) Through Cavalry Division.
16. 225 Siege Battery R.G.A.
17. Cavalry M.G. Squadron. (Through Cavalry Division)
18. VI Corps Cyclists.
19. C.R.A. Northern Division.
20. Brigade Signal Officer.
21. Staff Captain.
22. Brigade Transport Officer.
23.)
24.) War Diary.
25. File.

MARCH TABLE FOR J - 1 DAY.

Serial No.	Date.	Unit.	Starting Point.	Times at which head will pass S.P.	Destination.	Route.	Remarks.
1.	J - 1 day.	Composite Squadron Dragoons & 1 section M.G. Squadron.	Road Junction ½ ml. S. of second M in MULHEIM (just E. of MULHEIM BRGE.)	07.40 hr.	WERMELSKIRCHEN	SCHLEBUSCH	Units mentioned in Serial No.1&2 will march under C.O. "G" Bty. R.H.A. and will pass End. Northern Inf Bde. on road about 2½ miles N.E. of SCHLEBUSCH during halt which this Brigade will make for the purpose between 09.30 & 10.30 hours.
2.	do	"G" Battery R.H.A.	do	07.45. hr.	do	do	
3.	do	3rd. Northern Inf.Bde. Grp. in following Order of March. Brigade Headquarters. Signal Section. 1 Coy. 51st. D.L.I. 2 Sections D.Coy.3rd.M.G.Bn. 2 Sect.438 Field Coy. R.E. 52nd. D.L.I. 76th. T.M. Battery. 18 pdr. on lorry. D.Coy.3rd.M.G.Bn. (less 2 sects.) 20th. D.L.I. 438 Field Coy.R.E.(less 2 sects.) 51st. D.L.I.(less 1 Coy.) Bde. Ammunition Lorries. Supply lorries. Section 7th. Field Ambulance	Main entrance "C" Block RHINE Barracks.	12.30. hr	do	RHEIN STR. FLORA STR. Road along bank of the Rhine, KÖLN-MULHEIM BRGE. Road Junction ½ ml. S. of second M in MULHEIM.	Gaps of 30 yards will be maintained between each section of 12 lorries.
4.	do	236 Siege Battery R.G.A.	Road Junction ½ ml. S.E. of second M in DUNWALD.	14.15. hr	do	SCHLEBUSCH.	

3rd. Northern Bde. B3493/2.

    3rd. Northern Brigade letter B,3493/1 dated May 29th is cancelled, and the attached letter B.3493/2 in which amendments notified in G. 489 have been embodied is substituted.

[signature]
Captain,
Brigade Major, 3rd. Northern Brigade,

30/5/19.

SECRET.

3rd. Northern Bde.B.3493/2.

Reference Map : Sheet COLOGNE 1/200,000.

1. Herewith March Table for J - 1 day which cancels Serial Numbers 1, 2 and 3 of March Table issued with 3rd Northern Brigade B.3493 dated May 25th.

2. Transport and surplus personnel of 3rd Northern Infantry Brigade Group will move to TORRINGERT on J - 1 day under orders of 3rd M.G. Battalion.

3. Station Call for Brigade Headquarters will be W.D. and not C.N. as stated in para. 4 of Appendix "A" issued with B.3493 dated May 25th.

4. Brigade Headquarters will close at present location in COLOGNE at 11.30 hours on J - 1 day, and open at the CHATEAU near Bridge under Railway 200 yards from WERMELSKIRCHEN Station on arrival.

During the march Brigade Report Centre will be at the head of the main lorry column.

5. ACKNOWLEDGE.

Captain,
Brigade Major, 3rd Northern Brigade.

30/5/19.

Distribution.

1. G.O.C.
2. O.C. 20th. Bn. Durham L.I.
3. O.C. 51st.   "   "   "
4. O.C. 52nd.   "   "   "
5. O.C. 76th. T.M. Battery.
6. 3rd. M.G. Battalion.
7. O.C. 438 Field Company R.E.
8. O.C. 7th. Field Ambulance.
9. O.C. No. 2 Coy. Northern Div. Train.
10.)
11.) Northern Division.
12. 1st Northern Inf. Brigade.
13. 2nd. Northern Inf. Brigade.
14. "G" Battery R.H.A.   ) Through
15. Composite Dragoon Squadron) Cavalry
16. Cavalry M.G. Squadron.   ) Division.
17. 226 Siege Battery R.G.A.
18. VI Corps Cyclists.
19. C.R.A. Northern Division.
20. 12th. Squadron R.A.F.
21. Brigade Signal Officer.
22. Staff Captain.
23. Brigade Transport Officer.
24.)
25.) War Diary.
26. File.

MARCH TABLE FOR J - 1 DAY.

Serial No	Date.	Unit.	Starting Point.	Times at which head will pass S.P.	Destination.	Route.	Remarks.
1.	J - 1 day.	Composite Squadron Dragoons and one section M.G. Squadron.	Road junction ½ ml. S of second M in MULHEIM (just S. of MULHEIM BRIDGE)	07.40 hr.	MERHEISKIRCHEN	SCHLEBUSCH	Units mentioned in serial No.1&2 will march under O.C. J Bty.R.H.A. and will pass 2nd Northern Inf.Bde.on road about 2½ mls.N. of SCHLEBUSCH during which this Bde.will halt this Bde. for the purpose between 07.50 & 10.30 hours.
2.	do	"J" Battery R.H.A.	do	07.43 hr.	do	do	
3.	do	3rd. Northern Inf.Bde.Grp. In following order of march. 1 Coy. 51st. D.L.I. 2 Sec. D Coy. 3rd. M.G.Bn. Detch.VI Corps Cyc. 2 Sec. 428 Field Coy. R.E. 76th. M. Battery. 18 pdr. on lorry. 52nd. M.G.I. D Coy M.G.Bn.(less 2 secs.) 1 Coy. 20th. D.L.I. Brigade Headquarters. Signal section. 20th. D.L.I.(less 1 Coy) 438 Field Coy.R.E.(less 2 sects) 51st. D.L.I. (less 1 Coy). Ammunition lorries. 1 Sec. 7th. Field Ambulance. Supply lorries.	Main entrance "J" Block RLMH Barracks.	12.30 hr.	do	RIEHIER KEM- Road along bank of the Rhine, MUEHIM-HOHE.XM BDGE. Road junction ½ ml. S. of second M in MULHEIM.	Gaps of 50 yds. will be maintained between each sect. of 12 lorries.
4.	30	526 Siege Battery R.G.A.	Road junction ½ ml. S.E. of second D in MUHHEIM	14.15 hr.	do	SCHLEBUSCH.	

Appendix 3 to War Diary

<u>SECRET.</u> G.100/2/1.

To accompany 1st Northern Brigade Instructions No. 1.

NOTES on probable action of 1st Northern Brigade in advance on J day.
----

1.   are
The following notes on the present intention of the Brigadier Commanding 1st Northern Brigade for the advance of the Brigade Group on J day.

2.   <u>POSITION OF BRIGADE GROUP ON NIGHT J - 1/J.</u>

  (a) Mounted Troops at DELLING with patrols in the perimeter from LINDLAR to WIPPERFELD.
  (b) Brigade Headquarters KURTEN.
  (c) Remainder of Brigade along the road from road junction just South of N in KURTEN to DURSCHEID.

3.   <u>MOUNTED TROOPS.</u>

On J - 1 evening the O.C. Hussars Squadron will detail 1 Troop and O.C.Cyclist Detachment 1 section to report Brigade Headquarters for duty as Orderlies.
The Hussars Squadron (less 1 Troop), Machine Gun Squadron, Detachment Cyclists (less 1 section) will in future be known as the "Mounted Troops" and will be under the command of the Officer commanding Hussar Squadron.

4.   <u>FORMATION OF ADVANCE.</u>

The probable formation in which the 1st Northern Brigade Group will advance is as follows:-

      MOUNTED TROOPS.
1 lorry of Infantry with 2 L.G's.
1 sub-section "A" Coy. M.G.Bn.
1 lorry of Infantry
1 sub-section "A" Coy. M.G.Bn.
Remainder of "1" Coy, 53rd.Bn.N.F..
1 Lorry R.E. with demolition equipment.

      1,000 yards.

53rd.Bn.Northd.Fus, less 1 Company.
1 Ambulance lorry 142 Field Ambulance.
2 Ambulance Cars 142 Field Ambulance.

      1,000 yards.

"A" Coy, M.G.Bn.(less 1 section)
52nd.Bn.Northd.Fus. (less 2 Companies)
1 18pdr in lorry.
231 Fld. Coy. R.E.. (less lorry with demolition equipment.)
2 Companies 52nd Bn. Northd.Fus.
1st Northern Brigade Headquarters.
51st.Bn.Northd.Fus.
1 section 142 Fld Ambulance (less 1 lorry and 2 cars)

5. Method of Advance.

The advance will be made by bounds.
The lorry convoy halting for specified periods to allow the Cavalry to seize their various objectives.

6. Route of Advance.   WIPPERFURTH - HUCKESWAGEN - HALVER - LUDENSCHEID.

7. ACTION of the Mounted Troops.   The advance of the mounted troops will be carried out as follows:-

   1st Bound.   Line MARIENHEIDE - WIPPERFURTH - HUCKESWAGEN.

   2nd Bound.   Line MEINERZHGN - HALVER - RADEVORMVALD.

   3rd Bound.   HERSCHEID - ROSMART - EVINGSEN.

   Axis of march of mounted troops:-   KURTEN - WIPPERFURTH - HALVER - LUDENSCHEID.

8. Action on arrival at Objective.

   The 53rd.Bn.Northumberland Fusiliers will push on to ALTENA. The remainder of the Brigade Group will be concentrated around LUDENSCHEID.
   On the evening of J. day, the mounted troops less 5 guns of M.G. Squadron will be relieved by Infantry as follows, and will fall back on the ALTENA - LUDENSCHEID road.

   53rd.Bn.Northumberland Fusiliers.
   (a)   ½ Company to take up a suitable position between ALTENA and EVINGSEN to cover this road.
   (b)   ½ Company to a suitable position about 3 miles along the ALTENA - NEUENRADE road.
   (c)   1 Platoon along the LETMATHE road in vicinity of point where railway crosses the road 1½ miles North of E in ALTENA.
   (d)   An inlying picquet of 1 Company in ALTENA.

   52nd.Bn.Northumberland Fusiliers.
   (a)   ½ Company along LUDENSCHEID - HERSCHEID road in vicinity of junction of track and road just S.E. of Pt. 473.
   (b)   ½ Company to cover the LUDENSCHEID - WERDOHL road about the road junction 1½ miles South of M in ROSMART.
   (c)   1 platoon at the junction of road and track at Pt. 338 in LUDENSCHEID - HALVER road.
   (d)   An inlying picquet of 1 Company in LUDENSCHEID.

9. Headquarters.

   Brigade Headquarters will be established at LUDENSCHEID.

10.   The above will only be considered as notes for the advance on J day.
   Detailed orders will be issued as occasion arises.

   A. Sanderson
   Major,
   Brigade Major, 1st Northern Brigade.

30/5/19.

Distribution as for G.100/2 dated 28/5/19.

Northern Division "G".

Herewith War Diaries of Brigade Headquarters and three Battalions of this Brigade, for month of June.

W.G. Braithwaite
Brigadier-General,
Commanding 3rd Northern Brigade.

6 July 1919.

Army Form C. 2118.

WAR DIARY ORIGINAL
or
INTELLIGENCE SUMMARY.
(Erase heading not required)

Instructions regarding War Diaries and Intelligence
Summaries are contained in F.S. Regs., Part II.
and the Staff Manual respectively. Title pages
will be prepared in manuscript.

Place	Date	Hour	Summary of Events and Information	Remarks and references to Appendices
COLOGNE.	1st.		Weather fine.	
	2nd.		Weather fine.	
	3rd.		Weather unsettled. Some rain.	
	4th.		Weather unsettled. Some Rain.	
	5th.		Weather unsettled. Some rain.	
	6th.		Weather unsettled. Some rain. 20th. Bn. Durham L.I. relieved 51st. Bn. Durham L.I. on COLOGNE Garrison Guards.	
	7th.		Weather fine.	
	8th.		Weather fine.	
	9th.		Weather fine.	
	10th.		Weather fine. The Brigadier-General, Commanding, inspected the Transport of 20th. Bn. Durham L.I.	
	11th.		Weather fine and hot.	
	12th.		Weather fine and hot.	
	13th.		Weather fine and hot. 52nd. Bn. Durham L.I. relieved 20th. Bn. Durham L.I. on Garrison Guard Duties.	
	14th.		Weather fine.	
	15th.		Weather fine.	
	16th.		Weather fine.	

Army Form C. 2118.

Sheet 2.

WAR DIARY
or
INTELLIGENCE SUMMARY.

(Erase heading not required.)

JUNE 1919.

Instructions regarding War Diaries and Intelligence Summaries are contained in F. S. Regs., Part II. and the Staff Manual respectively. Title pages will be prepared in manuscript.

Place	Date	Hour	Summary of Events and Information	Remarks and references to Appendices
COLOGNE.	17th.		Weather fine. Notification was received that this date was "J" minus 3 day. B.3493/5 issued. (Copy attached).	
	18th.		Weather fine. 52nd. Bn. Durham L.I. relieved from Garrison Guards by 2nd. Light Brigade.	
WERMELSCIRCHEN.	19th.		Weather fine. Brigade Group moved to WERMELSCIRCHEN in accordance with B.3493/2 dated May 30th. (Copy attached to War Diary for May.)	
	20th.		Weather fine. Brigade remained in Billets in WERMELSCIRCHEN.	
	21st.		Weather unsettled and showery. Brigade remained in billets in WERMELSCIRCHEN.	
	22nd.		Weather unsettled. Brigade remained in billets in WERMELSCIRCHEN.	
	23rd.		Weather unsettled. Notification was received that June 24th would be "J" day, but this was cancelled shortly after being received.	
	24th.		Weather unsettled. Brigade remained in Billets in WERMELSCIRCHEN.	
	25th.		Weather unsettled. Brigade remained in billets in WERMELSCIRCHEN.	
	26th.		Weather unsettled. B.M. 133 issued. (Copy attached). Brigade remained in billets in WERMELSCIRCHEN.	
	27th.		Weather unsettled. Brigade remained in Billets at WERMELSCIRCHEN.	
	28th.		Weather unsettled. Division wire received stating that peace had been signed and that June 29th would be "A-1" day. Brigade remained in billets in WERMELSCIRCHEN.	
	29th.		Weather unsettled. 52nd. Bn. Durham L.I. moved into COLOGNE in accordance with March Table issued with B.M.133 dated June 26th.	

Sheet 3.   JUNE 1919.   Army Form C. 2118.

WAR DIARY
or
INTELLIGENCE SUMMARY.
(Erase heading not required.)

Instructions regarding War Diaries and Intelligence
Summaries are contained in F. S. Regs., Part II.
and the Staff Manual respectively. Title pages
will be prepared in manuscript.

Place	Date	Hour	Summary of Events and Information	Remarks and references to Appendices
WERMELS-KIRCHEN	30th.		Weather unsettled. Movements laid down in B.M.153 for "A" day carried out. 52nd. Bn. Durham L.I. relieved 2nd. Light Brigade on COLOGNE Garrison Guards.	

W Braithwaite

Brigadier-General,

Commanding 3rd Northern Brigade.

July 1919.

3rd Northern Brigade No.B.343/3

S E C R E T.

Reference this Office letter B.343/2 dated May 30th.

1. June 19th will be J - 1 day. March Table attached to above quoted letter will therefore be carried out on that day.

2. Brigade Headquarters will be established at WERMELSCIRCHEN in present Headquarters 15th Hampshire Regt. 60 yards East of the CHURCH on arrival on J - 1 day, and not at location previously stated.

3. A Conference will be held at the above mentioned Headquarters at 19.00 hours on J - 1 day, at which the following will attend:- Lieut.Colonel C. FANE, C.M.G., D.S.O., O.C's 20th, 51st and 52nd Battns. Durham Light Infantry, 438th Field Company R.E., 7th Field Ambulance, "D" Company 3rd Batth. M.G.C., 226th Siege Battery R.G.A., and Brigade Supply Officer.

4. On arrival at WERMELSCIRCHEN all Units will send an Orderly to Brigade Headquarters to report exact location of their Headquarters and to take orders etc, back to their Unit.

5. ACKNOWLEDGE.

Captain.

16th June 1919.   Brigade Major, 3rd Northern Brigade.

Distribution:-

1. G.O.C.
2. O.C. 20th Bn. Durham L.I.
3. 51st Bn. Durham L.I.
4. 52nd Bn. Durham L.I.
5. 76th T.M.Battery.
6. 3rd M.G.Battalion.
7. 438th Field Company. R.E.
8. 7th Field Ambulance.
9. No.2. Coy. "N" Divl. Train.
10.)
11.) Northern Division.
12. O.C. "G" Battery. R.H.A.
13. Lt.Col. C. FANE. C.M.G.,D.S.O., 12th Lancers.
14. Dragoon Brigade (for information of Composite Dragoon Squadron and Section Cavalry Division M.G. Squadron attached 3rd Northern Brigade.)
15. O.C. 226th Siege Battery. R.G.A.
16. VI Corps Cyclists.
17. C.R.E., Northern Division.
18. O.C. 12th Squadron R.A.F.
19. Brigade Signal Officer.
20. Staff Captain.
21. Brigade Transport Officer.
22.)
23.) War Diary.
24. File.

-2-

     (b)   ISERLOHN
            LANDHAU
            MENDEN
            HICKERLE
            WERL
            SOEST

and (c)   ISERLOHN
            MENDEN
            HUSTEN
            ARNSBERG

4.   Apart from the above, headquarters of leading formations should endeavour to establish communications with the rear, and laterally, on the German system which in many cases may not be damaged. The following information as regards this system is issued as a guide to establish communication in this way. There is a route from MARMELSKIRCHEN along the railway through LENNEP to SCHWELM. In the SCHWELM-HAGEN-SCHWERTE area there is a maze of telephone route, mainly along the railway.
Lateral routes which may be made use of
     SCHWELM-BRECKERFELD-HOLVER
     HAGEN-BRECKERFELD-HALVER
     HAGEN-LUDENSCHEID
     SCHWERTE-ISERLOHN

the above is not intended to be a complete list of all telephone routes in the area of the advance, but merely as a guide to possible requirements.

5.   If alterations have to be made on the German system they should be done by Signal Service personnel. As already laid down Battalion Signals will not interfere with the German system or make any disconnections in German Post offices.

6.   Supply of cable, to replace any expenditure during the advance, cannot be guaranteed. In this connection the following points will be observed as far as tactical situation permits.
    (a) Signal Office of Headquarters will be established at German post or telephone offices.
    (b) Unit Commanders and their Adjutants will select their headquarters close to their Signal Offices and were subscriber telephones exist.
    (c) Communication with the outpost system should be as far as possible by visual or runner.
    (d) If a cable has to be laid it must be picked up in good time before the advance is resumed unless taken over by an incoming unit.

                                                                  Captain.
1/6/19.   Brigade Major.   3rd Northern Brigade.

Copies to all recipients of B.3493 dated May 25th.

SECRET.   3rd Northern Brigade B.M.133.

```
20th B. Durham L.I.              Brigade Supply Officer.
51st B. Durham L.I.              Brigade Signal Officer.
52nd B. Durham L.I.              "G" Battery, R.H.A.
3rd Northern T.M.Battery.        Composite Dragoon Squadron.
"D" Coy. M.G.Battalion.          Lieut. Col. C. FANE. C.M.G., D.S.O.
438th Field Coy. R.E.            Detachment VI Corps Cyclists.
7th Field Ambulance.             226 Siege Battery, R.G.A.
Section Cav. M.G.Squad.          18 pdr. Gun.
```

2 Coy Tram
Bde Transport Off.   3rd M.G. Bn
                                  MAJOR ARMSTRONG M.C.

1.   In the event of Peace being signed without any further advance taking place, orders may be expected for all troops to resume their dispositions as they existed prior to "J" minus 3 day.

2.   The 3rd Northern Brigade Group will carry out the move in accordance with the attached March Table.

3.   If tents are wet they will be left standing under guards which will be arranged by the Brigade.

4.   Care will be taken to leave all camps and billets clean and in good order.

5.   The 52nd B. Durham L.I. will take over from the Light Division all guards previously found by them in accordance with attached Table.

6.   ACKNOWLEDGE.

                                                    Captain,
26th June 1919.   Brigade Major, 3rd Northern Brigade.

Copies to
    Northern Division.
    1st Northern Brigade.
    2nd Northern Brigade.
    2nd Light Brigade.
    3rd Southern Bde.

MARCH TABLE to accompany 3rd Northern Brigade B.M.133 dated June 25th.

Serial No.	Date.	Unit.	Starting Point.	Pass starting point.	Destination.	Route	Remarks.
1.	A - 1	52nd. Bn. Durham L.I.	Road junction ½ mile West of WERKELSKIR CHEN.	To be notified.	Portion of "C" Block RIEHL BARRACKS originally occupied.	SCHLEBUSCH & HOHENZOLLERN BRIDGE.	By Lorry. Orders may be issued later for this move to take Place on "A" day.
2.	A day.	52nd. Bn. Durham L.I.	do		Take over Garrison Guards shown on attached list from 2nd Light Brigade.		
3.	A day	"G" Battery R.H.A.	do	07.00.	Artillery Barracks MERHEIM.	SCHLEBUSCH & MULHEIM BRIDGE.	
4.	A day.	Dragoon Squadron & Sec. Cav. Divn. H.G. Squadron	do	07.35.	COLOGNE AREA.	SCHLEBUSCH.	
5.	A day	3rd Northern Inf. Bde. Group Transport. 7th Field Amb. Transport. 2 Coy.Train Transport. 438 Field Coy. R.E. Transport. 3rd Bn. M.G. Corps.	Road junction ½ mile south of DAHRINGHEN	cf 09.00.	TOERINKET	ODENTHAL	To move under orders to be issued by Capt. Roach M.C. 3rd M.G.B.

MARCH TABLE. (CONTINUED).

Serial No.	Date.	Unit.	Starting Point.	Pass starting Point.	Destination.	Route.	Remarks.
6.	A day.	51st Bn. Durham L.I.	Bridge carrying road over railway about 1½ miles S.W. of W in WERMELSKIRCHEN.	12.10.	RIEHL BARRACKS.	SCHLEBUSCH & HOHENZOLLERN BRIDGE.	By Lorry. Will occupy 9th D.L.I. Block in RIEHL BARRACKS on A/B night. O.C. 51st D.L.I. will commend column consisting of Units stated in serials No. 7,8,9 & 10 during march.
7.	A day.	1 Sec. 7th Field A.	do.	12.15.	do.	do.	By Lorry.
8.	A day.	"D" Coy. 3rd M.G.Bn.	do.	12.17.	do.	do.	By Lorry.
9.	A day.	Det. VI Corps Cyclists.	do.	12.18.	Original location in COLOGNE.	do.	By Lorry.
10.	A day.	18 pdr. on Lorry.	do.	12.19.	do.	do.	
11.	A day.	226th Siege Btty. R.G.A.	do.	12.25.	Original location in KALK.	SCHLEBUSCH	

MARCH TABLE (CONTINUED).

Serial No.	Date.	Unit.	Starting Point.	Pass starting point.	Destination	Route.	Remarks.
12.	B day.	H.Q. 3rd Northern Inf. Brigade.	Bridge carrying road over Rly. about 1½ mls. S.W. of W in WERSELS-KIRCHEN.	09.00	Original Location in COLOGNE.	SCHIEBUSCH & HOHENZOLLERN BRIDGE.	By Lorry.
13.	B day.	20th. Bn. Durham L.I.	do	09.01.	do	do	By Lorry. O.C. 20th. Bn. D.L.I. will command column consisting of Units stated in serial numbers 12, 13, 14, and 15.
14.	B day.	Personal 6th Field Coy. R.E.	do	09.06.	do	do	By Lorry.
15.	B day.	76 L.T.M. Battery.	do	09.03.	do	do	By Lorry.
16.	B day	3rd Northern Inf. Bde. Transport Group as T in serial No. 5.	Road junction N.W. of first T in TORRINGERT	08.00.	do	MULHEIM BRIDGE.	
17.	B day	Dragoon Squadron & Sec. Cav.M.G. Squad.			Cavalry Div. Area.	HOHENZOLLERN BRIDGE.	To march under the orders of O.C. Dragoon Squadron. To be clear of HOHENZOLLERN BRIDGE by 10.30 hours.

3rd NORTHERN INFANTRY BRIGADE.

No.	Details of Guards.	Offrs.	Strength. N.C.O's.	Men.
N.17.	MULHEIM BRIDGE.	1.	4.	20.
18.	Military Governor's House.		2.	8.
19.	Wireless Station.		2.	8.
20.	Refilling Point.		1.	3.
23.	Monopol Group (1.Coy minimum.)	3.	10.	65.
26.	ARSENAL.		2.	12.
27.	Military Police Barracks.		2.	8.
28.	Town Guard Room.		2.	12.
42.	Military Governor's Office.			
	Monopol Hotel :- Guard.		2.	8.
	Orderlies.		1.	8.

BEF

Northern Div
formerly 3 Div

3 Northern Inf Bde

20 Dur. L. I.

1919 Mar to 1919 June

From 41 Div 124 Bde

WAR DIARY
INTELLIGENCE SUMMARY.
(Erase heading not required.)

Army Form C. 2118.

Place	Date 1919	Hour	Summary of Events and Information	Remarks and references to Appendices
BARRACKS RIEHL.	MAR. 1.		Weather fine – Companies carried out interior economy during the morning – Afternoon – recreational training – Battalion football team played 6th Corps. anti-aircraft Battery – Result draw 1–1.	fw.
– do –	2.		Weather fine – Morning was devoted to general cleaning of billets equipment. etc. Afternoon – Battalion relieved the 2nd Bn SUFFOLK REGT on guard duties on Bridges over river RHINE at COLOGNE and various important points in the city – Voluntary R.C. service was held during the morning	fw.
– do –	3.		Weather fine during morning – showery during afternoon. Battn. remained on guard – Draft of 10 Officers + 163 O.R's reported during the evening from the 11th Bn. D.L.I	fw.
– do –	4.		Weather rainy – Battalion remained on guard – Commanding Officer inspected the draft during the morning – Afternoon – Battalion football team played 26th Royal Fusiliers for the third time in the Army competition. Result D.L.I 2 goals R.F's one goal.	fw.
– do –	5.		Weather showery – Battalion were relieved on guard duties by the 1st Battn. K.O. Liverpool Regiment	fw.

WAR DIARY

INTELLIGENCE SUMMARY.

(Erase heading not required.)

Army Form C. 2118.

Place	Date 1919 FEB	Hour	Summary of Events and Information	Remarks and references to Appendices
BARRACKS, RIEHL	6		Weather fine - Battalion were inspected during the morning by G.O.C. 76th Infantry Brigade - Afternoon - recreational training.	Hat. 1
-do-	7		Weather fine - Morning - Squad drill, ceremonial & physical training - Afternoon - Recreational training.	Hat. 1
-do-	8		Weather fine but dull - G.O.C. 3rd Division inspected the Battalion during the morning. Afternoon - Battn. Football team played the 41st Div. Ammunition Column in the semi final of the Divisional Championship for Completion. Result draw no goals were scored - Remainder of Battn. were employed on unloading stores at NIPPES Station.	Hat. 1
-do-	9		Weather fine - C.G. + R.C. Service were held during the morning	Hat 1
-do-	10		Weather fine but carried on in the morning with Physical training, ceremonial, company and squad drill. Afternoon - Bn. Football team played the 41st	
-do-	10		D.A.C. in the replay of the Divl. Semi final of the Army Cup etitions. Result:- 20 D.L.I. 4 41 D.A.C. 0.	*H.17.

Army Form C. 2118.

WAR DIARY
or
INTELLIGENCE SUMMARY.
(Erase heading not required.)

Instructions regarding War Diaries and Intelligence Summaries are contained in F. S. Regs., Part II. and the Staff Manual respectively. Title pages will be prepared in manuscript.

Place	Date	Hour	Summary of Events and Information	Remarks and references to Appendices
BARRACKS RIEHL.	MAR. 11		Weather fine. Morning was devoted to Physical Training, bayonet and Gas Drill, and Battalion Drill under the Commanding Officer.	W.W.
- do -	12		Weather fine. Bayonet course carried on under Physical Training, bayonet and Gas Drill, special attention being paid to the method of carrying arms in file formation.	W.W.
- do -	13		Weather has held well. Morning - bayonet course carried on with Physical Training, after which a lecture was given by Mr D. S. Tobin on "Industrial Peace after the War." The Bns. then packed Guard Mounting for the following day. Afternoon - the Bn. football team played the 12th East Surreys and the Divisional final of the Army bayonet... Result:- 10th D.L.I. 2 goals 12th E. Surreys 1 goal.	W.W.

WAR DIARY
INTELLIGENCE SUMMARY.
(Erase heading not required.)

Army Form C. 2118.

Place	Date	Hour	Summary of Events and Information	Remarks and references to Appendices
BARRACKS RIEHL.	MAR 14		Weather fine. Morning - Conferences carried out with Officers of Unit. Afternoon - the Bn. took over the Guard and other important duties at Cologne, relieving us front of the 51st and 52nd D.L.I. and	App.
	15		Weather fine. Morning - Remainder of Bn. carried out Interior Economy. It was a Guard Mounting Parade was held on the parade ground of the D.L.I. to illustrate the work of the H.C.C. on Guard. Afternoon - the Bn. football team played the Argyll and Sutherland Highlanders on the ground in front of the Army Expeditions at Worms, the Bn. losing by 1-0.	App.
	16		Weather fine. - Divine Services were held during the morning.	App.
	17		Weather showery. Remainder of companies carried out training as for training to-gamme. Afternoon recreational training	App.

Army Form C. 2118.

WAR DIARY
INTELLIGENCE SUMMARY.
(Erase heading not required.)

Place	Date 1918	Hour	Summary of Events and Information	Remarks and references to Appendices
BARRACKS. RIEHL	18		Weather fine – Morning – Remainder of Coys. carried out training as per Programme – Afternoon – Battalion were relieved on the COLOGNE GUARDS by the 52nd D.L.I. The Commanding Officer inspected the transport at 11 am.	AW
	19		Weather fine – The Battalion carried out a Route March during the morning – Afternoon Battalion football team played against the 51st D.L.I. Result 1 goal each.	AW
	20		Weather fine – Morning – training as per programme (Battalion Drill P[arade]). Education classes were also held – Afternoon – Recreational training	AW
	21		Weather showery. Morning – training as per Programme – Educational classes Afternoon recreational training.	AW
	22		Weather fine – Morning as per training programme – Guard of Honour were carried out ceremonial drill – Afternoon – recreational training	AW
	23		Weather fine – Divine Service were held during the morning. Afternoon Battalion took over the COLOGNE GUARDS from the 51st D.L.I.	AW
	24		Weather dull & showery – All men not on guard carried out training & education as per programme.	AW

Army Form C. 2118.

WAR DIARY
INTELLIGENCE SUMMARY.
(Erase heading not required.)

Place	Date 1919 MAR	Hour	Summary of Events and Information	Remarks and references to Appendices
BARRACKS RHEH.	25		Weather fine during morning - snow rain fell during afternoon - Men not on guard carried out training - education as per programme.	Aps 1
	26		Weather fine - Battalion were relieved on COLOGNE GUARDS by the 5-2nd D.L.I. - All men not on guard carried out training as per programme.	Aps 1
	27		Weather dull snow fell at intervals during the day - Troops carried out training - education as per programme.	Aps 1
	28		Weather dull - heavy fall of snow during morning - At 6.0 class was commenced under the last day's Troops carried out training as per programme.	Aps 1
	29		Weather dull - snow fell at intervals during the morning Troops carried out interior economy - Commanding Officer inspected billets during the morning - Afternoon recreational training	Aps 1
	30		Weather fine during the day - snow fell at night - Divine Service were held during the morning.	Aps 1

Army Form C. 2118.

WAR DIARY
INTELLIGENCE SUMMARY.
(Erase heading not required.)

Instructions regarding War Diaries and Intelligence Summaries are contained in F. S. Regs., Part II. and the Staff Manual respectively. Title pages will be prepared in manuscript.

Place	Date	Hour	Summary of Events and Information	Remarks and references to Appendices
BARRACKS RIEHL	1919 Dyte Mar 31.		Weather fine - Coys carried out Training & education as per Programme.	An

Cornall
Lt & Adjt
Commdg 20th Bn Devonshire

WAR DIARY
INTELLIGENCE SUMMARY.
(Erase heading not required.)

Army Form C. 2118.

20D/1 Vol II

Place	Date	Hour	Summary of Events and Information	Remarks and references to Appendices
BARRACKS. SIEGH.	1919 April 1.		Weather fine - Training & education were carried out as per programme by all men not on guards. Battalion relieved the 51st D.L.I. on the COLOGNE Guards - Brigadier General ADLERCRON, G.O.C. 124th Infantry Brigade presented caps & medals won by the Battalion whilst under his command. After the presentation the inspected the various guards and complimented them on their smart appearance, steadiness	A.1.
	2.		Weather fine - Training & education were carried out by all men not on guards	A.1.
	3.		Weather fine - do -	A.1.
	4.		Weather fine - Battalion were relieved on the COLOGNE Guards by the 52nd D.L.I. - All men not on guard carried out Training & education.	A.1.
	5.		Weather fine - Training & education were carried out as per programme. R.C.O's class recommenced under the Asst. Adjutant.	A.1.
	6.		Weather fine - Divine Services were held during the morning - Afternoon - C & D Coys paraded for baths	A.1.

WAR DIARY

INTELLIGENCE SUMMARY.

(Erase heading not required.)

Army Form C. 2118.

Place	Date	Hour	Summary of Events and Information	Remarks and references to Appendices
BARRACKS. RE1HL.	1919 APRIL	7.	Weather fine. Battalion carried out training education as per programme during the morning and Battalion drill during the afternoon.	Ans.
		8.	Weather fine. Training education as per programme. 1 draft of 1 coy joined the Battalion during the afternoon & were divided equally to coys.	Ans.
		9.	Weather fine. A + B coys carried out education during the morning. C + D coys carried out training as per programme. Afternoon no observed as a half holiday.	Ans.
		10.	Weather fine. Battalion took part in a rehearsal parade to practice ceremonial drill for a presentation of honours to American officers. The draft seen at the disposal of coy commanders.	Ans.
		11.	Weather fine. Battalion took part in a full dress rehearsal of the Divisional Commander. Afternoon coys carried out training as per programme.	Ans.
		12.	Weather showery. Battalion took part in the Brigade parade during the morning. Afternoon a guard mounting rehearsal was carried out	Ans.

WAR DIARY
INTELLIGENCE SUMMARY.
(Erase heading not required.)

Army Form C. 2118.

Place	Date 1919 APRIL	Hour	Summary of Events and Information	Remarks and references to Appendices
BARRACKS RIEHL	13		Weather fine during morning - afternoon rainy & windy - Divine Services were held during morning. Afternoon Battalion relieved 51st D.L.I. in the COLOGNE Guard.	For.
	14		Weather dull & showery - Battalion remained on guard.	For.
	15		Weather dull & showery - Battalion remained on guard.	For.
	16		Weather fine during morning - showery remainder of day - Battalion were relieved by 52nd D.L.I. on COLOGNE GUARDS in the afternoon.	For.
	17		Weather fine - Battalion carried out training as per programme during morning and afternoon.	For.
	18		Weather fine - cold wind - Divine services were held during the morning - Afternoon was observed as a holiday - Lt. Col. A.S. BEAUMONT D.S.O. took over command of the Battalion.	For.
	19		Weather fine - Companies carried out drill & minor economy. Battalion football team played against the 9th D.L.I. - Result draw 2 goals each.	For.

Army Form C. 2118.

WAR DIARY
or
INTELLIGENCE SUMMARY.
(Erase heading not required.)

Instructions regarding War Diaries and Intelligence Summaries are contained in F. S. Regs., Part II. and the Staff Manual respectively. Title pages will be prepared in manuscript.

Place	Date APRIL	Hour	Summary of Events and Information	Remarks and references to Appendices
RIEHL BARRACKS	20		Weather fine – Divine Services were held during the morning ensuing.	Her.
	21		Weather fine – Troops carried out training during the morning – Afternoon guard mounting rehearsal took place.	Her.
	22		Weather fine but chilly – Battalion relieved the 51st Battalion, Durham L.I. on the COLOGNE guards – during the afternoon cos carried out training as per programme during the morning. – The Commanding Officer inspected the guards before they moved off.	Her.
	23		Weather showery – All men not on guard attended the educational classes	Her.
	24		Weather snow fell slightly during early morning, remainder of day fine but chilly. All men not on guard attended educational classes	Her.
	25		Weather fine – The Commanding Officer inspected the transport during the morning – Afternoon the Battalion were relieved on COLOGNE guards by the 15-2nd Durham L.I.	Her.
	26		Weather rain fell during early morning + during afternoon very heavy showers fell. – Battalion carried out a route march during the morning – Afternoon HOLIDAY. Battalion football team played the 3rd Battn M.G.C.	Her.

Army Form C. 2118.

WAR DIARY
or
INTELLIGENCE SUMMARY.
(Erase heading not required.)

Place	Date	Hour	Summary of Events and Information	Remarks and references to Appendices
BARRACKS RIEHL	1919 April 26		Brigade football League Results. Battalion 3 - M.G.C. 1 goal	Fine
	27		Weather fine. Battalion paraded for Divine Service in the morning - Voluntary service in the evening. The Commanding Officer lectured to officers after Divine Service	Fine
	28		Weather fine but chilly. Boys carried out training during the morning. Afternoon - all men who did not wish to attend London Divisional Race Meeting paraded for education	Fine
	29		Weather fine. Battalion took part in a Brigade rehearsal Parade during the morning - All men who did not wish to attend London Div: Race Meeting paraded for education	Fine
	30		Weather fine and warm. Battalion carried out training as per programme during the morning. Afternoon, Inter-Coy: run of 4 miles took place. "B" Coy. winning	Fine

1/5/1919.

O B Beauman Lieut Col
20th Bn Durham Light Infantry

Army Form C. 2118.

WAR DIARY
INTELLIGENCE SUMMARY.
(Erase heading not required.)

Instructions regarding War Diaries and Intelligence Summaries are contained in F. S. Regs., Part II. and the Staff Manual respectively. Title pages will be prepared in manuscript.

Place	Date	Hour	Summary of Events and Information	Remarks and references to Appendices
BARRACKS RIEHL	1919 MAY 1		Weather very chilly. The Battalion took over the COLOGNE Guards from the 51st Division. U.S during the afternoon. Training education were carried out during the morning.	Apx.
	2		Weather very heavy showers following the afternoon morning. Battalion remained on guard.	Apx. 1
	3		Weather fine. Tent drill. Battalion remained on guard.	Apx.
	4		Weather fair. Divine services were held during the morning. afternoon the Battalion were relieved on COLOGNE Guards by the 2nd D.L.I.	Apx.
	5		Weather fine. The Battalion took part in a Divisional Rehearsal March. Practised marching past. Bands were present. Afternoon training as per programme.	Apx. 1
	6		Weather fine with fog wind. "C" and "D" Coys carried out range practice on the Bayard Range. "B" Coy acted as butt markers. "A" Coy training as per programme during morning afternoon education.	Apx. 1
	7		Weather fine. "A" & "B" Coys fired on the Range. "B" Coy carried out training in table. Gym. Boxing. Fighting Drill. Afternoon	Apx. 1

WAR DIARY

INTELLIGENCE SUMMARY

Army Form C. 2118.

Place	Date	Hour	Summary of Events and Information	Remarks and references to Appendices
BARRACKS RIEHL	1919 MAY 8		Weather fine. Battalion took part in a Divisional Parade and was inspected and addressed by Field Marshal H.R.H. the Duke of Connaught. R.G., R.I., R.P. etc.	Att.
	9		Weather fine – A.C. & D Coys fired on the range and B Coy acted as butt markers – Lewis gun & signalling classes as usual.	Att.
	10		During the morning rifle exercises. Weather fine – cloudy during evening – A&D Coys carried out drill & interior economy & attended a lecture on "United States of America" by the Sandhurst lecturer – B & C Coys carried out education & int. ec. economy. The Battalion football team played against 1st Bn D.L.I. in the Rhine Cup League & lost by 3 goals to nil.	Att. 1
	11		Weather fine during morning – short thunderstorm during the afternoon – Battalion paraded for Divine Service during the morning. Afterwards attended a lecture by Major Super D.S.O. on "War Givings."	Att.
	12		Weather fine – "A" & "D" Coy carried out range practices on Rele range. B Coy acted as butt markers. "C" Coy carried out	Att.

Army Form C. 2118.

WAR DIARY
INTELLIGENCE SUMMARY.
(Erase heading not required.)

Instructions regarding War Diaries and Intelligence Summaries are contained in F. S. Regs., Part II. and the Staff Manual respectively. Title pages will be prepared in manuscript.

Place	Date	Hour	Summary of Events and Information	Remarks and references to Appendices
BARRACKS. RIEHL.	1919 12/May		Training and education as per programme.	
	13		Weather fine - A & D Companies carried out range practice - C coy acted as butt markers - B coy carried out training according to programme & attended a lecture during the afternoon by Mr Seaver Hills on the "Panama Canal." D coy were allotted the Turnol baths - A shooting competition was held during the evening on the Brigade range.	
	14		Weather fine - A coy carried out a Route march during the morning - B, C & D coys carried out training in Drill, Lewis gunnery, musketry and attack movements - Afternoon - a cross country run was held in which Officers & 50 ORs from B,C, & D coys took part.	Stat. 1
	15		Weather fine - B & C companies carried out range practice - A coy acted as butt markers - D coy carried out a route march. Afternoon - Boys were allotted the Turnol baths - A.C. & D coys carried out education.	

Army Form C. 2118.

WAR DIARY
INTELLIGENCE SUMMARY.
(Erase heading not required.)

Place	Date	Hour	Summary of Events and Information	Remarks and references to Appendices
BARRACKS RIEHL	1919 MAY 16		Weather fine - MARSHAL FOCH. visited COLOGNE and the route along the left bank of the RIVER RHINE during the morning. The Battalion relieved the 51st D.L.I. as the important COLOGNE GUARDS during the afternoon.	Apx. 1
	17.		Weather fine - All men not on guard attended educational classes	Apx. 1
	18.		Weather fine - All men not on guard attended Divine Service during the morning.	Apx. 1
	19		Weather fine - Lewis gun class assembled during the morning - afternoon. A lecture was given to all men not on guard by Brig. Gen. Hy. Stone, C.M.G. on "Lessons past in the seven years' war" - afternoon educations was carried out.	Apx. 1
	20		Weather fine - Lewis gun instruction, education were carried on & all men not on guard.	Apx. 1
	21		Weather fine - Lewis gun instruction was carried out by all men not on guard. Afternoon - Recreational Training - 1st Battn Bgde Band Wagon A coy 52nd D.L.I. at football. Band beat by Yorks to one	Apx. 1

Army Form C. 2118.

WAR DIARY

INTELLIGENCE SUMMARY.

(Erase heading not required.)

Instructions regarding War Diaries and Intelligence Summaries are contained in F.S. Regs., Part II. and the Staff Manual respectively. Title pages will be prepared in manuscript.

Place	Date 1919	Hour	Summary of Events and Information	Remarks and references to Appendices
BARRACKS. RIEHL.	May 22.		Weather fine – Lewis gun instruction carried out during the morning – All employed men and Batn. H.Qrs. attended educational classes in the afternoon.	Hts.
	23.		Weather fine – Lewis gun instruction carried out during the morning – all employed men – Batn. H.Qrs. attended educational classes in the afternoon.	Hts.
	24.		Weather fine – Lewis gun instruction – interior economy were carried out during the morning – The Battalion were released in Cologne grounds by 2nd Batn. D.L.I. during the evening. The H.Qrs. Guard & Pickets from the 32nd Batn. D.L.I. during the evening. Batn. turned for Divine Service.	Hts.
	25.		Weather fine during day – showery at night. Batn. turned for Divine Service. Voluntary Divine Services were held during the evening.	Hts.
	26.		Weather fine – The boys towards neglected Parades during the morning – boys carried out advance guard outpost scheme returned & practiced. A. B. & C. Coys education – C. Coy. & H.Qrs. Coy attended educational classes – Platoons were allotted the Batn.	Hts.
	27.		Weather fine – boys carried out training in advance guards, attack schemes, outposts, Lewis gunnery, gas drill and arms drill during the morning.	Hts.

Army Form C. 2118.

WAR DIARY

INTELLIGENCE SUMMARY.

(Erase heading not required.)

Instructions regarding War Diaries and Intelligence Summaries are contained in F. S. Regs., Part II. and the Staff Manual respectively. Title pages will be prepared in manuscript.

Place	Date 1919	Hour	Summary of Events and Information	Remarks and references to Appendices
BARRACKS RIEHL	May 27		Afternoon - A + B companies attended educational classes. C + D coys were allotted the Barrack Baths. - A shooting competition was held this evening.	No.
	28.		Weather fine. - B + C coys fired practice on Brigade Range. - A coy acting as fatigue parties. D coy satisfy carried out Gunnery in attack, advance guard, and outpost scheme, large gunnery and bombing. - Afternoon - Recreational training	No. 1
	29.		Weather fine. - Battalion carried a route march during the morning. The Commanding Officer lectured all Officers & NCOs in the Bn. Lecture Hall on the "Attack". C + D coys carried out education. A + B coys bathing	No.
	30.		Weather fine.- B + C coys carried out range practice on Brigade Range. "D" coy acting as markers. A coy attended the funeral of Pte. Abbott who was accidently shot on the 27th inst in his barrack room. Afternoon - A coy carried out education.	No.
	31.		Weather fine.- A coy fired range practices from 8.30 to 9.30 and afterwards marked for B + C coys who fired from 9.30 until 1 pm. D coy	No. 1

Army Form C. 2118.

WAR DIARY.
INTELLIGENCE SUMMARY.
(Erase heading not required.)

Instructions regarding War Diaries and Intelligence Summaries are contained in F. S. Regs., Part II. and the Staff Manual respectively. Title pages will be prepared in manuscript.

Place	Date	Hour	Summary of Events and Information	Remarks and references to Appendices
BARRACKS RIEHL	1919 MAY 31		Carried out education and interior economy. - Afternoon - holiday.	Ap./1

18/6/19.

O.R.Beaumont Lieut Col
Commdg 20th Bn Durham L.I.

WAR DIARY
INTELLIGENCE SUMMARY
(Erase heading not required.)

Army Form C. 2118.

Place	Date	Hour	Summary of Events and Information	Remarks and references to Appendices
BARRACKS RIEHL.	1919. JUNE 1.		Weather fine - The Battalion paraded for Divine Service during the morning - Voluntary Service were held during the evening.	/s/
	2.		Weather showery with high wind - B - 6 coys. carried out musketry practice on Bde. Engl. - A coy acted as Batt. markers - D coy carried out training in attack, advance rear guards, musketry & Lewis gun training - 2nd. Lieut. Ernst Egglestoe, A coy, was killed in the performance of his duty on the range while acting as O.C. of Batt. markers.	/s/
	3.		Weather fine during morning - showery in afternoon. The Battalion took part in a Bde. tournamt. to celebrate the C.I.G's Birthday - Everyone of the Holiday.	/s/
	4.		Weather chilly and dull - The Battalion attended the funeral of 2nd. Lieut. E. Egglestoe who was buried at SUDFRIEDHOF, COLOGNE. Afternoon A General Inspection - Evening a Battalion Boxing contest took place in the State Theatre Hofgarten was very keen.	/s/

Army Form C. 2118.

WAR DIARY
INTELLIGENCE SUMMARY.
(Erase heading not required.)

Instructions regarding War Diaries and Intelligence
Summaries are contained in F. S. Regs., Part II.
and the Staff Manual respectively. Title pages
will be prepared in manuscript.

Place	Date	Hour	Summary of Events and Information	Remarks and references to Appendices
BARRACKS RIEHL	June 5		Weather showery & chilly wind – B. T. C. boys carried out musketry practices on Butt Range. B. Coy acted as Butt Markers. A. Coy carried out training in Company Drill, musketry & Lewis gun training, Grenade & Gas drill.	
	6		Weather dull & warm – Battalion mounted Cologne Guards.	Tell.
	7		Weather fine – The Battalion remained on Cologne Guards. Captain D. Bird R.A.M.C. and Lieut E. Russell left The Battalion to be demobilised. Capt. Montgomery, R.A.M.C reported to the Battalion.	Tell.
	8		Weather fine – The Battalion paraded for Divine Service during the morning. Voluntary Services were held during the evening – The Battalion remained on Cologne Guards.	Tell.
	9		Weather fine – Battalion remained on Cologne Guards – Being Whit Monday there was no training.	Tell.
	10		Weather fine – Battalion remained on Cologne Guards. The Lewis Gun, Scout & Education Classes were held during the morning.)	Tell.

Army Form C. 2118.

WAR DIARY
INTELLIGENCE SUMMARY.
(Erase heading not required.)

Instructions regarding War Diaries and Intelligence Summaries are contained in F. S. Regs., Part II. and the Staff Manual respectively. Title pages will be prepared in manuscript.

Place	Date	Hour	Summary of Events and Information	Remarks and references to Appendices
BARRACKS RIEHL	JUNE 11		Weather fine – The Battalion remained on Bologn guards. The Lewis gun, Scout and Education Classes were held during the morning.	
	12		Weather fine during morning, thunderstorm in evening – The Battalion remained on Bologn Guards. The Lewis gun, Scout and Education classes were held during the morning.	T&U
	13		Weather fine – Battalion were relieved of Bologn guards – The Lewis Gun Scouts & Education Classes were held during the morning.	T&U
	14		Weather fine – All boys ran on Interior Economy, and also attended Education Classes in the morning.	T&U
	15		Weather fine – The Battalion paraded for Divine Service during the morning – Voluntary services were held during the evening.	T&U
	16		Weather fine – A & B Coys carried out Tactical Educational Training – C & D Coys Squad Drill, Musketry, Gun Drill & Educational – Coy D Coys Kneels firing on Range during morning.	T&U

(51175) Wt W355/P360 60,000 12/17 D. D. & L. Sch. 52a. Forms/C2118/5.

Army Form C. 2118.

WAR DIARY
INTELLIGENCE SUMMARY.
(Erase heading not required.)

Instructions regarding War Diaries and Intelligence
Summaries are contained in F. S. Regs., Part II
and the Staff Manual respectively. Title pages
will be prepared in manuscript.

Place	Date	Hour	Summary of Events and Information	Remarks and references to Appendices
BARRACKS RIEHL	JUNE 17		Weather fine – 'A' & 'D' Coys carried out Tactical & Educational Training. 'B' & 'C' Coys Educational, Squad Drill, Musketry, Gas Drill – 'A' & 'B' Coys casuals firing on Range during morning	JU
	18		Weather fine – The Battalion prepared to move forward on the 19th inst.	JU
	19		Weather fine. The Battalion left RIEHL BARRACKS by motor bus at 12.30 hours and proceeded to WERMELSKIRCHEN, arriving there at 18.00 hours.	JU
BILLETS WERMELSKIRCHEN	20		Weather fine – Companies were at disposal of Company Commanders for cleaning up parades – Bathing parades were held during the afternoon.	JU
do –	21		Weather dull & showery – Companies at disposal of Company Commanders for smartening up drill – Bathing parades were held during the afternoon	JU
do –	22		Weather fine – The Battalion paraded for Divine Service in the morning – Voluntary Service was held in the evening	JU

Army Form C. 2118.

WAR DIARY

INTELLIGENCE SUMMARY.

(Erase heading not required.)

Place	Date	Hour	Summary of Events and Information	Remarks and references to Appendices
BILLETS WERMELSKIRCHEN	JUNE 23		Weather wet. The Battalion carried out Musketry, Lewis Gun, Bombing & Gas training, and musketry and drill in the morning. Bathing parade was held during the afternoon.	TEU
	24		Weather wet. The Battalion carried out Musketry, Lewis Gun, Bombing & Gas training, and musketry and drill in the morning. Bathing parade was held during the afternoon.	TEU
	25		Weather wet. The Battalion paraded for a Route March in the morning. Bathing parades were held during the afternoon.	TEU
	26		Weather wet. The Battalion carried out Company & Platoon Tactical Training in the morning. Bathing parade was held during the afternoon. Captain Turnbull M.C. was thrown from his horse whilst in execution of his duty, and was evacuated to Hospital with a broken collar bone.	TEU
	27		Weather wet. The Battalion carried out Company & Platoon Tactical Training in the morning. Bathing parades were held during the afternoon.	TEU

Army Form C. 2118.

WAR DIARY
INTELLIGENCE SUMMARY.
(Erase heading not required.)

Instructions regarding War Diaries and Intelligence Summaries are contained in F. S. Regs., Part II. and the Staff Manual respectively. Title pages will be prepared in manuscript.

Place	Date	Hour	Summary of Events and Information	Remarks and references to Appendices
BILLETS WERMELSKIRCHEN	JUNE 28		Weather wet - The Battalion carried out Company & Platoon Tactical Training in the morning -	Jell.
	29		Weather showery - The Battalion paraded for Divine Service in the morning - Voluntary Services were held in the evening.	Jell.
	30		Weather dull - The Battalion carried out Company & Platoon Tactical Training in the morning - Bathing parades were held during the afternoon.	Jell.

A.R.Bryan mar Lieut Col
Comdg 20th Durham Light Infantry.

SECRET.　　　　　　20TH BN. DURHAM LIGHT INFANTRY.　　　Copy No. 12
　　　　　　　　　　　　OPERATION ORDER NO. 116.
　　　　　　　　　*****************************

1. The Battalion will return to Riehl Barracks, Cologne by Lorries, and occupy previous billets on "B" Day. (Tuesday July 1st).

2. The head of the column will pass the starting point (Bridge carrying road over Railway 1½ miles South West of W in Wermelskirchen at 06.46 hours.
Companies will be embussed by 06.00 hours.
The lorries will then proceed to the Starting Point under orders of the R.A.S.C. Officer in charge and form up in the following order:-
Headquarters, A., B., C., D., Stores, Tents.

3. Lorries as far as possible should be packed the night before to minimise any delay.
A Spare Lorry will be parked outside Battalion Headquarters Mess to convey Officers' Valises which must be loaded by 05.45 hours.
Care must be taken that no trench stores or ammunition is left behind.
Detonators should be removed from Bombs and carefully repacked.
Certificates to this effect will be rendered to this Office by 05.45 hours.

4. The unconsumed portion of the days rations will be carried on the man.
Rations for consumption on "C" Day will be drawn from Refilling Point, Reihl Barracks, on evening of "B" Day.
All Iron Rations will be returned to Q.M. Stores on arrival at Riehl Barracks.

5. All Personnel from Reception Camp will rejoin Companies on arrival.

6. Companies will render a certificate to this Office by 05.45 hours stating that billets at Wermelskirchen have been left in a clean and sanitary condition.

7. On arrival all trench stores, ammunition, bombs etc., will be stacked in Company Stores till orders are received to return them to Q.M. Stores.

8. All Box Respirators haversacks will be scrubbed and khaki blancoed. Box Respirators will then be stored in Company Store Room.

9. ACKNOWLEDGE.

　　　　　　　　　　　　　　　　　　　　　　A. Graham
　　　　　　　　　　　　　　　　　　　　　　Lieut. A/Adjutant,
30/6/19.　　　　　　　　　　　　　　　20th Bn. Durham Light Infantry.

No. 1.　File.
　　2.　A. Coy.
　　3.　B. "
　　4.　C. "
　　5.　D. "
　　6.　Headquarters.
　　7.　Quartermaster.
　　8.　Medical Officer.
　　9.　Signal Officer.
　　10.　Major Armstrong.
　　11.　R.S.M.
　　12.　War Diary.

SECRET.   OPERATION ORDERS.   20th Bn Durham Light Infantry
                                    114

1. The Battalion will be prepared to move forward tomorrow 19th inst
    J - 1 day by motor bus at 12.30 hours.
    Lorries will park in the square "O" Block today Z - 2 day about
    18.00 hours.
    20 O.R's will be allotted to each lorry which will be under the
    charge of an Officer or Senior N.C.O.
    The lorries for the Battalion will be marked "B" Group.
    Spare lorries will be marked "S".
    Supply   "   "   "   "   "Supply"
    These lorries will be kept throughout the move.
    The Battalion will parade outside billets at 11.30 hours ready
    to embus.
    Dress - Full Marching Order.

2. All barrack stores will be handed over to the Light Division on
    relief and receipts for same plus cleanliness receipts will be
    forwarded to this Office as early as possible.

3. The unconsumed portion of the days rations, plus Iron Rations will
    be carried on the man. Rations for J day will be carried on the
    lorries provided for personnel of Units.

4. The Buglers attached to each Company will act as stretcher bearers
    and carry the Company stretchers.

5. The Transport will move in accordance with instructions received
    from O.C. 3rd Bn. Machine Gun Corps.

6. A billetting party of 1 N.C.O. per Company and the Battalion
    Interpreter will report to 2/Lieut. T.E.UPTON outside Orderly Room
    at 07.40 hours tomorrow 19th inst., This party will billet during
    the whole of the move.

7. The rear party already detailed will report to Lieut. C.A.HEPPELL
    at 10.00 hours outside Orderly Room, 52nd D.L.I. to take charge of
    stores in cellars under 52nd D.L.I. Orderly Room. This party will
    be under the charge of Major C.B.NICHOL, O.C. Northern Divisional
    Reception Camp. 2 days rations will be left behind with this party,
    they will then be attached to the 2nd Brigade, Light Division for
    Rations, accommodation etc.

8. All surplus blankets, stores, Officers and Men's kits will be
    stacked in cellars under 52nd D.L.I. Orderly Room. Blankets to be
    rolled in bundles of ten and labelled. All stores will be clearly
    labelled and an inventory taken which should be forwarded to this
    Office as early as possible showing approximate weight and cubic
    capacity of articles dumped. Cellar doors will be locked and the
    keys retained by Lieut. C.A.HEPPELL.

9. 120 rounds S.A.A. will be carried on the man.   and men
    24 rounds Ammunition will be carried by all Officers armed with
    revolvers.
    1 box of Grenades will be carried in each lorry.
    All Lewis Guns in canvas carriers with 25 filled magazines per gun
    will be carried on lorries.
    Anti- Aircraft Lewis Guns will be carried on first line Transport.

10. As many filled water tins as possible will be carried on the lorries
    and these should not be touched without the permission of the C.O.

Continued.

11. All ranks must be in possession of a Field Dressing. Two Medical panniers per Battalion will be taken on lorries.

12. All available camp kettles will be carried on lorries.

13. Signal apparatus as already detailed will be carried on the lorries. One bycycle will be issued to each Company to be carried on Company lorry.

14. O.C. "D" Company will move off immediately behind 3rd M.G.Corps followed by Brigade H.Q., Brigade Signals and 20th D.L.I. (less 1 Company).

15. Companies, Q.M. and Headquarters will render parade states to this Office by 09.00 hours.

16. Acknowledge.

A Graham
Lieut. A/Adjutant,
20th Bn. Durham Light Infantry.

18/6/19.

No. 1 File.
2. A.Company.
3. B.   "
4. C   "
5. D   "
6. Headquarters.
7. Signal Officer.
8. Quartermaster.
9. Transport Officer.
10. War Diary.

BEF

Northern Div
formerly 3 Div

3 Northern Bde.

51 Dur L.I.

1919 Mar to 1919 June

Army Form C. 2118.

WAR DIARY
or
INTELLIGENCE SUMMARY.
(Erase heading not required.)

Place	Date	Hour	Summary of Events and Information	Remarks and references to Appendices
HAREWELL CAMP CATTERICK	1919 1 Mch			
	2 -			
	3 -	1030	Batt's marched direct from WOKINGHAM Station early on 4th. All Bn's less except Blanket party returned during the day.	
		1700	Train detail received from R.T.O	
	4 "	0245	Reveille. Blankets collected at Company H.Q.	
		0330	Breakfast	
		0430	Batt'n paraded and marched to RICHMOND S'tn and entrained 0520 arrived DOVER in two trains 1800	
			Spent night in Rest Camp No 1. Strength 40 Officers 742 OR.	
	5 -	1100	Paraded at Rest Camp and marched to Quay - embarked 1230 on Princess ELIZABETH. Strength 40 Officers 742 OR	
		1500	Arrived DUNKIRK - accommodated in No 3 Rest Camp - Officers in Huts OR in Tents	
	6 -	12.00	Entrained for COLOGNE at SAND SIDING. Strength 40 Officers 742 OR - 4 40 Trucks. 3 Blankets per Officer & 1 issued	
	7 -			
COLOGNE	8 -	0930	Arrived COLOGNE detrained & marched to REIHL Bks	
	9 -		2 Coys in Bath during day - rest was spent in Cleaning up and settling down	
	10	1000	Army Corps Commander inspected the Batt'n in Marching Order. Drew Transport & Mot-Scoot, from 2E 8th Batt'n during afternoon	
	11	1400	Took over COLOGNE guards from 52nd DLI. MM W & X Coys	

WAR DIARY
or
INTELLIGENCE SUMMARY.
(Erase heading not required.)

Army Form C. 2118.

Place	Date	Hour	Summary of Events and Information	Remarks and references to Appendices
COLOGNE	12 Wed			
	13 -			
	14 -		Transport inspected by the Brigadier. 10000 COLOGNE gds dismantled - relieved by 20th DLI during afternoon	
	15			
	16 -	9.40	Church Parade for service in REIHL R[?]	
	17			
	18			
	19			
	20	1400	Relieved 20 DLI on COLOGNE gds	
	21		African Men Slashed to Reihl R[?]	
	22		52 m DLI relieved COLOGNE G[?]	
	23			
	24/25	15.35	Batt: Bonfirid STBOS - mobilised - all clear 21.35"	
	25/26	1500	do Y Coy sent to DOM rehired 21.35	
	27			
	28			
	29	1400	Relieved 20th DLI on COLOGNE Gd.	
	30			
	31			

J.A. Tropman
Major
OC 5/7th 8th Durham LI

WAR DIARY
or
INTELLIGENCE SUMMARY.

(Erase heading not required.)

Army Form C. 2118.

Place	Date	Hour	Summary of Events and Information	Remarks and references to Appendices
	1919.			
COLOGNE	1st April		COLOGNE Guards relieved during afternoon. 3 Officers reported from 2/6 D.L.I. from	2nd D.L.I
"	2nd "		1 Officer reported from 2nd D.L.I. Lecture in Boxing Hall 200 o.rs attended	
"	"		1 Officer evacuated to U.K. sick.	
"	4th "		Lt. Col. J. A. Yupman relinquishes command of the Battalion - Lt. Col. B.J. Cowling D.S.O. assumes command of the Bn. forthwith.	
"	6th "		200 Officers and O.R's provided on River trip up the Rhine. 1 N.C.O and 25 men proceeded to Base on Arrival Collecting duty.	
"	5th "		Lt. Col. Yupman struck off strength of Bn and proceeded to U.K. 1 Officer evacuated from Base to U.K.	
"	7th "		Battalion moved into accommodation on "C" Block RIEHL Barracks.	
"	8th "		Took over COLOGNE Guards from 52nd D.L.I.	
"	9th "		13 Officers reported and taken on strength from 53rd Bn. D.L.I. on that Bn being reduced to Cadre strength also 217 o.rs transferred from 53rd D.L.I.	
"	12th "		Capt. W. J. Jull, M.C. reported for duty as Adjutant and took over duties as such	
"	13th "		Capt. F. R. K. Hine relinquishes his appointment of Adjutant of the Bn. and takes over command and payment of W. Coy.	

Army Form C. 2118.

WAR DIARY
or
INTELLIGENCE SUMMARY.
(Erase heading not required.)

Instructions regarding War Diaries and Intelligence Summaries are contained in F. S. Regs., Part II. and the Staff Manual respectively. Title pages will be prepared in manuscript.

Place	Date	Hour	Summary of Events and Information	Remarks and references to Appendices
COLOGNE	April 15th		Transport inspected by Brigade Commander. Unit awarded 3rd prize in lottery competition. Revd P.T. Hutchinson reported and attached to the Bn.	
	16th		1 OR admitted 4th Field Ambulance Cellos Spinal Meningitis Isolated Isolated.	
	17th		Major J. Bjamiron M.C. arrives from 9th D.L.I. takes over command of "Z" Coy.	
	18th		1 Officer demobilised.	
	19th		COLOGNE Guards – Bn relieved by 52nd D.L.I. 1 Officer to UK for dispersal.	
	20th		4 Officers proceeded to No 1 Concentration Camp COLOGNE for dispersal. 1 Officer to UK for service with Regular Unit.	
	21st		1 Officer joined from Hospital and posted from 53rd D.L.I. 2 Officers proceeded to UK for leave previous to joining Regular Bn.	
	22nd		Guards relieved in COLOGNE by 20th D.L.I.	
	23rd		1 Officer proceeded to join 2nd NORTHERN BRIGADE. "Z" Coy isolation on account of 2 cases of measles. Major Unthank reports arrival on 2nd in Command	
	24th			
	25th		Rhine Trip up the Rhine Major Unthank proceeds home to England.	

for 200 ORs.

Army Form C. 2118.

WAR DIARY
or
INTELLIGENCE SUMMARY.

(Erase heading not required.)

Instructions regarding War Diaries and Intelligence Summaries are contained in F. S. Regs., Part II. and the Staff Manual respectively. Title pages will be prepared in manuscript.

Place	Date	Hour	Summary of Events and Information	Remarks and references to Appendices
COLOGNE	April 26th		3 ORs posted to No1 Concentration Camp for demobilization lecture.	
			Lt 150 ORs by Mr Markman Smith on "Policy of Germany since 1865".	
			1 OR's admitted to F.A. (measles) Contacts isolated.	
"	27th		4 Officers proceeded to join 46th D.L.I. at DUNKIRK. 10 Officers to 61st Div. St RIQUIER.	
"	28th		Advance Party dogs arrived from the Base in dispersing of 3rd Echelon.	
			Bn Runners arrived from ROUEN.	
"	29th		"Z" Coy and composite Coy practised ceremonial parade on ground between AMSTERDAMER STRASSE and the RHINE. I.OR died at 61"CCS	
"	30th		of Cerebro Spinal meningitis.	

B.J. Curry
Lieut Col.
Commanding 5th Yth Durham Light Infantry.

VI Corps:- A/1564

NORTHERN Division.

The attached War Diary of the 51st
Bn. Durham Light Infantry is returned for
disposal in accordance with G.R.O.2814.

A.A. & Q.M.G.,
NORTHERN
DIVISION.

No. A104
Date 4/6/19

4/6/19.

Major,
D.A.A.G., VI Corps.

AA9.
a of the R.

Army Form C. 2118.

WAR DIARY
or
INTELLIGENCE SUMMARY.
(Erase heading not required.)

Instructions regarding War Diaries and Intelligence Summaries are contained in F.S. Regs., Part II. and the Staff Manual respectively. Title pages will be prepared in manuscript.

Place	Date	Hour	Summary of Events and Information	Remarks and references to Appendices
Cologne	May 1		Relieved on Cologne Guards by 20th D.L.I. 1 Officer attached to D.A.D.R.T. Zoothesthal	
	3rd.		Commander-in-Chief inspects Barracks "Y" + "Z" Coys. start musketry	
	4th.		13 Officers dispatched to Louville from 1/9th H.L.I.	
	5th.		1 Officer " " " " " "	
	"		Lecture for 50 other ranks of "W" Coy in Lecture Hall. RIEHL BARRACKS on "Labour and the Church"	
	8th.		Duke of Connaught inspects the 3rd Northern Div. in EXERCIZER PLATZ, MERHEIM. Battalion relieve 52nd D.L.I. Cologne Guards.	
	9th.			
	10th.		Lecture in Theatre on "The United States of America" by 2/Lt. Sandon Perkins	
	"		50 Other Ranks attended of "Y" Coy. 1 Officer returned from Hospital.	
	12th.		Lt. Col Curling D.S.O. proceeded on leave to U.K. - Major Winton assumes 2nd in Command.	
	13th.		Major Maitland joins Battn from leave and takes over command of Bn.	
	14th.		Entries for Brigade Boxing Tournament sent in	
	15th.		Brigadier General inspects Battn transport	
	16th.		Marshall Foch visits Cologne - Bn. line river bank near Hohenzollern bridge	

Army Form C. 2118.

WAR DIARY
or
INTELLIGENCE SUMMARY.
(Erase heading not required.)

Instructions regarding War Diaries and Intelligence Summaries are contained in F. S. Regs., Part II. and the Staff Manual respectively. Title pages will be prepared in manuscript.

Place	Date	Hour	Summary of Events and Information	Remarks and references to Appendices
Cologne	17th		100 Other Ranks attended a lecture on "Hanover" by Capt Edgar Bellingham in the Lecture Hall at 11:15 A.M.	
	19th		"Y" & "Z" Coys Commence to fire L.M.G. & officers appointed Discipline Offr. E.F.C. Cologne.	
	20th		Inspection by Brigadier and address to officers of Battalion	
	22nd		Lt. Col. B.J. Curling D.S.O. returns from leave	
	24th		100 Other Ranks attend Lecture in Durham House at 11 A.M.	
	26th		Inspection of Barracks by Corps Commander at 09.45 hours.	
	27th		Lecture on "CONSTANTINOPLE" by Rev J A Douglas in Lecture Room. 100 other ranks attended.	
	31st		Lecture by 2th A.G. Phillips Lecture Room at 11.00 hours. 100 other ranks attended.	

Cologne.
31.5.19.

M Watty Carr
Lieut Colonel
Commanding 51st Bn. The Durham Light Infantry

Army Form C. 2118.

WAR DIARY
or
INTELLIGENCE SUMMARY.
(Erase heading not required.)

Instructions regarding War Diaries and Intelligence Summaries are contained in F. S. Regs., Part II. and the Staff Manual respectively. Title pages will be prepared in manuscript.

51/DLI

Place	Date	Hour	Summary of Events and Information	Remarks and references to Appendices
Cologne	June 3rd		Battalion parades with remainder of Brigade to celebrate birthday of H.M the King	
"	4th		Lieut Colonel B. f. Curling D.S.O. proceeds to U.K. on duty. Major J.S. Unthank D.S.O. assumes command.	
"	5th		Battalion v 53rd Sherwood Foresters at cricket at Siveck.	
"	6th		The Battalion is relieved from Guards in Cologne by 20. D.L.I	
"	9th		Major J.S. Unthank D.S.O proceeds to U.K on leave. Major T.G. Davison assumes command	
"	9th		Holiday for all ranks.	
"	10th		Lecture in Barracks by the 6.6. book 50 O.Rs from "X" "Y" attnd	
"	11th		Lt. Col B. f. Curling D.S.O returns from U.K.	
"	12th		Div Gas Officer inspects gas arrangements in Battalions, cricket match with Barracks Siers Guat.	
"	14th		Capt the Gratin Ramsvroud to U.K. on leave. The Batt. goes on Rhine Trip.	
"	15th		Capt D. T. Tully proceeds to U.K. on leave.	
"	17th		Conference with Company Commanders re move. This is J-3 day	
"	18th		J-2 day. Batt prepares to move to Wemilshirchen. 34 lorries arrive at night & are packed in Barrack Square	

WAR DIARY
or
INTELLIGENCE SUMMARY.
(Erase heading not required.)

Army Form C. 2118.

Place	Date	Hour	Summary of Events and Information	Remarks and references to Appendices
	June			
	19th		J -1 day Billeting Party moves to Wemelskirchen at 8 am. The Battn less 1 Officer details, follow at 12.45 hrs. Strength 22 Offrs 647 O.Rs. Arrive at 18.00 hrs. Battn billets in Dabringhausen Strasse & area. Battn finds guards for supply column. Transport proceeds to Dabringhausen.	
	20th		J - 1 day. Transport arrives at Dabringhausen	
	21st		J - 1 day. Bn do tactical scheme in morning. Capt W. Gething M.C. R.A.M.C. recalled	
	26th		German civilian wounded in face by 2 carbine shots of X Coy.	
	27th		Court of enquiry held on case of the 26th inst.	
	28th		Received news of signing of peace	
	29th		Church Parade in Protestant Church, Wermelskirchen. Prepare for move back to Bologne.	
	30th		A - 1 day. Battn moves by lorry to Buhl Barracks. Transport leaves Dabringhausen at 07.30 hrs for Tourcoing. Battalion occupies 9th D.L.I. quarters.	

B. J. Curling
Lt. Col.

BEF

NORTHERN DIV

formerly 3 DIV

3 NORTHERN INF BDE

52 DUR L.I.

1919 MAR to 1919 JUNE

WAR DIARY

52nd BATTN. D.L.I

March 1919

Army Form C. 2118.

WAR DIARY
or
INTELLIGENCE SUMMARY.
(Erase heading not required.)

Instructions regarding War Diaries and Intelligence Summaries are contained in F. S. Regs., Part II. and the Staff Manual respectively. Title pages will be prepared in manuscript.

Place	Date	Hour	Summary of Events and Information	Remarks and references to Appendices
Catterick	Mar 2nd 1919	21.30	Entrained CALIFORNIA CAMP STATION in two hours, detained CATTERICK BRIDGE: Movement orders attached	1
		23.10	Detained CATTERICK BRIDGE. Arrived port of Embarkation attached.	2
			Marching-out strength 33 officers 981 other ranks.	
	3rd	11.20	Arrived DOVER & Embarked on S.S. SCOTIA. Sailed 1315 hours and arrived DUNKIRK 1630 hours.	
FRANCE			Disembarked and marched to No 4 Rest Camp.	
	4th	11.30	Marched to SANDSIDING and entrained for COLOGNE	
		12.50	Departed SANDSIDING.	
		16.40	Arrived MERRIS detrained & men had hot stew.	
		17.35	Departed MERRIS	
		23.54	Arrived BAISEUX but did not stop for Hot Soup & tea	
Belgium	5th	11.25	Arrived CHARLEROI issued rations on the train	
		13.00	Departed CHARLEROI	
		15.50	Arrived NAMUR	
		17.35	Departed NAMUR	
		20.20	Arrived HUY Marched to Rest Camp & gave men cold meat & tea. We arrived back at train 20 minutes before train was due to depart, but before men had started to entrain, the train moved out but the R.T.O. had it brought back & the battalion entrained, however the train	5

WAR DIARY
or
INTELLIGENCE SUMMARY.

(Erase heading not required.)

Army Form C. 2118.

Place	Date 1919	Hour	Summary of Events and Information	Remarks and references to Appendices
BELGIUM GERMANY	Mar 5th – 6th	20.20 / 07.30	(continued) Stocks again moved off before time & 8 men were left behind but joined the Battalion next day. Arrived NIPPES Station COLOGNE but had to wait until an outgoing train of Grenadier Guards had left before we could detrain.	
	7th	0930	Debussed and marched to RHIEL BARRACKS occupied by 2nd Batt SUFFOLK REGIMENT	
		1100	Inspected by Brigadier General F.E. METCALFE C.M.G. D.S.O.	
	8th	10.30	Formally inspected by Major General C.J. DEVERELL C.B. COMDG. NORTHERN DIVISION Took over COLOGNE TOWN GUARDS. We were the 1st Grenadier of Young Soldiers Battalion to perform this duty and the Army Commander GENERAL SIR HERBERT C.O. PLUMER, G.C.B., G.C.M.G., G.C.V.O, A.D.C. Commanding Second Army, sent the following message to the Commanding Officer after he had inspected the Guards "Tell your Commanding Officer that your Guards are very clean and smart & soldierly" This was only 3 days after we had arrived & come off a two days train journey in trucks.	
	10th / 11th	11.45	Inspected by Army Commander GENERAL SIR HERBERT C.O. PLUMER G.C.B., G.C.M.G., G.C.V.O. A.D.C. Commanding Second Army.	
	11th		Handed over Guards to 51st Durham Light Infantry.	
	15th		6th Division became Northern Division.	
	17th		Took over Guards from 20th Durham Light Infantry.	
	18		Battalion Guards inspected by MAJOR GENERAL. C.J. DEVERELL, C.B. COMDG. NORTHERN DIVISION	
	25		Message received from BRIGADE at 14.55 that civil disturbances were expected & that we were to send One Coy to BRIGADE H.Q. stores, this Coy-D.Coy- moved off from Barracks complete with Lewis Guns Left an hour after receipt of message. ½ Coy were also sent to reinforce the Guards of 20th D.L.I. all men were notified to return to Barracks at about 21.00 hrs as the civil population quieted down.	

WAR DIARY
or
INTELLIGENCE SUMMARY.
(Erase heading not required.)

Army Form C. 2118.

Instructions regarding War Diaries and Intelligence Summaries are contained in F. S. Regs., Part II. and the Staff Manual respectively. Title pages will be prepared in manuscript.

Place	Date 1919	Hour	Summary of Events and Information	Remarks and references to Appendices
Cologne	March 28		Warned that COMMANDER-IN-CHIEF was to visit barracks during morning, but he did not come.	
Cologne	31		Strength of Battalion.	
			Officers W.O. Sergts. Cpls. Other Ranks. Total	
			R.Q. 61 6 39 23 716 843	

John B Mueer
LIEUT. COL.
COMDG. 52nd Bn DURHAM L.I.

MOVEMENT ORDERS. Appendix 1.

by.

LIEUT.COLONEL J.B. LIUR D.S.O.
COMMANDING 52nd BN. DURHAM LIGHT INFANTRY.

GENERAL ORDERS. March 1st 1919.

The Battalion will move Overseas to-morrow the 2nd inst., by the 23.10 train from Catterick Bridge.

Vans for baggage will be at Catterick Bridge Station at 19.10.

SPECIAL ORDERS.

(1) All Baggage and kit Bags will be stacked in Hut No 43 by 12 noon 2nd inst.

(2) All Barrack Stores will be handed into Quartermaster's Stores at the following times.

"A" Coy. 9 a.m.
"B" Coy. 11.a.m.
"C" Coy. 1 p.m.
"D" Coy. 3 p.m.

Blankets will be rolled in Bundles of 20.

BAGGAGE PARTY.
(3) Lieut. Fowler will be in charge of the party for loading the baggage vans at the Station and will take the Regimental Transport Personnel as his loading party.
The R.S.M. will detail a party of 20 men and 2 N.C.Os. to load the lorries and waggons at the camp at a time to be notified later.
All baggage and kit bags will be labelled with the Coy or H.Q. label — this to include Officers Kits.

(4) PACKS.
The packs and rifles of the Band and any category men unable to carry back will be stacked, clearly marked, in Hut 43 by 12 noon 2nd inst.

(5) ENTRAINING
Lieut. Cain is appointed Entraining Officer and will report to this Office at 12 noon 2nd inst for instructions.

(6) MESSING.
The Messing Officer will provide a good tea meal at 18-30 and also a heversack ration to be carried on the men.
The rations for the 3rd inst., will be taken in bulk, this ration to be a preserved one, and will be stacked in Hut 43 by 12 noon. Cpl.Walker and Pte Hughes will be in charge of these ration.

(7) CLEANING.
O.C. Coys will take steps to ensure that all Huts and Quarters vacated by them are left thoroughly clean and tidy and will render a certificate to this effect to this Office before moving off.

(8) PARADE.
The Battalion will parade ready to move off at 21.15.
O.C. Coys will ensure that all men parade with Water Bottles full.

Capt.& Adjt.,
52nd Batt. Durham L.I.

Appendix 2

52nd Battn. DURHAM LIGHT INFANTRY.

NOMINAL ROLL OF OFFICERS.

Lieut.Colonel, J.B.Muir D.S.O.	Royal Highlanders	Commdg.Officer.
Major T.H. Russell	West.York. Regt.	2nd i/c Command.
Capt. A.B. Mawer	Durham Light Infy.	Adjutant.
Lieut. W.O. Williams	Welch Regt.	Asst.Adjt.
Lieut. W. Fowler	Yorkshire Regt.	Transport Officer
Capt. & QM E.L.Pears	North'd Fusrs.	Q.M.
Lieut. P. Waldron	Leicester Regt.	Signalling Officer.
Lieut. H. Martin	Durham L.I.	Scout Officer.
Capt. F.G. Beatty	R.A.M.C.	M.O.
Lieut. W.V. Palethorpe	Durham L.I.	Comdg. A Coy.
" S. Cooper	Sherw. Fors.	A Coy.
2/Lieut. E.A. Machen	Durham L.I.	do.
" S. Morris	do.	do.
" L.W. Allen	do.	do.
" G.E. Wood,	Sherw. Fors.	do.
Capt. F. Brunt	Durham L.I.	Comdg. B Coy.
Lieut. F.D. Morris	do.	B Coy.
" W.C. Black	Highland L.I.	do.
2/Lt. G.R. Oliver	Durham L.I.	do.
2/Lt. A. Nottingham	Durham L.I.	do.
" F. Nurse	Sherw. Fors.	do.
Captain A. Knox-Gore	North'd Fusrs.	Comdg. C Coy.
A/Capt. F.P. Robson	Durham L.I.	C Coy.
Lieut. T.E. Bare	Oxf. & Bucks L.I.	do.
" B.C. Holding	Sherw. Fors.	do.
2/Lt. W. Harding	Durham L.I.	do.
" D.A. Beardall	Sherw. Fors.	do.
Captain T.G. Saint	Durham L.I.	Comdg. D Coy.
Lieut. C.P. Sansom	York & Lancs.	D Coy.
" M.S. Robertson	Cheshire Regt.	do.
" R.H. Cain	Lanc. Fus.	do.
2/Lt. J.P. Anslowç	Durham L.I.	do.
" P. Kirk	Sherw. Fors.	do.

52nd Battalion Durham Light Infantry.

ROLL OF OFFICERS JOINED DURING MONTH OF MARCH.

Captain	E.O. Brown	U.S.M.C.	24.3.1919
Lieut.	C.B. Mills	U.S.M.C.	26.3.1919
T.2nd.Lieut.	J.E. Walton	15th D.L.I.	26.3.1919
do	C.F. Anderson	do	do
do	W.J. Bowl	do	do
do	J.H.L. Dacey	do	do
do	A. Argyle	13th D.L.I.	27.3.1919
do	W.M. Wardle	do	do
do	J.W. Willey M.C.	do	do
do	T.A.B. Allison M.C.	do	do
do	A.G. Waters	do	do
do	H.H. Mennell	do	do
do	T.G. Walton	do	do
A/Capt.	R.H. Farrier	do	do
T.2nd.Lieut.	H. Shelpey	19th D.L.I.	do
do	R. Wood	do	do
do	S. Colpitts	do	do
do	G. Hobson	do	do
do	L.F. Simms	do	do
A/Capt.	H.A. Wareham	do	do
T.Lieut.	A.S. Carroll	do	do
Capt.	D.O. MacDonald	R.A.M.C.	11.3.1919

Roll of OFFICERS LEFT DURING MONTH OF MARCH.

Capt.	F. Beaty	R.A.M.C.	12.3.1919
Capt.	E.O. Brown	U.S.M.C.	25.3.1919
Capt.	D.O. MacDonald	R.A.M.C.	23.3.1919

Vol II 52nd Bn. D.L.I.
War Diary
for
April 1919

WAR DIARY
or
INTELLIGENCE SUMMARY.

(Erase heading not required.)

Army Form C. 2118.

Place	Date	Hour	Summary of Events and Information	Remarks and references to Appendices
Cologne	4th April		Just when Brigade friends from 20th Durham L.I.	
	5.		H C.L.W. Tryell D.S.O. M.C. reported on arrival & assumed command of the Battalion	
	9.		53rd Y.S. Battalion Durham L.I. arrived from England & were accommodated in Rhul Barnes.	
	10.		14 Officers & 205 O.R.s transferred from 53rd Durham L.I. to the Battalion	
	12.		General Sir Herbert C.O. Plumer G.C.B, G.C.M.G, G.C.V.O, A.D.C. Commanding Second Army held a parade for the distribution of English decorations to heads to General Officers & others of the American Army. The 76th Brigade formed the troops for the ceremony. Battalions represented were 20th Batt. the Durham Light Infantry, 52nd Batt. the Durham Light Infantry & 3rd Batt. Machine Gun Corps. Numbers of the Battalion on parade were 29 Officers & 530 O.R.s excluding draft of 53rd Batt. Durham O.R.s who were on parade. The General Officer commanding Second Army sent a message of thanks through the G.O.C. Brigade for the bearing of the troops on the parade.	
	15.		Official program of the Brigade changed from 76th Brigade to 3rd Brigade	Appendix I

WAR DIARY
or
INTELLIGENCE SUMMARY.
(Erase heading not required.)

Army Form C. 2118.

Place	Date	Hour	Summary of Events and Information	Remarks and references to Appendices
	16?		Northern Division	
			Took over Brigade fronts from 20th Yeomanry L.S.	
	25?		Took over Brigade fronts from 20th Yeomanry L.S.	
	22?		General Sir William Robertson G.C.B. K.C.V.O.) So: A.I.C assumed Command	
			of British Army in the Rhine	
	23?		The Head Quarters of the British Army of the Rhine leaves General Headquarters	Appendix 2
			List of officers on establishment during month of April	

C. S. Bingham Lt Col

C O P Y   APPENDIX I.

O.C. 52nd Bn. Durham L.I.

    The Army Commander wishes his thanks conveyed to all ranks for their smart appearance and for the excellent manner in which all movements were carried out on parade to-day.

    The American General Officers present were much impressed by the soldierly appearance of the troops in the march past, and the steadiness in the ranks and good handling of arms earned most favourable comment.

    It gives the Brigade Commander very great pleasure to convey the Army Commander's Message to the Battalions concerned, and he wishes to add his congratulations to all Ranks on having carried out a difficult performance at such short notice in such a manner as to reflect the highest credit on the Division and Brigade to which they belong.

12.4.19.

(Sgd.) T.F. FURNELL, Captain,
Staff Captain, 76th Inf. Bde.

52nd Battalion Durham Light Infantry

NOMINAL ROLL OF OFFICERS LEFT THE BATTALION DURING APRIL, 1919.

Rank & Name		Date of Leaving
A/Capt. F.P. Robson	Durham L.I.	9.4.1919.
T/2/Lt. A. Nottingham	do.	do.
T/3/Lt. F. Nurse	Notts & Derby	11.4.1919.
Lt.Col. J.B. Muir, DSO.	Royal Highlanders	12.4.1919.
T/Lt. W.S. Hutchins	Manchester	do.
T/Capt. F. Brunt	Durham L.I.	14.4.1919.
T/Lt. C.A.T. Lawrence	E. Surrey Regt.	do.
T/Lieut. B.C. Holding	Notts & Derby	20.4.1919.
T/Capt. N. Howard	do.	21.4.1919
T/2/Lt. S.L. Martin	do.	do.
T/Lt. P. Waldron	Leicester Regt.	do.
T/Lieut. J. McCarthy	Durham L.I.	do.
T/Lieut. M.S. Robertson	Cheshire Regt.	20.4.1919.
T/2/Lt. D.A. Beardall	Notts & Derby	21.4.1919.
T/Capt. A.St.G. Knox-Gore	North'd Fusiliers	23.4.1919.
T/Lt. C.P. Sansom	York & Lancs.	23.4.1919.
T/Lieut. J.S. Wilson	Lincolnshire	19.4.1919.
Lieut. T.E. Bore	Oxf. & Bucks (TF)	21.4.1919.

COLOGNE.
1.5.1919.

Lieut.-Colonel,
Commanding 52nd Bn. Durham L.I.

52nd Battalion Durham Light Infantry

NOMINAL ROLL OF OFFICERS JOINED THE BATTALION DURING APRIL, 1919.

Rank & Name			Date of Joining
T/Capt. A.E. Owles, M.C.	Durham L.I.	(Volunteer)	3.4.1919.
T/Lt.Col. C.W. Frizell, DSO, MC.	R. Berks Regt.	"	7.4.1919.
T/Lieut R. England	Oxf. & Bucks	"	4.4.1919.
T/Lt. A.S Maitland	Durham L.I.	"	4.4.1919.
T/Lt. C.A.T. Lawrence	E. Surrey Regt.	"	2.4.1919.
T/Capt. A.T. Carr-West	Durham L.I.	(Volunteer)	6.4.1919.
T/Lieut. J.G. Wilson	Lincolnshire	"	7.4.1919.
T/Capt. H. McDine	North'd Fus.	"	8.4.1919.
T/Capt. N. Howard	Notts & Derby	"	do.
T/Lieut. J. McCarthy	Durham L.I.	"	do.
Lieut. S.F. Ireland	Derby. Yeomanry (TF)	"	do.
Lt S. Benson Cooper	Notts Yeomanry (TF)	"	do.
T/Lieut W.S Hutchins	Manchester	"	do.
Lt. F.O. Springmann	R.A.S.C. (TF)	"	do.
T/Lt. J.B. Robertson, M.C.	Argyle & Sutherland	"	do.
T/2/Lt. W. C. Wright	Durham L.I.	"	do.
" N. L. Sheppard	Manchester	"	do.
" F. Hemstock	Notts & Derby	"	do.
" S. L. Martin	do.	"	do.
" G. S. L. Profit	dd.	"	do.
" J. S. V. Brown	Durham L.I.	"	do.

COLOGNE.
1.5.1919.

Lieut.-Colonel,
Commanding 52nd Bn. Durham L.I.

WAR DIARY or INTELLIGENCE SUMMARY

Army Form C. 2118.

5/2 D.L.I.

Place	Date	Hour	Summary of Events and Information	Remarks and references to Appendices
Cologne	1/5/19		Company training	
"	2/5/19		"	
"	4/5/19		Battalion relieved 20th D.L.I. on Town Guard.	
"	9/5/19		Battalion relieved by 21st D.L.I. on Town Guard.	
"	10/5/19	09.25	Church parade.	
"	12/5/19		2/Lt D.A. BEARDALL, Sherwood Foresters joined Battalion	
"	16/5/19		Battalion proceeds to quay S. of HOHENZOLLERN BRIDGE to witness arrival of MARSHALL FOCH who arrived by boat at 11:15 hours.	
			Bt Col. (T/B.G.) W.G. BRAITHWAITE C.B. C.M.G. D.S.O. 9/19/of Welch Fusiliers arrives.	
			Command of 3rd Northern Brigade.	
"	18/5/19		Bath: Hockey match v. 3rd Batt'n: Machine Gun Corps.	
"	24/5/19		Batt. War Service total for week ending 24.5.19. 2.53 · 13.05.	
"	23/5/19		Battalion relieved on Town Guard by 20th D.L.I.	
"	30/5/19		Batt. relieves on town guard by 51st D.L.I.	
"	30/5/19		Major Burnell DSO DCM joined Battalion & took over duties of 2/i/c Command.	

LIEUT. COL.
COMDG 5/2

Army Form C. 2118.

WAR DIARY
or
INTELLIGENCE SUMMARY.
(Erase heading not required.)

Instructions regarding War Diaries and Intelligence Summaries are contained in F. S. Regs., Part II. and the Staff Manual respectively. Title pages will be prepared in manuscript.

52 DL1

Place	Date	Hour	Summary of Events and Information	Remarks and references to Appendices
Cologne	June 3rd		Bn. ceremonial parade in honour of His Majesty the King's birthday.	
	4th		Remainder of day general holiday.	
	5th		Batt. Route march @ 09.00 hrs.	
	6th		Company training & education	
	7th		— do — — do —	
	8th		Church Parade	
	9th		General Holiday. Whit Monday.	
	10th		Batt. wrote Church	
	13th		Batt. took over guard duties from 20th Batt. D.L.I.	
	15		Church parade.	
	19		Batt. details & transport moved at 08-15 hrs. in preparation for 3 day the Batt. entrained at 12-00 hrs. and arrived at WERMELSKIRCHEN at 17-30 hrs.	
WERMELS- KIRCHEN	20.		Bn. at disposal of Bde Commander	
	21		Training under Coy arrangements.	
	22.		Church parade.	
	24.		Batt. received orders to be ready to move forward. These were afterwards cancelled	

Army Form C. 2118.

WAR DIARY
or
INTELLIGENCE SUMMARY.
(Erase heading not required.)

Instructions regarding War Diaries and Intelligence Summaries are contained in F. S. Regs., Part II, and the Staff Manual respectively. Title pages will be prepared in manuscript.

Place	Date	Hour	Summary of Events and Information	Remarks and references to Appendices
Wimbushon	June 25		Training under coy arrangements	
	26		do	
	27		Batt received orders to be ready to move forward then were afterwards cancelled.	
	28th		Capt. W Bagshaw DSO. MC RE. Lieut I. H Bagshaw MC came over to Bn HQ	
	29th		Entrained @ 09.00 hrs and returned to RIGHT Division BARRACKS.	
Cologne	30th		Took over guards and duties from the Right Division.	

C. W. Frizell
Lieut. Colonel
Comg 52nd Bn R.E.

www.ingramcontent.com/pod-product-compliance
Lightning Source LLC
Chambersburg PA
CBHW081425300426
44108CB00016BA/2303